The Rise
and Fall
of Strategic
Planning

The Rise
and Fall
of Strategic
Planning

Reconceiving Roles for
Planning, Plans, Planners

HENRY MINTZBERG

THE FREE PRESS

The Free Press
A Division of Simon & Schuster Inc.
1230 Avenue of the Americas
New York, N.Y. 10020

Printed in the United States of America

printing number

8 9 10

Library of Congress Cataloging-in-Publication Data

Mintzberg, Henry.
   The rise and fall of strategic planning: reconceiving roles for planning, plans, planners / Henry Mintzberg.
      p.   cm.
   Includes bibliographical references and index.
   ISBN 0-02-921605-2
   1. Strategic planning.   I. Title.
HD30.28.M56   1994
658.4'012—dc20   93-27323
                                  CIP

Credits

The author and publisher of this volume wish to acknowledge the following sources for material:

From H. I. Ansoff, *Corporate Strategy* (McGraw-Hill, 1965). Excerpts and diagrams used with permission of the author.

From H. I. Ansoff, *Implanting Strategic Management*, © 1984. Reprinted by permission of Prentice Hall, Englewood Cliffs, New Jersey.

Reproduced from *The Politics of Expertise* by A. Benveniste (Glendessary Press, 1972) with the permission of South-Western Publishing Co. Copyright 1972 by South-Western Publishing Co. All rights reserved.

From Joseph L. Bower, *Managing the Resource Allocation Process: A Study of Corporate Planning and Investment*. Boston: Division of Research, Harvard Business School, 1970. Reprinted as a Harvard Business School Classic. Boston: Harvard Business School Press, 1986.

From *A Behavioral Theory of the Firm* by R. M. Cyert and J. G. March (Prentice Hall, 1963; revised edition, 1992). Reprinted with permission of R. M. Cyert.

From *Planning in Practice: Essays in Aircraft Planning in War-Time* by E. Devons (Cambridge University Press, 1950). Reprinted with permission from Cambridge University Press.

Diagram from *Strategic Management: A Stakeholder Approach* by R. E. Freeman (Pitman Publishing, 1984). Reprinted with the permission of author.

From "Organizing Competitor Analysis Systems" by S. Ghoshal and D. E. Westney (*Strategic Management Journal*, 1991, 12:17–31). Reprinted with permission.

From *Institutionalizing Innovation* by M. Jelinek, pp. 136–141. © 1979 by Marian Jelinek. Published 1979 by Praeger Publishers, an imprint of Greenwood Publishing Group, Inc., Westport, CT. Reprinted with permission.

Reprinted from *Long Range Planning*, vol. 21, no. 3. A. Langley, "The Roles of Formal Strategic Planning," pp. 40–50. Copyright 1988 with permission from Pergamon Press Ltd., Headington Hill Hall, Oxford OX3 0BW, UK.

Not to our fantasies
—may they mostly fall
as fast as they rise—
but to the wonders of reality

Contents

Acknowledgments

I always get irked when authors finish this piece with: despite all this wonderful help and advice, everything that is wrong is really my fault. I should hope so! For there is almost no mass-produced product in society so personal as a book. Of course, the content does depend critically on the work and good-will of other people—the authors who came before as well as the advisors who appeared during. In production, however, the author is wholly dependent on others (and can, in fact, blame them, although, happily, I have no need to do that here).

I must thank a few special people who did try to set me straight on the content. I did listen, I assure you, even if sometimes I either disagreed or else was just too pig-headed. Ann Langley read the entire manuscript very carefully and provided a great deal of sensible advice, some of it too sensible for the likes of me. But if you find the tone of parts of the discussion that follows a bit strident, just imagine how it read before Ann made her comments! Similarly helpful comments were made by Bob Simons, who like Ann, even throughout doctoral studies, has always been a wonderfully sympathetic and stimulating colleague.

George Sawyer not only provided helpful feedback but championed this book right from the start in a way that I found most encouraging, especially given his active role in the planning field and The Planning Forum in particular. We shall all miss him.

I did take every bit of advice—I wouldn't dare not—from Kate Maguire-Devlin, who manages my professional life and managed the preparation of this manuscript, as well as from Jody Bessner and David Myles, who dealt with all the picky details of it, which at times became a minor nightmare. I know it was all an excuse to shmooze in the outer office, gang, but I am grateful nonetheless—I love it too!

At The Free Press in New York, one of those rare publishing houses that does things the old way—i.e., with commitment and care—it often seemed like I was the one giving the advice. But I did win one—look at this design and compare it with their old way! Of course, I had Cathy Peck on my side, who was part of a similar publishing activity on the other side of the Atlantic, at Prentice-Hall International, which is doing the book overseas. I thank her and Bob Wallace as well as Celia Knight and Lisa Cuff at The Free Press for their considerate support.

McGill continues to support me wonderfully well, and I write this while at INSEAD, which is most kind to let me "hang out" when the urge to be back in France overwhelms me once again.

Finally, I dedicated my first book to Susie and Lisa "who manage me" and "who well know that [their father] writes books in the basement and that he is not to be disturbed. Shhh . . ." Well, little did they know that exactly two decades later, it was I who would be disturbing them from France, sending them repeatedly down into the basement to dig out all kinds of obscure references and quotes, which they did most goodnaturedly. Believe me kids, that wasn't the plan.

Fontainebleau, France
May 1993

A Note to the Reader

I would be delighted to know that everybody read everything. And dismayed to find that nobody read anything. My suspicion, however, is that most of you will read something. So let me at least try to encourage you to read as much of direct relevance to yourself as possible.

This book consists mostly of rather long chapters. I know I should have had sixteen chapters instead of six—we all feel a sense of accomplishment at having finished a chapter, and so this book could have provided a lot more accomplishment. But, frankly, that would not have made it any shorter, or better, and there was just no logical way to slice it differently. (No thirty-minute planners here, let alone one-minute managers.) There are six basic themes represented in the chapters of this book that build up to the fifth, and then consider the consequences in the sixth: an introduction to the concepts (chapter 1), a review of what strategic planning has been (2), evidence on its performance (3), two sets of criticisms of the process, one of its more evident "pitfalls" (4), the other of its deeper "fallacies" (5), and, finally, what planners might do about all this (6).

The real heart of the argument is contained in Chapter 5, on the fallacies. I like to think there are a number of important points here, that go well beyond the practice of planning, in fact. And so, if you have bothered to buy this book, or even to have borrowed it, I urge you to read this chapter, more or less completely. There are a few sections of it that could be skipped, such as "Forecasting as Magic" and "Forecasting and 'Turbulence' " (both actually quite fun, I believe), "Scenarios Instead of Forecasts," "Contingency Planning Instead of Deterministic Planning," and " 'Marketing Myopia' Myopia" (also good fun).

But, please, no matter what else you read, skip neither the Introduction to the book nor Chapter 1. These are not very long, and should be read carefully. Otherwise you will be scratching your head throughout and wondering what in the world I mean by planning or by strategy or by the positioning school, etc.

Beyond this, you can pick and choose according to your own needs. Chapter 2 reviews the basic structure and models of the process known as strategic planning, as depicted in the literature. If you know this, you might want to skip or at least scan much of this chapter. But I do urge you to read the tiny subsection called "A Missing Detail," and to look at the following section called "Sorting Out the Four Hierarchies," which presents these processes in a different way. Read especially the introduction to this section, and its final subsection called "The 'Great Divide' of Planning." You might also consider the following section that presents "Forms of 'Strategic Planning' " in this new perspective.

Chapter 3 goes through some evidence on planning, followed by the response of planners to this evidence. The "Survey Evidence on 'Does Planning Pay?' " concludes that it does not necessarily. It may be of interest if you wish to know how academics can tie themselves into knots. The "Anecdotal Evidence" is brief and fun to read, but by this time you will know what I have in mind. The "Deeper Evidence" is just that, and should be of greater interest, especially "Some Evidence on Capital Budgeting," which I suspect contains important points. The last section, on "Planners' Responses to the Evidence," shows how some of them can be just as bad as academics. (See especially the subsections called "Planned Politics" and "Calculating Culture.") Mostly this material is light and easy to read (unless, of course, you are the target). The subsection on "Ansoff's Elaborations" was necessary to include and is necessarily long, but might be of special interest to readers who know well the work of this important author.

Chapter 4 reconceives the classic "pitfalls" of planning. (You will have to read the last subsection of Chapter 3 on the "Pitfalls: 'Them not us' " to understand this.) It shows how some of the planners' favorite arguments can be turned around to demonstrate how planning can discourage commitment, impede serious change, and encourage politics. This could all be skipped and Chapter 5 would still make sense, but I think there are a number of points worthy of careful consideration here. This chapter is a bit of a portfolio of problems with planning, so feel free to pick and choose. The subsections I like best include "Commitment at the Top" and "Commitment Lower Down," "Commitment Versus Calculation," "Flexible Planning: Wanting Things Both Ways," "The Biases of Objectivity," "Obsession with Control," "Our age is turbulent, Chicken Little" (don't skip this one!), and "Illusion of Control?"

Chapter 6 is written especially for planners and for people who work closely with them. It presents a kind of reconceived model of the roles for planning, plans, and planners, summarized in the short section about two-thirds of the way through called "A Plan for Planners." I would also urge you to read the brief section that follows it called "A Planner for Each Side of the Brain." Aside from this, the introductory section on "Coupling Analysis and Intuition" is short and sets up what follows. The discussion of the various roles, quite detailed, will be of greatest interest to practitioners and can otherwise be easily skimmed (with the help of the various diagrams). The subsection on "Strategic Control" presents a different perspective of this process, while the proposed "First Role of Planners: Finders of Strategy" is unusual. I believe the discussion of the "Third Role of Planners: Catalysts" should be noted, as it is nuanced somewhat differently from the usual discussion of this subject. I also believe that the subsections here on the "Role of Formalization" and "The Formalization Edge" are of particular importance. In the last section, on "Planners in Context," read the brief introductory "Forms of Organizations," and then choose your own context(s) for reading accordingly.

Beyond this, don't plan excessively. Just read!

Introduction: The "Planning School" in Context

"I was in a warm bed, and suddenly I'm part of a plan."
Woody Allen in *Shadows and Fog*

This is a history book of sorts about so-called strategic planning. Through its literature we trace the story of that concept, from its origins around 1965 through its rise to prominence and its subsequent fall. In so doing, we seek to learn about planning, about strategy, and about the relationship between the two. We also seek to understand, more narrowly, about how the literature of management can sometimes get so carried away; more broadly, about the appropriate place for analysis in organizations; and more practically, about the useful roles that can be played in today's organizations by planners and plans as well as by planning. The story of the rise and fall of strategic planning, in other words, teaches us not only about formal technique itself but also about how organizations function and how managers do and don't cope with that functioning, also about how we, as human beings, think and sometimes stop thinking.

This book began as one piece of a larger work. In 1968, I set out to write a text called *The Theory of Management Policy*, to draw together the research-based literature that helps to describe the processes of general management. There were to be chapters on managerial work, organization structure, and organization power among others, as well as a chapter on the process of strategy formation. But after each of those first three individual chapters became a book in itself (Mintzberg, 1973, 1979a, 1983), it stood to reason that the remaining one would also constitute a book. But it did not. In outline it proved too long for one book, so it was split into two volumes, one to be called *Strategy Formation: Schools of Thought*, the other, *Strategy Formation: Toward a General Theory*. The first volume went well until I did the third chapter, on the "planning school." That too ran rather long. Hence the present publication, a book within a book within a book within a book.

Setting this book into its context may help to explain its specific focus, which some readers may find narrow, especially with regard to its view of planning. But while I do restrict the bounds of planning here, I believe the narrow definition I ascribe to the process is appropriate. One problem, as we shall see, has been an unwillingness by the proponents of planning to bound the concept at all. Indeed, in another respect this book tries to be rather broad, by addressing tentatively that most fundamental issue of all: the place of analysis, not only in our organizations but also in our cognitive makeup as human beings. Confounding analysis with "rationality"—calling it "systematic," "objective," "logical," and other good things—has narrowed our view of the world, sometimes with disastrous consequences. The narrowness I prefer to be accused of here is in seeking to push analytical processes that slight our abilities to synthesize back to the side of human cognition (the left hemisphere of the brain?) where they belong.

A word on all ten schools of thought on strategy formation is in order before we begin (see Table 1, also Mintzberg, 1990b). Three are prescriptive, seeking to explain the "proper" ways of going about the making of strategy. The first I call the "design school," which considers strategy making as an informal process of conception, typically in a leader's conscious mind. The design school model, sometimes called SWOT (for internal strengths and weaknesses to be compared with external opportunities and threats), also underlies the second, which I call the "planning school" and which accepts the premises of the former, save two (to be discussed in Chapter 1)—that the process be informal and the chief executive be the key actor. These differences may seem subtle, but we shall see that they are fundamental. The third, which I call the "positioning school," focuses on the content of strategies (differentiation, diversification, etc.) more than on the processes by which they are prescribed to be made (which are generally assumed, often implicitly, to be those of the planning school). In other words, the positioning school simply extrapolates the messages of the planning school into the domain of actual strategy content. As I shall save my comments on that school for a later volume, I ask the reader to please forgive the paucity of references here to Boston Consulting Group (BCG) dogs, PIMS homilies about market share, etc., and Michael Porter's more substantive ideas. I shall get to them in due course.

I shall not write a great deal at this point about the seven other schools of strategy formation, schools more *descriptive* than prescriptive in nature, because that might give away a theme that underlies the conclusions of this book (which is—cover your eyes—that there must be other ways besides planning to make strategy). But let me just note them: the "cognitive school" considers what happens in a human head that tries to cope with strategy; the "entrepreneurial school" depicts strategy making as the visionary process of a strong leader; the "learning school" finds strategy to emerge in a process of collective learning; the "political

Table 1: **Schools of Thought on Strategy Formation**
(from Mintzberg, 1990b)

School	View of Process
Design	Conceptual
Planning	Formal
Positioning	Analytical
Cognitive	Mental
Entrepreneurial	Visionary
Learning	Emergent
Political	Power
Cultural	Ideological
Environmental	Passive
Configurational	Episodic

school" focuses on conflict and the exploitation of power in the process; the "cultural school" considers the collective, cooperative dimension of the process; the "environmental school" sees strategy making as a passive response to external forces; and the "configurational school" seeks to put all the other schools into the contexts of specific episodes in the process. This book will refer to some of these schools occasionally, will also occasionally refer to their concepts of culture and politics, among others, and will especially make pointed comparisons between strategy making as a process of planning and one of vision and especially of learning. In this history of the rise and fall of the process known as strategic planning, told through its literature, we seek the lessons that can be drawn from these experiences.

The mid-1990s is perhaps the right time to publish such a book. It might have been dismissed before 1973, when planning could do no wrong, and after that submerged in the wave of anti-planning sentiment that continued for a decade or more. Following the buffeting that planning received, perhaps now people are more inclined to consider it in a more reasonable way, as neither a panacea nor the pits but a process with particular benefit in particular contexts. I believe, in other words, that we are now ready to extract the planning baby from all that strategic planning bathwater. It makes no more sense to fire all the planners in great bloodbaths than it does to expect their systems to make strategy for everyone else. It is time to settle on a set of balanced roles for planning, plans, and planners in organizations.

One final point: A certain cynicism of tone pervades much of this book. Perhaps the reader will forgive it when bearing in mind that he or she has to see only this final result of my work. I, in turn, had to read huge quantities of some awfully banal literature. In the midst of doing that, I heard an item on Canadian radio news about the opening of a new mine from which the owners expected to extract about three-quarters of an ounce of gold for every ton of ore. My immediate reaction was—if only I had been able to do as well with this literature! But I did find some gold, which has enabled me to close this book on a positive note. There are indeed ways to couple the skills and inclinations of the planners with the authority and flexibility of the managers to assure a strategy making process that is informed, integrative, and responsive to changes in an organization's environment.

1

Planning and Strategy

What is the relationship between planning and strategy? Is strategy making simply a process of planning, as the proponents of planning have so vigorously insisted? Or, at the other extreme, is strategic planning simply another oxymoron, like progressive conservative or jumbo shrimp (or civil engineer?). In other words, should strategy always be planned, never be planned, or sometimes be planned? Or should it relate to planning in some other way?

Barely anything written about planning or strategy provides considered answers to these questions. This book seeks to do so. We begin in this chapter by addressing some other basic questions. First we ask, "What is planning anyway?" After considering a variety of popular answers, we narrow them down to a definition of our own. Next we ask, "Why plan?" and provide the answers according to planners. (Our own answers come later.) Finally we ask, "And what is strategy?" and answer in a way that is opposite to planning by insisting on the need for several definitions. Then, after considering briefly planning, plans, and planners, we conclude this opening chapter with the plan for the rest of the book.

What Is Planning Anyway?

This may seem like a strange question to ask as the twentieth century draws to a close, given the long popularity of planning, especially (ironically) in both Corporate America and Communist Europe. Largely a budget exercise in the America of the 1950s, it began to spread quickly, having become firmly installed in most large corporations by the mid-1960s (Gilmore, 1970:16; Chamberlain, 1968:151). At that point the notion of strategic planning took hold, to become within a decade a virtual obsession among American corporations (and in American government, in the form of the Planning-Programming-Budgeting System, or PPBS).

In fact, however, the concept dates much farther back. There is even a reference to a "Director of Strategic Planning" in Sun Tzu's *The Art of War* (1971:146), originally written about 2,400 years ago (although a Chinese student of mine considers this title too loose a translation from the Chinese). But there is no doubt about the translation of Henri Fayol's work. Writing of his experiences as a French mining chief executive in the last century, he noted the existence of "ten-yearly forecasts . . . revised every five years" (1949:47). Despite all this attention, the fact remains that the question, "What is planning anyway?", has never been properly answered—indeed, seldom seriously addressed—in planning's own literature.

In 1967, in what remains one of the few carefully reasoned articles on the subject, Loasby wrote that "the word 'planning' is currently used in so many and various senses that it is in some danger of degenerating into an emotive noise" (1967:300). At about the same time, one of the more impressive assemblages of planning people took place at Bellagio, Italy, (Jantsch, 1969) under the auspices of the OECD. Jay Forrester's "reflection" on the conference included the comment that "efforts to define the terms [planning and long-range forecasting] failed" (1969a:503). They have failed ever since.

Aaron Wildavsky, a political scientist well-known for his criticisms of planning, concluded that in trying to be everything, planning became nothing:

> Planning protrudes in so many directions, the planner can no longer discern its shape. He may be economist, political scientist, sociologist, architect or scientist. Yet the essence of his calling— planning—escapes him. He finds it everywhere in general and nowhere in particular. Why is planning so elusive? (1973:127)

"Planning" may be so elusive because its proponents have been more concerned with promoting vague ideals than achieving viable positions, more concerned with what planning might be than what it actually became. As a result, planning has lacked a clear definition of its own place in organizations and in the state. Yet it is our belief that planning has, nevertheless, carved out a viable niche for itself, through its own successes and failures. The need, therefore, is not to create a place for planning so much as to recognize the place it already does occupy.

This book seeks to describe that place with regard to strategy—in effect, to develop an *operational* definition of planning in the context of strategy making. But we do not begin with the assumption that planning is whatever people called planners happen to do, or that planning is any process that generates formal plans. People called planners can sometimes do strange things, just as strategies can sometimes result from strange processes. We need to delineate the word carefully if it is not to be eventually dropped from the management literature as hopelessly contaminated. We begin here by considering *formal* definitions of planning; the rest of this book is about the operational definition.

To some people **(1) planning is future thinking,** simply taking the future into account. "Planning denotes thinking about the future," wrote Bolan (1974:15). Or in the more poetic words of Sawyer, "Planning is action laid out in advance" (1983:1).

The problem with this definition is that it cannot be bounded. What organizational activity, no matter how short-term or reactive, does not take the future into account? Newman acknowledged the problem back in 1951 when he quoted Dennison that "Almost all work, in order to be done at all, must be planned, at the least informally and a few minutes ahead" (1951:56). By this definition, planning includes ordering a sandwich for lunch as much as establishing a division to flood the market with sandwiches. In fact, Fayol understood this breadth of the term back in 1916 when he wrote that:

> The maxim, "managing means looking ahead," gives some idea of the importance attached to planning in the business world, and it is true that if foresight is not the whole of management at least it is an essential part of it. (1949:43, published in French in 1916)

But if this is true—if, as Dror put it more baldly, "planning, in a word, is management" (1971:105)—why bother to use the word "planning" when "management" works just fine?

To others, **(2) planning is controlling the future,** not just thinking about it but acting on it, or as Weick (1979) is fond of saying, *en*acting it. "Planning is the design of a desired future and of effective ways of bringing it about," Ackoff wrote (1970:1). Others expressed the same thought when they defined the purpose of planning as "to create controlled change in the environment" (Ozbekhan, 1969:152), or, more pointedly, "the design of social systems" (Forrester, 1969b:237). In this regard, John Kenneth Galbraith argued in his book, *The New Industrial State*, that big business engages in planning to "replace the market," to "exercise control over what is sold . . . [and] what is supplied" (1967:24).

But this second definition of planning, really just the other side of the coin from the first, suffers from the same problem of excessive breadth. By associating planning with free will, it becomes synonymous again with popular uses of the word management and so loses distinctive meaning.

> Since practically all actions with future consequences are planned actions, planning is everything, and nonplanning can hardly be said to exist. Nonplanning only exists when people have no objectives, when their actions are random and not goal-directed. If everybody plans (well, almost) it is not possible to distinguish planned from unplanned actions. (Wildavsky, 1973:130)

Schumacher (1974) provides some conceptual help here. By distinguishing the past from the future, acts from events, and certainty from uncertainty, eight possible cases are constructed:

1. act-past-certain
2. act-future-certain
3. act-past-uncertain
4. act-future-uncertain
5. event-past-certain
6. event-future-certain
7. event-past-uncertain
8. event-future-uncertain (188–189)

This approach is used to clarify such words as "plan," "forecast," and "estimate," and we can use it here to help position planning. The first two definitions in the list appear to place planning in cases 2 and 4—how to act in the future, whether certain or uncertain, or how to make it certain by enacting it. Anything to do with events—things that "simply happen"—is outside of the realm of planning: "to apply the word 'planning' to matters outside the planner's control is absurd," although that can be a part of "forecasting" (189). Thus planning is precluded, for example, from cases 5 and 8, the given past and the uncertain, uncontrollable future, although the author noted the frequency with which case 8 forecasts are "presented as if they were plans" (189). Alternately, " 'estimates' are put forward which upon inspection turn out to be plans" (190). As for the past (e.g., case 1), planning would hardly seem to have a role to play here, although, as we shall see near the end of this book, planners themselves may have roles in that studies of past behavior can influence future events (cases 2 and 4).

Still, we need a definition of planning that tells us not *that* we have to think about the future, not even that we should try to control it, but *how* these things are done. In other words, planning has to be defined by the *process* it represents. In this regard, a number of writers have proposed, sometimes inadvertently, that **(3) planning is decision making.** As far back as 1949, Goetz defined planning as "fundamentally choosing" (in Steiner, 1979:346), and in 1958 Koontz defined it as "the conscious determination of courses of action designed to accomplish purposes. Planning is, then, deciding" (1958:48). Likewise, Snyder and Glueck, without labeling it decision making, defined planning as "those activities which are concerned specifically with determining in advance what actions and/or human and physical resources are required to reach a goal. It includes identifying alternatives, analyzing each one, and selecting the best ones" (1980:73). Similarly, in certain literature of the public sector (so-called public planning), the term planning has been used as a virtual synonym for decision making and project management (see, for example, the various writings of Nutt [e.g., 1983, 1984]). Others tried to nuance this definition: Drucker, for example, by discussing the "futurity of present decisions" (1959:239), and Ozbekhan, by describing the "future directed decision process" (1969:151).

But unless anyone can think of a decision process that is not future-directed, these nuances are of little help.[1] Assuming that

---

[1] As are those of Dror, who described planning as "a means of improving decisions" (1971:105), and Ansoff and Brandenburg, who characterized it as "a process of setting formal guidelines and constraints for the behavior of the firm" (1967:B220).

decision means commitment to action (see Mintzberg, Raisinghani, and Théorêt, 1976), every decision takes the future into consideration by a vow to act, whether it be to market a product in ten years or ship one in ten minutes. Rice recognized this when he argued that "*all* decisions are made with forethought," that every decision maker has "a reason for making his decision," which amounts to a "plan" (1983:60).[2]

Thus, this third definition really reduces to the first and, because commitment is an act of free will, to the second as well. Accordingly, planning again becomes synonymous with everything managers do, "part of the intellectual process the policy maker employs to reach his decision," even if "informal, unstructured" (Cooper, 1975:229). In fact, to make their case that managers do indeed plan, Snyder and Glueck used the example of a school superintendent dealing with the efforts of a councilman to disrupt school board meetings and discredit him. But if planning is reacting to such pressures in the short term, then what isn't planning? Indeed, these authors quoted George (1972) that:

> *Planning*, of course, is not a separate, recognizable act. . . . Every managerial act, mental or physical is inexorably intertwined with planning. It is as much a part of every managerial act as breathing is to the living human. (1980:75, italics in original)

But if that is true, why describe what organizations do as planning, any more than describe what people do as breathing? In other words, who needs the planning label when decision making or even managing does the job? As Sayles noted, planning (presumably by any of these first definitions) and decision making "are inextricably bound up in the warp and woof of the [manager's] interaction pattern, and it is a false abstraction to separate them" (1964:2087).[3]

---

[2] Rice, however, went on, like the others quoted above, to equate planning with decision making. "By looking at the existence of strategic decisions, it is possible to infer that strategic planning actually occurred, even though that strategic planning may not have been extensive, formalized or accurate" (1983:60).

[3] Corresponding to the confusion of planning and decision making is the confusing of plans and decisions. At the age of eight, my daughter Susie said, "I have a plan. Every night, whenever I have time, I'll chop the ice in the window and take it

Let us, therefore, begin to consider more bounded definitions of planning as a process. **(4) Planning is integrated decision making.** To Schwendiman, it is an "integrated decision structure" (1973:32). To van Gunsteren, it "means fitting together of ongoing activities into a meaningful whole" (1976:2): "Planning implies getting somewhat more organized. . . . It means making a feasible commitment around which already available courses of action get organized" (2–3).

The last definition may seem close to the preceding one. But because it is concerned not so much with the making of decisions as with the conscious attempt to integrate different ones, it is fundamentally different and begins to identify a position for planning. Consider the words of Ackoff:

> Planning is required when the future state that we desire involves a set of interdependent decisions; that is, a system of decisions. . . . the principal complexity in planning derives from the interrelatedness of the decisions rather than from the decisions themselves. . . . (1970:2, 3)

This view of planning finally takes us into the realm of strategy making, since that process also deals with the interrelationships among decisions (important ones) in an organization. But because this normally has to take place over time, such coordination among decisions is rendered difficult. Planning as integrated decision making imposes a particularly stringent requirement, however: that the decisions in question be batched—be drawn together periodically into a single, tightly coupled process so that they can all be made (or at least approved) at a single point in time. As Ozbekhan noted of the result, " 'Plan' refers to an integrative hierarchically organized action constraint in which various kinds of decisions are functionally ordered" (1969:153).

It is this requirement that may help to explain why planning is

---

away." (The roof was leaking. Like many plans, incidentally, this one was longer on intentions than on actions.) What did she mean? A year later, asked what a plan was, she said, "A plan is when you get something ready." Her sister Lisa, at the age of seven, was clearer: "A plan is something you're going to do." In other words, it is a commitment to action—a decision. (Susie and Lisa were just reflecting popular sentiment, ones I hope they had not picked up from their father!)

sometimes treated as synonymous with decision making. If different decisions have to be batched, they may come to resemble a single decision. Hence planning writers have tended to confuse decision making with strategy making by assuming that the latter necessarily involves the selection of a single course of action—the choice of an integrated strategy at one point in time. Normann, in fact, made this point about Igor Ansoff's well-known writings on planning:

> Ansoff regards the choice of strategy and the formulation of policy chiefly as a decision process: first, goals are established, after which (using a series of analytical techniques) alternatives are evolved and (still using analytical techniques) a choice made among them, possibly after some adjustments in the original goals. (1977:8–9)

But since, as we shall see, there are other ways in which to make strategy, notably dynamically *over* time, the process of integrating decisions at a point in time becomes, not strategy making, but simply *planning's approach* to strategy making, the situation to which it restricts *itself*. Thus its position becomes clearer. However, it is still not clear enough. Visionary leaders likewise integrate decisions, in their cases informally, or, if you prefer, intuitively. Yet to encompass their behavior under the planning label would again seem to broaden it beyond reasonable (and current) usage. (Indeed, as we shall see, some of the most influential writers in this field pit planning process *against* managerial intuition.) Thus something more is needed to identify planning.

That something, in our view, is the key to understanding planning—formalization. **(5) Planning is a formalized procedure to produce an articulated result, in the form of an integrated system of decisions.** What to us captures the notion of planning above all—most clearly distinguishes its literature and differentiates its practice from other processes—is its emphasis on formalization, the systemization of the phenomenon to which planning is meant to apply. Thus Bryson referred to strategic planning as a "disciplined effort," in fact, "simply a set of concepts, procedures and tests" (1988:512), while in some of the research literature the term FSP was substituted for strategic planning, with the f for formal (e.g., Pearce et al., 1987).

Formalization here would seem to mean three things, especially

(a) to decompose, (b) to articulate, and especially (c) to rationalize the processes by which decisions are made and integrated in organizations.

An emphasis on formal *rationality* permeates the literature of planning. Denning contrasted the "systematic" with the "haphazard" (1973:26–27), while Steiner argued that "Plans can and should be to the fullest possible extent objective, factual, logical, and realistic in establishing objectives and devising means to obtain them" (1969:20). Similarly, Dror claimed that in the public sector "planning is at present the most structured and professionalized mode of policy making," given its "explicit attention to internal consistency" and its "effort to supply structured rationality" (1971:93).

Rationality of this formal kind is, of course, rooted in analysis, not synthesis. Above all, planning is characterized by the decompositional nature of analysis—reducing states and processes to their component parts. Thus the process is formally reductionist in nature. This may seem curious, given that the intention of planning is to *integrate* decisions. But the performance of planning has been curious too and for this very reason, as we shall see. Here, in any event, we seek to characterize planning by the nature of its process, not by its intended results. In fact, the key, if implicit, assumption underlying strategic planning is that *analysis will produce synthesis:* decomposition of the process of strategy making into a series of articulated steps, each to be carried out as specified in sequence, will produce integrated strategies. This, in fact and not incidentally, is the old "machine" assumption, the one that underlies the design of the manufacturing assembly line—itself a kind of machine of human steps. If every component is produced by the machine as specified and assembled in the order prescribed, an integrated product will appear at the end of the line. Indeed, as we shall see, this analogy underlies some of the most important thinking in the field of planning, and has proved to be patently false. Organizational strategies cannot be created by the logic used to assemble automobiles.

Along with rationality and decomposition, articulation is the third key component of formalization. The product of planning—the plans themselves—after being carefully decomposed into strategies and substrategies, programs, budgets, and objectives, must be clearly and explicitly labeled—by words and, preferably, numbers on sheets of paper. Thus Zan, in a carefully reasoned paper called "What Is Left for Formal Planning?," concluded that "the common characteristic" of various planning systems is "the process of rendering things explicit," in terms of both processes and their consequences (1987:193). George Steiner, probably the most prolific of the business planning writers, noted that the word planning comes from the Latin *planum*, "meaning flat surface" (1969:5). Leaving aside the prophetic powers of the Romans with regard to a literature that was to follow in two millennia, Steiner went on to note that the word "entered the English language in the Seventeenth Century, referring principally to forms, such as maps or blueprints, that were drawn on flat surfaces" (1969:5–6). Thus, the word has long been associated with formalized documents.

So now we seem to have a more operational definition of planning, since the word can be identified with two observable phenomenon in organizations—the use of formalized procedure and the existence of articulated result, specifically concerning an integrated system of decisions.

This may seem to some people an unnecessarily restricted definition of the term. We think not. This book's introduction suggested that planning is one proposed approach to strategy making among several that are possible. It certainly does not encompass the whole process. The theoreticians of planning may have intended a broader definition of the word, but the reality of planning—its actual practice, let alone its tangible accomplishments—tell a much different story. Our claim, which we believe to be demonstrated in the rest of this book, is that the definition proposed here is, by virtue of planners' own behaviors, closest to the one that planning has created for itself, and, indeed, has chosen for itself, however implicitly. In other words, in this book planning is defined by what it *is* (and that, it should be noted parenthetically in a departure from Wildavsky, is something!).

To some people, when corporate executives go off to a mountain retreat to discuss strategy, that is planning. To others, adapting to external pressures informally over time is also planning. In principle, there is no problem with this. In practice, however, it creates all kinds of confusion. For example, the planners may not understand why the executives at the retreat did not structure their discussions more systematically. Had they simply called their retreat "strategic thinking," this would not happen. Because the word planning, implicitly when not explicitly, is associated with formalization, use of it presupposes the requisite decomposition, articulation, and rationalization. But for those readers who are still not persuaded by our use of the term, we suggest that every time we write planning, you read formal planning. Eventually you will probably drop the adjective, because, we hope, you begin to agree with us rather than out of just plain weariness.

Obviously, formalization is a relative, not an absolute, term. And obviously, planners carry out a range of activities, some more, some less formal. But as a process, we argue here that planning sits toward the formal end of the continuum of organizational behavior. (We shall specify this in the last chapter.) It must be seen, not as decision making, not as strategy making, and certainly not as management, or as the preferred way of doing any of these things, but simply as the effort to formalize parts of them—through decomposition, articulation, and rationalization.

Why Plan (According to Planners)?

Given that this is planning, the question then becomes—why do it? In a word, why formalize? And correspondingly, why decompose, why articulate, and why rationalize? The answer must extend throughout our discussion: in a sense, that is what this book is about—why and why not do these things. But at this point, it is appropriate to consider how planners themselves have answered the question.

We shall discuss these answers in the form of imperatives, for this is how they tend to be found in so much of the literature of planning. To many of its writers, planning became not just *an* approach to managing the organization's future but the *only* conceivable one, at the limit a virtual religion to be promulgated with the fervor of missionaries. "If you say, 'Is every part of GE planned strategically?' I have to say no," commented one man who headed this function in what was once known as America's most planning-oriented company. He concluded, "Some SBUs [Strategic Business Units] do not have good strategies"! (Rothschild in Cohen, 1982:8) In a legacy—and a phrase—inherited from Frederick Taylor, who developed the initial practice of "scientific management," and

honed through half a century of increasingly rationalistic approaches to management, planning anointed itself as the "one best
way."

1. Organizations must plan to coordinate their activities. "Coordinate," "integrate," and "comprehensive" are words generously
used in the vocabulary of planning. A major argument in favor of
planning, as suggested in the third definition presented earlier, is
that decisions made together formally in a single process will ensure that the efforts of the organization are properly coordinated.
Thus Porter claimed in the Introduction to his book, *Competitive
Strategy:*

> The emphasis being placed on strategic planning today in firms in
> the United States and abroad reflects the proposition that there are
> significant benefits to gain through an *explicit* process of formulat-
> ing strategy, to insure that at least the policies (if not the actions) of
> functional departments are coordinated and directed at some com-
> mon set of goals. (1980:xiii, italics in original)

When the different activities of an organization take place at
cross-purposes—the salespeople have sold but the factory cannot
produce, or the office tower built yesterday is too small today—the
problem is usually attributed to the lack of (effective) planning. By
decomposing a strategy, or its consequences, into intentions attrib-
utable to each part of the organization, we ensure that the overall
job will get done—so long, of course, as each carries out (that is,
"implements") his, her, or its plan. Here, again, we have that old
machine assumption.

Moreover, the articulation of plans provides a mechanism of
communication that promotes coordination across the different
parts of the organization. Sawyer, for example, wrote of "the need
[through planning] to bring the management process of the organization out of the individual minds of one or a few leaders and
into a forum amongst a management group" (1983:5), where it can
be shared and discussed, perhaps, as Zan suggested, helping to
create consensus (1987:192). Some writers, in fact, have claimed
that planning is of value in and of itself ("it's the process that
counts") because of its capacity to enhance communication in the
organization, for example, by "enriching [people's] common un-

derstanding of corporate objectives and businesses" (Hax and Majluf, 1984:66). Fayol even claimed that "The Plan . . . builds unity, and mutual confidence," and that it "leads to . . . a broadened outlook" (1949:xi).

There can be little doubt that plans and planning can serve as important mechanisms to knit disparate activities together. But to consider this an imperative or, as Weick characterized the underlying assumption, that "organizations are rational arrangements of people and props which are held together by plans" (1969:101), is another matter. Coordination can be effected in other ways too—through informal communication among different actors (called "mutual adjustment"), through the sharing of the norms and beliefs of a common culture, also through the direct supervision by a single leader (see Mintzberg, 1979a:2–7). And even when plans do serve in a coordinating role, it cannot be assumed that planning (that is, formalized procedure) has created those plans. As for the claim that the planning process naturally enhances communication, well, meetings held for any purpose can do that!

2. Organizations must plan to ensure that the future is taken into account. "The first reason for looking at the future in a systematic way is to understand the future implications of present decisions," also "the present implications of future events" (Loasby, 1967:301). What planning does specifically in this regard is to introduce "a *discipline* for long-term thinking in the firm" (Hax and Majluf, 1984:66, italics added).

The future can be taken into account in three basic ways (paraphrasing Starr, 1971:315):

1. preparing for the inevitable
2. preempting the undesirable
3. controlling the controllable

Clearly, no self-respecting manager would be caught avoiding any of these things. There is good reason to try to take the future into account. But need that be done systematically and formally, that is, through planning? In many cases, no doubt, it should be. But always? The future can be taken into account in other ways too, for example, informally, by an insightful individual, indeed, even by instinct. The squirrel gathering nuts for the winter certainly takes the future into account. Indeed, it does all three things on the above list concurrently, since winter is inevitable, hunger is undesirable, and nuts are controllable! Are we to conclude, therefore, that squirrels are more sophisticated than we might have thought, or planning is less so?

An obvious response to this—common in the literature—is that managers (unlike squirrels, perhaps) have so many things on their minds that they risk forgetting about the long-term future. Planning can at least be "a means for getting topics on the agenda" (Loasby, 1967:303). As March and Simon claimed in their " 'Gresham's Law' of Planning": "Daily routine drives out planning" (1958:185), or, as they restated it, highly programmed tasks tend to take precedence over highly unprogrammed ones. Planning thus becomes a means to program the unprogrammed: in the words of one General Electric planner, it "program[s] an executive's time" (Hekhuis, 1979:242). But does that resolve the problem: does forcing formal recognition of the future, let alone formalizing how it is dealt with, necessarily mean the future is properly taken into account?

3. Organizations must plan to be "rational." The prime reason put forth for engaging in planning is that it is simply a superior form of management: formalized decision making is better than nonformalized decision making. In Schwendiman's words, it "force[s] deeper thinking" (1973:64). "Strategic thinking rarely occurs spontaneously," claimed Michael Porter in *The Economist* (1987:17). Setting aside the fact that no evidence was offered for this astonishing statement, is there likewise any evidence that strategic thinking is promoted by strategic planning? "Without guidelines," Porter went on, "few managers knew what constituted strategic thinking" (17). Was he really claiming that with such guidelines they suddenly knew what it was? Was it that easy? Did the managers really need planners to tell them about strategic thinking? Again Wildavsky captured the sentiment well.

> Planning is not really defended for what it does but for what it symbolizes. Planning, identified with reason, is conceived to be the way in which intelligence is applied to social problems. The efforts of planners are presumably better than other people's because they result in policy proposals that are systematic, efficient, coordinated,

consistent, and rational. It is words like these that convey the superiority of planning. The virtue of planning is that it embodies universal norms of rational choice. (1973:141)

The literature has been quick to point out what is gained by formalizing behavior, though seldom with supporting evidence. But it almost never addressed what might be lost. Typical was a comment by Charles Hitch, to justify one of the greatest planning efforts (and failures) of all time, his installation of PPBS in the U.S. military and later the rest of the government in the 1960s. Hitch's point was that managers are not only busy but also overwhelmed with information and so cannot make decisions effectively without the aid of formal analysis.

> Almost never do we find one person who has an intuitive grasp of all the fields of knowledge that are relevant to a major defense problem. . . . in general, and especially when the choice is not between two but among many alternatives, systematic analysis is essential. . . . And wherever the relevant factors are diverse and complex, as they usually are in defense problems, unaided intuition is incapable of weighing them and reaching a sound decision. (1965:56)

But is "systematic analysis" capable of so doing? To what extent does it not aid intuition but impede it? Even if it were true that planning focuses "on the right set of issues," as claimed by two well-known writers in the field (Lorange and Vancil: 1977:x), again without supporting evidence, could we be sure that it focuses on them in the right way? Indeed, is there evidence that the "attention-direction, pace setting mechanism" called planning (Yavitz and Newman, 1982:109) really does encourage thinking about the long term? And, above all, do we improve unprogrammed thinking by programming it? The evidence we shall cite later in this book, including that of the failure of Hitch's PPBS exercise (see Chapter 3), will throw into question the inclination of the planning literature to assume consistently favorable responses to all of these questions.

4. Organizations must plan to control. Using planning to control is a touchy subject in this literature, because planning is also claimed to motivate, to encourage participation, and to facilitate consensus. Yet the purpose of planning in order to effect control (the two words are often used concurrently, if not interchangeably, as in "planning and control systems"), is never far below the surface, and often right on it. "Planning is an activity by which man in society endeavors to gain mastery over himself and to shape his collective future by power of his reason" (Dror, 1971:105).

Control through planning extends itself in all directions, as is evident in the reasons for planning given earlier. To be sure, planning is meant to control others in the organization, namely those whose work is "coordinated." Thus among the "primary responsibilities" of the planning staff, Schwendiman lists:

1. The corporate planning staff should be responsible for planning the "system" and seeing that the steps are carried out in the proper sequence.
2. The staff should ensure quality, accuracy, and completeness in the planning done by others.
3. The staff should be responsible for coordinating the overall planning effort and pulling the individual pieces together. (1973:50)

Note that it is not only those down in the hierarchy whose work is controlled; if planning formalizes strategy making, it controls some of the work of top management as well. But control in planning does not stop there. Planning is also meant to control the future of the organization and, therefore, the environment outside the organization. "If the market is unreliable," as John Kenneth Galbraith wrote, the firm "cannot plan." Therefore, "much of what the firm regards as planning consists in minimizing or getting rid of market influences" (1967:26). Indeed, as in the quotation from Dror about "mastery over himself," planning even controls the planners, whose intuitive inclinations are preempted by their rational procedures. And when Zan wrote of planning "as a means of reducing external complexity to 'manageable' forms" (1987:192), he meant *conceptual* control—rendering the world simple enough to comprehend. Thus Lorange, in a paper entitled "Roles of the C.E.O. in Strategic Planning and Control Processes," noted that while the chief executive "typically cannot carry out the implementation of the design issues himself, he has to be sufficiently involved so as to control the processes" (1980b:1), which, of course, he must do through planning. "He might even in fact conclude that this . . . is his only realistic option for managing a large, complex organization" (2). Perhaps Lorange should have called it *"remote* control"!

Jelinek's Case for Planning

In her book, *Institutionalizing Innovation*, Mariann Jelinek presented one of the few carefully reasoned arguments in favor of strategic planning. Tackling the issue head-on, Jelinek sought to make the case for formalization per se, rooting her argument in the historical development of management science, or, more precisely, scientific management, as that term was coined early in this century for the work of Frederick Taylor.

As Jelinek pointed out, Taylor's contribution in his famous experiments in the formal study and routinization of manual work was not only to vastly improve procedures but to initiate a true revolution in the way that work was organized—"the codification of routine tasks." Taylor "for the first time made possible the large-scale coordination of details—planning and policy-level thinking, above and beyond the details of the task itself" (1979:136). This led to a fundamental division of labor—between the performance of the task and its coordination. And this in turn enabled management to be "abstracted," removed from the day-to-day operations, so that it "could concentrate on exceptions" (137).

Jelinek went on to point out that Taylor's efforts were extended into the administration function by Alexander Hamilton Church, in the area of cost accounting, "provid[ing] the means for abstracting management by making possible the description and monitoring of performance" (138). Then the work was extended to the most senior level of management through the introduction of the divisionalized form of structure, initially in Du Pont and then in General Motors. This innovation formalized the separation between operating a business and developing a corporate strategy.

> [This] made possible for the first time concerted coordination . . . and true policy for such organizations. So long as management is

overwhelmed by the details of task performance, planning and policy will not occur . . . That is, until what is routine is systematized and performance replicable without extensive management attention, management attention will necessarily focus on the routine. By the time of Du Pont and General Motors, the specification of task had moved from codifying workers' routine activities to codifying managers' routine activities. (138–139)

This led Jelinek to her basic point: The revolution that Taylor initiated in the factory was in the process of being repeated at the apex of the hierarchy, and *it would be fundamentally no different.* And the motor for this new revolution—the equivalent of Taylor's work-study methods although on a higher level of abstraction— was that set of formal systems of strategic planning and control: "It is through administrative systems that planning and policy are made possible, because the systems capture knowledge *about* the task . . ." (139). Such systems "create a shared pattern of thought, with focus explicitly shifted to the *pattern,* rather than the specific content"; they "generalize knowledge far beyond its original discoverer or discovery situation"; and "in generalizing the insights they codify, also make them accessible to change and refinement." Thus "true management by exception, and true policy direction are now possible, solely because management is no longer wholly immersed in the details of the task itself" (139, italics in original).

Jelinek's book is about a system called OST (Objectives, Strategies and Tactics) developed at the Texas Instruments company in the early 1960s and constituting, in her view, another step in the century-old sequence, this one "concerned with a higher logical level":

Rather than coordinating multiple routine tasks, the OST is focused on generating new tasks which may eventually themselves become routine. . . . As a system, the OST generalizes a procedure for acquiring the requisite new knowledge, creating a shared pattern of thought *regarding innovation.* . . . The OST specifies how to proceed, monitor, and evaluate. (141)

Thus, Jelinek highlighted some central premises that underlie the practice of strategic planning: the management of strategy can be sharply separated from the management of operations, and the strategy formation process itself can be programmed—in her words, "institutionalized"—by the use of formal systems; indeed, only through such institutionalization does that separation become possible. What Taylor accomplished in the factory, planning systems could now accomplish by extrapolation in the executive suite. By virtue of its powers of formalization, planning becomes the means to create as well as to operationalize strategy. In other words, strategic planning *is* strategy formation, at least in best practice. Hence the common tendency to use the two terms interchangeably.

Jelinek's argument is a fundamental one, perhaps the boldest one in the literature and certainly among the most sophisticated. It exposes the key premises that, if true, provide the basis for supporting planning, and if false, undermine some of its most active efforts. We shall, therefore, return to her arguments (as well as her own later views) at a key point in our discussion. At this point, by asking one last question, we wish to begin consideration of the premise that strategic planning and strategy formation are synonymous, at least in best practice.

And What Is Strategy?

Ask anyone, planner or otherwise, What is strategy? and you will almost certainly be told that **(a) strategy is a plan,** or something equivalent—a direction, a guide or course of action into the future, a path to get from here to there, etc. Then ask that person to describe the strategy that their organization or a competitive one has actually pursued over the past five years, and you will find that most people are perfectly happy to answer that question, oblivious to the fact that it violates their very own definition of the term.

It turns out that strategy is one of those words that we inevitably define in one way yet often use in another. **(b) Strategy is also a pattern,** that is, consistency in behavior over time. A company that perpetually markets the most expensive products in its industry pursues what is commonly called a high-end strategy, just as a person who always accepts the most challenging of jobs may be described as pursuing a high-risk strategy.

Now, both definitions seem to be valid—organizations develop

pl   ᵊy also evolve patterns out of their past.
We   ᵗategy and the other *realized* strategy.
The ᵢ   becomes: must realized strategies always

Ther   way to find out: Just ask those people who happily   u their (realized) strategies over the past five years what theiᵣ intended strategies were five years earlier. A few may claim that their intentions were realized perfectly. Suspect their honesty. A few others may claim that their realizations had nothing to do with their intentions. Suspect their behavior. Most, we propose, will give an answer that falls between these two extremes. For, after all, perfect realization implies brilliant foresight, not to mention inflexibility, while no realization implies mindlessness. The real world inevitably involves some thinking ahead of time as well as some adaptation en route.

As shown in Figure 1–1, intentions that are fully realized can be called *deliberate* strategies. Those that are not realized at all can be called *unrealized* strategies. The literature of planning recognizes both cases, with an obvious preference for the former. What it does

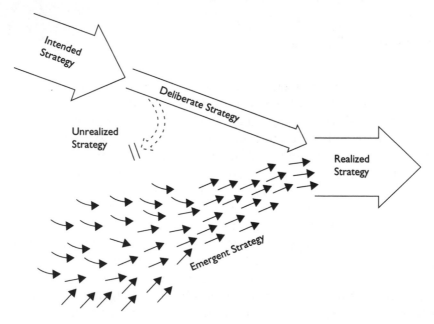

Figure 1–1
Forms of Strategy

not recognize is the third case, which we call *emergent* strategy—where a realized pattern was not expressly intended. Actions were taken, one by one, which converged in time in some sort of consistency or pattern. For example, rather than pursuing a strategy (read plan) of diversification, a company simply makes diversification decisions one by one, in effect testing the market. First it buys an urban hotel, next a restaurant, then a resort hotel, then another urban hotel with restaurant, and then another of these, etc., until the strategy (pattern) of diversifying into urban hotels with restaurants finally emerges.

As implied earlier, few, if any, strategies can be purely deliberate, and few can be purely emergent. One suggests no learning, the other, no control. All real-world strategies need to mix these in some way—to attempt to control without stopping the learning process. Organizations, for example, often pursue what may be called *umbrella* strategies: the broad outlines are deliberate while the details are allowed to emerge within them. Thus emergent strategies are not necessarily bad and deliberate ones good; effective strategies mix these characteristics in ways that reflect the conditions at hand, notably the ability to predict as well as the need to react to unexpected events.

Yet the literature of planning, including that book by Jelinek, considers effective strategy making a fully deliberate process, to the virtual exclusion of emergent elements. There is talk occasionally about flexible planning, but as with a pregnant virgin, the obvious contradiction is seldom addressed—except, of course, by those who believe in planning as immaculate conception.

Walter Kiechel of *Fortune* magazine once polled consultants who claimed that less than ten percent of strategies are successfully implemented; Tom Peters referred to that figure as "wildly inflated"! (in Kiechel, 1984:8). Often, when a strategy fails, those at the top of the hierarchy blame it on implementation lower down: "If only you dumbbells appreciated the brilliance of the strategy we formulated . . ." Well, those dumbbells down below might well respond: "If you're so smart, why didn't you take into account the fact that we are dumbbells?" In other words, every failure of implementation is, by definition, also a failure of formulation. If there is to be a separation between the two, so that one side thinks before the other side acts, then clearly, the capacity to act has to be taken into consideration in the thinking process.

But how smart can any thinker be? In other words, might the real problem not so much be in either poor implementation or weak formulation as in forcing an artificial separation between the two? If the formulators get closer to their implementation (which is typical for entrepreneurs), or the implementers have greater influence over formulation (which is what *intra*preneurship means), perhaps there can be greater successes in strategy making. Deliberate strategy relies on this artificial separation, while emergent strategy does not. Indeed, in the case of emergent strategy, the term form*u*lation has to be replaced by *formation* because here strategies can form without being formulated. Thus, we shall use the term strategy formation in the rest of this book, not because strategies have to be purely emergent but simply to allow for the fact that they can be, or, more realistically, almost inevitably *partially* are.

There is another important implication of emergent strategy, also slighted in most of the planning literature. Strategies need not emanate from a center. Implicit in deliberate strategy is the belief that strategy derives all at once from some central place—namely general management (or else the planning department). In the popular metaphors, the head thinks and the body acts, or the architect designs (on paper) so that the builders can construct with bricks and mortar. But in the case of emergent strategy, because big strategies can grow from little ideas (initiatives), and in strange places, not to mention at unexpected times, almost anyone in the organization can prove to be a strategist. All he or she needs is a good idea and the freedom and resources required to pursue it. Indeed, even the pervasion of a strategic initiative throughout the entire organization (to become a broadly-based strategy) need not be centrally controlled, let alone centrally planned, in some formal process on some formal schedule. For example, a salesperson may have an idea to sell an existing product to some new customers. As other salespeople realize what that person is doing, they begin to do so too, and one day, months later, management discovers that the company has entered a new market. The new pattern certainly was not planned. Rather, to introduce a distinction we shall make much of in this book, it was *learned*, in a collective process. But is that bad? Sometimes yes, sometimes no, just as is true of behaviors that are carefully planned.

One final implication of emergent strategy: In the planning literature there is a long tradition, inherited from the military, of distinguishing strategies from tactics. That is a convenient distinction for a literature that likes to decompose and determine the importance of things a priori. Strategies refer to the important things, tactics to the mere details. But the very meaning of emergent strategy is that one can never be sure in advance which will prove to be which. In other words, mere details can eventually prove to be strategic. After all, as was pointed out in that old nursery rhyme, the war could well have been lost all for want of a nail in the shoe of a horse. Care must therefore be taken not to leap into labeling things as intrinsically tactical or strategic. (The company in the earlier diversification example may have bought its first urban hotel inadvertently.) To quote Richard Rumelt, "one person's strategy is another's tactics—that what is strategic depends on where you sit" (1979a:197). It also depends on *when* you sit, because what seemed tactical yesterday might prove strategic tomorrow. Thus, the term tactical will not be used in this book, while strategic will be used as an adjective to mean relatively consequential, in patterns after actions are taken as well as in intentions that precede them.

We are not yet finished with definitions of strategies, for alongside *p*lan and *p*attern, we can add at least two more "p" words. Some years ago, McDonald's introduced a new product called Egg McMuffin—the American breakfast in a bun. This was to encourage the use of the restaurant facilities in the morning. If you ask a group of managers whether Egg McMuffin was a strategic change for McDonald's, you will inevitably hear two answers: "Yes, of course; it brought them into the breakfast market," and "Aw, come on, it's the same old stuff—the McDonald's way—just in a different package." In our view, these managers differ not so much as to whether this was a strategic change but in how they implicitly define the content of strategy in the first place.

To some people, notably Porter (1980, 1985) and his followers, **(c) strategy is position,** namely the determination of particular products in particular markets. To others, however, **(d) strategy is perspective,** namely an organization's way of doing things, in Peter Drucker's phrase, its concept of the business. As position, strategy looks *down*—to the "x" that marks the spot where the product meets the customer—and it looks *out*—to the external marketplace. As perspective, in contrast, strategy looks *in*—inside the organization, indeed, inside the head of the collective strategists—but it also looks *up*—to the grand vision of the enterprise (that forest seen above the trees, or is it the clouds that are being perceived?!).

As we shall see, the tendency in the planning literature has been to favor position over perspective. Claims notwithstanding, as soon as the practicalities of formalizing things come into play, strategy inevitably reduces to a set of positions. All those "x's" can be marked easily—identified and articulated—while perspective does not lend itself easily to decomposition.

Again, however, we need both definitions. McDonald's introduced Egg McMuffin successfully because the new position was consistent with the existing perspective. The executives of McDonald's seemed to understand well (though not necessarily in these terms) that one does not casually ignore perspective. (Anyone for McDuckling à l'Orange?) Changing position within perspective may be easy; changing perspective, even while maintaining position, is not. (Just ask the Swiss watchmakers about the introduction of quartz technology.) Figure 1–2 illustrates examples of this.

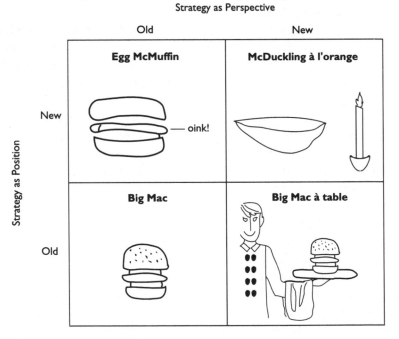

Figure 1–2
Strategy as Perspective Versus Strategy as Position

Clearly, organizations have to consider both positions and perspective in their strategy formation. A literature that favors one over the other does a disservice to that process.[4]

But the literature of planning does exactly that, as does it favor plan over pattern. Our conclusion is that "strategic planning" cannot be synonymous with strategy formation, which encompasses all of these, and certainly not with effectiveness in that process. The implication of this is that planning may have less to do with strategy making than is often claimed, but also that planners probably have more work to do than they sometimes realize!

Planners, Plans, and Planning

Many writers on business planning discuss the importance of top management in strategy formation, the fact that the chief executive is the foremost planner. But much else that is written reveals quite a different point of view. If intuition really is haphazard and unreliable, as is often claimed in this literature (as we shall see), then the role of managers must be circumscribed; if, as is also claimed, managers really are too busy to plan, then they cannot play the key role in the process of planning; if formal systems really should be used to make strategy, then perhaps managers should not; and if strategy really must be separated from operations, through the use of systems like OST and PPBS, then perhaps planning should also be separated from management.

In an early report published by the Boston Consulting Group and entitled "The Impact of Strategic Planning on Executive Behavior," Robert Mainer contrasted "the work of *planning* . . . with the work of *managing* a business that is traditional to the organization":

> The crux of the matter is that the behavioral requirements of planning as a management task are often different from, or in conflict

---

[4] A fifth "p," in common usage for the word strategy, could be added here— **strategy as ploy**, a specific maneuver intended to outwit an opponent or competitor (as in Schelling's [1980] book, *The Strategy of Conflict*; see also Porter's chapters on "Market Signals" and "Competitive Moves" in his book, *Competitive Strategy* [1980]).

with, the processes and content of management work normally prevalent in the organization. . . . To a very real extent, planning is a new kind of management activity. (1965:1)

Enter, therefore, the planner. The role of this actor in the strategy formation process was seldom made precise and has hardly ever been studied systematically. Instead, what comes through in the writings is the fact that the planner is an individual, or part of a specialized department, with no responsibility for line operations per se but with some vague mandate with respect to planning— whether to do it, encourage it, or simply coordinate its being done by others. Of course, since formal power lies with the line management, the writers were usually careful to relegate the planner's formal role to a secondary one of support:

[One] cardinal principle of planning theory is that "planning is always done by the line." The planning staff is to serve in a supportive role to line managers and is generally charged with keeping the planning "system" operative. (Schwendiman, 1973:43)

But the real sentiments in this literature lay elsewhere—with the planners themselves. Thus Steiner claimed that "if there is an intuitive genius at the helm, no formal planning is needed." One might surmise, therefore, that organizations led by ordinary people must plan. Not quite. "Even among companies not so blessed, success has been achieved without formal planning. For instance, a company may be lucky" (1979:44). Steiner's message is clear, however, for those companies that happen to lack genius as well as the right configuration of the stars.

Occasionally writers became even bolder. Leontiades, for example, questioned "the prescription that corporate planning staffs exist only to help managers plan," pointing out situations where "it may be the line managers who play a secondary role in fulfilling the overall corporate objective" (1979–80:22, 25–26). But one can almost hear his colleagues urging Professor Leontiades to bite his tongue. Even into the 1990s, the head of planning at one of America's major corporations (Bell & Howell) referred to strategic planners as being *"in charge* of guiding the direction for the company" (Marquardt, 1990:8, italics added).[5]

But Leontiades and Marquardt may be the honest ones. For if planning is designed to program strategy formation, and if that programming is to be accomplished by formal systems, then surely the design as well as the running of these systems has to fall to people with the requisite time as well as technical skills to be able to do so. And by any title, that means the planners. Thus, when this literature gets down to specifics, the roles intended for managers and planners do become clearer. Consider Pennington's guidelines to planners, which include: "involve the doers in planning" and "involve top management at key points, only at key points" (1972:3). What this meant in his example of a major steel company was that the chief executive's "important involvement" amounted to "only four points in the planning process, 1 day at a time": In October the CEO "reviews" the forecast (following which, the corporate plans are prepared by others); in February the CEO "participates" in a planning conference that examines gaps between performance and objectives; in June the CEO "reviews" the updated five-year plan and "gives it his blessing"; and in September the CEO "reviews and approves—sometimes after modification—the annual plans" (5). Lucy once told Charlie Brown that great art cannot be done in half an hour; it takes at least forty-five minutes. Four days every year from the CEO on the future of the company! Isn't that the natural consequence of Jelinek's process of institutionalization?

So far in this introduction we have discussed planning and introduced the planners. As noted earlier, we take the noun *planning* to mean formalized procedure to produce articulated result, in the form of an integrated system of decisions. As for *planners*, we

---

[5] Better still is Keane's example in an article about "the strategic planning external facilitator." The president "commissioned a strategic planning consultant" to develop a plan. The consultant launched a large consumer research study, interviewed all the relevant people, conducted an environment study, and organized and moderated a series of strategic planning sessions with the top executives. "All this cumulated in the company's first strategic plan"—*"entirely composed by the outside consultant."* Keane went on to boast that "in the process the consultant fulfilled to varying degree most of the roles depicted in this article" (1985:155, italics added). Some "facilitator"!

shall take them to be people with that title (or something similar) but without line (operating) responsibilities and so with time on their hands to worry about the future of the organization that employs them (although many get caught up running planning systems that don't always do that). Another term that figures prominently in our discussion is plan. We shall take the noun *plan* to mean an explicit statement of intentions (written on a flat surface!), usually considered in the planning literature to be specific, elaborated, and documented (Chamberlain, 1968:63). We shall use the verb *plan*, however, to mean simply taking the future into account, whether formally *or* informally.

A major assumption of the strategic planning literature, to summarize our argument to this point, is that all of these terms necessarily go together: **Strategy formation is a planning process, designed or supported by planners, to plan in order to produce plans.** Thus, to quote Steiner, who in turn quoted J. O. McKinsey of 1932: "a plan . . . is 'tangible evidence of the thinking of management.' It results from planning" (Steiner, 1969:8). But Sawyer did provide a notable and welcome exception to this in his planning monograph: "formal systems are only a means to an end—they do not cause planning to occur, and can even prevent it when their emphasis is too much on form instead of substance" (1983:145).

In contrast, we shall proceed on the assumption that all these terms can be independent of each other: An organization can plan (consider its future) without engaging in planning (formal procedure) even if it produces plans (explicit intentions); alternately, an organization can engage in planning (formalized procedure) yet not plan (consider its future); and planners may do all or some of these things, sometimes none of them, yet, as we shall see in conclusion, still serve the organization.

A Plan for This Book

If this attempt to clarify the basic terms has served to confuse the reader, then welcome aboard: it has been no different from the rest of this introduction. Indeed, in this accomplishment, however modest, we take pride. That was our plan.[6] Social psychologists have concluded that to change someone, you must first "unfreeze" his or her basic beliefs. Since everyone knows *what* planning is, *how* it should be done, and *that* it is obviously good ("like motherhood," Wildavsky has written, "everyone is for it because it seems so virtuous" [1973:149]), we have made this introduction an effort at unfreezing. The rest of the book will be directed to the two stages that are supposed to follow: "changing" the beliefs, and "refreezing" around the new ones.

We shall proceed by describing, in Chapter 2, the basic model of strategic planning as proposed in the literature, with some of its better-known variants. After reviewing its various steps, including one missing detail (the source of strategies themselves), we shall consider this model and its variants in terms of a framework of four hierarchies—objectives, budgets, strategies, and programs.

Chapter 3 considers the evidence—survey, anecdotal, intensive—indicating whether this model really works. That evidence is not very encouraging. Nor is the planning writers' response to it, which we consider next. Much of that response resembles what psychologists call "flight": planners fall back on faith, hope for salvation, propose elaborations, or revert to the "basics." But the most popular reaction has been to blame "them," usually under the label of "pitfalls": the managers who don't support planning as they should or the organizations that house climates uncongenial to planning. In Chapter 4, we consider these pitfalls at some length, launching into our serious critique of the planning school. We turn the pitfalls around, to present some "pitfall characteristics of planning"—it can impede commitment, discourage major change, and promote politics within

---

[6] Lorange, in contrast, an insider with respect to this literature who presumably had no such plan, was forced to conclude his review of the empirically-based literature with the comment that:

> Having gone through a considerable body of literature for the purpose of this survey, we are left with the uncomfortable feeling that it is difficult to fit the bits and pieces together. There seems to be a considerable lack of consensus in the literature when it comes to such central questions as what are the critical elements of the nature of planning systems, what constitute relevant empirical areas of research, and so on. (1979:240)

organizations. An "obsession with control" is described as being at the root of these difficulties.

Since "an expert is a person who knows enough about the subject to avoid all the many pitfalls on his or her way to the grand fallacy," we turn in Chapter 5 to a consideration of the fundamental fallacies of planning—what we believe to be the real reasons for the failure of strategic planning. We discuss the fallacies of predetermination (predicting the future), of detachment (of strategy from operations and managers from the things they are supposed to manage), and, ultimately, of formalization, all of which amounts to the grand fallacy: that analysis can produce synthesis. This will be the essence of our critique.

At that point in the book, we put the negative tone of our discussion behind us. Chapter 6 sets out to position planning as well as plans and planners. We consider first the effective role of planning, probing further into its meaning and its appropriate use. Then we take up the roles that we believe are effectively played by plans as well as planners, including roles quite independent of planning itself. In conclusion, we suggest that a different type of planner may exist for each side of the brain. The book closes with a discussion of the context of planning—what circumstances and types of organizations seem to favor the various roles of planning, plans, planners.

This is our plan for the book; we planned it that way—without the aid of planning or planners.

2

Models of the Strategic Planning Process

Beginning perhaps in 1962, if not earlier, with a *Harvard Business Review* article by Gilmore and Brandenburg entitled "Anatomy of Corporate Planning," the literature of planning has offered literally hundreds of models of a process by which strategy could supposedly be formally developed and operationalized. In fact, however, with some specific exceptions (notably capital budgeting and its governmental equivalent, PPBS), these built on a single conceptual framework, or basic model, differing less in fundamentals than in levels of detail. They have ranged from the simple elaboration of that framework to the highly detailed specification of its steps, using all kinds of checklists, tables, diagrams, and techniques.

We shall begin our discussion with that basic model and then present two popular renditions of it. After that, we shall decompose strategic planning in two ways, first into the basic steps delineated by its own authors, then into our own set of four distinct hierarchies that seem to underlie it—of objectives, budgets, strategies, and programs. This latter decomposition will enable us to reconstruct various distinct forms of strategic planning at the end of this chapter.

The Basic Planning Model

The Core "Design School" Model

One single set of concepts underlies virtually all the proposals to formalize the process of strategy formation. Sometimes called the SWOT model (for strengths and weaknesses, opportunities and threats), and most popularly known in the writings of the Harvard business policy people (especially Kenneth Andrews, in his own books [1971, 1980] and a textbook with his various colleagues [Learned et al., 1965; Christensen et al., 1982, etc.]), the basic ideas can be traced back at least to Philip Selznick's influential little book, *Leadership in Administration* (1957).

We prefer to call this the design school model (see Mintzberg, 1990a), because it is built on the belief that strategy formation is a process of conception—the use of a few basic ideas to design strategy. Of these, the most essential is that of congruence, or fit, between external and organizational factors. In Andrews's words, "Economic strategy will be seen as the match between qualifications and opportunity that positions a firm in its environment" (in Christensen et al., 1982:164). "Capture success" seems to be the motto.

As shown in Figure 2–1 in our rendition of the model, similar to others, strategy is created at the intersection of an external appraisal of the threats and opportunities facing an organization in its environment, considered in terms of key factors for success, and an internal appraisal of the strengths and weaknesses of the organization itself, distilled into a set of distinctive competences. Outside opportunities are exploited by inside strengths, while threats are avoided and weaknesses circumvented. Taken into consideration, both in the creation of the strategies and their subsequent evaluation to choose the best, are the values of the leadership as well as the ethics of the society and other aspects of so-called social responsibility. And once a strategy has been chosen, it is implemented.

That is essentially all there is to it—a simple "informing idea," so claimed Andrews, who did not even like to call it a model (in

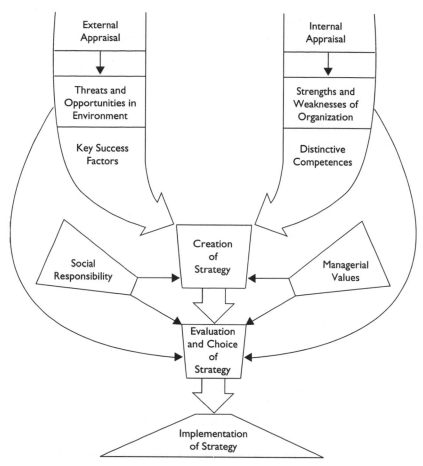

Figure 2–1
Core "Design School" Model of Strategy Formation

Christensen et al., 1982:12, although he and his colleagues did argue that its use was not natural but had to be learned, formally, preferably in a case-study classroom [6]).

Premises of the Design School

A number of premises underlie what we nonetheless prefer to refer to as this model, as promulgated by members of what we call the design school of strategic management—those who stayed with this model in its simplest form (rather than elaborating it in the spirit of the planning school). Below we list these premises with the corresponding references all from the 1982 version of the Harvard textbook (Christensen et al., which contains the Andrews text), unless otherwise noted.

1. Strategy formation should be a controlled, conscious process of thought (6, 94, 185, 543). It is not action that receives the attention here so much as reason—strategies formed through a tightly controlled process of conscious human thought. (Action is assumed to follow, once strategies have been formulated.) Thus strategies should be developed neither intuitively nor in emergent fashion; instead, they must be as "deliberate as possible" (Andrews, 1981:24). Andrews also wrote of the need to change "intuitive skill" into "conscious skill" (105–106), and he contrasted "purpose" with "improvisation" and "planned progress" with "drifting" (20), dismissing emergent strategy in one place as "erosion" (544) and in another, under the label "opportunism," as "the conceptual enemy of strategy" (829).

2. Responsibility for the process must rest with the chief executive officer: that person is THE strategist (3, 19, 545). (Hayes has referred to this as the "command and control mentality" [1985:117]). "Architect" has been a favorite metaphor of this literature, since the chief executive is seen as the designer whose plans everyone else builds (19). Other members of the organization are thus relegated to subordinate roles in the process, as are external actors (aside from the directors who advise the CEO). Hence, the emphasis on social responsibility: it is the leader who accounts for the needs of society, not society that exerts influence on the organization, at least not if the leader is voluntarily socially responsible.

3. The model of strategy formation must be kept simple and informal (12, 14). Strict proponents of this school stand opposed to the elaboration of the model. Ultimately, it is "an act of judgment" (108).

4. Strategies should be unique: the best ones result from a process of creative design (107, 186, 187). Strategies are built on *distinctive* (now called *core*) competences, leading Hofer and Schendel to refer to this approach as the "situational philosophy" (1978:203).

5. Strategies must come out of the design process fully developed. Formulation comes to an end with the delineation and choice of a particular strategy. Thus Andrews referred repeatedly to the "choice" of a strategy, and to strategy formation, as a process of "decision" (e.g., xiv). The result was, in a sense, biblical: the appearance of grand strategy all at once, fully formed. Hence, our characterization of the process as one of conception!

6. The strategies should be made explicit and, if possible, articulated, which means they have to be kept simple (105–106, 554, 835). That way they can be "tested or contested" (105). Thus, "Simplicity is the essence of good art; a conception of strategy brings simplicity to complex organizations" (554). Or, to quote a General Electric planner, "A good strategy can be explained in two pages. And if it can't, it's not a good strategy" (Michael Carpenter, quoted in Allio, 1985:20).

7. Finally, once these unique, full-blown, explicit, and simple strategies are fully formulated, they must then be implemented. For example, structure must follow strategy (543, 551), presumably to be reconsidered anew each time a new strategy is formulated. And a host of administrative mechanisms—budgets, schedules, incentives, etc.—are brought into play for implementation.

Premises of the Planning Literature

The planning literature developed alongside this design school literature—indeed, its best-known early book (Ansoff, 1965) was published in the same year as the original Harvard textbook. As already noted, the basic model shown in Figure 2–1 served as the basis for the planning school as well, with perhaps the only real difference being an emphasis on the setting of formal objectives in place of the implicit incorporation of managerial values. Even many of the premises were common, notably the depiction of strategy formation as a deliberate, cerebral process, which produces its strategies full-blown, then to be articulated and formally implemented. But there were differences too in the premises—one (keeping the process simple and informal) in particular, a second (the CEO as *the* strategist) in deeds if not always words, and a third (on strategies having to be unique) in effect.

Where the two literatures most decidedly parted company was in the premise of keeping the process simple and informal. As already noted, planning is characterized above all by efforts to formalize process. Thus, what was to the design people a loose conceptual framework, with elements delineated on paper but not clearly separated in practice (except for implementation[1]), became in the planning literature a highly formalized procedure, decomposed into an elaborated sequence of steps supported by techniques, at the limit executed almost mechanically. The well-known Ansoff model, for example (reproduced in Figure 2–2), contains fifty-seven boxes. Thus, one year after the appearance of the two initial books, Learned, the lead author of the Harvard textbook, wrote with his colleague Sproat:

> A . . . distinctive difference between Ansoff and the Harvard group may be found in the former's attempt to routinize—so far as possible—the process of strategic decision making. This he does by providing rather detailed checklists of factors that the strategy maker must consider, plus pointers on weighting these factors and on establishing priorities among them, plus numerous decision-flow diagrams and choice rules. (1966:95–96)

This divergence between the two literatures, despite their sharing of the same basic model, is perhaps best illustrated by Andrews's efforts to distance his own writings from those of the planning people: his text, he claimed, is not "a how-to-do-it checklist for corporate planners. In fact, it virtually ignores the mechanisms of planning on the grounds that, detached from strategy, they miss their mark" (in Christensen et al., 1982:10).

The premise of the chief executive as architect of strategy was not so much dismissed as sidestepped. As already noted, while lip service was paid to the top line manager in this regard, a good deal

---

[1] See Mintzberg (1990a:179–180) for discussion of Andrews's claims to the contrary and our rejoinder.

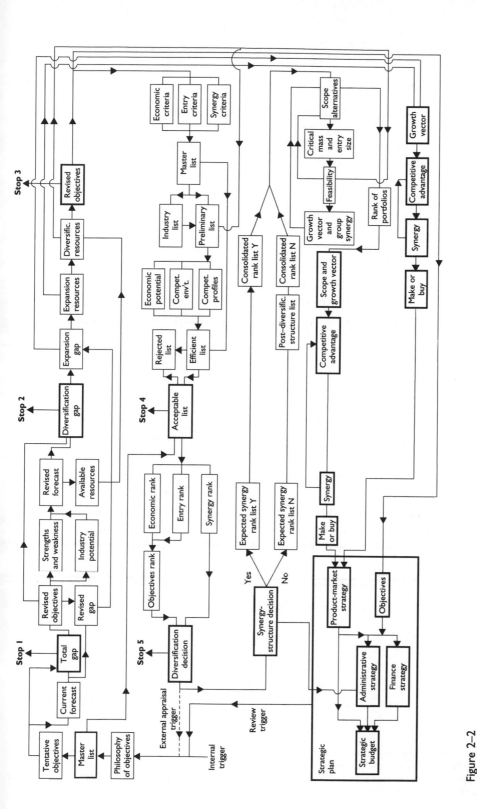

Figure 2–2
The Ansoff Model of Strategic Planning
(From Ansoff, 1965: 202–203)
Note: double-lined boxes represent points of management decision.

of the literature implicitly brought the planner front and center—as we shall see, sometimes as an advisor with more than passive influence, sometimes as the designer of the system of strategy making, or even of strategies themselves (which could relegate the CEO/architect to the role of approving rather than designing strategies), and sometimes as the police officer who ensured that everyone else planned (meaning carried out the designated planning procedures).

Finally, while the premise of keeping strategies unique was not often addressed directly—this is a literature about the process of planning more than the content of plans—as we shall argue in Chapter 4, the very nature of that process, based on formalization, often undermined creativity and so promoted strategies that were more generic than unique.[2]

We can thus summarize the basic premises of the planning school as follows:

1. Strategy formation should be controlled and conscious as well as a formalized and elaborated process, decomposed into distinct steps, each delineated by checklists and supported by techniques.
2. Responsibility for the overall process rests with the chief executive in principle; responsibility for its execution rests with the staff planners in practice.
3. Strategies come out of this process fully developed, typically as generic positions, to be explicated so that they can then be implemented through detailed attention to objectives, budgets, programs, and operating plans of various kinds.

The reader in search of models of such a process will find an enormous choice. We have no intention of presenting here any significant number of them. Rather we shall begin with just two, one early, significant in its impact, and a prime example of detailed elaboration, the other, later, most popular when the literature of

---

[2] Of course, here again we are separating the positioning school literature from that of planning, the former growing out of the latter. But the former's concentration on strategy content does not change our conclusion: in fact, the term generic strategy is one of the most popular in the literature of positioning (e.g., Porter, 1980, 1985).

strategic planning was at the height of its own popularity, and a good example of less extensive elaboration.

The Initial Ansoff Model

The publication of the book, *Corporate Strategy*, by H. Igor Ansoff was a major event in the 1965 world of management. As early as it came in this literature, the book represented a kind of crescendo in the development of strategic planning theory, offering a degree of elaboration seldom attempted since (at least in published form). Curiously, Ansoff did not address the process of strategic planning in general; rather he focused his model on the more narrow issue of corporate expansion and diversification—a reflection of the bullish mood of the 1960s—which he set into the context of product-market strategy.

> The end product of strategic decisions is deceptively simple; a combination of products and markets is selected for the firm. This combination is arrived at by addition of new product-markets, divestment from some old ones, and expansion of the present position. (1965:12).

Ansoff's view of strategy, characteristic of the planning literature in general, was as position (and, of course, plan), but not perspective: "Strategy is viewed as an 'operator' which is designed to transform the firm from the present position to the position described by the objectives, subject to the constraints of the capabilities and the potential" (205).

Ansoff subtitled his book *An Analytical Approach to Business Policy for Growth and Expansion*, although in an article published the previous year, he referred to the approach as "quasi-analytic." In contrast to the "earliest effort [that] took the form of check-off lists for the important ingredients of the strategic problem," his effort "gives [these] items a logical relationship, structures the internal analysis within each, and provides an overall methodology" (1964:74).

Figure 2–2 gives some idea of the intricacy of the Ansoff model; this is a reproduction of his own summary of the various diagrams presented throughout his book.[3] Ansoff characterized his model as a "cascade of decisions, starting with highly aggregated ones and proceeding toward the more specific" (1965:201). As he noted earlier in the book, "This gives the appearance of solving the problem several times over, but with immensely more precise results" (24). The first step is to decide whether or not to diversify the firm, the second to choose a broad product-market scope, and the third to refine that scope. Ansoff linked this sequence to his summary diagram as follows:

> The decision flow proceeds from the first preliminary diversification decisions [Step 1] through three successive preliminary stages based on successively greater information [Step 2], [Step 3], and [Step 4] to the final diversification decision [Step 5]. Following this, a major decision is made on the firm's organizational strategy (synergy-structure decision) followed by successive decisions on four components of strategy (product-market scope, growth vector, synergy, competitive advantage) and culminated in the make or buy decision. (201)

While we cannot review here the whole process, which gets incredibly detailed in places, we do wish to capture its essence. Two concepts are central to its understanding. The first is *gap* analysis.

> The procedure within each step of the cascade is similar. (1) A set of objectives is established. (2) The difference (the "gap") between the current position of the firm and the objectives is estimated. (3) One or more courses of action (strategy) is proposed. (4) These are tested for their "gap-reducing properties." A course is accepted if it substantially closes the gaps; if it does not, new alternatives are tried. (25–26)

The second is *synergy*, a concept that subsequently became so popular in management that it probably stands as the book's most sustained contribution.[4] The *Random House Dictionary* defines synergy as "combined" or "cooperative action," as between nerves in

---

[3] Note that Ansoff's "simplified schematic of this diagram" (28), Figure 2–1 on page 27 of his own book, is very similar to our core design school model (Fig. 2–1 of this book).

[4] Synergy is actually mentioned in the 1962 paper by Gilmore and Brandenburg, but these authors thank Ansoff for the term.

a body or drugs in chemistry. Ansoff used it to help explain the basic notion to fit in the design of organizational strategy. He first referred to it "as the '2 +2 = 5' effect to denote the fact that the firm seeks a product-market posture with a combined performance that is greater than the sum of its parts" (75). Later Ansoff broadened his definition of the concept to include any "effect which can produce a combined return on the firm's resources greater than the sum of its parts" (79). (Hofer and Schendel referred more concisely to "joint effects" [1978:25]). Of course, as Ansoff noted, synergy can also be negative (which Loasby labeled "allergy" [1967:301]).

In essence, synergy serves an an attractive label (or perhaps measure) for the most basic concept of the design school model, namely fit or congruence, the linking of components to gain competitive advantage. In Ansoff's words, the "measurement of synergy is similar in many ways to what is frequently called 'evaluation of strengths and weaknesses' " (76).

Ansoff developed his model in several steps. First, he devoted a great deal of attention to objectives, especially to the development of "A practical system of objectives," the title of the second of his two chapters on the subject. Under his "hierarchy" of long-term return-on-investment objectives alone, he listed 19 of them. In his model, these objectives are supposed to be developed tentatively and then revised according to the results of the internal and external appraisals.

Another important step is the construction of "capability profiles," in "order to accommodate synergy and strengths and weaknesses within the same analytic framework" (91). The appraisals follow. The "internal appraisal is concerned with whether the firm can solve its problems without diversifying" (140), that is, whether it can meet its objectives through the growth and expansion opportunities offered by its current product-market strategies. If the objectives cannot be met, the "external appraisal" is undertaken. This "calls for a survey of opportunities outside the firm's present product-market scope" (140), including the development of the firm's capability profile in each possible industry to assess the potential synergy. Ansoff provides detailed checklists throughout this section (for example, a 29-item list for doing "industry analysis," [146]), and the text becomes terribly intricate.

Finally, "alternate portfolios of product-market entries" are constructed and, after careful evaluation of each in terms of the objectives, taking decision theory into account, a total product-market strategy, and the financial, administrative, and budgeting consequences of it, are elaborated (all of which Ansoff referred to as the "strategic plan," as can be seen at the bottom left of Figure 2–2).

There is much more to *Corporate Strategy* than we have outlined here (besides the much greater detail for each of the steps). A good deal of wisdom is interspersed throughout the text (e.g., "it is important to avoid mistaking an abundant competence for an outstanding one" [194]), and the discussion of the "concept of strategy" itself, in a chapter by that title, remains among the best in the business literature. That chapter, and others, also developed some interesting notions of generic-type strategy (see, for example, pp. 109 and 132) long before that concept became popular in the literature (with publication of Porter's *Competitive Strategy* in 1980), although aside from the distinction between expansion and diversification strategies, these were not really pursued as central themes in the Ansoff model.

The main thrust of the book is, of course, the model itself, which in the words of the book's original dust jacket, achieved an analytical scope unlike that of any other book, one "which provides an *over-all* conceptual and methodological framework for solving the firm's *total* strategic problem." The first part, about the scope, may still be true. (The book, it should be noted, was reissued in 1988 as *The New Corporate Strategy;* we refer to this edition later in our discussion.) The outstanding question is whether or not this ever worked, whether Ansoff did indeed solve any "strategy problem," let alone the "total" one. Did he contribute a viable model for strategy making or simply (but by no means merely) a number of interesting ideas, a good bit of wisdom, and a body of useful vocabulary?

The Mainline Steiner Model

In sheer number of pages on strict planning, George Steiner has been more prolific than Igor Ansoff (who, we shall see, moved on to a somewhat different perspective), and probably than anyone else in this literature for that matter. His main book, *Top Management Planning*, published in 1969, falls just short of 800 pages, and was preceded and followed by several others. Yet the model

Steiner presented is less developed than that of Ansoff, and by almost any account more conventional and less sophisticated. In a sense, Steiner was less a groundbreaker than a popularizer of generally accepted views of planning: indeed, his 1979 book, *Strategic Planning,* is subtitled, *What Every Manager Must Know.* We summarize briefly here Steiner's model in his 1969 book, as the essence of mainline thinking in the field during the 1970s.

After a four-chapter introduction (on the nature of planning, introduction to the model, the importance of comprehensive planning, and top management's role in it), Steiner devoted seven chapters to "the process of developing plans," covering such topics as organization for planning, corporate aims (two chapters), environmental appraisal, the nature of strategies, policies, and procedures, and getting from planning to action. A third section of the book deals with "tools for more rational planning," including quantitative ones and management information systems, while a fourth deals with planning in a number of functional areas, including marketing, finance, and diversification.

The model around which Steiner built his discussion is reproduced in Figure 2–3.[5] While it looks very much like that of the design school, except for a breakdown of the steps that follow implementation, it is in the presumptions about its comprehensiveness, the tight sequencing of its steps, and the detailing of their execution, that it differs markedly. (This is perhaps best indicated by Steiner's detailed table of contents, labeled "Analytical Contents," which runs to ten pages!) To quote from sections of his introduction to the model:

> The subject matter that may be covered in strategic planning includes every type of activity of concern to an enterprise. Among the areas are profits, capital expenditures, organization, pricing, labor relations, production, marketing, finance, personnel, public relations, advertising, technological capabilities, product improvement, research and development, legal matters, management selection and training, political activities and so on. (34)

---

[5] His 1979 rendition of this model (17) relabeled some of the boxes—for example, "purpose" and "values" became "expectations of major outside" and "inside interests," and "strategic planning" and "plans" became "master strategies" and "program strategies"; also in 1979, "the plan to plan" was added at the front of it all.

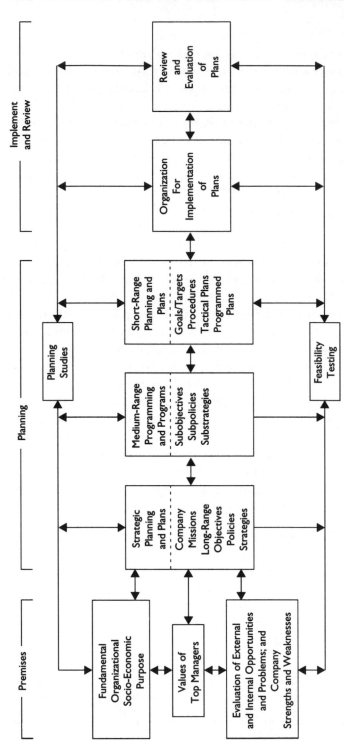

Figure 2–3
The Steiner Model of Strategic Planning
(From Steiner, 1969:33)

Medium-range programming is the process in which detailed, co-ordinated, and comprehensive plans are made for selected functions of a business to deploy resources to reach objectives by following policies and strategies laid down in the strategic planning process. All medium-range programs and plans for a company cover the same period of time, usually five years. Whatever the period covered, plans are worked out in considerable detail for each year of the planning period. (35)

Short-term budgets and detailed functional plans include such matters as short range targets for salesmen, budgets for material purchases, short-term advertising plans, inventory replenishment, and employment schedules. (35)

Any doubt about the result fitting into what we call the planning school can be dispelled in Figure 2–4, which reproduces Steiner's figure on planning at one major corporation.

The reader interested in a public-sector rendition of the basic planning model of the same period might wish to glance at Figure 2–5. This presents strategic planning in the U.S. Army, circa 1970, a truly astonishing collection of acronyms. (For those who may be interested, JSOP, for example, means Joint Strategic Objectives Plan, ASA means Army Strategic Appraisal, and so on.) No wonder that a Japanese planner who had just been shown the comprehensive, computer-assisted strategic planning process of a U.S. firm commented, "My goodness, it looks as complicated as building a chemical plant!" (quoted in Ohmae, 1982:224)

Decomposing the Basic Model

Every box on these charts, and each acronym, was usually backed up by considerable detail, which could sometimes be taken to extreme lengths—in the case of the U.S. Army, probably rooms full of documents. At the very least, checklists were provided, sometimes with clearly specified sequences; beyond that, especially from the mid-1970s, systematic management science techniques

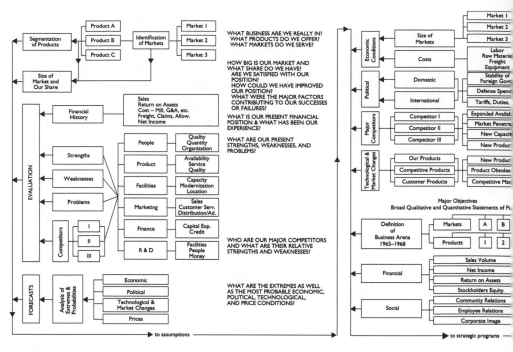

Figure 2–4
The Planning Process at Kaiser Aluminum, Circa 1964
(Reproduced from Steiner, 1969:50–52)

were proposed to deal with many of the issues in question.[6] Drucker may have had reason to try to argue that strategic planning "is not a box of tricks, a bundle of techniques" (1973:123), but his claim would not have meant much to people like Rea, who wrote that "The general approach to the design of forecasting and planning systems is (1) to identify the functions that must be carried out in the resource allocation process, (2) to search for analytical tools that can be employed to carry out these functions, (3) to analyze the inputs, outputs, benefits, and costs of each tool, (4) to evaluate their requirements and performance in terms of estab-

[6] The book, *Strategic Formulation: Analytical Concepts,* by Hofer and Schendel (1978) provided an extensive list of the techniques available in the late 1970s (see also Huff and Reger [1987] for some of the later literature on techniques in strategic planning). In fact, the Hofer and Schendel book may be considered to stand near the transition of attention from the planning school to the positioning school, advancing beyond the specification of processes to the application of technique, but not really organized around the articulation of content. That, however, followed shortly.

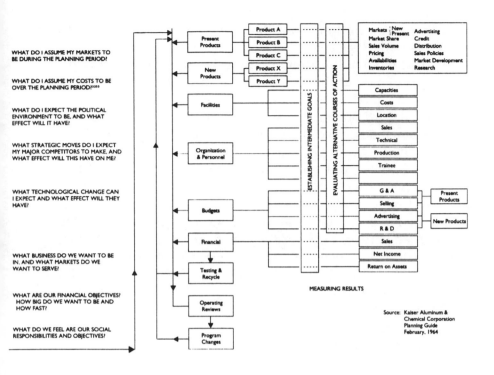

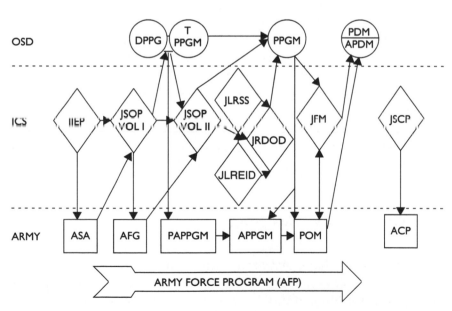

Figure 2–5
Strategic Planning in the U.S. Army
(From Chapman and Gabrielli, 1976–77:280)

lished criteria, and (5) to choose the best combination of tools to form the system" (1968:205).

But no matter what the attention to technique, there was virtually full agreement that the different steps must be sharply delineated and then linked in clearly prescribed sequences. Thus Steiner referred to his 1979 book as "a step-by-step guide," while Linneman and Kennell described the purpose of their 1977 *Harvard Business Review* article as "to give a simplified ten-step approach to developing flexible strategies through what we call multiple-scenario analysis" (e.g., "Step 3: take a hard look at the past . . . Step 7: build scenarios," 142). In a later survey of almost a thousand U.S. planners, Ginter et al. found strong agreement on the underlying sequence of steps (as they characterized them: mission, objectives, external analysis, internal analysis, development of strategic alternatives, strategy selection, implementation, and control of the strategy, with only mission receiving rather low emphasis in importance). They concluded:

> Even though the normative model of strategic management appears idealistic and excessively mechanistic in the sense that it appears to progress sequentially from one well defined stage to another, contrary to the expectations of some, this does not confuse or intimidate those who are actually engaged in strategic management in contemporary organizations. On the contrary, they appear to identify very easily with the normative model. (1985:588)

Below we review briefly (with one exception) the main stages of the basic model, in their usually prescribed sequence. (We call them stages because typically each of them clusters a great many "steps.")

The Objectives-Setting Stage

Planning writers have elaborated the simple notion of accounting for values in strategy formation by developing extensive procedures for explicating and, wherever possible, quantifying the goals of the organization (generally referred to in numerical form as objectives). We have already seen the attention to the setting of objectives in Ansoff's and Steiner's work. Others gave it similar treatment, in some cases drawing on loose techniques such as the Delphi method (which ascertains and encourages consensus among the beliefs of a number of participants through successive estimations for one or more parameters).

In their well-known book, *Strategic Management,* based on a key conference in the field held in 1977, Schendel, and Hofer (1979:16) made an issue of the distinction between "(1) those [models] that separate the goal and strategy formulation tasks (Ansoff, 1965; Cannon, 1968; McNichols, 1972; Paine and Naumes, 1974; Glueck, 1976; Hofer and Schendel, 1978); and (2) those that combine them (Learned et al., 1965; Katz, 1970; Newman and Logan, 1971; Uyter-hoeven et al., 1977)." As it happens, the first group consists for the most part of people who wrote from a planning perspective, while those in the second were subscribers to the design school. In other words, people predisposed to the planning approach are more likely to try to distinguish goals from strategies.

This distinction can presumably be made only if there is some reasonably clear point where goals end and strategies begin. One might think such a point easy to identify. But when such prominent planning writers as Ansoff (1965) included "expansion of product lines" and "merger" under the list of objectives while Lorange (1980a) used the word objectives to mean strategies,[7] one is not very encouraged. A distinction that may sometimes be clear at the extremes seems to break down in the wide margin in between, much as does the distinction between strategies and tactics.

Schendel and Hofer "favor separation of goal and strategy formulation processes because it is clear that these processes are, in fact, separate in a number of organizations and because personal values and social mores are almost always much more influential in goal formulation than in strategy formulation" (1979:16). But the first claim is not clear at all—and no evidence was provided to back it up—and this renders the second claim questionable at least. How, in any event, can such claims be made, unless, of course, one has partitioned the world into arbitrary categories? Organizations can certainly define on paper whatever they choose to be goals and

---

[7] "The first stage, objectives setting, serves primarily to identify relevant strategic alternatives, where or in what strategic direction the firm as a whole as well as its organizational subunits should go" (1980:31).

strategies. But what have the labels to do with real phenomena and working processes? How can anyone, for example, deny the impact of values on strategy making, indeed even measure it?

What we have in this supposed issue reflects a major tendency in the planning approach itself, indeed a reflection of one of *its* own values: that a phenomenon has been captured because it is written down, labeled, and put in a box, ideally represented by numbers. As Wildavsky put it about objectives in government: "each one neatly labelled as if they came out of a great national sausage machine in the sky" (1973:134).

In fact, values are the least operational of the elements of the planning model, especially in the collective context of organizations. Quantification, as we shall see in Chapter 5, while possible in principle—anyone can put a number against anything they care to on a piece of paper—can do a terrible injustice in practice to the complex set of values contained in the human system called organization. Nonetheless, the planning model devotes a great deal of energy to just such an exercise. Indeed, we shall see that much so-called strategic planning activity reduces to not much more than the quantification of goals as a means of control.

The External Audit Stage

Once the objectives have been set, the next two stages, as in the design school model, are to assess the external and internal conditions of the organization. In the spirit of the formalized, systematic approach of planning, we shall refer to these as audits.

A major element of the audit of the organization's external environment is the set of forecasts made about future conditions. Planning theorists have long been preoccupied with such forecasting, because, short of being able to control the environment, an inability to predict its course amounts to an inability to engage in planning. Thus "predict and prepare" (Ackoff, 1983:59) became the motto of this school of thought. Extensive checklists were proposed, to cover every conceivable external factor, and a myriad of techniques were developed, ranging from the simple (moving averages, etc.) to the immensely complex (see Makridakis and Wheelwright [1981] for a review of forecasting methods). Particularly popular in more recent years has been scenario building (e.g.,

Porter, 1985:Chapter 13; Wack, 1985a and b; discussed in Chapter 5), in which alternative views of the possible states of an organization's future environment are postulated. We shall discuss this at greater length in Chapter 5.

In addition to the subject of forecasting per se, a certain literature grew up on strategic intelligence, oriented in good part to broader but looser methods for gathering information about the external environment (see Huff, 1979, for a good review of it up to that time). Most of the planning models present checklists of factors to consider in the external audit, often categorized as economic, social, political, and technological. In addition, a significant literature grew up in the 1980s around what is generally referred to as industry and competitor analysis, stimulated in particular by Porter's 1980 book, *Competitive Strategy*. Figure 2–6 shows his basic framework for conducting competitor analysis. Despite all this attention and effort, however, one study of the experiences of large firms considered to be leaders in this area found that they had "difficulty in doing en-

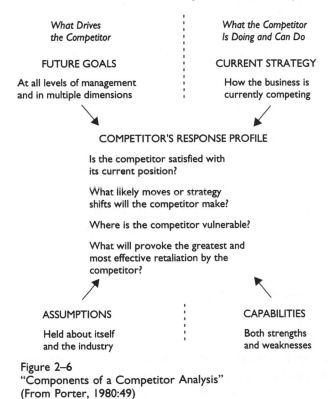

Figure 2–6
"Components of a Competitor Analysis"
(From Porter, 1980:49)

vironmental analysis, fitting in to the planning process, and evaluating its contributions" (Lenz and Engledow, 1986:82); in a follow-up study actually published in the previous year (Engledow and Lenz, 1985), these researchers found diminished attention to the formal practice.

The Internal Audit Stage

In keeping with the spirit of the planning approach, once again the study of strengths and weaknesses was subjected to extensive decomposition, although here the use of technique generally gave way to simpler checklists and tables of various kinds, what Jelinek and Amar referred to as "corporate strategy by laundry lists" (1983:1). Perhaps the assessment of *distinctive* competence is inherently more judgmental and therefore less amenable to rigorous analysis (if not to efforts at decomposition).

Ansoff's framework for the "competence profile," a matrix of functional areas and types of organizational capabilities (personnel, facilities and equipment, etc.), seems to have set the standard for much of the work that followed. We reproduce it in Figure 2–7 from his 1965 book. Among the few innovations since that time were efforts stimulated by the Boston Consulting Group and the McKinsey Company together with General Electric to plot the position of a business on a matrix of competitive strengths and market attributes (giving rise to BCG's famous stable of dogs, cash cows, wildcats, etc. [see Henderson, 1979]). Overall, however, the internal audit hardly advanced since Ansoff's book, and by remaining not much more than judgment supported by checklist, is not very different from the general statements in the core design school model.

The Strategy Evaluation Stage

In this next stage, the evaluation of strategies, the planning literature made up for what it lost in the last one. Techniques abounded simply because the process of evaluation naturally lends itself to elaboration and qualification, ranging from the simple early no-

Figure 2–7
Grid for Capability Profile
(From Ansoff, 1965:98–99)

	Facilities and equipment	Personnel skills	Organizational capabilities	Management capabilities
General management & finance	Data processing equipment	Depth of general management Finance Industrial Relations Legal Personnel recruitment and training Accounting Planning	Multidivisional structure Consumer financing Industrial financing Planning and control Automated business data processing	Investment management Centralized control Large systems management Decentralized control R&D intensive business Capital-equipment intensive business Merchandising intensive business Cyclical business Many customers Few customers
Research and development	Special lab equipment General lab equipment Test facilities	Areas of specialization Advanced research Applied research Product design: industrial consumer military specifications Systems design Industrial design: consumer industrial	Systems development Product development industrial consumer process Military specifications compliance	Utilization of advanced state of the art Application of current state of the art Cost-performance optimization

Figure 2–7 (continued)

	Facilities and equipment	Personnel skills	Organizational capabilities	Management capabilities
Oper-ations	General machine shop Precision machinery Process equipment Automated production Large high-bay facilities Controlled environment	Machine operation Tool making Assembly Precision machinery Close tolerance work Process operation Product planning	Mass production Continuous flow process Batch process Job shop Large complex product assembly Subsystems integration Complex product control Quality control Purchasing	Operation under cyclic demand Military specifications quality Tight cost control Tight scheduling
Market-ing	Warehousing Retail outlets Sales offices Service offices Transportation equipment	Door-to-door selling Retail selling Wholesale selling Direct industry selling Department of Defense selling Cross-industry selling Applications engineering Advertising Sales promotion Servicing Contract administration Sales analysis	Direct sales Distributor chain Retail chain Consumer service organization Industrial service organization Department of Defense product support Inventory distribution and control	Industrial marketing Consumer merchandising Department of Defense marketing State and municipality marketing

tions of return-on-investment analysis to a rash of more recent techniques such as "competitive strategy valuation" (Williams, 1984), "risk analysis" (Hertz and Thomas, 1984), "the value curve" (Strategic Planning Associates, 1984), and the various methods of "shareholder value" (Rappaport, 1986).

As is evident in the labels of the techniques mentioned above, most are oriented to financial analysis, as if only the monetary consequences of strategy (or performance, since strategy too is sometimes forgotten) really matter, and these can be measured directly. Thus "value creation" became a popular term in the planning literature, considering such issues as the market-to-book value of the firm and the cost of equity capital (Hax and Majluf, 1984:Chapter 10). The underlying assumption seems to be that firms make money by calculating money, free of the confounding factors of products and markets and customers. Later we shall argue that this obsession with financial quantification can have exactly the opposite effect, that putting the financial carriage ahead of the strategy horse may, in fact, worsen the actual performance of the firm.

In any event, we see here particularly that whereas the design approach merely sought to get a broad sense of whether a proposed strategy might work, the planning approach favored precise calculation of the viability of proposed strategies. Once again, one formalized what the other merely addressed. But that produced in its consequences a difference of kind, not just of degree.

There was some attention over the years to another approach to the evaluation of strategies, perhaps more sensible in principle though more difficult to execute in practice. This was the attempt to use comprehensive computer simulations of the firm to test the consequences of proposed strategies. These first appeared in the late 1960s (e.g., Gershefski, 1969) and ran into problems in the 1970s (see W. Hall, 1972/1973), although their proponents renewed their enthusiasm in the 1980s (e.g., Shim and McGlade, 1984). But one wonders if the literature had gotten too far ahead of the practice here, in that the proponents of these simulations seemed more interested in developing than in applying them, as in Shim and McGlade's citation of one study's finding that "the end users of the models were usually strategic planning groups, the Treasurer's department and the Controller's department" [1984:887]). One notable exception was an article by Hall and Menzies (1983), which detailed the use of a systems dynamics model in, of all places, a sports club, to test what effect various strategies would have on the membership. In response to the simulation, the club reportedly altered a number of its key strategies.[8]

It must be borne in mind what the strategy evaluation stage assumes: that strategies are not evolved or developed so much as *delineated*, at a particular point in time. And not one but several are delineated, so that these can be evaluated and one chosen definitively. Sawyer's comments are indicative in this regard:

> Just as in planning the conquest of France the German general staff defined a series of alternative strategies and prepared a complete battle plan for each strategy before making its choice, it is often necessary to consider the results various business alternatives might yield, before a specific strategy can be chosen and put in motion. (1983:14)

The Strategy Operationalization Stage

Here is where most of the models become very detailed (Ansoff's being a notable exception), almost as if the planning process suddenly passed through the strategy formulation neck of a wind tunnel to accelerate into the seemingly open spaces of implementation. In fact, the reality of strategy making would seem to be exactly the opposite: formulation should be the open-ended, divergent process (in which imagination can flourish in the creation of new strategies), while implementation should be the closed-ended, convergent one (in which these given strategies are subjected to the constraints of operationalization). But because of planning's need for formalization, ironically it is formulation that becomes tightly constrained, while implementation provides the freedom to decompose, elaborate, and rationalize, down the ever-widening hierarchy. (The consequence, as we shall see, is that, under planning, formulation lost its creative potential while implementation provided great powers of control.) Thus, from the difficulties of assessing the external environment, the ambiguities

---

[8] Such computer models might, of course, also be used in the external audit stage, to get a sense of the workings of the environment, assuming the critical parameters can be quantified. Roger Hall's (1976) simulation of the fortunes of the *Saturday Evening Post* magazine, done retrospectively, showed how such models might be used as a diagnostic tool.

of identifying distinctive competencies, and the arbitrariness of imposing technique on the evaluation of strategies, the planning model arrives with great relish at the concrete details of making strategies operational—so naturally amenable to formalization.

Decomposition was clearly the order of the day. As Steiner noted, "All strategies must be broken down into substrategies for successful implementation" (1979:177), as if no other means of implementing strategy (for example, by the metaphoric conveyance of vision) is conceivable. Bower referred to the whole result as a "deductive cascade" (1970a:286), while Normann and Rhenman (1975) called this the "means-ends model." They attributed it to Herbert Simon, whose "notion, which has greatly attracted the disciples of 'rational' planning techniques, [is] that a planning problem can be solved by a rational partitioning of the whole issue into ends and means, ordered in a hierarchy" (13).

The operationalization of strategies gives rise to a whole set of hierarchies, thought to exist on different levels and with different time perspectives. Long-term, comprehensive, or "strategic" plans sit on top, looking out several years (usually five), medium-term plans follow, looking perhaps two or three years out, and operating or short-term plans rest at the bottom, for the next year. Slicing this vertically produces, first, a hierarchy of objectives, in which the basic goals to be accomplished by the whole organization are broken down into specific targets, partitioned into a hierarchy of subobjectives. The consequences of these are translated in turn into a whole hierarchy of budgets, which impose the financial constraints (or motivational incentives, depending on how you see it) on each unit of the organization.

Meanwhile, the strategies themselves are elaborated into a whole hierarchy of the substrategies Steiner talked about. This is now generally conceived to exist on three levels—*corporate* strategies to consider the overall business portfolio of the diversified firm (i.e., its set of positions in different industries), *business* strategies to describe the product-market positions of each individual business (or SBU—strategic business unit—as the term was coined for the General Electric planning of the early 1970s [Hamermesh, 1986:188][9]), and *functional* strategies to define the approaches of

---

[9] SBUs may or may not correspond to formal divisions, some of which encompass a variety of SBUs.

marketing, manufacturing, research, and so on. The consequences of all these substrategies—as positions, not perspective—are translated in turn into another hierarchy, of action programs: to introduce particular new products, launch specific advertising campaigns, build new plants, etc., each with a specific timetable.

Finally, the whole works—objectives, budgets, strategies, programs—is brought together into a whole array of operating plans, carefully integrated, sometimes referred to as the "master plan." "The essential characteristics of such a master plan are that it is *comprehensive*—that is, it covers all major elements of the business—and that it is *integrated* into a balanced and synchronized program for the entire operation" (Newman, Summer, and Warren, 1972:396). Needless to say, this could become awfully elaborate, as suggested in Figure 2–8, which shows the Stanford Research Institute's widely publicized "System of Plans."

The label for all this effort at operationalization was *planning*, but the intention was really *control*. Each budget, subobjective, operating plan, and action program was overlaid on a distinct entity of the organization—some unit, be it division, department, or branch, or else an individual—to be carried out as specified. As Loasby put it, responsibilities were allocated "in a pretty watertight way" (1967:304). Steiner argued that "all strategies must be broken down into substrategies for successful implementation" because of his assumption that everyone must be given precise intentions in order to accomplish his or her own job: "the final step in implementation concerns controlling and motivating people to take actions in conformance with plans" (1979:215). If the decomposition were done correctly, all these individual tasks would add up to the accomplishment of the overall strategic intentions of the organizations. All very neat and tidy, as machine-like as the assembly line.

Scheduling the Whole Process

Not only were all the steps in the planning process ostensibly programmed, but so too was the timetable by which they were supposedly carried out (not to mention the results themselves, the plans, which were supposed to impose a timetable on all programs and a time period on all budgets). In his 1979 book, Steiner added to the front of his whole model an initial step called the "plan to

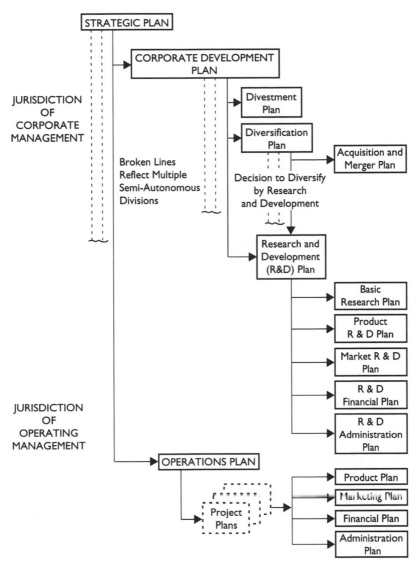

Figure 2–8
Stanford Research Institute's proposed "System of Plans"
(From Stewart, 1963:i)

plan": if planning is good, it must be good for planners too. Figure 2–9 shows the annual planning schedule that General Electric used (circa 1980), which began on January 3 and ended on December 6. Another General Electric planner described the process around the same time as follows:

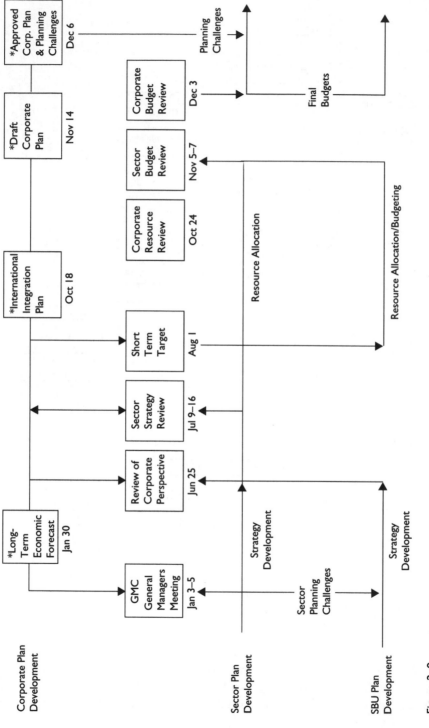

Figure 2–9
Annual Planning Cycle at General Electric (From Rothschild, 1980:13)

1. *January:* A corporate-level review of the environment identifies issues of corporate-level concern across the company, such as the impact of double-digit inflation or of an energy crisis. SBUs receive corporate-level guidelines indicating the company's major priorities and goals.

2. *February-June:* Each Strategic Business Unit (SBU) updates its five-year strategic plan. A major focus is on enhancing its long range competitive position. In addition, it determines its response to corporate guidelines.

3. *July-September:* The Corporate Management Committee, comprised of the Chairman, Vice Chairmen, and top staff officers review the SBU plans. They judge plan quality, assess risks, and decide on resource allocation priorities. Corporate management concentrates on objectives and resource requirements, minimizing its involvement in specific SBU strategies to achieve objectives.

4. *October-December:* Each SBU develops detailed operating programs and budgets for the coming year.

5. *December:* SBU budgets receive final approval at corporate level; they provide the basis for measuring operations in the coming year. (Hekhuis, 1979:242–243)

What this suggests—although not really so well as some charts and descriptions that spell out everything in minute detail—is the lockstep nature of such scheduling, designed to program when specific things will happen. "By the middle of June," wrote Lorange and Vancil of planning in a large diversified multinational, "top management has prepared an explicit statement of corporate strategy and goals" (1977:31). One can almost see the executives sitting around a table at 11:00 p.m. on the 14th of June, working frantically to complete their strategy. Although Lorange claimed that the planning model "specifies a logical sequence of steps that should be carried out in order to make the process come alive within a corporation" (1980a:54–55) one is led to wonder how much of corporate life it killed instead.

A Missing Detail

This whole planning exercise, as we have seen, was programmed in great detail: the delineation of steps, the application of checklists and techniques to each of these, the scheduling of this whole thing, everything nicely accounted for. Except for one minor detail: *strategy formation itself*. Somehow the ostensible object of the whole exercise got lost in the exercise. Nowhere was anyone told how to create strategy. How to collect information, yes. How to evaluate strategy, yes. How to implement it, for sure. But not how to create it in the first place. Every writer literally talked around that step. When Malmlow, in a 1972 article in the journal *Long Range Planning*, put boxes onto his planning chart labeled "Apprehend Inputs" and "Add Insights," he was merely presenting the worst example of a problem symptomatic of the entire literature: assuming that a phenomenon has been captured, that action will take place, simply because it has been labeled in a box on a piece of paper. With all that decomposition, there never was any integration. Ansoff's talk of synergy notwithstanding, the Humpty Dumpty of planning lay in pieces on its flat surface. Of course, this was all to be taken care of in one step, called formulating strategy. But they forgot to specify that step—no decomposition, no articulation, no rationalization, indeed, no description!

In fact, our understanding of how strategy does or should get made was not advanced one iota by all these efforts. If anything, they may have served mostly to deflect some talented individuals from coming to grips with the thorny problems of creating strategy. Thus Steiner, after all that writing, all that concern with formalization, admitted in his 1979 text that "although a good bit of progress has been made in developing analytical tools to identify and evaluate strategies, the process is still mostly an art" (178). Back we went, it seems, to the design school model![10]

But if the process remained an art, then where did planning come in? If formalization is the essence of planning, and if the

---

[10] That model itself offered no more help. As Bryson commented, "The main weakness of the Harvard model is that it does not offer specific advice on how to develop strategies, except to note that effective strategies will build on strengths, take advantage of opportunities, and overcome or minimize weaknesses and threats" (1988:31).

creation of strategy cannot be formalized, then what was "strategic planning" doing all those years? Did it have to be relegated to the setting of objectives on the front end and the operationalizing of strategies (wherever they came from) on the back end, where formalization is possible?

Sorting Out the Four Hierarchies:
Objectives, Budgets, Strategies, Programs

That missing detail aside, all the neat order of the planning model belies a good deal of confusion in the whole process. In particular, the system offers a whole series of components, the relationships among which have never been made clear in practice. Objectives, budgets, strategies, and programs do not mesh quite so cleanly as assumed in the basic model. Ansoff told us about implementation that:

> The next step is to convert the planned levels into coordinated action programs for various units of the firm. These programs specify the schedules of actions, goals and quotas, the checkpoints, and the milestones. The action programs are then translated into resource budgets in terms of men, materials, money, and space needed to support the programs. The action programs and the resource budgets form the basis for profit budgets—measures of the net cost—accomplishment effectiveness of the proposed performance levels. (1967:6–7).

But somehow no one ever came to grips with how all this translation is supposed to take place. Practice, therefore, often led to different results, generating all kinds of complaints about the rarity of successful implementation (recall Peters's comment about that "wildly inflated" ten percent success rate in strategy implementation). Another consequence has been the popularity of less ambitious and less comprehensive models, such as capital budgeting, which proved more practical to apply. In part, these problems likely reflect the underspecification of the basic model—all the relationships that remained unresolved or ambiguous. But more significantly, we believe it reflects erroneous assumptions in the model itself.

According to the comprehensive model, organizations begin with objectives that are supposed to emanate from the top (as a reflection of the basic values of the top management) and flow down the hierarchy in that deductive cascade. If, however, they are part of that once-fashionable system called MBO (management by objectives), then they are also supposed to flow up the hierarchy in cumulative fashion, in which case it becomes unclear where over-all values enter the picture. In any event, the objectives are sup-posed to stimulate the development of strategies (as in Ansoff's gap analyses), although Steiner seemed to maintain that objectives can also derive from strategies ("the planning process may begin with strategies. Once credible strategies are formulated it is easy to determine the objectives that will be achieved if the strategies are properly implemented" [1979:173]).[11] Then there is to come a cas-cade of strategies, which should give rise to another cascade of programs. However, in capital budgeting, which is often more entrenched than conventional strategic planning, the assumption is that programs are initiated from below and flow up the hierar-chy for approval, in which case it is not clear where the strategies come in. A third cascade of budgets is considered to flow out of the objectives in a routine manner, quite independent of strategies (leaving aside the problem that budgets, like objectives, are often negotiated in a bottom-up manner). Yet budgets are supposed to reflect changes in strategy as well, presumably on an ad hoc basis (since that is how strategies themselves change). In fact, the rela-tionship between routine budgets and ad hoc strategies never seems to have been addressed in any substantive manner.

What, then, has really been going on in this process? Planners who have lived with specific planning systems in specific situa-tions may know the answer in particular. In other words, they may have worked things out for their own organization—made their own compromises. But does anyone know in general? Is there

---

[11] More confusing is yet another alternative, that "through analysis of company opportunities, threats, strengths, and weaknesses managers and staff will identify alternative objectives and strategies from which firm objectives eventually will be established for the company" (172).

really any clear conceptual knowledge here? Or has the planning literature only confused presumption with practice?

Let us try another tack, in an effort to sort some of this out. Objectives, budgets, strategies, and programs appear to be very different phenomena that do not link quite as conveniently as the planning literature has suggested. More likely, the linkages are either formally absent or far more complex than indicated. It seems reasonable enough to conclude that particular strategies sometimes evoke ad hoc programs, or that objectives help to determine budgets. But it is not reasonable to conclude that any of these hierarchies conveniently nest within each other—for example, that of budgets emanating from that of strategies (or vice versa). How programs, essentially ad hoc, get incorporated into budgets, essentially routine, is far less clear; it is no more clear how objectives stimulate the creation of strategies. Moreover, as mentioned earlier, the prescribed flow in the basic model seems to be contradicted by systems such as MBO or capital budgeting, which can flow in quite opposite directions. These contradictions all remain to be reconciled.

To make some headway through this confusion, we feel the need to engage in some decomposition of our own. But we shall slice things vertically, so to speak, completely separating the four hierarchies of objectives, budgets, strategies, and programs in order to consider afresh what some of the links between them might be in practice. We use the word "might" because here we can only speculate; anything further will require some very careful empirical research. Figure 2–10 shows these four hierarchies so delineated, at different levels of management—corporate, business, functional, and operating—although any hierarchy of structural units could be substituted. Along the bottom of the figure are shown the actions taken by the organization, the target of all this effort.

Figure 2–11 overlays on this the full-blown planning model *in theory*. (See Lorange [1980a:55–58] for an example of a step-by-step process roughly consistent with this.) The starting point is the delineation of the overall objectives of the firm (#1), which on one hand gives rise to a whole system of subobjectives (1a–1c), on the other hand evokes the development of a top-down cascade of strategies (2a–2c), which leads in turn to a hierarchy of capital and operating programs (3a–3c), which determines the organization's

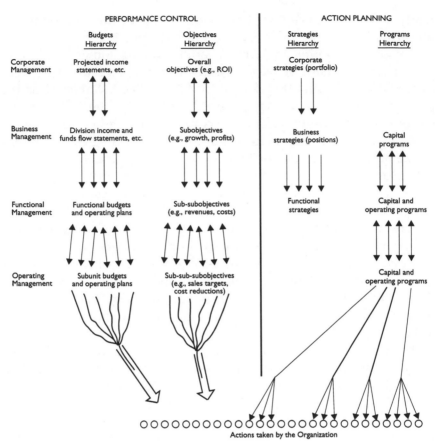

Figure 2–10
Four Planning Hierarchies

actions. Meanwhile, the objectives and subobjectives feed into the budgeting process at various levels (4a–4d), as do the consequences of the various programs, whose effects on budgets must be taken into consideration. This, roughly, is how the whole system is supposed to tie together.[12] Let us now take a closer look at its components before returning to this issue. We review each of the four hierarchies and then consider their interrelationships.

---

[12] As we shall discuss later, the PPBS exercise in the U.S. government in the 1960s proceeded in much the same way, except that it had more of a bottom-up, capital budgeting flavor to it and was even more ambitious in its presumed comprehensiveness.

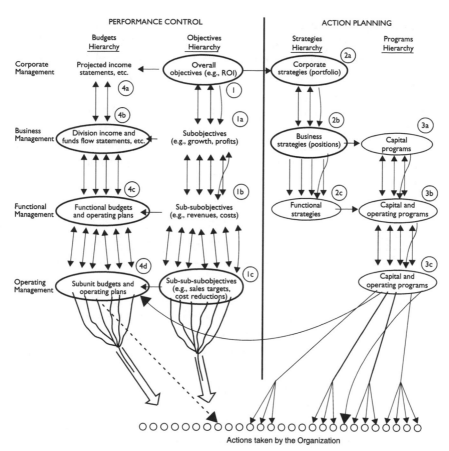

Figure 2–11
Conventional Full-Blown Planning Model

Hierarchy of Objectives

The assumption of strategic planning seems to be that objectives are decided upon by the top management for the entire organization, which in turn evoke the process of formulating strategy, and, themselves, cascade down the structural hierarchy, as devices of motivation and control—that is, to provide incentives as well as means against which to assess performance. But if the objectives truly exist to motivate, then according to behavioral scientists, people have to be involved in the setting of their own ones. So instead of cascading down, objectives have to be made in different places and then aggregated up. But if so, how can they relate to strategies? With one aggregating up and the other cascading down, how do they get together? To quote Eigerman, "In a purely bottom up system, the integration of strategy across units is achieved with a stapler"! (1988:41).

Thus, aside from some very general impressions in the literature, the link between the setting of objectives and the creation of strategies remains unspecified. It is one thing to describe strategy as being driven by values in a general sense, as does the design school model, quite another to establish a link with formal, quantitative targets.

Hierarchy of Budgets

Budgets are not so different from objectives, in that they are integrated sets of (primarily financial) targets, decomposed according to units in the hierarchy. (Here we might also include operating plans of various kinds, concerning finances, manpower, material, and other resources, as well as funds flows and pro forma income statements.) Like objectives, budgets may cascade down the structural hierarchy, aggregate up it, or flow both ways through a process of negotiation. Likewise, budgets are designed primarily for control (but perhaps less so for motivation) and tend to be applied to every subunit of the organization. And similarly, they tend to be established on a regular basis (e.g., annually) even if reviewed at more frequent intervals (e.g., monthly or quarterly).

That budgets are crucial elements of almost every organization few would deny: they are inevitably prime devices for resource allocation and control. As Siegel noted in the context of government:

> The budget is the single most important policy statement of any government. The expenditure side of the budget tells us "who gets what" in public funds, and the revenue side of the budget tells us "who pays the cost". There are few government activities or programs which do not require an expenditure of funds, and no public funds may be spent without budgetary authorization. . . . Budgets determine what programs and policies are to be increased, de-

creased, lapsed, initiated, or renewed. The budget lies at the heart
of public policy. (1977:45)

But the open question in response to this last statement is: how
and in what form? Do budgets make strategy, express strategy,
respond to strategy, or even exist free of strategy? Few writers
looked beyond the obvious issues associated with budgeting—the
frictions and political maneuverings, the various games played to
increase budgets, the tendencies toward knee-jerk extrapolation of
budgets from one year to the next. One exception was Wildavsky,
who offered one of the most sophisticated studies of public-sector
budgeting in his book, *The Politics of the Budgetary Process*. He
opened his discussion with some thoughts on what a budget really
is—a prediction, a plan, a contract, a precedent. His comments are
worth quoting at length:

> Presumably, those who make a budget intend that there will be a
> direct connection between what is written in it and future events.
> Hence we might conceive of a budget as intended behavior, as a
> prediction. . . . The budget . . . becomes a link between financial
> resources and human behavior to accomplish policy objectives . . .
>
> A budget [may also] be characterized as a series of goals with
> price tags attached. Since funds are limited and have to be divided
> in one way or another, the budget becomes a mechanism for mak-
> ing choices among alternative expenditures. When the choices are
> coordinated so as to achieve desired goals, a budget may be called
> a plan. . . .
>
> Viewed in another light, a budget may be regarded as a con-
> tract. Congress and the President promise to supply funds under
> specified conditions, and the agencies agree to spend them in ways
> that have been agreed upon. . . .
>
> Once enacted, a budget becomes a precedent; the fact that some-
> thing has been done once vastly increases the chances that it will be
> done again. Since only substantial departures from the previous
> year's budget are normally given intensive scrutiny, an item that
> remains unchanged will probably be carried along the following
> year as a matter of course. . . .

It should now be apparent that the purposes of budgets are as varied as the purposes of men. (1974:1–4)

All of these definitions do seem to have one common element: they suggest that budgets are expressions of public policy, in other words, the *outcomes* of the strategy formation process. As Wildavsky put it, "the budget records the outcome of [the] struggle" for control of national policy. "If one asks, 'who gets what the government has to give?' then the answers for a moment in time are recorded in the budget" (4). But they can also be inputs: the strategies that can be formulated (or, more to the point, the ones that cannot) are significantly influenced by the budgets that have been allocated, especially when the latter are tight. But either way, how is the translation between strategies and budgets made?

Shank et al. (1973:91) discussed three forms of linkage between planning and budgeting cycles, that is, "between strategy formulation and the quantified explanation of that strategy": content linkage (of the data of plans and budgets, where they noted the problem of format differences between the two documents), organizational linkage (between units responsible for both, especially, the role of the controller, responsible for budgets, vis-à-vis that of the planner), and timing linkage (concerning the sequencing of the two, particularly which is done first). The authors then compared loose linking (planning first) with tight linking (budgeting first, planning soon after). Tight linking "can undermine strategic activity" by excessive attention to cost cutting and control (Jelinek and Schoonhoven, 1990:221), while loose linking may allow the freedom for creative strategy formation but leaves unanswered the question of how, rather than how close, to make the connection.

Hierarchy of Strategies

As noted earlier, the strategy hierarchy is conventionally described to flow from corporate strategies (intentions concerning the portfolio of businesses), to business strategies (intended positions on specific product-markets), to functional strategies (intentions concerning marketing, production, sourcing, etc.). The assumption apparent in the strategic planning model is that all of this is put into question each time the exercise is undertaken, typically annually, on a well-defined schedule, starting with corporate strategies at the top and working down. There is, however, no reason to believe that strategies should, can, or actually do change on a regular schedule, let alone an annual one. Indeed, all evidence (some of which is cited in the next chapter), is to the contrary: real strategic change is ad hoc and irregular, with strategies often remaining stable over long periods of time and then suddenly changing all at once. Everyone may be all set for that meeting on June 14 to finalize the strategies. But that might include the key competitor, who simply initiates its moves on June 15. Then what? Should the firm wait until next June 14 to respond?

Nor is there any evidence of a smoothly flowing deductive cascade of strategies. Budgets easily divide and add up arithmetically; strategies do not. How could they, when even the planning literature has failed to distinguish objectives from strategies? Strategies are not sharply-defined entities to be stacked up like crates in a warehouse. They are unique conceptions that exist only in people's minds. So adjectives like corporate, business, and functional may sound good on paper, but they are far from clear in reality, any more than are the distinctions between strategies and tactics, which they in fact reflect. Likewise, budgets overlie naturally on the structural hierarchy, while strategies do not. No one has ever explained the relation of corporate strategies to business strategies or business strategies to functional ones. And when one considers the process from an emergent point of view, even greater problems arise, because initiatives lower down in the hierarchy can cause strategic changes higher up—unintended and therefore unplanned.

Hierarchy of Programs

Programs seem clear enough—ad hoc clusters of activities, for example, to acquire a foreign firm, market a new product, expand the factory, or staff it, typically with a time specification called a schedule. Even the hierarchical relationships may seem clear—for example, the program to expand the factory at the level of the manufacturing department leading to the program to staff it at the level of the factory manager. Some programs are considered to be of a *capital* nature (the former), some of an *operating* nature (the latter).

Programs can, of course, be initiated independently at any level of the hierarchy (for example, to replace a maintenance machine in a factory shop), although those involving major capital expenditures usually have to be approved at senior levels in the hierarchy. Upward flow in the hierarchy is, therefore, common among programs, and, when subjected to common reporting formats and schedules, including their concurrent consideration at certain times of the year, they become part of the formal system known as capital budgeting. This form of budgeting, which deals with *ad hoc* projects, is not, however, to be confused with the regular budgeting by subunits discussed earlier. (So-called zero-based budgeting seems to combine the two: the continued existence of each budget unit is reconsidered at regular intervals as if it were like a capital project, for example, in the case of a government that is supposed to decide each year whether it wishes to continue having a police force.)

In conventional strategic planning, top-down in nature, intended strategies are simply converted into the capital and operating programs required to implement them, as when a strategy of expansion in the automobile business evokes a program of acquiring competitors in order to get their factories. But where does strategizing end and programming begin? What if the company, because it was forced to acquire a particular firm in order to get a particularly desirable plant, finds that it also bought a hog farm, and, later, as its automobile business falters, that the hog farming does marvelously well and saves it? Did the program not cause a change in the strategy? Or should we call expansion the objective and hog farming the strategy? Grossman and Lindhe have insisted that "Capital budgeting decisions should be made in the context of the long-term strategy of an organization" (1984:105). But why? Because that makes things neater for the planners? Even when something unexpected in the project can lead to a better strategy? Must everything always be so centrally deliberate? And what if the CEO had a thing about raising pigs, and really bought that firm to satisfy his (her?) secret wish? Should strategies and objectives change places?

Our point is not *where* to draw the line; it is *how* can such lines be drawn in the first place. Or, more to the point, *why* must such lines be drawn at all. Planning theory, by trying to draw arbitrary lines all over the place, has often served more to confuse issues than to clarify them. If strategy is meant to outsmart the competitors, or simply to deposit the organization in a secure niche, then it is a creative phenomenon that depends more on redrawing lines than on respecting them.

And what about the relation between capital budgeting and strategy? Duffy claimed that "the programming phase . . . bridges the gap between the planning and budgeting phases" (1989:167). But Camillus (1981) argued that the link between strategies and programs themselves is among the weakest in the literature. Are capital projects advanced with existing strategies in mind? Is so, how do these strategies get into minds in the first place? And what if they do not come to mind? What if a project is advanced quite independently of existing strategies? How does it get linked to the strategies? Indeed, what happens when the programs drive the strategies, as in our hog farming example?

In a small, insightful monograph on capital budgeting, Marsh et al. (1988) asked "Which comes first, the strategy or the projects?" Claims in the literature notwithstanding, they found the issue "far from self evident." What they called strategic investment decision making "is a long and complex process of learning and exploration, including extensive concern with operational details. These details determine how appropriate and implementable the strategy is" (15). Thus, they found "only very tenuous links between . . . 'group strategies' and the three division projects [they] monitored"; indeed in one case the two "seemed largely inconsistent" (17). They concluded that "it is almost impossible to answer" the question they posed, the only thing being "clear [was] that the project did not flow out of any *formal* process of planning" (20, italics in original). They even suggested that perhaps the term strategic accommodation might be more accurate.

And, looking the other way, how does the hierarchy of programs relate to that of budgets? Conventional planning suggests that the former gets incorporated into the latter, that the ad hoc plans for specific activities work their way into the routine plans for whole units. But no one has ever explained how.

The "Great Divide" of Planning

To summarize our discussion, albeit tentatively, when we probe into the neat relationship among these four hierarchies, we uncover all kinds of vagaries and confusions. In particular, we seem to have two solitudes in planning, two isolated sets of activities, separated by what we might call the "great divide" of planning. In Figure 2–10, one is labeled *performance control*, the other *action planning* (discussed earlier in Mintzberg, 1979a:Chapter 9).

On the left are the two hierarchies of objectives and budgets. These are routine in nature, logically carried out on a regular basis, quantitative in approach and largely the concern of the accounting people, easily mapped onto the existing structure, and geared to motivation and control—hence the label *performance control*. Each period, every unit in the organization finds itself receiving or negotiating a budget and set of objectives intended to evoke a certain level of performance, against which its results can be measured. Note that here control is after-the-fact. In other words, objectives and budgets are not concerned with predetermining *specific* actions but with controlling overall performance, that is, with the cumulative consequences of many actions. Thus, they have little to do with the formulation of strategy *per se*. Rather, performance control constitutes an *indirect* way to influence the actions taken by an organization. The operating plans, objectives, and budgets outline only the general results expected from whole series of actions by particular units; for example, that everything done by the hog farming division during the next year will produce a profit of $1 million. Hence the broad lines coming down the left side of Figure 2–10 stop short of the actions designated at the bottom of the figure.

On the right side are the hierarchies of strategies and programs. Together these are labeled *action planning* because the intention is before-the-fact specification of behavior: strategies are supposed to evoke programs that are supposed to prescribe the execution of tangible actions (as in an intended strategy of expansion manifested in a program of acquisition leading to the addition of particular factories). Hence, we have the direct lines from the program hierarchy to specific actions at the bottom of Figure 2–10 (and so Newman et al. referred to these as "single-use plans" as opposed to the performance "standing plans" [1982:56]). In contrast with objectives and budgets, strategies and programs tend to be, if not nonquantitative, then at least less so, and more the purview of the line managers, supported perhaps by the planners. Linkages here are far less specified.

But however direct the link between programs and actions, there is in general no direct connection between programs and structural units in the hierarchy. A particular unit may, of course, be charged with a particular program, but not necessarily. Indeed, forcing that correspondence can prove artificial—tangible programs of actions have their own needs, often quite independent of how the organization happens to be structured (which is equally true of particular business or functional strategies). Thus, action planning simply does not overlie conveniently on structural hierarchy (as planners discovered in their efforts to apply the SBU concept in business and PPBS in government).

Lewis has made a distinction similar to ours in his contrast of "planning by inducement" with "planning by direction." He found the former, where planning influences behavior indirectly (as in performance control), more common in governmental economic planning in Western Europe, where the budget "is the principal instrument of planning." The latter, where specific orders flow down from the top of the hierarchy (as in action planning), was more common in economic planning in the Eastern European states under Communist rule:

> The Soviet Union is a "command" economy. This means that if the plan specifies that x million tons of nails are to be produced in 1968, an order goes out from the government to each factory making nails telling it how many tons of nails are its quota, how many employees it may have, from whom it shall buy iron, and to whom it shall sell the nails. (1969:iv)

Keeping the two sides separate, by concentrating control in one or the other, appears to be easy enough. The real problems arise when efforts are made to combine them. Consider the words of Novick (who, by "plan" seemed to mean what we call action plan):

> It is quite commonplace in the literature on budgeting for business to say, "the budget is the financial expression of a plan." . . . None-

theless, we are all familiar with the budget that was developed without a plan (particularly a long-range plan). In fact, it is probably fair to say that in most budgets such planning as there is, is a projection of the status quo with increments added on the basis of the most current experience. Turning to the other side of the coin, we all know of plans that never get translated into budgets. (1968:208)

Thus, enter the great divide in planning: how to cross from performance controls on one side to action plans on the other, or vice versa—how to link general objectives and/or budgets to tangible strategies and/or programs.

Lorange, in an article with Murphy, acknowledged the "problem" of the "assumption that the budget indeed is adequately linked to the strategic plan." Many budgets are *"not* explicit reflections of the strategies" but rather merely annual "percentage updates" (1983:126). To planning theorists, this was a situation to be rectified. But they seldom explained how. As Gray noted, "the conflict between strategic plans and budgets is the most commonly perceived area of dissonance" (1986:95). "Most CEOs yearn" for budgets that will show them the consequences of their strategies, but "the same CEOs are told such budgets are not possible without disrupting the whole accounting system" (96).

In a 1981 article, Camillus sought to provide an "integrative conceptual framework" to "define the stages in the transition from strategy to action" (1981:257, 253). But it remained just that—a delineation of the stages as black boxes (from "business strategy" to "action planning" to "budgeting" to "executive action"), with little insight into the practical functioning of the linkages. In fact, the Camillus article provided a large bibliography (76 items)— much of it inserted into a matrix of these four stages by the "linkage dimensions" of "structure," "process," and "content." But almost all of this is, like his own article, conceptual rather than empirical, meaning that it is rooted in beliefs about planning rather than in its practice. Camillus never really went beyond telling his reader that "the structure and content linkages between action planning and budgeting" are among "the weakest . . . of the relevant literature" (255).

In a thoughtful article, Piercy and Thomas noted that "a number of studies suggest that ineffective integration [of corporate planning and budgeting] is a source of planning failures . . . and that corporate plans may become remote from the decision making centre arguably through a weak budgeting link" (1984:51). "At the most extreme" is the point of view that the two "require separate treatment" (53). But in general, "neither in the literature of corporate planning nor of budgeting is there any substantial explicit attention to integrating the two systems" (54). These authors pointed out various conceptual differences between the two: judgmental versus quantitative (or evaluative), long-term versus short-term, rational versus political, goal-directed versus activity-focused, nonincremental versus incremental, and "broad brush" versus narrower data. They then considered efforts to bridge the divide, generally "attempt[s] to extend what amounts to a budgeting framework into corporate planning" (57), as in the PPBS exercise in government. Among the "integrating mechanisms," they found in one example were "the use of program budgets, the financial model, and implicitly the rotation of staff between the corporate planning unit and operations or other staff functions" (61), which they referred to as "full 'textbook' integration" (66). They concluded with the call for "further investigation" (66).

In general, however, the literature has remained at the level of Bryson, who commented in his book of 1988 that, although "special efforts will be necessary to make sure the important connections are made, and incompatibilities reduced," this "should not unduly hamper the process" (65). But why not? Because he says so? While the links on each side of our divide may seem clear—for example, between objectives and budgets—the crossovers between the two sides are more often assumed than specified. Let us consider some of these in the context of different kinds of planning.

Forms of Strategic Planning

We can now use the four hierarchies to map the flows of different sets of procedures that have been promoted under the label of strategic planning.

A. Conventional Strategic Planning

Conventional strategic planning would not normally be shown in terms of our Figure 2–10 because the different hierarchies would be considered in hierarchical relationship *to each other*, for example, programs subordinate to strategies. Figure 2–12 shows their interrelationships more conventionally, with objectives over strategies (together called formulation) and these over programs, all three of them driving budgets (the latter two conventionally labeled implementation, although real implementation—that is, actually taking physical actions—never seems to figure in the discussion of the process at all!). It is, however, instructive to consider the conventional view overlaid on our diagram of the four hierarchies, and adjusted for its ambiguities, which we show in Figure 2–13.

We begin with overall objectives joined to the strategy hierarchy with a dotted line to signify that while one is supposed to drive the other, that linkage is indirect and, in fact, not well understood. Then, rather than showing a hierarchical cascade of strategies, we circle the whole strategy hierarchy to suggest that its inner workings constitute a mysterious "black box" of strategy formation difficult to get inside and understand formally. Intended strategies (however formulated) are then shown evoking programs, which are elaborated down that hierarchy, leading eventually to organizational actions (all therefore shown in solid lines). But since pro-

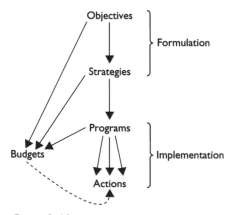

Figure 2–12
Conventional Strategic Planning

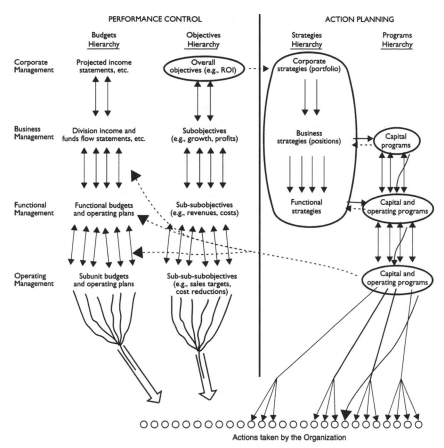

Figure 2–13
Conventional "Strategic Planning"

grams can also evoke strategies, we show a dotted line back as well. Finally, the consequences of these ad hoc programmatic changes must be incorporated into routine financial budgeting, somehow and somewhere. But because we know neither how nor where, we indicate this link as a dotted line too.

B. Strategic Planning as a Numbers Game

Meanwhile, back on the side of performance control another planning procedure occurs, one that in fact seems to be more common even though sometimes mistakenly given the name strategic planning. The reason it is more common is that it is much easier to do; the reason it is given the same name may reflect either wishful thinking (the hope that objectives will magically produce strategies, sometimes even the assumption that objectives *are* strategies), or wishful acting (that going through the motions of something called strategic planning is tantamount to creating strategies).

In any event, the process is the one we have described on the left side of the diagram and is shown in Figure 2–14: the development of a hierarchy of objectives and a hierarchy of budgets (each either top-down, bottom-up, or negotiated), with the objectives at each level feeding in as one determinate of the budget. This kind of per-

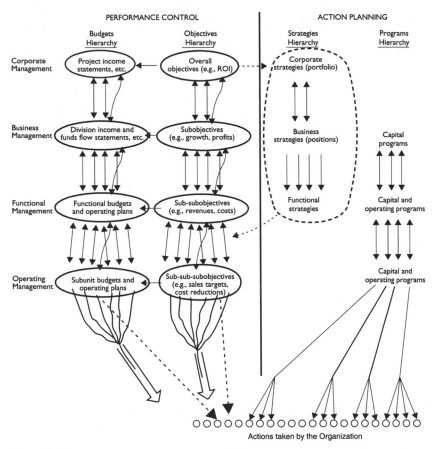

Figure 2–14
Planning as a "Numbers Game"

formance control is certainly easier to understand and to do then the conventional strategic planning of Figure 2–13; indeed, it is not uncommon for organizations to attempt the full process but end up with only this. In other words, what are called strategic planning exercises often reduce to the generation of numbers, not ideas—objectives and budgets but not strategies. From the perspective of strategy formation, therefore, this constitutes a numbers game, a label that has had a certain currency in organizations themselves.

Gray found this game still very common in the mid-1980s: "Approximately seven out of ten companies in our sample do not carry the formulation of strategy much beyond some general statement of thrust such as market penetration or internal efficiency and some generalized goal such as excellence" (1986:94). These "half-baked" or "financial" strategies were often found to be developed without consideration of such strategic issues as "competitive reactions . . . and other problems lying beneath the numbers. . . . Financial strategy is not reconciled with other strategies but preempts them as the final arbiters of corporate resource allocation" (95). Gray's findings were consistent with earlier ones of Franklin et al. that 55 percent of "planners identified most heavily" with an approach that sounds much like this, with only 59 percent opting for something akin to what we called conventional strategic planning and 10 percent with the core design school (what they call the Harvard) approach (some respondents chose more than one approach to corporate planning and some none). These authors also found that "70% of the corporate planners mentioned having pro-forma financial statements of some type in their plans. Sixty percent of the corporate plans included *specific* plans and budgets for such areas as personnel, plant and equipment, R&D, etc." (1981:16). But no mention was made of how many of the plans contained strategies!

Of course, when taken for what it is—a system of performance control—this is not a game at all but perhaps one valid means of motivating employees and regulating their behavior. Thus Allaire and Firsirotu commented on what they called "numbers-driven planning": "Whatever else may be included in the plan, the essence of planning here boils down to preparing and monitoring a set of numbers which can be tied to a compensation package" (1990:109). This is a game only when it is confused with strategy formation: that is, when organizations pretend that an annual ritual of producing reams of numbers satisfies their need to engage in strategic thinking, moreover, when they believe that to establish controls is to set direction (and not just to maintain it). To quote the same authors in an earlier monograph: such "strategic plans . . . are but euphemistic operational plans with the words strategy and strategic thrown in for dramatic effect every couple of sentences" (1988:63). That the numbers game is something different from strategic thinking—by our definitions, that to engage in "planning" is not necessarily "to plan"—was pointed out by Tilles early in this whole literature:

> For far too many companies, what little thinking goes on about the future is done primarily in money terms. There is nothing wrong with financial planning. Most companies should do more of it. But there is a basic fallacy in confusing a financial plan with thinking about the kind of company you want yours to become. It is like saying, "When I'm 40, I'm going to be *rich*." (1963:112)

The numbers game can, in fact, impede strategic thinking by focusing so much attention on extrapolations from the status quo that serious change in strategy is never even entertained. Bear in mind that performance control, unlike action planning, overlies naturally on the *existing* organizational structure; this makes it difficult to consider changes that reconfigure that structure, as serious shifts in strategy generally do. Thus, the whole numbers game usually amounts to an exercise in repeating what everyone already knows, geared to the generation of a set of targets and standards within the context of the existing strategies (and even ignoring what changes in strategy might be taking place in emergent fashion). In an early book that delineated different forms of "planning and control systems," Anthony was one of the few to recognize this:

> Actually, the characteristics of the long-range planning process resemble more closely the characteristics we have identified with the management control process than they do those of the strategic planning process. A five-year plan usually is a projection of the costs and revenues that are anticipated under policies and programs *already approved*, rather than a device for consideration of, and decision on, new policies and programs. The five-year plan

reflects strategic decisions already taken; it is not the essence of the process of making new decisions. (1965:57–58)

Indeed, a good deal of the so-called strategic planning through the 1970s turned out to be just this: ritualistic strategy formation overlaid on more serious "numbers crunching" that actually impeded strategic change. Rogers referred to this as "strictly financial forecasting and budgeting" even though it involved "often lengthy and complex forms" to be filled in (for example, 20 pages for each division manager at Motorola), commenting that:

Often the paper work disguised the fact that financial planning was predominant. The sheets to be filled in might well include complex market forecasts, competitive analyses, or detailed plans for all functional areas; only the experienced divisional manager knew "what the head office was really interested in." (1975:59)

C. Capital Budgeting as Ad Hoc Control

Our third form of strategic planning sits on the action planning side of our diagram, but because it flows up rather than down, and because it ultimately bypasses that mysterious process of strategy formation altogether, it is able to function roughly as specified. This is capital budgeting, a system to handle the approval of major capital expenditures. (For a review of its popular use in business, based on surveys in 1970, 1975, and 1980, see Klammer and Walker, 1984.)

As indicated in Figure 2–15, a new project (such as the creation of a new facility or the purchase of a new piece of machinery) is conceived by a sponsor at some level down in the hierarchy (most often, by far, within a functional department, according to Yavitz and Newman [1982:189]). There, an assessment is made of its costs and benefits over time, normally in quantitative terms, ideally as discounted cash flow, so that its overall performance can be estimated (e.g., as return on investment). The program is then proposed to one or more successively higher levels in the hierarchy, where it is supposed to be compared with projects and funded if it ranks sufficiently high to deserve receiving whatever remains in the capital budget.

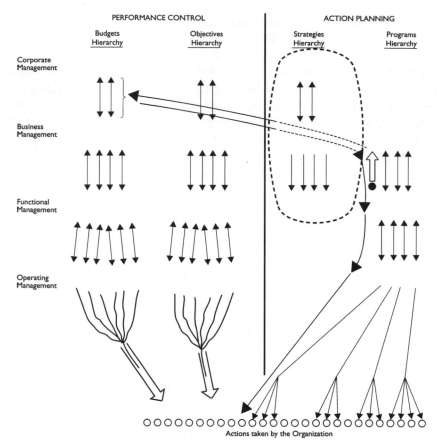

Figure 2–15
Capital Budgeting as Ad Hoc Control

That projects are generated and evaluated in this way and flow up the hierarchy for review appears to be true; but not that the assessments of them are objective (these being done amidst all kinds of future uncertainties by their own biased sponsors) or that the appraisal is a straightforward process (given all the political effort invested in getting them that far, e.g., Bower, 1970b). Moreover, while capital budgeting has been associated with strategy making (Berg, for example, titled his 1965 *Harvard Business Review* article on the subject, "Strategic Planning in Conglomerate Companies"), the links between the two processes are far from clear. How strategy making influences the generation and selection of projects, or how the projects influence the formation of strategies (or even which way the influence should flow), has never been specified with any precision.

Thus we show the capital budgeting procedure in Figure 2–15 starting within the program hierarchy and skipping through the black box of strategy formation on its way to the budgeting hierarchy, where the monetary constraint is imposed on proposed programs before the successful ones return to be implemented down the hierarchy of programs. Indeed, capital budgeting seems primarily to be a means to control capital spending—specifically, to review the financial impact of individual projects. To quote the opening sentence of Bower's well-known empirical study of the process, it is a "problem of efficient allocation of resources" (1970b:1). Even the set of decisions about the different projects is not integrated in any way except to ensure that together they do not violate capital constraints. (Back to Eigerman's integration by stapler.) To quote Yavitz and Newman, "the model assumes that projects bubble up from the bottom and that selection can be based on estimated rate of return with little or no attention to long-run strategy" (1982:189).

Later we shall review some of the evidence on capital budgeting in relation to strategy formation as well as the associated PPBS experience in government. The latter, a more ambitious attempt to link strategy formation with a kind of capital budgeting as well as regular budgeting (altogether probably the greatest effort ever made to apply the full-blown planning model, but with bottom-up elements), reverted to both a numbers game and a capital budgeting exercise; it failed as strategy formation process.

To summarize this discussion, what remains of strategic planning is in fact a set of three independent approaches—a kind of portfolio of planning techniques, if you like. On one side is a numbers game, geared to motivation and control but not to strategy formation. On the other is capital budgeting, a portfolio technique to control capital spending through decision making but not strategy making. And in between is a process that seems to be about strategy making, but more in name than in content, for this remains largely unspecified. The black box of strategy creation was never opened, nor were its linkages to the other hierarchies specified.

Our discussion suggests that the planning approach's very nature of emphasizing decomposition has led to the decomposition of its own efforts into these three independent approaches. Some planning writers (for example, Gluck et al., 1980, and Ansoff, 1967, 1984:258) claimed that these approaches built on each other over time to emerge as one integrated system. First came the numbers game, then forecasting techniques, later the introduction of methods to formulate strategy, and so on, resulting finally in a comprehensive planning system encompassing all these elements (see, for example, Lorange, 1980a:55–58). But outside of textbooks and planning manuals, it is difficult to find systematic evidence that any of this really ever did happen. We have, in other words, found nothing yet to link planning directly with strategy formation. To probe further into this, we turn now to a review of the evidence on the performance of planning itself.

3

Evidence on Planning

What has been the performance of planning itself? In this chapter we present three forms of evidence: survey, anecdotal, and intensive. Then we look at some evidence of how planners themselves have dealt with this evidence.

Planners have been notably reluctant to study their own efforts—not only what they really *do* but, more important, what they and their processes of planning really *get done,* in terms of impact on the functioning and effectiveness of their organizations. Planners have been so busy calling on everyone else to collect data and to be objective that they have seldom gotten around to doing so about their own activities. Starbuck, for example, could not find any study that has "assessed the consequences of adhering to or deviating from long-range plans" (1985:371). And Lorange, who, at the end of planning's heady decades of the 1960s and 1970s, sought "to survey the empirically based research literature on long-range formal planning processes for corporations" (1979:226), was able to cite fewer than thirty empirical studies in his bibliography, which consisted almost entirely of questionnaire surveys from a distance on "Does planning pay?". (A few were experimental studies that ostensibly simulated planning in a laboratory setting.) Consider this in terms of the length of the bibliography in Steiner's book, *Top Management Planning:* it numbers 38 *pages*—and that is only the 1969 edition!

Nonetheless, there is no shortage of anecdotal evidence on the performance of planning in specific settings, especially from the early 1980s when the planning community came under severe fire. And here and there, usually buried in some obscure corner of the management (not planning) literature, is an intensive study of what planning really did (or failed to do) in one or a very few particular settings. We review these different sets of evidence in turn.

Survey Evidence on "Does Planning Pay?"

If planning produces higher profits, how could anyone possibly criticize it? Accordingly, beginning in the late 1960s a number of academics set out to prove that planning pays. For the most part, their biases were that blatant.[1]

The approach was simple. You measured performance, which was easy enough, at least if you restricted yourself to conventional short-term measures of economic performance in business (or better still, the respondents' subjective ranking of their firms' performance, as some studies did). And you measured planning, which also seemed easy enough: you simply mailed a questionnaire to the head of planning (or to the chief executive, who was most likely to give it to the planners anyway, unless he or she threw it away instead[2]), asking the respondent to tell you on seven-point scales or the like how much planning took place in the firm. Then

---

[1] I recall attending one conference presentation at the Academy of Management in which the researcher explained how he tried the data one way and the desired relationship did not appear, so he tried another and another and another, always without success (in his terms). And so he concluded publicly that his methodology must have been at fault, never even entertaining the possibility that his original hypothesis might have been flawed.

[2] In a 1972 survey on a slightly different subject (the "pitfalls" of planning), George Steiner mailed questionnaires to 600 companies "intend[ing] to get responses from a representative group of chief executives, division managers, and managers of headquarters staff." Of the 215 replies, *"unexpectedly* . . . most companies [75 percent] decided to have only the corporate planner complete the form" (1979:287–288, italics added).

you dumped all the responses into a computer and sat back and read correlation coefficients. You never even had to leave your office at the university.[3] And that meant you never had to face all the distortions inherent in such research.

The first of these is the question of the reliability of the reporting. Answers come cheap on seven-point scales. But how objective can planners be in assessing planning? To quote from Starbuck's critique of these studies: "Nearly all of these studies gathered their data by mail questionnaires that could be filled out quickly ["in a few minutes," to quote one study] and that were filled out by self-selected respondents who had little reason to respond accurately and who may not have known what they were talking about" (1985:370). Starbuck also documented the low response rates of these mailed surveys, generally in the range of 20 percent but some as low as 7 percent. In one study, Welch explained his use of a mailed questionnaire as being better to "acquire factual information rather than to examine the planning process in detail" (1984:144). Among the "factual information" he gathered: whether the firm "identified and analyzed alternative strategic options" and "planned courses of direction subject" to such factors!

Second is the problem of measuring planning (Foster, 1986). As Pearce et al. pointed out in their review of eighteen of these studies, "although the term *formal strategic planning* was used liberally throughout their work, the authors of only 1 of the 18 articles provided a conceptual definition (1987:659).[4] Indeed, Armstrong, who also reviewed some of these studies, commented that "in fact, I was unable, in most studies, to find *any* description of the planning process" (1982:204).[5] Even leaving this aside, does producing

---

[3] In a notable exception, Grinyer and Norburn (1974) supplemented their mailed questionnaire with interviews. But they did not reflect the biases of many of the other researchers.

[4] Grinyer and Norburn (1974) again.

[5] He added: One study, by Leontiades and Tezel, treated this lack of definition as an advantage. They asked chief executives to rate the importance of planning, but they did not provide the executives with a definition nor did they ask them for a definition. They claimed that, "An advantage of our approach . . . is that it eliminated the necessity to make an outside judgment on the quality of formal planning" (Armstrong, 1982:204). But given the vagaries of the word itself (as noted at the outset of our discussion), this is truly an astonishing claim.

documents called plans, or claiming to use a whole raft of procedures and techniques, or even having a department called planning or people called planners, really indicate that the organization has internalized "planning" (by any reasonable definition)? As Wildavsky put it, "Attempts to plan are no more planning than the desire to be wise may be called wisdom or the wish to be rich entitles a man to be called wealthy" (1973:129). Even Lorange criticized the treatment of formal planning in these studies "as a broad phenomenon" with "little effort ... made to distinguish what sort of formal planning one was dealing with" (1979:230).

In their study of capital budgeting techniques, which they probed deeply in three cases, Marsh et al. claimed that "all three would have shown up in [survey studies] as 'using' [discounted cash flow] techniques, and all three would have been at the most sophisticated end of the spectrum," yet "there were widespread differences between the formal systems and reality" (1988:27). The best that can be said for the equivalent research on planning in general is that it did not even get so far as to reveal such problems!

Third and perhaps most important is the problem of inferring cause. These were studies of correlation, not causation. A positive correlation between planning and performance allows no one to conclude that planning pays. Causation may also go the other way: only rich organizations can afford planning, or at least planners. Starbuck (1985:370–371) raised another possibility here: firms that do well naturally emphasize their planning activities (since they made or exceeded their targets) while those that do poorly become unsure of them and so underemphasize them. And then again, planning and performance may be independent of each other, both driven by some common third force (say, smart managers, who improve performance by other means and also know that they better have planning, even if only to impress the stock market analysts). Overall, the assumption that the final number on some remote "bottom line" has an identifiable and therefore measurable relation to some process the organization happens to use—one among hundreds—would appear to be, if not extraordinarily arrogant, then surprisingly naïve.

All these problems notwithstanding, these studies did not even prove their own point. Some supported the relationship while others did not. The overall results were "inconclusive" to quote one review (Bresser and Bishop, 1983:588), "inconsistent and often contradicting," to quote another (Pearce et al., 1987:671, who titled their article "The Tenuous Link Between Formal Strategic Planning and Financial Performance"; see also Shrader, Taylor, and Dalton, 1984, for another thorough review that drew the same conclusion). Or in Lorange's conclusion, "a problem still remains in deciding what type of formal planning activities proved advantageous" (1979:230).

One of the first studies, published in 1970, probably the most widely cited—and one of the more careful ones—was carried out by Thune and House. Their findings were strongly favorable. But their measure of formal planning should be noted: "questionnaire responses indicat[ing] that [the firm] determined corporate strategy and goals for at least three years ahead, and if they established specific action programs, projects, and procedures for achieving the goals" (82). Ansoff and his colleagues published another study in the same year indicating that firms engaging in acquisition activity in a "systematic planned" way achieved higher performance and more predictable performance on average, although "several of the non-planners had performances that surpassed the best performance in the group of planners" (1970:6). When Herold supported these findings two years later (1972), everything looked quite rosy for planning.

But 1973 was not a good year for planning, even leaving aside the energy crisis. The first crack appeared in a paper by Rue and Fulmer (1973; see also Fulmer and Rue, 1974), which concluded that while planning paid in durable goods businesses, a lack of planning paid in service businesses, and it was not clear which paid in nondurable goods businesses. From there, the relationship was up for grabs. In 1975, Malik and Karger found favorable results, while Sheehan (1975) and Grinyer and Norburn (1974, "probably the best study . . . to date" according to Starbuck [1985:371]), did not. Later Wood and LaForge (1979) found a positive relationship for large banks, followed by Robinson and Pearce who found (1983) no such relationship for small banks. Shapiro and Kallman (1978) found no relation between planning and performance for motor carriers, nor could Leontiades and Tezel find one for a more general sample, "no matter how the data were manipulated" (1980:74), nor did Kudla, although he observed that planning did seem to provide a "transitory" reduction in riskiness (1980:5).

In a 1986 study of small firms in a "stable, mature environment" (dry cleaning business), in which the authors distinguished "structured strategic plans" from "structured operational," "intuitive," and "unstructured" ones, Bracker and Pearson found that higher growth performance was associated with the first of these (and the other three could not be distinguished from each other with respect to performance). But would the more intuitive types, especially the most successful, be inclined to fill out questionnaires in the first place? Of the association members surveyed, 53 percent did not respond, despite repeated contacts by mail and even telephone. In the same year, Rhyne (1986) found among Fortune 1000 companies that those with more of a "strategic planning" orientation (as opposed to "long-range planning," "annual planning," etc.) exhibited higher performance, although there was some variation from year to year.

The research continued, with the addition of more and more variables, seeking ever more contingent relationships. The following year Rhyne reported again, finding "no relationship" with formality but that high performers "appeared to develop less complex planning systems" (1987:380); Javidan (1987) went into some detail about the effectiveness of different roles that planners perform; Ramanujam and Venkatraman suggested that "resistance to planning" and "resources provided for planning" had "the dominant impact on planning system effectiveness, broadly construed" (1987:453); and Rule (1987), a Canadian consultant, found that the self-rated effective planners earned a higher return on equity.

In 1988, an article by Bracker et al. about "planning process sophistication" and performance of small firms in a growth industry claimed to support the results of previous research that "opportunistic entrepreneurs who employ structured strategic planning processes may be better prepared to develop a framework for anticipating and coping with change," although "the remaining firms are not necessarily doomed"! (602) Robinson and Pearce presented a complex study with the analyses relating "strategic orientation" (consistency of and commitment to strategy) and "planning sophistication," which found the highest performers strong on both. Other types of studies appeared in 1989 (e.g., Kukalis on the relationship between firm and planning characteristics [see also Kukalis, 1988]), and in 1990 (e.g., Sinha on the contribution of formal planning to different types of decisions).

Finally, as this book was nearing completion, Boyd published a long and detailed "meta-analytic review" of these studies. He found 49 journal articles and book chapters in all, some reviews, some repeats of each other, some of whose authors answered his request with the claim that the necessary backup data were "unavailable" (1991:356). Narrowing down to 29 the number of empirical studies he could use, which sampled 2,496 organizations in all, Boyd found "the overall effect of planning on performance . . . very weak" (362). With sufficient breakdown of the performance measures (into nine types), however, the correlations were labeled "modest" (353). But "extensive measurement problems suggest that these findings *under*estimate the *true* relationship between planning and performance" (353, italics added). Moreover, "while the average effect size is small, many firms do report significant quantifiable benefits from participating in the strategic planning process" (369). So much for scientific objectivity! Boyd closed with a call for "more rigorous measurement," "more controls," and "separate analyses" (369). Good idea!

More evidence will, no doubt, come, providing elaboration if not insight. What Pearce at al. referred to in 1987, after seventeen years of research, as "a problematic and unresolved issue" remains problematic and unresolved. At the very least, we have found that planning is not "the one best way," that it certainly does not pay in general, and that at best, it may have some suitability in particular contexts, such as larger organizations, those in mass production, etc.

Anecdotal Evidence

As good scientists, we are all expected to rely on hard data systematically collected. Anecdotal evidence is supposed to be soft, biased, and superficial. Yet we have just seen exactly the same about hard data—that these have a decidedly soft underbelly. The systematic collection of data about ill-specified processes does not provide much insight into what is going on out there.

Let us therefore turn to some anecdotal evidence, not to resolve any issue so much as to gain a bit of insight into several of them. The following choice of anecdotes may suggest our own biases, since we have selected them to highlight the problems with planning. But it also seems that the more specific an anecdote about planning in the popular press, the more likely it is to be negative: praise tends to come in generalized commentaries, criticism in pointed examples.

The evidence we are citing goes back to the early years of strategic planning, starting as a trickle that grew into an important stream of its own in the mid-1970s, which had become a veritable flood by the 1980s. The anecdotes reproduced here tell this story.

- 1970: On the first page of what was to become a widely read book on planning, one of America's most dedicated technocrats wrote: "Recently I asked three corporate executives what decisions they had made in the last year that they would not have made were it not for their corporate plans. All had difficulty in identifying one such decision. Since each of their plans were marked 'secret' or 'confidential', I asked them how their competitors might benefit from the possession of their plans. Each answered with embarrassment that their competitors would not benefit. Yet these executives were strong advocates of corporate planning" (Ackoff, 1970:1). So too was this author, who followed this comment, not with an investigation of its causes, but with 144 pages on the glories and procedures of corporate planning.
- 1972: A well-known proponent of planning, having visited a wide variety of European and American companies between 1967 and 1972, concluded in a leading planning journal: "most companies find formal planning has not been the panacea or solution originally thought. Success in planning does not come easy ... not only in the United States and Europe but also in Japan, the Communist countries, and even the developing nations [that have] embraced, often with great enthusiasm" the concept of organized corporate planning (Ringbakk, 1972:10). This journal nonetheless continued to embrace the concept, always with great enthusiasm.
- 1972: The Vice-president of a U.S. corporation, writing in the same journal in the same year, was more blunt: "In practice, planning has been a resounding and expensive failure" (Pennington, 1972:2).
- 1973: A bashful academic who, in the late 1960s, had grit-

ted his teeth and ventured out of the protected environment of the university to observe what real, live managers in America really do, came back to tell the tale: "with few exceptions managerial activities in my study concerned specific rather than general issues. During working hours it was rare to see a chief executive participating in abstract discussion or carrying out general planning. . . . Clearly, the classic view of the manager as planner is not in accord with reality. If the manager does indeed plan, it is not by locking his door, puffing on his pipe, and thinking great thoughts" (Mintzberg, 1973:37).

• 1972: Another academic ventured out of his university to find out whether top managers really find computer models for planning useful. His conclusion, in brief: "No." In many cases, development efforts had been reduced or stopped; many of those efforts that were finished had not been implemented; and most that had been implemented were not significantly influencing the actual strategy making process within the firm (Hall, 1972/73:33).

• 1977: An academic renowned in this field, who spent much time working with practitioners, spoke up. More than a decade after his pathbreaking book, Igor Ansoff commented that "in spite of almost twenty years of existence of the strategic planning technology, a majority of firms today engage in the far less threatening and perturbing extrapolative long-range planning" (1977:20).

• 1977: To return to that leading planning journal some years later, two academics, after noting that "there are few axioms in the management literature more generally accepted without question than that stating the necessity for sound strategic planning," a point on which "academics and researchers are . . . virtually unanimous" ("virtually," as usual, encompassing a good deal of evidence to the contrary), found, like Ansoff, that none of the five "major" U.S. corporations studied "engaged in true strategic planning" (Saunders and Tuggle, 1977:19).

• 1978: A French professor who surveyed several European firms after the energy crisis of 1973, some of which reduced their planning horizon or abandoned planning altogether as a result, quoted one executive of a 7000-person enterprise:

"Those who say that they make plans and that these work are liars. The term planning is imbecilic; everything can change tomorrow." Said another executive, "The crisis showed us that long-term planning is useless" (Horowitz, 1978:49, our translation from the French).

• 1980: Not only did firms seem not to do strategic planning as prescribed, but some seemed to go out of their way to avoid it. One group of consultants noted that line managers even took the unheard-of step of surrendering formal authority so as not to have to plan. "Division managers have been known to attempt to escape from the burden of 'useless' annual planning by proposing that they fold their businesses into other SBUs, at least for planning purposes" (Gluck, Kaufman, and Walleck, 1980:159).

• 1985: Javidan asked the managers of fifteen firms how satisfied they were with the performance of their planning staffs. "Not very" was the short answer (1985:89). None considered them "very successful," half the chief executives considered them "somewhat unsuccessful." (The planning managers surveyed were somewhat more positive [p.93]). Many of the respondents considered planning to have a "negative effect" on the firm's strategic decisions and on its managerial innovativeness (91).

• 1985: Harvard Business School professor Robert Hayes reported on "a recurring theme in the explanations [that innumerable line managers] give for their companies' competitive difficulties": "Again and again they argue that many of those difficulties—particularly in their manufacturing organizations—stem from their companies' strategic planning processes. Their complaint, however, is not about the *mis*functioning of strategic planning but about the harmful aspects of its *proper* functioning"! (1985:111)

• 1987: In an article in *The Economist*, Michael Porter commented that "The criticism of strategic planning was well deserved. Strategic planning in most companies has not contributed to strategic thinking" (17). His solution: "strategic planning needs to be rethought" (by planning?).

• 1988: Walter Schaffir, Strategic Planning Conference Program Director for The Conference Board, referred to strategic planning as having been "formalized and systematized, criticized, reshaped, misunderstood, oversold (and overbought), once again redefined, misapplied, discarded . . . and revitalized." He claimed it to be "alive and well in the real world of business," noting that "still—strategic planning had gotten a bad name in some quarters—and often deservedly so," referring to "the perfunctory nature of the 'exercise' . . . without real meaning" (1988:xiii).

The General Electric FIFO Experience

In 1984, Lauenstein noted that "companies such as International Harvester and AM International were bragging in their annual reports about their strategic planning systems shortly before they met disaster" (1984:89). The phenomenon, in fact, proved all too common. In a 1975 article, Ansoff noted that

> In the mid-1960's, the management of one of the world's largest conglomerates proudly displayed its planning and control. A week after the public display, the same management made a red-faced admission to two multimillion-dollar surprises: a major overrun in its office furniture division and another in its shipbuilding division. (1975a:21)

Ansoff nonetheless argued in a later book that "the history of management systems is a succession of inventions," some of which "failed," others "succeeded," but in general constituting a progression toward better practice. "For example, today's leading practitioner of strategic planning, the American General Electric Company, has tried and regressed twice before the currently successful process was established as a part of the firm's general management" (1984:188).

Ansoff's timing was, however, also unfortunate, because that "successful process" had just come apart too, this time with a great deal of publicity.

In 1984, as the criticisms of planning intensified, *Business Week* capped the discussion with a cover story that carried a strong and unrelenting attack on planning: "After more than a decade of near-dictatorial sway over the future of U.S. corporations, the reign of the strategic planner may be at an end"; "few of the supposedly brilliant strategies concocted by planners were successfully implemented"; the CEO of General Motors, after three "unsuccessful tries" at establishing a headquarters planning system, was quoted as saying that "we got these great plans together, put them on the shelf, and marched off to do what we would be doing anyway. It took us a little while to realize that wasn't getting us anywhere." To *Business Week,* the upheaval was "nothing less" than "a bloody battle between planners and managers" (1984a:62); "the end result is that strategic planners disrupt a company's ability to assess the outside world and to create strategies for a sustainable competitive advantage" (64).

One organization dominated the *Business Week* article, as it had the lore of planning almost from the very beginning: the General Electric Company. Accountants would probably not be uncomfortable with our giving GE's experience with planning the label FIFO (first in–first out).

To the advocates of planning, General Electric had always been the exemplary firm (e.g., Blass, 1983:6–7, alongside Ansoff). An impressive number of the concepts and techniques that became widely accepted saw the light of day in the planning department of this firm: the strategic business unit (SBU), the PIMS project, the 3 × 3 matrix of industry attractiveness/business strength, and so on. General Electric's planners were among the most prolific in the literature (e.g., Wilson, 1974; Allen, 1977; Rothschild, 1976, 1979, 1980; see also interviews with GE planners Rothschild [Cohen, 1982] and Carpenter [Allio, 1985]). To quote a *Washington Post* article, "G.E. literally wrote the book on the subject" (Potts, 1984).

Planning at GE received its great impetus from Reginald Jones, chief executive from 1972 to 1981. In a 1979 article, he traced the origins of "the era of strategic planning at General Electric" to a recentralization of power after the debacle of the company's sortie into the computer business. As Hamermesh recounted the story, lackluster profits in the late 1960s plus threats to GE's "sacred" triple-A bond rating encouraged the company to "begin to look for new forms of strategic planning" (1986:183).

Hamermesh described the development of planning under Jones's tutelage in considerable detail, noting, for example, that by 1980 there were approximately 200 senior level planners in the company (193), all of them along with SBU general managers required to attend special strategic planning seminars (at which they received slide and tape shows to carry the word to their own people). His description depicted an organization continually searching for the right formula to enable a senior management with limited time to understand a complex and diversified company. For example, Jones was very excited about the concept of "sectors" (clusters of strategic business units, originally 6 in all for 43 of the latter) introduced in 1977. "I could look at six planning books and understand them well enough to ask the right questions" (202).

The hoopla associated with what really amounted to GE's trials and tribulations with planning (rather than the perfectly-honed system depicted in the literature) continued through the 1970s, so that when the new senior vice-president for planning visited the Defense Department to find out about an extensive survey that had been done on planning systems, he was told that he "was probably inheriting the world's most effective strategic planning system and that Number Two was pretty far behind" (Hamermesh, 181).

There was one problem however. As *Fortune* writer Walter Kiechel put it, while "strategic planning was the gospel" at GE, its "stock traded at about the same moribund level all through the seventies, with the PE gradually declining" (1984:8).

Thus in the early 1980s, soon after he arrived on the scene as Chairman and CEO, Jack Welch—a very different kind of manager—dismantled the system. To return to that *Business Week* article (1984a), Welch "slashed the corporate planning group from 57 to 33, and scores of planners have been purged in GE's operating sectors, groups, and divisions" (62).

The Major Appliances Business Group was a case in point. Its vice-president was quoted in *Business Week* on " 'gaining ownership of the business, grabbing hold of it' from 'an isolated bureaucracy' of planners" (62). To the *Business Week* writers, the experiences of his Group "serve as an excellent case study of how disruptive strategic planning can be" (64). The Group's planners, who numbered 50 by the late 1970s, many of them former consultants, generated a " 'natural resistance' that escalated into out-and-out hostility" to the line managers. Among the problems "was the planners' obsession with predicting the unpredictable—such as oil prices—and then hastily reacting when events did not turn out as expected" (65). Another problem was a reliance "on data, not market instincts, to make judgments," which created bad assumptions that led to some bad strategies. Most telling is the comment that "top management, which also lacked contact with the market, did not see that the planners' data failed to tell the true story" (65).

Thus, the more "bureaucratic" the process of planning became, the more "managers began to confuse strategy with planning and implementation." *Business Week* claimed that *no* planners were left with the Group Vice-President for Major Appliances in 1984![6]

This Group vice-president's anger with planning was not unusual. In our own experiences, we frequently come into contact with organizations going through formalized planning processes, and we recall no middle line manager we ever met who claimed to actually enjoy the process! But there has been no shortage of those who hated everything about it, and who would be most favorable to the characterization of it as "some sort of perverse management hazing" (Eckhert in Bryson, 1988:66).

Some Deeper Evidence

The survey research we discussed earlier reviewed planning from a distance, in a detached way, and so revealed hardly anything about its actual performance in context. Even the anecdotal evi-

---

[6] Given this change, it is interesting to go back two years to a *Planning Review* interview with GE planner Rothschild, inopportunely titled "For GE, Planning Crowned with Success" (Cohen, 1982). The interviewer seemed to be unaware that the axe was about to fall—his questions reflected the upbeat attitude about planning at GE ("everyone is thinking strategically and the planning system works" [8]). But one got hints of what was to come in some of Rothschild's responses, for example, his parting comment in answer to "Where is GE headed now?":

> The challenge in my job is to help Jack Welch find some others. I like being challenged, and I like people to argue with me. By the way, that happens to be what our new chairman likes too. The new buzz-word here is contention management. I'd say that's where we are and where we're going. (11)

But other comments by Rothschild may help to explain why GE line managers eventually revolted. In response to why the GE system worked, in contrast with the "many examples of planning systems that self-destruct, or perhaps, worse, provide no value," Rothschild responded in part: "I can assure you that a guy who doesn't implement the strategy can be in big trouble," and later, "We tell the CEO when a manager is not on plan" (10). (Later, in reply to "What do SBU managers have to say about [planning integration]?", Rothschild cited a survey indicating that 85 percent of them claimed they would continue to do strategic planning if the company itself stopped doing it; a repeat three years later pushed that figure up to 90 percent. "So yes, our strategic planning really is part of the culture" [11]. Another example of the reliance "on data, not market instincts"!!)

dence, while telling a story, did not really get inside the issues. Clearly, what all this evidence cries out for is in-depth investigation of planning itself. After all those years of clocking workers in the factories, wasn't it time someone subjected those high-priced planners to the same scrutiny, to find out what they themselves did and really got done? "Analyst, study thyself," implored Wildavsky (1979:10).

Unfortunately, few did, at least close up. Lorange's own call for "clinically based research design, emphasizing an in-depth assessment of planning needs and capabilities for the given firm" (1979:230) was never heeded within the planning field, by him or anyone else. From the outside, however, a few researchers did dig into the process, to find out what really went on, sometimes to their own surprise. Here we review some of those studies.

Sarrazin's Study of Exemplary Planning

Two most interesting studies were carried out in France as rather obscure theses. The French have long been enamored of formal planning, perhaps because of their Cartesian traditions that emphasize rationality and order. Jacques Sarrazin (1975, 1977/1978), then a young management researcher at Ecole Polytechnique, the very center of such thinking, set out to document the planning process in France's equivalent of General Electric, the firm most renowned for its planning. He came in for his share of surprises. In a nutshell, he concluded that planning was an ineffective process for making strategic decisions but was retained as a tool for control, perhaps of a political nature—to centralize power in the organization.

Sarrazin found that the planning process did not integrate the results of specific strategic studies; these studies were simply not ready on schedule. "The firm cannot allow itself to wait every year for the month of February to address its problems" (1975:79).[7] Thus, "few of the critical decisions for the organization were taken during the planning cycle" (78). Nor did the process allow for

---

[7] I have translated quotations from Sarrazin's 1975 thesis; his 1977/78 article is a summary of the findings in English.

"genuine integration" (56): it simply could not handle the associated complexities. ". . . the complexity of the environment makes it almost impossible, in the case of larger corporations, to define the plan as a decision process covering all of their future activities"; there was simply too much data involved and too little of it available for planning. At its best, the plan offered an "integration after the fact" (137), or "official sanction for actions already decided upon and hardly subject to review and revision at that point" (1977/78:48). These served not to avoid upcoming inconsistencies so much as to uncover ones that already existed (1975:137).[8]

The problem with achieving integration is that the organization consists, not of the "single decision making center" presupposed in the classical planning model (1977/78:48), but of multiple centers of decision and various "logics of action": managers "make greater use of their own personal views of company strategy than they do of real strategy as envisaged by the top executives" (50). Thus instead of integrating the efforts of people, planning enhances conflict between them.

Why then did the organization engage in the planning process? For one thing, it "formalizes a certain number of decisions taken elsewhere"; in that respect, the plan allows "certain things to be recorded in black and white" as well as to commit managers to certain principles of action (1975:146). Second, planning provided a means to gather information systematically about the organization's activities. Third, planning, by exposing certain gaps, did help to initiate certain strategic studies. Finally, planning was used as a tool by top management to try to regain control of its organization:

> The top managers try to utilize the existing planning process to regain control of strategic decision-making that has been lost because of the multiplicity of real decision centers, and also to achieve a minimal degree of coherence between those decisions and the company's strategy. (1977/78:56)

---

[8] In light of our discussion of budgets versus strategies, it is interesting to note Sarrazin's comment that "In reality, it seems that the plan-budget synthesis is difficult," in his view primarily because budgeting is a separate procedure from planning, usually already functioning with its own needs when strategic planning is introduced and not modified to accommodate it (1977/78:52).

In Sarrazin's view, "this provides a possible explanation of the fact that the larger French companies often maintain planning procedures in spite of cost and evident failure" (56).

Gomer's Study of Planning Under Crisis

The second thesis was written in France by a Swede, Hakan Gomer (1973, 1974, see also 1976), who was particularly interested in the role of planning systems in response to the energy crisis of 1973—the drastic rise in oil prices due to the creation of the OPEC cartel. Gomer studied three major firms in his country (one in insurance, a second diversified from a base in primary industry, and a third manufacturing equipment for mining and other industries), all of whose planning activities "reflected the general planning model" (1976:10).

In essence, Gomer concluded that "formal planning lent some *evaluative* support to problem-solving activities related to the crisis, but did not provide 'early warning' or otherwise make the organization more sensitive to environmental change" (1). In other words, "planners did not contribute to the *recognition phase* of the response process," for which senior managers took responsibility (8). Instead, planning emerged from this study as a "lagging system" (1), more concerned with the output *from* strategy making than the input *to* it. Gomer found that planners were used to estimate the impact of the crisis on standards of performance, to carry out special studies, to summarize estimates made by various managers, to suggest emerging measures, and to evaluate division budgets. At the division level, plans and budgets served also as models, for example to estimate the impact of price increases on performance.

Thus, while *planners* were of help in dealing with the crisis, *planning*, as conventionally conceived, was not. It "seems to have rather little use as a method for problem solving, being more related to the implementation of measures" (16). In fact, Gomer referred to the "overall contribution" of planning as "relatively insignificant," after noting that "in more than 12 hours of non-directive interviewing with line managers about their organization's response to the crisis, [formal planning system] components or related subjects surfaced less than eight minutes" (16).

Quinn's Findings on Planning Under "Logical Incrementalism"

Sarrazin and Gomer studied planning directly; others who focused more on the strategy formation process also found planning conspicuous by its absence. One of these was James Brian Quinn, whose probes into that process in a number of large firms (mostly American) led to its description in his 1980 book as "logical incrementalism"—a process of the gradual evolution of strategy driven by conscious managerial thought. On planning, Quinn concluded:

> My data suggest that when well-managed major organizations make significant changes in strategy, the approaches they use frequently bear little resemblance to the rational, analytical systems so often described in the planning literature. (1980a:14)

More to the point, "formal planning systems rarely formulated a corporation's central strategy" (38).

Consistent with Gomer, Quinn found that "the annual planning process itself was rarely (if ever in the study) the source of new key issues or radical departures into entirely different product/market realms. These almost always came from precipitating events, special studies, or conceptions implanted" in other ways, "although individual staff planners might identify potential problems and bring them to top management's attention" (40). Indeed, Quinn concluded that "formal planning practices themselves usually institutionalized a form of incrementalism" (40), quite "properly" in his view (41).

Quinn offered two reasons for planning's own inclination to be incremental. First, most planning was carried out bottom-up by managers responding to the narrow needs of their units' products, services, or processes within a long-standing framework of assumptions, etc. And second, plans were "properly designed" by most managements to be flexible, "intended only as frameworks to guide and provide consistency for future decisions made incrementally during shorter term operating cycles" (40–41).

In fact, however, whereas the plans were made by management to be flexible, formal planning itself proved inflexible:

> Horizon scanning frequently became a routine designed primarily to justify ongoing plans, and contingency plans became precap-

suled (and shelved) programs to respond in precise ways to stimuli that never quite occurred as expected. . . . Even R&D plans showed all people committed for a year in advance, thus assuming (often predictably) that nothing new would happen to require a change. (122)

Too often, formal planning resulted "primarily in either formless wordy statements of principle or detailed budgeting plans"; it "mitigate[s] against generating the coordinated cross-divisional thrusts and commitment patterns that are the essence of strategy"; it "overemphasizes financial analysis methodologies that foreclose meaningful strategic options, encourage short-term attitudes and behavior, drive out potential major innovations, misdirect resource allocations, and actively undercut the enterprise's intended strategies"; and, finally, it "converts planning departments into bureaucratized agencies grinding out annual plans rather than catalyst groups intervening properly in the incremental processes that determine strategy" (154). Quite a list of ailments from an author who considers himself sympathetic to the planning process! Nevertheless, Quinn did find a role for planning, one similar to those suggested by Sarrazin and Gomer. It "provided a mechanism through which earlier strategic decisions were confirmed"; in other words, planning helped to codify as well as formalize and calibrate "agreed-upon goals, commitment patterns, and action sequences" (41, 38). In the decision making sphere, it also "provided a systematic means for evaluating and fine-tuning annual budgets," "formed a basis to protect long-term investments and commitments," and "helped to implement strategic changes once decided upon." In the " 'process' realm," it "created a network of information," extended the perspective of operating managers and helped reduce their uncertainty about the future, and "stimulated long-term 'special studies' " (38–39).

The McGill Research on "Tracking Strategies"

Our own studies at McGill University, in which we tracked the strategies of several organizations to find out how these formed and changed, reinforce a number of these conclusions. In general, we found strategy making to be a complex, interactive, and evolutionary process, best described as one of adaptive learning. Strategic change was found to be uneven and unpredictable, with major strategies often remaining relatively stable for long periods of time, sometimes decades, and then suddenly undergoing massive change. The process was often significantly emergent, especially when the organization faced unpredicted shifts in the environment, and all kinds of people could be significantly involved in the creation of new strategies. Indeed, strategies appeared in all kinds of strange ways in the organizations studied. Many of the most important seemed to grow up from the "grass roots" (much as weeds that might appear in a garden are later found to bear useful fruit), rather than all having to be imposed from the top down, in "hothouse" style (Mintzberg and McHugh, 1985).

The apt metaphor for the process, in sharp contrast with the one of architecture in the design school and keeping a ship on course in the planning school, might well be crafting. To quote from a summary article on this research, entitled "Crafting Strategy":

> Imagine someone planning strategy. What likely springs to mind is an image of orderly thinking: a senior manager, or a group of them, sitting in an office formulating courses of action that everyone else will implement on schedule. The keynote is reason—rational control, the systematic analysis of competitors and markets, of company strengths and weaknesses, the combination of these analyses producing clear, explicit, full-blown strategies.
>
> Now imagine someone *crafting* strategy. A wholly different image likely results, as different from planning as craft is from mechanization. Craft evokes traditional skill, dedication, perfection through the mastery of detail. What springs to mind is not so much thinking and reason as involvement, a feeling of intimacy and harmony with the materials at hand, developed through long experience and commitment. Formulation and implementation merge into a fluid process of learning through which creative strategies evolve.
>
> My thesis is simple: the crafting image better captures the process by which effective strategies come to be. The planning image, long popular in the literature, distorts these processes and thereby misguides organizations that embrace it unreservedly. (Mintzberg, 1987:66)

The McGill studies did not research planning processes per se. Indeed, it was our feeling that to find out about the role of planning in strategy making, one should study the strategy making process directly and infer where planning did (and did not) enter the picture (much as in the Gomer study). It appeared in two of our studies in particular, as well as in a third, associated study.

In our study of Steinberg Inc. (Mintzberg and Waters, 1982), a large, entrepreneurial supermarket chain, we found that formal planning was introduced to satisfy an external need of the organization. When the firm wished to go to capital markets for the first time, it simply had to issue plans. Its founder and chief executive could not write in his prospectus, "Look, I'm Sam Steinberg, with this incredible track record. So please give me five million of your dollars." Rather, he had to show plans to the financial markets. But these did not reflect any formal process for arriving at a strategy; the firm already had its strategy, in the vision of its leader (to expand the chain of large supermarkets in Quebec, primarily through the construction of shopping centers). All the plan did was to articulate the strategy—explicate it, justify it, elaborate it (the number of stores to be built, on what particular schedule, etc.). We concluded, therefore, that planning did not create strategy so much as program a strategy that already existed:

> . . . companies plan when they *have* intended strategies, not in order to get them. In other words, one plans not a strategy but the consequences of it. Planning gives order to vision, and puts form on it for the sake of formalized structure and environmental expectation. One can say that planning operationalizes strategy. (498)

But the consequences of this were not incidental: "the inevitable result of programming the entrepreneur's vision is to constrain it":

> The entrepreneur, by keeping his vision personal, is able to adapt it at will to a changing environment. By being forced to articulate and program it, he loses that flexibility. The danger, ultimately, is that . . . procedure tends to replace vision, so that strategy making becomes more extrapolation than invention. . . . In the absence of a vision, planning comes to extrapolate the status quo, leading at best to marginal changes in current practice. (498)

Another of these studies concerned Air Canada (Mintzberg, Brunet, and Waters, 1986), a company that lacked a tradition of entrepreneurship but built up a very strong one of planning, at least in the operating and administrative spheres. This reflected its paramount need for precise coordination (in aircraft operations, among craft, route schedules, flight crews, etc., and in capital expenditures, between the arrival of new equipment and the development of the route structure), as well as its concerns about safety, the high capital costs of new aircraft, and the long lead times in adding new routes. These needs resulted in patterns of action that were remarkably orderly and stable.

Figure 3–1, for example, shows the pattern of aircraft acquisition (and disposal) over time. Note the steady, systematic arrival of new aircraft after the mid-1950s (by which time the detailed planning procedures were firmly established), compared with their stepped arrival in blocks before then. Indeed, a curiosity of the graph is that, as we stacked up the figures for the different aircraft in chronological order, we found that two close parallel lines encompassed almost all the aircraft acquired after 1955, except for the DC8s and 747s, both of which arrived at slower pace, although even more regularly, likely a reflection of the massive capital outlays they involved.

But Air Canada exhibited another interesting characteristic: after planning became prevalent, strategies hardly changed (to the end of our study period in 1976). We concluded that the two factors were related, specifically that formal planning, as well as the forces that encouraged it, not only did not constitute strategy making but in fact positively discouraged it, impeding strategic thinking and strategic change. "The more the organization relied on detailed, systematic, routine specification of its existing procedures, the less its people were encouraged to think beyond those procedures to new orientations . . ." (36). Strategy as perspective, even as position, was assumed within the plan, not thrown into question by it.[9]

---

[9] In a study of another airline, Air France, Hafsi and Thomas drew a conclusion that in one place at least reinforced ours about Air Canada, as well as about planning as programming by the Steinberg supermarket chain: "Planning was, as a matter of course, a highly technical tool and not a strategy-related one. The important thing was to be able to predict traffic, costs, etc. and conduct an orderly business within

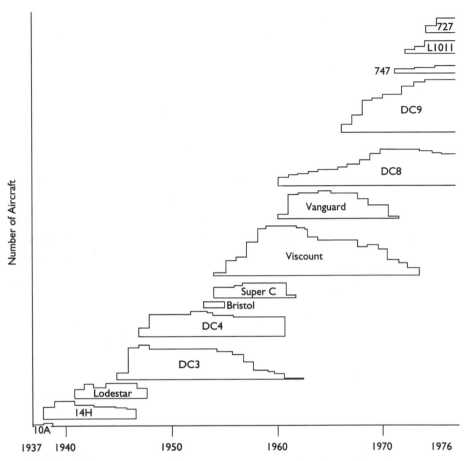

Figure 3–1
The Pattern of Aircraft Acquisition and Disposal at Air Canada, 1937–1976

There was one excellent example of this, concerning the decomposition of the organization into five operating sectors for the purpose of planning. (This began in 1955 and continued at least through 1976.) Referred to as the "five little airlines," these included one labeled southern "thin" routes (from Canadian cities to the Caribbean islands, etc.). Note the effect of the label: the southern routes are thin, implying a stable strategy or at least encour-

the confines of the precise instructions coming from the bureaucracy" (1985:16).
The same impression was given by Guiriec and Thyreau's (1984) description of the
communication role that planning played in Air France.

aging the stabilization of strategy. In effect, planning imposed (or at least used) categories that reified the existing strategy—locked it into place. As we concluded our report:

> Formal planning, and the associated forces that encourage it, may discourage the very mental state required to conceive new strategies—a state of openness and easy flexibility that encourages people to step back from operating reality and question accepted beliefs. In short, formal strategic management may prove incompatible with real strategic thinking. (40)

This did prove to have one unexpected benefit, however. When, as a result of a consulting intervention, the organization underwent a massive disruptive reorganization that paralysed its top management ranks for a substantial period of time, the routine imposed by the planning system maintained its continuity. As one planning executive put it to us: "During the McKinsey crisis, the detailed plans, implemented faithfully by the operations people, saved the day. Management did not know which way to turn for a time but the planes kept on flying" (28).

Related to the McGill research was an MBA thesis written by Claude Dubé on the strategy making behavior of the Canadian armed forces after World War II. His findings were rather intriguing. In brief, the organization either planned or it acted; otherwise the two seemed unrelated. When the military had nothing to do, it planned, almost as an end in itself:

> One of the unique characteristics of this organization is that its major occupation is to get ready for action. But most of the time there is no need to get into action (no war). And so, much activity is devoted to search for an active role during those waiting periods, in fact to search for a "raison d'être" for the time being. One way by which this organization has attempted to solve this problem has been to institutionalize the planning process so that existing plans are constantly revised, new ones introduced, [with] the more sophisticated methods of planning replacing the old ones. All these plans attempt to take into consideration all eventualities. This is a never-ending enterprise as it is impossible to plan for everything ... (1973:71–72)

But when the Canadian military did have something to do (such as fight in Korea), it threw its plans aside and acted. Much as in the Gomer study, the organization did not foresee the contingencies or scenarios that really did arise. As for formal planning, it seems better suited to the tranquilities of peacetime than the disruptiveness of war, especially unforeseen war. To quote one military writer, "where 'preparation for war' deals in fixed values, physical quantities and unilateral action, 'war proper' is concerned with variable quantities, intangible forces and effects, and a continual interaction of opposites" (Summers, 1981:114), hardly the most favorable conditions for planning. One implication of Dubé's study is that organizations plan formally to have something to do when they otherwise lack a raison d'être!

Koch's Study of the "Façade" of French Government Planning

The military is, of course, one arm of government. And while big business has hardly been indifferent to planning, big government has been especially interested in it. This may have been especially so in Communist Eastern Europe, but the same inclinations have hardly been absent in the West. Like the Steinberg supermarket chain when it went public, but far more so, big government must be publicly accountable for its actions; like Air Canada, it must coordinate the allocation of huge quantities of resources and be especially sensitive to losses (money, if not lives); like the managers of General Electric, its leaders must try to come to grips with things they know little about. Formal planning seems to provide that accountability, to effect that coordination, to avoid that loss, to supply that knowledge. The important question, of course, is whether it improves the quality of public policy making.

Unfortunately, with the goals of government so vague, the measures of performance so poor, and the recipients of policies so dispersed, the question is virtually unanswerable in any systematic way. And so governments have persisted in trying to plan formally despite the steady evidence attesting to planning's failures.

Probably no government that we in the West would call democratic has been more obsessed with planning than that of France, at least until several years ago. Koch documented France's highly publicized efforts at comprehensive national planning, which he referred to as a democratic "façade": "Contrary to the image propagated by the executive, the French plan fits a model of nondemocratic nonplanning" (1976:374).

In Koch's view, it was simply impossible to succeed in the effort, because of the nonviability of the assumption that all the relevant information could be brought to one place and integrated into a single framework. There was simply no way to assemble the requisite expertise and give it sufficient time to produce usable results, no matter how much was invested in the effort. The result "was a political hodgepodge of soundly-based elitist aims, inadequately-based general aims, sincere commitments and empty promises ... certainly not a 'plan' but neither was it widely acceptable"; "it simply could not predict the economic and social future with any accuracy" (thus "planners could only sit hopelessly by while phenomena such as the energy crisis wreaked havoc with their predictions"); "it could not control the actions of the multiple international and private national actors who affected its execution"; and, overall, "the Plan was never executed accordingly to Plan" (381, 382). Thus Leon Trotsky, who experienced national economic planning in a society dependent on its success, once commented:

> If there existed the universal mind that projected itself into the scientific fancy of Laplace; a mind that would register simultaneously all the processes of nature and society, that could measure the dynamics of their motion, that could forecast the results of their inter-reactions, such a mind, of course, could *a priori* draw up a faultless and exhaustive economic plan, beginning with the number of hectares of wheat and down to the last button for a vest. In truth, the bureaucracy often conceives that just such a mind is at its disposal; that is why it so easily frees itself from the control of the market and of Soviet democracy. (in Lewis, 1969:19)

Some Evidence on the PPBS Experience

Governments in the Anglo-Saxon tradition may have been less inclined to engage in national economic planning. But they have been hardly less interested in other forms of planning. The U.S. government in the heady days of President Kennedy's 1960s must rank next to the French experience for intensity of effort as well as sheer failure. This was the time when Robert McNamara brought PPBS along with his whiz kids (whom Halberstam [1972] dubbed "the best and the brightest") to Washington from the halls of Harvard University and the Rand Corporation. Because the experience was so widely publicized, it has also been widely assessed and criticized; hence, here we review not a single study but the broader evidence of several.

As Kennedy's Secretary of Defense, McNamara imposed PPBS on the military establishment; later President Johnson decreed its use throughout the government and from there it went to the state governments and imitators in other countries. In his acclaimed book, *The Politics of the Budgetary Process,* Aaron Wildavsky summarized the experience succinctly: "PPBS has failed everywhere and at all times" (1974:205).

PPBS represented a formal attempt to couple strategic planning with programming and budgeting in a single system. According to Alain Enthoven (1969a: 273), McNamara's chief analyst, this was to be done on the basis of "outputs" rather than "inputs"—"mission-oriented building blocks" such as Strategic Retaliatory Forces or Civil Defense instead of internal structural divisions such as the Army, Navy, or Air Force. Thus, planning was not to be conducted around existing departments but around strategic thrusts (governmental SBUs, if you like, or "market missions," as Smalter and Ruggles referred to them in a *Harvard Business Review* article intended to bring the "lessons from the Pentagon" to business [1966:65]). These, of course, came to take on a life of their own too, much as did Air Canada's five little airlines. To quote Enthoven, "PPBS enables the Secretary of Defense, the President, and the Congress to focus their attention on the major missions of the Department of Defense, rather than on lists of unrelated items of expenditure" (1969a:274).

All of this was supposed to generate strategic thinking as well as enable strategic planning to be tied to capital and operational budgeting. But, of course, in government no overall measure is available that relates costs directly to benefits to allow a numerical comparison of different projects (which the return on investment measure does in the capital budgeting process of business). So to get as close as possible to this, government planners placed heavy emphasis on the quantification of costs and benefits, each in their own terms, so that at least alternatives could be compared within missions (e.g., missiles versus bombers in terms of the "greatest bang for the buck" within the strategic retaliatory forces mission).

Van Gunsteren has described the "core idea" of PPBS as "to tie analysis, planning, strategic decision-making and day-to-day budgetary decision-making together into a unified structure of information and power in order to make planning and analysis more relevant and effective, and budgeting more rational and informed" (1976:54). He went on to delineate the steps in PPBS as follows:

> Formulate the ultimate objectives of government activities or of segments of government activity. Relate program outputs (favorable impacts of program) to these objectives. Relate outputs to program inputs (unfavorable impacts). Put values, preferably money, on outputs and inputs. Aggregate the outputs of a program and call them total benefits. Aggregate the inputs of the same program and call them costs. Do this for the total expected lifetime of the program. Establish the benefit-cost ratio of the program and the net difference between benefits and costs. Consider existing programs, and invent and design new alternative programs. Go through the same sequence with the alternative programs, beginning with the relating of outputs to objectives. Choose between alternative programs. Establish this whole sequence as part of the regular budget review procedure. (54)

Much of the responsibility for the implementation of PPBS in McNamara's defense establishment fell on Enthoven's shoulders; he expressed his faith in it in his article as follows:

> ... decision making on strategy, forces, programs, and budgets is now unified. . . . The *machinery* by which this is done is the Planning-Programming-Budgeting System. . . . The Secretary of Defense reviews the data on [mission plans] with the Joint Chiefs of Staff and the Services; obtains their advice, and makes decisions on the forces. From there on, the breakdown of the budget by Service and appropriation title is largely derivative, a process left mostly to the staff. (1969a:273–274, italics added)

There are a number of interesting things about these comments: the assumption that the System—the "machinery"—did the job, the belief that budgeting somehow got done in linkage with strategy, the implied separation between formulation and implementation. Indeed, the latter distinction stood at the heart of PPBS, as it does in the design school model. McNamara was depicted as sitting back in his office and making these complex decisions after being briefed, much as he did years earlier as a student in the case study classes of the Harvard Business School. Enthoven pointed out that, "of course, the approach makes great demands on the Secretary of Defense." But so too, of course, did the MBA program at Harvard, in much the same way: he was forced "to become acquainted in detail with the merits of many proposals," and he "must have a systematic flow of information on the needs, effectiveness, and cost of alternative programs." But fear not, Enthoven hastened to add, "we are organized to provide this information" (273). It all came neatly packaged in "Draft Presidential Memorandums," which "summarize the relevant information on the threat, our objectives, the effectiveness, and cost of the alternatives he has considered and his tentative conclusions" (274). To protect the "free world," they were writing case studies for McNamara in the Pentagon! Also what Harvard people call WACs (written analysis of cases). After all, they had the "machinery."

Enthoven's article was published in 1969, another prophetic date since that was exactly when the whole effort was coming apart in the rice paddies of Vietnam. The System, the machinery, McNamara and his whiz kids, were leading America to its most humiliating military debacle ever.

Colonel Harry Summers Jr. of the U.S. Army later considered this experience from the perspective of the line officers, in a book entitled *On Strategy: The Vietnam War in Context*. Like Dubé, he distinguished between "merely preparation for war" and "war proper" (1981:28, quoting Clausewitz, 1966). PPBS, in his opinion, covered "only half the equation," the former (28), while for the latter, it reflected "an educated incapacity to see war in its true light" (29). Yet McNamara's planners captured control of the preparation for the war as well as the war proper, for example, by blocking the access of senior military officers to the President (31).

Summers's argument, built on themes we have discussed earlier, is that planning proved inflexible as well as incremental, not suited to "an animate object that *reacts*" (to quote Clausewitz again, 29), better known as an enemy, with a will of its own:

> The rationalistic approach is . . . characterized by the pretention to universality of its solutions, its intolerance of tradition and authority, quantification, simplification, and lack of flexibility. Its very efficiency prevents flexibility by eliminating what does not contribute to achieving the current objective so that alternative means are not available if the objective is changed. (29, quoting British defense analyst Gregory Palmer)

In Summers's view, "the fatal flaw was that *consistency* was a premise of rationalist policy, and the one thing that war is not is consistent." Or in the more colorful words of a U.S. Army Officer: "Any damn fool can write a plan. It's the execution that gets you all screwed up" (29). Thus, "the military found themselves designing weapons on the basis of abstract criteria, carrying out strategies in which they did not really believe, and ultimately conducting a war that they did not understand" (Henry Kissinger, quoted on 30). Moreover, the policy procedures, being essentially economic in nature, "direct the inquiry exclusively toward physical quantities, whereas all military action is intertwined with psychological forces and effects," notably will and commitment (quoting Clausewitz [32], whose "words could have been written about the PPBS approach to the Vietnam War").

It is interesting that Halberstam (1972) used many of the same arguments about PPBS to make the case *against* the war effort (for example, that military and intelligence people in the field realized the futility of the war long before the detached planners in Washington did). In other words, planning proved to be an impediment to effective strategic thinking and action, whether one favored hawkish military strategies or dovish political ones. Summers quoted Smith and Enthoven on their "disingenuous" comment that:

> PPBS was not involved in the really crucial issues of the Vietnam war. Should the United States have gone into Vietnam in the first place? Did we go in at the right time, in the right way, and on the right scale? What force level should we have had, and how should

these troops have been used? What timetable should we have set up for withdrawals? How can we best achieve a speedy and just settlement? (1981:32).

Like all conventional staff planners, they were trying to distance their procedures from the political choices that had to be made by line managers. But again, like all such planners, they were deluding themselves: the problem was not that PPBS tried to dictate these choices directly so much as that, by virtue of how it necessarily worked—what planning excluded as well as included—it influenced strongly how others made those choices.

Thus, after all the dust settled—and a great deal of it was scattered in the 1960s—for all the hoopla about PPBS, it proved no more adept at realizing its intentions than did any other planning model. Stating an intention to plan strategically and to couple this with programming and budgeting did not achieve anything; indeed, because it was such an ambitious effort applied so massively, PPBS simply fell all that much harder.

By 1974, Wildavsky—America's leading student of public-sector budgeting—could write, following his "PPBS has failed everywhere and at all times" comment, that:

Nowhere has PPBS (1) been established and (2) influenced governmental decisions (3) according to its own principles. The program structures do not make sense to anyone. They are not, in fact, used to make decisions of any importance. (1974:205)[10]

Later he would write that "the wholesale introduction of PPBS presented insuperable difficulties of calculation"; in essence, "no-one knows how to do" it; there is not even any "agreement on what the words mean" (1979:201). Similarly, in summing up the Canadian experience, French referred to PPBS as a "sterile attempt to frame the current and future actions of government" that was "completely unable to come to grips with the realities of governing at the national level" (1980:18, 27).

The simple fact is that they never did put P and PB together into

---

[10] Perhaps Wildavsky should have added the adjective "successful" before "decisions," with reference to the Vietnam experience.

an S that worked. Thus, Wildavsky called for an annulment of the "shotgun marriage between policy analysis and budgeting" [1974:205].) Nor did they ever get that first P straight. Planning—the creation of strategy—remained an article of faith, or as in the Sarrazin study, a front for political control. Exercise that control Secretary McNamara certainly did, but in a fashion that proved—in its biggest test of all—arbitrary and ineffective, not "rational" even in his own terms. (Halberstam pointed out that McNamara himself distorted reports to Congress on the costs of the war during the period 1965–1967, with the excuse: "Do you really think that if I had estimated the cost of the war correctly, Congress would have given any more for schools and housing?" [1972:610].) "The plans," as Charles Lindblom noted later, were "for the most part no more than proposals for capital investments" (1977:317). In other words, the system really reduced to capital budgeting—or perhaps we should say, never rose above it. PPBS was really pPBS, or perhaps more to the point, ppBS.

Some Evidence on Capital Budgeting

If PPBS—as well as some practices in business referred to as strategic planning—never amounted to much more than capital budgeting, the next obvious question is whether capital budgeting itself constitutes a form of strategy making. Let us consider some evidence on it.

Capital budgeting, as already noted, is a procedure by which unit managers (division heads, functional managers, etc.) propose individual projects up the hierarchy for approval. These are supposed to be assessed in terms of their costs and benefits (combined in business to indicate return on investment) so that the general managers can assess each, compare and rank them, and accept only as many as the capital funding available for a given period will allow.[11] Because of the impetus of the flow from unit manag-

---

[11] It might be noted in passing that while this kind of control on the front end—in approving the project—receives considerable attention, control on the back end—whether the finished project ever actually achieved its stated objectives—remains almost completely ignored.

ers to general managers, capital budgeting is sometimes referred to as bottom-up strategic planning.

Evidence on the actual practice of capital budgeting tells a very different story, and calls into question its relationship to strategy formation. In one of the best-known studies, an intensive probe into the process in one large divisionalized firm, Bower found that the general management had a propensity to approve all the projects that reached its level.

> Projects that have the approval of a division general manager are seldom turned down by his group—although minor modifications are frequently requested—and projects reaching the executive committee are almost never rejected. (1970a:57)

"The important question," wrote Bower, "was whether that group of officers which possessed the power to move proposals through the funding process chose to identify a particular proposal for sponsorship" (322)—because once that happened, proposals had more or less free passage.

In a later study, Marsh et al. looked carefully at three firms that used the capital budgeting procedure. (They noted in reviewing the literature that in one "respected" finance textbook, only two of one thousand empirical studies cited "related to real investment decisions" [1988:3]). Although, as we noted earlier, "all three firms would have [shown up on survey research as having] been at the most sophisticated end of the spectrum" of use of this technique (27), the researchers found all kinds of problems. For one thing, their procedure manuals on the process "proved quite hard to locate!" (22); for another, the presentation to the divisional board in one firm "was described as 'a con job'," in another, "group approval as 'rubber stamping' " (23). Errors in the application of the technique (23), and "hard-to-qualify costs and benefits were excluded from the financial analysis." As for the quantitative data, there were references to "chang[ing] the financial model to give you the answers you want"—after all, "project proposers . . . knew it would be hard for those above them to check out the detailed forecasts" (28).

A particularly strong critique of capital budgeting was contained in the popular textbook, *Dynamic Manufacturing*, by Hayes, Wheelwright, and Clark, who bristled at the negative effects the process has had on the competitiveness of American manufacturing firms. They, too, discussed the problems of excluding soft data that "might trigger suspicion" among the "skeptic[al]" corporate staff (1988:69).

> To leave [soft considerations] out of the analysis simply because they are not readily quantifiable or to avoid introducing "personal judgements," clearly biases decisions against investments that are likely to have a significant impact on such important considerations as the quality of one's product, delivery speed and reliability, and the rapidity with which new products can be introduced. (77)

But the most severe criticism of these observers concerned the artificiality of the decomposition forced on the organization by capital budgets. "By focusing on the various expansion proposals one by one, and evaluating each over a short time period, the analysis ignored a number of the strategic aspects of the situation" (72). "Companies," they noted, "are not simply collections of tangible assets; they are also collections of people, interlinked by complex bonds and loyalties that reflect understandings and commitments developed over a long period of time" (78). Of course, "several projects [could] be treated as one big project and evaluated together." But "as the interdependencies between projects get more numerous and complicated, it is difficult to see where to stop. Taken to its logical extreme, one should combine each new project with all previous and future projects" (81).

Hayes et al. also noted "a bias toward big projects," even given the requirement of preparing the analysis (87). And that also encouraged staff domination of decision making about investment: thus "divisions develop their own staffs (proposal advocates) to deal with the corporate staff (protectors of the purse)," the two of which "often engage in an almost ritualistic mating dance" (86). Meanwhile, necessarily incremental investments that "tend to bubble up, in an entrepreneurial fashion" (87) get slighted, and this "tends to insulate lower levels of the organizations from strategic issues" (78).

These problems seemed to be built right into the technique of capital budgeting itself, and, in fact, revealed some important weaknesses of planning in general. In capital budgeting, the information about the projects rests with the sponsors below, not the reviewers above. The former conceive the projects, carry out the cost-benefit analyses, and commit themselves to managing the approved projects on an intensive basis, usually for years. They truly are "champions." The reviewers have neither much time nor much commitment to give to any single project; they must review many. So they remain essentially uninformed, or at least have only superficial knowledge of any project. In discussing this as "the span of knowledge" required to review projects (1988:29), Marsh et al. referred to a group deputy chairman who claimed to have spent "at least a whole day" on a major project. Imagine that! (The division manager in charge of the project "estimated that he spent eight months [full-time equivalent]" on it prior to approval, and "his team members spent a further two man-years"!) In another case, the researchers themselves accumulated over 2,000 pages of documents on a project that ended up as "a two-page summary for the Group Board"! (30)

Of course, the very assumption underlying capital budgeting is that a few figures reinforced by such a brief summary can give senior management the information it needs to review the project. (That was clear in Enthoven's comments that "we are organized to do it," "we" meaning the small office of the Secretary of Defense, "it" meaning the review of all the many PPBS programs of the U.S. military.) The concurrent assumption is that the analysis is objective, the numbers are accurate. In fact, as we have seen, neither is assured.

A great deal of subjective judgment must go into the projections of costs and benefits: these are forecasts, and as Spyros Makridakis, a leading authority on forecasting, has pointed out in this context, the "forecasting and planning considerations" of many capital investments "usually defy analytical treatment" (1990:132). The longer the projection, of course, the greater the subjectivity, especially, as Bower argued (1970a:20), of the estimates of sales volumes and prices.

> While everyone realizes that long-run return is the object, the only credible quantitative data is short run, so that observed behavior usually consists of various sorts of short-term suboptimizations and/or a limited number of major moves justified by judgments of long-run strategic consequences. (1970b:6)

Add to this the fact that those responsible for the analyses are the sponsors themselves—hardly unbiased (let us say enthusiastic, when not outright manipulative)—and you can easily get unreliable estimates. Almost any plausible project can be made to look good. And looking good can mean more than just ensuring that the numbers are right. "In one incident, that still rankles" Jack Welch, CEO of General Electric, "managers in the light bulb business spent $30,000 putting together a slick film to demonstrate some production equipment they wanted" (Allaire and Firsirotu [1990:112], quoting *Business Week*). Indeed, Broms and Gahmberg who cited evidence of capital projects in some Finnish and Swedish firms "regularly miss[ing] the mark" (e.g., requiring 25 percent return on investment while consistently getting about 7 percent), went so far as to describe these plans as "mantras," which "organizations read to themselves, saying time and time again: 'This is what we should look like!' " He referred to "this self-deception" as "socially accepted fact" (1987:121).

Now, senior mangers are not stupid—they were once champions of projects themselves. They know the game, and realize they cannot win—at least not as specified in the formal procedures. They do, however, have one way to make these tricky choices. They can choose the champions, if not the projects. In other words, while they may not be able to get to know and judge the projects, they are paid to get to know and judge the people. Their job thus becomes to ensure that they have trustworthy people proposing projects; then they can rubber-stamp their proposals. Rejection of a proposal thus becomes tantamount to rejection of the sponsor. As Bower noted when considering an intermediate level in the review process:

> Once a project is sponsored, it is almost always approved by top management. They are loathe to second guess the judgments of the men selected for intermediate-level management precisely on the basis of their ability to evaluate the technical-economic content of product-market subunit plans and projects. That is why batting average is so important. It reflects the ability of middle-level managers to judge lower-level generalists. (1970b:6)

The Links Between Capital Budgeting and Strategy Formation. In our diagram of four hierarchies (Figure 2–10), we show capital budgeting—in theory—as bottom-up planning. We must clarify that here. For one thing, the crossover from programs at one level to budgets at the next is tenuous at best and really should be dotted. For another, a dotted line should be added from objectives to programs to suggest that how sponsors take objectives into account may be implicit at best.

But what about the link from programs to the strategy hierarchy? In other words, what is the relationship between strategy formation and capital budgeting? Nothing we have seen so far gives any indication that capital budgeting represents a process to plan strategy. Rather, it appears to be a formal means to structure the consideration of projects and to inform senior management about upcoming projects and their costs, also perhaps an informal means to control spending by virtue of the projects that reluctant sponsors never propose in the first place.

In fact, three possibilities present themselves in the relationship between capital budgeting and strategic planning: that new or existing strategies influence the capital projects proposed, that the proposed projects influence the strategies pursued, or that the two exist quite independently of each other. Since the third possibility depends on the absence of the other two, let us consider these.

Planning theorists who do not claim that capital budgeting is a process for formulating strategy presumably still believe that it should take its cue from intended strategies, however they are formulated. To quote Marsh et al., in most of the work on capital budgeting there "is an assumption that investment projects can somehow be subordinated to prior definitions of strategy, and that this is primarily the domain of top management" (1988:4). In other words, programs are supposed to be proposed in the light of the strategies explicitly formulated by the senior management. Much as the sponsors are supposed to be influenced by the objectives of the organization, so too is their behavior supposed to be driven by its existing strategies. It makes little sense, for example, to propose the building of a new laboratory to do basic product research when the senior management has just decided to pursue a cost leadership strategy predicated on undifferentiated products.

But *how* this link is established is another question. That it might work *informally*—as sponsors try to take the senior management's intentions implicitly into account in the projects they propose (implying a dotted line from strategy to programs)—is easy to imagine, so long as those intentions are somehow conveyed to the sponsors down the line. But that it works *formally*—that the projects proposed are somehow determined by the strategies intended (suggesting a solid line in Figure 2–15)—is not the same thing. Of course, in conveying their intended strategies to subordinate managers, senior managers may call for projects in response, even outline (in the spirit of what we referred to earlier as umbrella strategy) the broad areas in which they hope to see such projects forthcoming.

Our own suspicion, however, is that the links are typically informal at best, that, in fact, most capital budgeting takes place in the context of existing strategies that are implied rather than new ones that are explicated. What this means is that most capital budgeting probably takes place in the absence of any fresh strategy formulation activity at all, perhaps even any discussion of strategy per se. Strategy is implicitly assumed to be a given. If the demand for widgets increases, a plant expansion is proposed: everyone knows the company is in the widget business to stay. (In effect, strategy as position gets reified as perspective.) As Yavitz and Newman noted:

> Triggered by a need related to existing activities, few [capital expenditure proposals] deviate very much from the status quo. Some of these bottom-up proposals are for necessary projects—replacement of a faltering elevator, for instance. Others propose better ways to perform present activities, such as computer control of accounts receivable. Still others may deal with natural expansion— say, a West Coast sales branch or acquisition of an additional coal mine by a utility company. If the business-unit wishes to pursue its existing strategy, such proposals are quite appropriate. (1982:189)

Strategy may influence capital budgeting in these ways, but the capital projects proposed can also influence the strategy pursued. We see this happening in two ways. First, as suggested earlier, by functioning within a given strategic context, capital budgeting can reinforce the actual (i.e., realized) strategy already being pursued—in other words, the proposed projects extrapolate the patterns already formed. But a second way may be more important. A capital project may break an established pattern and thereby create a precedent that changes strategy. When the vice-president of R&D proposes and gets his new basic research laboratory in spite of an established strategy of cost leadership, he may be driving in the wedge for an upcoming strategy of product differentiation. If senior management does not realize what is happening—perhaps it approves the project merely to keep its R&D vice-president happy—then the strategic change has to be considered emergent.

What this means is that the capital budgeting process can drive the strategy formation process inadvertently, through the emergence of strategy. The organization, in other words, simply makes its decisions on an ad hoc basis, project by project; during this process, patterns form to become strategies. New projects not quite consistent with existing strategies may create precedents that lead to new patterns. Put another way, a small opening through capital budgeting can stimulate a large, if unexpected, change in strategy. Thus can capital budgeting become a factor in the processes by which strategies form but are not formulated.

Of course, sponsors don't have to read this to know that. Those intent on changing a strategy in the face of top management resistance have long used capital budgeting in this way—we can call it political—so much so that it even has a label in the budgeting literature: the "foot-in-the-door" technique. Create a small opening through an initial capital investment and then keep pushing incrementally until the door is wide open—until the pattern is firmly established. In effect, in proposing the project, the sponsor is really championing a strategy, but in a clandestine manner. It is deliberate for him or her but not (yet) for the organization at large.[12]

Perhaps then, a key, if implicit, role of capital budgeting—given that it is not particularly effective at its assigned role—can be to offer senior managers the possibility of screening proposals for these effects, so as to catch those that may cause *strategic deviations* (if we may be permitted to coin that term). Of course, once found, such proposals need not be stopped; senior management can play the game too, leaving the door open just enough to test the initiative, while being prepared to shut it tight later if necessary.

Thus we can conclude that when strategies change deliberately, some proposed programs are likely to follow these changes,

---

[12] For a discussion of this type of behavior in the context of "internal corporate venturing" in diversified corporations, see Burgelman (1983a:232, 237–238).

though the connection is informal and poorly understood. But when programs are proposed in isolation, independent of strategy formation activity or in the absence of it, then strategies may be reinforced or changed as a consequence. The ironic conclusion is that, in the first situation, where capital budgeting works more or less as specified in the formal model, it falls outside the process of strategy formation, while in the second, where it works outside the formal model, it can enter into that process but contribute to the formation of emergent rather than deliberate strategies.

There remains one last point: the effect of the technique itself on the propensity of organizations to undertake strategic change. Here we wish to argue and present evidence that, both at the sponsor and reviewer level, capital budgeting normally acts to impede such change and to discourage strategic thinking.

Our argument is rooted in the essential characteristic of all planning systems—formalization through decomposition. To formalize requires analysis, specifically the reduction of a process to a procedure, a series of steps, each concerning a well-defined category. Moreover, the result of the process must itself be decomposed in the form of plans. In capital budgeting, this manifests itself in the separation of projects from each other. In other words, capital budgeting is a disjointed process, or, more to the point, a *disjointing* one. Programs are expected to be proposed along departmental or divisional lines. (Indeed, if Yavitz and Newman were right that "by far the largest number of capital expenditure proposals originate in the functional departments of a business-unit..." [1982:189], where concerns are especially parochial, then the problem becomes that much more serious.[13]) Any joint effects that different proposals may have—any synergies that may naturally exist or might be encouraged among them—have to be ignored for the convenience of formal analysis (unless, as noted by Hayes et al. earlier, all proposals are to be combined into one large one). But since synergy is the very essence of creative strategy—the realiza-

---

[13] PPBS was, of course, an effort to move from functional concerns to mission concerns (as was the concept of the SBU), but it suffered from the same problem of decomposition, as we saw. So did a series of later techniques known as "portfolio planning," which tried to categorize whole businesses according to their performance potential and thereby to provide senior managers with another yardstick for assessment.

tion of new, advantageous combinations—then capital budgeting has to discourage creative strategic thinking. As Bower noted in his study of the process:

> Water will flow and combine as pictured [in the mechanical concept of capital budgeting], but ideas will not. Unless higher-level management intervenes, the sum of initiating-level plans is more likely to be a meaningless catalog than anything else. (1970a:336)

As discussed earlier, capital budgeting is essentially a decision making process: it focuses on particular resource allocation choices. And decision making is not strategy making. One deals with single commitments to action, the other with the connection of different commitments over time. Thus capital budgeting violates strategy making, by separating the very things that have to be connected. It reduces to a portfolio technique, in other words a means to review independent projects.[14]

In his critique of formal planning, Quinn argued that "certain analytical procedures undermine the very strategies they are supposed to create" (1980a:169). Here he had capital budgeting in mind as a prime culprit. Among his reasons were what he found to be the dysfunctional effects of relying on quantitative measures, which eliminate from consideration whole classes of potentially beneficial options (such as reforestation or basic research). "If followed rigorously, [the practice of capital budgeting] quickly drives out of consideration most options with payoffs or costs that: (1) are beyond a time horizon of four to five years or (2) defy reasonable quantification in financial terms" (171). Quinn also noted that capital budgeting "essentially foreclose[s] radical internal innovation" (171). Given a typical lead time of "7 to 13 years from first discovery to profitability," and "given the cost of capital and probability assessments usually imposed by large enterprises, few radical innovations could survive formal screening practices" (173–174).

---

[14] In a critique of capital budgeting, in the context of "capacity expansions" as decisions, Porter argued that its "essence" is "not financial analysis," "not the discounted cash flow calculation," but the "numbers that go into it," which must encompass industry and competitor analysis and take account of uncertainty (1980:325). But this addresses neither the need to integrate this decision with others and connect them to strategy formation, nor the need to encompass factors that are not quantifiable.

If the key players had acted on the rational financial information available at the time, there would have been no xerography, no metal skis, no aircraft, no jet engines, no television, no computers, no wireless communications, no float glass, and so on ad infinitum. In each case, standard financial calculations (including estimated markets, probabilities of technical success, lead times, and investment returns) would have directed funds toward less risky or more profitable options. (174)

Picture yourself as a senior manager reviewing capital proposals on the basis of financial performance projections. How are you to think strategically when everything comes to you split into bits and pieces, in concise, numerical, and essentially detached terms? It is all so neatly packaged; all you need do is sit back passively and render judgment, on schedule. What incentive do you have to get involved, to stimulate the creative centers of your brain? Even if you wish to, how can you ferret out the richness of the idea from the poverty of its presentation? As Quinn noted, the techniques "interdict the balancing of operating units' commitments into a cohesive pattern across all divisions" (171). Moreover, the practice of using "capital cutoff points" or "hurdle rates" will "usually destroy any strategic patterns top management may have selected earlier" (172).

Now picture yourself as the project sponsor, sitting behind your calculator. You are not being asked to conceive strategies, not even to think about the future of your organization. No, all they want from you is quantitative justification for the moves you wish to make, each one separated into a nice neat package for the convenient comprehension of your superiors. And these packages had better come on schedule. The plant may have just burned down, but (in theory at least) they are not considering proposals for another eight months. Everything must be held up for that "grand ranking," as Yavitz and Newman put it (1982:189). Ironically, however, the pressures on you are to produce sooner, not later. "The world of operating managers and design engineers is filled with current, local problems, and rewards typically are tied to short-run solutions of these problems. Thus proposals from the bottom naturally have a short-run bent" (Yavitz and Newman, 1982:190). So you revert to your bureaucratic box and play their game, with the machinery in place. If you do happen to be a strategic thinker, you had better not let anyone know. Instead you propose isolated projects that serve your own unit, even if they undercut the one next door. Who will even know, given that the technique is expressly designed to preclude synergy. The whole exercise takes on what Quinn calls an "operational-extrapolative" mode (1980a:174).

To conclude our discussion of capital budgeting, taken seriously, at its own word, we find that not only is it not strategy formation, it decidedly impedes strategy formation. But taken by its effects, it can sometimes have an inadvertent influence on the strategies that organizations do pursue, in contradiction to the dictates of its own model. Managers who are stuck with it had better take it seriously, at least to mitigate its negative consequences.

Concluding the Deeper Evidence

What then do we conclude from this whole review of the more serious evidence about the performance of planning itself? In the widely publicized Bellagio Declaration on Planning (Jantsch, 1969), the participants in this "OECD Working Symposium on Long-Range Forecasting and Planning" made a variety of ambitious pronouncements, including the following:

- Planning must be concerned with the structural design of the system itself and involved in the formation of policy. Mere modification of policies already proved to be inadequate will not result in what is right. . . .
- The scope of planning must be expanded to encompass the formulation of alternative policies and the examination, analysis and explicit stipulation of the underlying values and norms.
- Planning must cope with new situations and devise new institutions. . . . (8)

In contrast with these views of what planning *must* do—its own such list—is Wildavsky's assessment of what planning *has* done:

From old American cities to British new towns, from the richest countries to the poorest, planners have difficulty in explaining who

they are and what they should be expected to do. If they are supposed to doctor sick societies, the patient never seems to get well.
Why can't the planners ever seem to do the right thing? (1973:127)

"So far, so bad," concluded Wildavsky (128).

The evidence we have cited in this chapter would hardly encourage anyone to challenge Wildavsky. A number of biased researchers set out to prove that planning paid, and collectively they
proved no such thing. All kinds of anecdotes have highlighted a
litany of problems with planning, and the facts about leading-edge
efforts to apply planning, whether "strategic planning" at General
Electric or PPBS in the U.S. government, proved even more discouraging. Deeper probes into the process, including a reasonable
amount of evidence about capital budgeting, widened the gap and
compounded the relations between planning and strategy formation.

But we need not to be quite so pessimistic. Our review has also
suggested that planning does have a number of viable roles to play
in organizations, even if these differ from the stated intentions of
its proponents and, in fact, seem to exist outside the strategy making process. Likewise, planners may have roles to play close to that
process even if these do not constitute planning per se. Indeed,
there has emerged recently a small literature that makes a good
case for both of these possibilities—that other, useful things are
going on in the world of analysis, outside of formalized strategic
planning.

In a sophisticated study of the role of formal analysis in organizations, Langley (1986; see also 1988, 1989) found important roles
quite different from those usually claimed in the planning literature—"roles peripheral to the strategy development and implementation process"—which she labeled "public relations,
information, group therapy, and direction and control" (1988:40).
Similarly, in a series of papers, Simons (1987, 1988, 1990, 1991) has
argued that senior managers tend to make one type of analytical
control system "interactive" to guide the emergence of new strategies, for example, as an "attention focusing" mechanism to force
analysis, and focus debate. In their 1988 monograph, Marsh et al.
found similar purposes for capital budgeting. And finally, even
Jelinek, in her later work with Schoonhoven, described the interaction of formal processes with informal ones "that work on ideas
'in the air' " (1990:194).

We shall return to the conclusions of these studies in Chapter 6. But to understand what might be right about these different approaches, we must first understand what has gone wrong with the conventional ones. In the present chapter we have tried to indicate that something has indeed gone wrong. Chapters 4 and 5 seek to explain what has gone wrong. But first we should consider how planners themselves have responded to the types of evidence presented here. Their responses—one in particular—will lead us into the Chapter 4 discussion of some important characteristics of the planning process. And that will prepare us to consider in Chapter 5 what may be fundamentally wrong with the concept of strategic planning.

Planners' Responses to the Evidence

How did planners respond to this evidence, the failure to prove that planning paid amidst the many stories in the popular press as well as the occasional deeper research study that strategic planning was not working as prescribed? Given this litany of difficulties, one might have expected them to rush out and seek the roots of the problem. But that never happened—the planners never studied planning. A useful bit of advice from Anthony in one of the first books on planning was never heeded: "No matter how many theorists have advocated a procedure, if the procedure has been given a thorough trial and then abandoned, there is a strong presumption that it is unsound" (1965:166).

Instead of questioning planning, conventional planners retreated into a set of behaviors that psychologists might label various forms of "flight"—withdrawal, fantasy, projection. They denied the problem, falling back on faith; they acknowledged some superficial difficulties, but promoted the process anyway; they accepted the failures to date, but insisted that more planning would resolve them; and finally they projected the difficulties onto others, notably "unsupportive" managers and "uncongenial" climates, under the label of the "pitfalls" of planning. Let us consider these responses briefly before probing the last of them for what the so-called pitfalls reveal about the basic characteristics of planning itself. Then we shall be prepared to discuss some more fundamental "fallacies" of planning. We ask the reader to forgive us the negative tone of what follows: we believe it is justified by the behaviors in question.

Faith: "There is no problem"

Some advocates of planning simply closed their eyes, denying any evidence unfavorable to planning. For example, some reviewers of the "Does planning pay?" research cited only the favorable studies. Bresser and Bishop (1983:588) named Donnelly et al. (1981) and Thompson and Strickland (1980) as "authors [that] cite evidence supporting formal planning as a cause of success while disregarding non-supporting results." To these must be added Steiner, who acknowledged only one of the studies that had mixed results in his book of 1979 (see 1979:43 and 350), and Ansoff, who referenced only one study, his own, to support his claim in 1988 of "put[ting[. . . to rest" the argument that strategy formulation must be an informal process, commenting that "a number of subsequent research studies confirmed our findings, namely that explicit strategy formulation can improve performance" (80, 81).[15]

Then there are those who read the evidence and dismissed it in one way or another. Lorange, who did review the range of "Does planning pay?" studies, nevertheless managed to conclude that strategic planning "seems to pay off for the corporations that use it and is therefore a useful management tool" (1979:238). Or in the bolder words of an Arthur D. Little consultant:

> Evidence like this does not say that planning has failed. Let's say that it just has not succeeded in ways that can be directly measured and credited to planning in the multi-variate corporate system. (Wright, 1973:615–616)

---

[15] Another inclination has been to dismiss the unfavorable studies as weaker methodologically. Armstrong rated the studies on various factors, concluding that "overall, the studies rated poorly," 1.5 against the ideal score of 6, but that the relatively better methodologies showed more positive results for planning (1982:207, 208; see Foster [1986] for a critique of Armstrong's rating scheme). But Starbuck, taking account of Armstrong's conclusion, argued that "the worst studies find the strongest relationship between planning and performance, whereas the best studies find no significant relationship" (1985:369).

At the same level of logic are Lorange and Vancil, who, after estimating the "decimation" or "elimination" of between a quarter and a third of corporate planning departments during the 1970–71 recession, concluded that "the survivors knew that they had 'arrived'—that the planning activity had been carefully reexamined and found to earn its keep" (1977:xi). But given the energy crisis two years later, followed by the next decimation of planners, the timing of this comment too was a bit unfortunate.

To "abandon planning . . . obviously this is irresponsible nonsense," wrote Higgins from academia (1976:41), while Unterman, a businessman turned academic, suggested that "any kind of strategic planning is better for an organization than no planning at all" (1974:47). And their sentiments were fully reflected in practice, where Gray's survey of U.S. multibusiness firms found that "most companies in our sample remain firmly committed to strategic planning, even though 87 percent report feelings of disappointment and frustration with their systems" (1986:90). No wonder Wildavsky commented that planners "are confirmed in their beliefs no matter what happens. Planning is good if it succeeds and society is bad if it fails. That is why planners so often fail to learn from experience. To learn one must make mistakes and planning cannot be one of them" (1973:151). Thus he referred to planners as people "of secular faith."

Had planning crowned its truest believer of the 1970s, it may well have been George Steiner, who wrote that "The best planning is most likely to take place in organizations with the best management" (1979:103) although Steiner never did bother to mention what constitutes the best management, except that it overcomes "anti-planning biases." Runners-up might have been Roach and Allen, who referred to "the strict duty to plan strategically," in order to honor "the obligation inherent in management" (1983:7–44). And for the 1980s, Ansoff may well have regained his 1960s mantle with the comment that although "doubts were voiced about feasibility of systematic strategic analysis" when he published his book in 1965, "since then doubts have disappeared and practice of systematic strategy formulation has flourished" (1988:22). Maybe this has been because, to quote one of the truly astounding statements in this literature of astounding statements, "formal long-range planning seemed almost like a godsend to [the top executives of organizations facing increased complexity]. . . . Announcing that his organization would undertake a formal program of strategic planning was almost like a public announcement that he was going to quit smoking. It forced the chief executive to attempt to change his own behavior in a way that he knew was desirable" (Lorange and Vancil, 1977:x). But the prize for blind faith must go to Ekman, whose pitch for planning was preceded by the comment that:

> There are very few people today who would question the value of long-range planning even though we in fact know rather little about the real contributions of planning and planning technology to the advancement of government, business and other activities. We know even less of what damage planning has caused, and that might have been considerable. (1972:609)

Salvation: "It's the process that counts"

Proponents of planning also responded in a slightly more pragmatic but no less devout way: planning is not utopia, only the road to it. In its most popular rendition—"It's the process that counts"— one is reminded of the clergy whose sole purpose is to get people inside the door, no matter what happens inside.[16]

Steiner told his readers it is not the plans that count "but the development of intellectual skills," a "thought . . . captured in an old maxim: 'Plans are sometimes useless but the planning process is always indispensable' " (1983:15). Ackoff urged his readers to treat planning as "not an act but a process . . . that has no natural conclusion or end point" (1970:3). Does that mean it does not generate plans? (Even Steiner admitted that "planning without plans is a waste of time" [1969:8]—presumably even when the plans are "useless"!) And then there was the Ringbakk comment on one of the "reasons why planning fails": the apparently strange misperception in many companies that management actually "ex-

---

[16] Allaire and Firsirotu responded much as we do but with a different metaphor: "perhaps planning is the managerial equivalent of jogging; it is not an efficient means to get anywhere nor is it really intended to; but if practiced regularly, it will make you feel better" (1988:50).

pects that the plans as developed will be realized" (1971:21). Imagine that!

Taking a cue from this perhaps, some years ago the office of the Auditor General of the Government of Canada became intent on conducting "comprehensive audits" of Canadian government departments, to assess their overall effectiveness (studies that became known as "value of money"). But finding itself stymied frequently by performance that could not be measured, the office fell back instead on the ascertainment of the presence of good management technique, including systematic planning. In other words, if the department in question planned, it had to be effective. It was the process that counted. As Wildavsky noted, "defining planning as applied rationality" directs attention "to the internal qualities of the decisions and not to their external effects." The result is that "Planning is good . . . not so much for what it does but for how it goes about not doing it" (1973:130, 139). Is it any wonder that Quinn commented:

> A good deal of the corporate planning I have observed is like a ritual rain dance; it has no effect on the weather that follows, but those who engage in it think it does. Moreover, it seems to me that much of the advice and instruction related to corporate planning is directed at improving the dancing, not the weather. (1980a:122)

Elaboration: "Just you wait"

A little more sophisticated—and slightly less enamored of the status quo—were those who acknowledged the evidence but promised that salvation was just around the corner. "Just you wait," they pleaded, "we're working on it; soon all the problems will be solved." Thus, fourteen years after Ansoff published *Corporate Strategy*, he claimed:

> The book continues to sell well. But many practical applications of prescriptions similar to mine have come to grief, the spread of strategic planning has been slow, and it is only now, ten [sic] years later, that the practice of genuine strategic planning is emerging. (1979:65)

One is reminded here of that old joke about the doctor who examines Mrs. Jones, finds her to be a virgin, and wonders how this can be. "Every night," she explains, "my husband sits on the edge of the bed and tells me how good it's going to be!" But this is no joke for many of the subjects of planning, for example, the city dwellers whose lives were significantly affected by urban planners who believed they could design an acceptable city from scratch. Some years ago, in *The New York Times*, a writer on the subject referred to these comprehensive urban planning exercises as "such a conspicuous failure in the last 15 years that doctrinaire planning, and its adherents, are in considerable disrepute and disarray. The impressive theories and presentations that seem so intellectually compelling go up in smoke when faced with the human and political equation" (Ada Louise Huxtable, quoted in Chandler and Sayles, 1971:42).

Yet they kept trying, each time claiming that the last failure revealed the true problems, which would be solved next time. Never put into question were the premises that underlaid the whole exercise: that planners, or at least their systems, can be smart enough to figure out centrally the dynamics of an entire city, the comprehensive future of an entire enterprise, the integrated policies of an entire government.

There was, however, one important consequence to this response: every time they failed, the planners upped the ante. More resources become necessary—more planners, more managerial time for planning, more technology, more documents. While the planners ran around plugging up the holes in their practice, everyone else had to pay the bill. If it hadn't stopped, we would all be doing nothing but planning. (Indeed, in what became the world's ultimate planning system, the Soviet Union, one estimate for 1969 put the number of economists, "mostly administrative staff connected with planning," at 800,000! [Lewis, 1969:19])

Forecasting is a good case in point. When simple extrapolations didn't work, the forecasters developed more and more convoluted mathematical techniques; when single predictions failed, multiple "scenarios" had to be concocted; when short-term estimates proved unreliable, planners had to look to the ever-longer term. To quote Godet:

The considerable promise of futures and prospective studies, following the failure of classical forecasting . . . has not thus far come up to expectations. Growing uncertainty about the future points to the need for increased effort in futures studies and, at the same time, identified the current practical limitations of such efforts. (1987:xiv)

Every failure led to the inclusion of new factors, each encouraging the proliferation of planners and planning. Thus at one point, the failure of planning was attributed to the fact that planners didn't plan for themselves, hence the proposal for "meta-planning" ("the plan to plan") so as to change "a relatively ineffective planning activity into something that meets the characteristics prescribed by planning theorists" (Emshoff, 1978:1095). When operating planning did not suffice, we got functional planning—marketing planning, product planning, financial planning, R&D planning, international planning, manufacturing planning, organization planning, public relation planning, even diversification planning (all in Steiner, 1969, Section IV). Then it was all to come together in business planning, later long-range planning, still later strategic planning. After that we got corporate planning and portfolio planning. When political forces were deemed the problem, "stakeholder" planning was added: shortly after that, as the competition from Japan became severe (in the opinion of Pascale [1984], because the Japanese had fewer pretences about formal planning), cultural planning became the imperative. (Ansoff captured much of this proliferation graphically, as reproduced in Figure 3–2—and this tabulated only to 1974!)

Let us consider these last two elaborations (in theory at least; it is hard to believe that many firms took them seriously in practice), because they seem, to this observer at least, to reflect the bizarre proportions reached in this elaboration response.

Planned Politics: Stakeholder Analysis. In so-called stakeholder analysis, the wants and needs of the different influencer groups surrounding the organization were to be calculated systematically and factored into the planning process, in some neat way that would pave over all the messy affairs of power and politics. Consider Bryson's description:

A complete stakeholder analysis will require the strategic planning team to identify the organization's stakeholders, their stake in the organization or its output, their criteria for judging the performance of the organization, how well the organization performs against those criteria, how the stakeholders influence the organization, and in general how important the various stakeholders are. (1988:52)

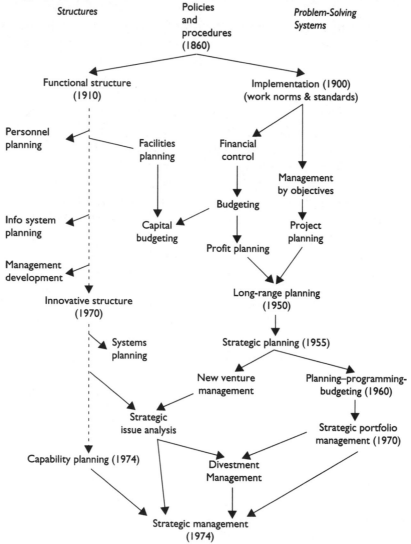

Figure 3–2
Proliferation of Forms of Planning
(From Ansoff, 1984:258)

Figure 3–3 shows Freeman's model of the "Stakeholder Strategy Formulation Process," in which "Stakeholder Behavioral Analysis," "Stakeholder Behavioral Explanation," and "Coalition Analysis" lead to "Generic Strategies," which gives rise to "Specific Programs for Stakeholders" and an "Integrative Stakeholder Program."

It all seemed so logical—just an elaboration of those boxes called "values" and "ethics" on the original design school model (to quote Freeman: "explicate the intrinsic values" of the executives and of the organization itself, "analyze the differences" between the two, being "explicit about where there are conflicts and inconsistencies," repeat for the stakeholders, and so on [1984:98–99]). Except that it was so mechanistic that one has to wonder if logic became the problem instead of the solution. Even if planners really did exhibit the assumed objectivity to stand aside (or above) and

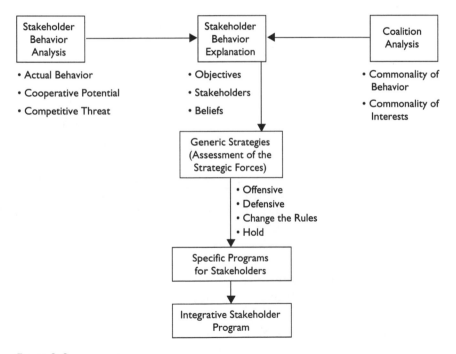

Figure 3–3
"Stakeholder Strategy Formulation Process"
(From Freeman, 1984:131)

calculate everybody else's needs, even if such calculations were possible in the first place (two assumptions almost certainly false), the result would be so sterile that any stakeholder with a shred of sensitivity would reject the whole exercise out of hand. Consider one case in point:

> New England Telephone adopted a stakeholder approach to implementing a plan for charging for Directory Assistance in Massachusetts (Emshoff and Freeman, 1979). The rational analysis of the stakeholder environment was sound and the planning process used to chart out an implementation scenario was successful. However, its transactions with several key stakeholders, most notably and ironically, its own union, as well as the State Legislature, were not successful. The union got a piece of legislation prohibiting the company's plan passed in the state legislature, and even though the company was successful in persuading the Governor of Massachusetts to veto the legislation, as there was no public support, the state legislature overrode the Governor's veto, at the cost of $20 million to the customers of New England Telephone. (Freeman, 1984:70)

The analysis was "sound," the process "successful"; it was just that some nasty stakeholders got in the way and scuttled it. Ironically, Freeman told the story to make a classic case for the "elaboration" response: perhaps "the transactions between company and stakeholders have not given the strategy and process a fair test" (70). In fact, they may have done just the opposite: granted a generous test to an unfair procedure. (Did the planners work for management or the union?) In other words, did such an exercise do more than encourage an unnecessary political battle and then lose it trying to fight fire with frivolity?

Calculating Culture. When the Japanese upset American ways of doing business, the planning pendulum swung back to economic competition. But not in the old ways. With the Japanese decimating their markets, some American planners turned their attention to culture. And so a new set of factors was duly plugged into the planning formulae, in four easy steps of course,

Step 1:   Define the relevant culture and subcultures of the organization. . . .

Step 2:   Organize these statements about the firm's culture in terms of managers, tasks and their key relationships. . . .

Step 3:   Assess the risk that the company's culture presents to the realization of the planned strategic effort. . . .

Step 4:   Identify and focus on those specific aspects of the company's culture that are both highly important to strategic successes and incompatible with the organizational approaches that are planned (Schwartz and Davis, 1981:47).

It was all so simple, making this "a part of the corporation's strategic planning process" (47). All it needed was lots of resources (especially for the consultants who concocted these procedures) and a blind eye to how it violated the natural functioning of the organization. Somehow, imagining that you could sit down and calculate coalitions seems silly enough, but to take culture—so deeply rooted in the history and traditions of an organization, and, for the Japanese at least, in the long evolution of a society—and work it into the pat procedures of the planning cycle seems extraordinarily naïve. One is hard-pressed to imagine the Japanese quaking in their geisha houses at the thought of Americans doing such planning. But then again, this probably never amounted to more than a marginal distraction in any event.

Ansoff's Elaborations. In a way, since the publication of his classic book on planning in 1965, Ansoff became part of this elaboration response, although once again in his own unique and interesting manner. This is well worth reviewing, for what it reveals about planning, about the field of strategic management in general, and, not incidentally, about H. Igor. Ansoff himself, the generally recognized father of the field.

Ansoff published steadily after 1965, developing his ideas in stages that were often confusing to the reader (this one at least). While never quite repudiating his earlier work on strategic planning, he nevertheless opened up the whole process (under what came to be his preferred label of strategic management) to what he considered the increasingly turbulent environment of business and, therefore, the need to provide increasingly flexible but nevertheless proactive and institutionalized responses. "Today, c. 1977, this problem [of rapid change in the shape of the strategic problem] is significantly different from ten years ago, when my first book on the subject made its appearance." Important "new conditions of turbulence" have appeared, in the form of "commercial linkages, socio-political interaction with the environment and competition for scarce resources" (1979a:5). In 1984, Ansoff drew all his ideas together in a book titled *Implanting Strategic Management.*

This is an interesting book, full of novel ideas and with a major message to convey, but difficult to follow in places. For our purposes here, it ended up in a most curious relationship with the planning process. That is because Ansoff all but let go of planning at points, yet in the end clung tenaciously to it. Ultimately, he believed that he could reconcile the need for flexible response with the decomposition and institutionalization of procedure, in other words, with the planning approach. We believe that he never did reconcile the two, and we conclude (based on arguments developed later in this book) that he could not. Ansoff wanted both ways, that which we believe, in the final analysis, is an incompatibility.

On one hand, Ansoff firmly believed that turbulence required flexible response and that the traditional forms of planning—he called them "long range planning" and "strategic planning"—did not allow for it. And so he proposed alternate ways to manage strategy, which he called in a summary chapter "modes of strategic behavior," including "ad hoc management," "strategic posture management," and "strategic learning" (1984:459–469).

Ansoff's text becomes confusing, however, about how and when these methods should be used. Broadly, he suggested what organization theorists call a "contingency" approach: the mode used (including conventional planning) should depend on the degrees of predictability, complexity, and novelty of the conditions faced. But that is mitigated by his belief, repeated in various places in the book, that business in general has moved toward conditions of increased turbulence. Earlier in the book, for example, he tracked the "turbulent level" of organizations from "stable" or "repetitive" around 1900, through "reactive" and "expanding" in the middle of the century, to more "discontinuous" in recent years and "surpriseful" in the near future. Thus, Ansoff, seemed to favor the more flexible modes, such as "strategic learning."

But that was not quite his final stand either, for ultimately, he came down in favor of ever increasing comprehensiveness: he wanted firms to combine all these approaches, comprehensive planning for some parts and what he called "strategic issues management" for others (348). Indeed, at the end of the book he predicted that the " 'planning of planning'—a foresightful development of new systematic approaches, will be increasingly used in the 1980's" (470).

Moreover, while recognizing these alternate modes of strategic behavior, Ansoff nonetheless set even the most flexible of these (at least the ones he favored, not "unmanaged organic adaptation" [459–460]) into a framework that clearly falls within the planning approach, in terms of the basic premises we outlined in our Chapter 1. To Ansoff, the strategy process must always be controlled and conscious and clearly proactive ("unmanaged firms are poor profit makers and are prone to strategic surprises" [460], a condition he equated with "intuitive managing" [460]); strategies must always be made explicit (31ff); and the analyst or planner has a major role to play in the process, although the senior managers are the acknowledged formulators of strategy (e.g., in a 1975 article, "the planning staff detects, tracks, and analyzes strategic issues; general management keeps up to date the list of important strategic issues, assigns specific issues for planning, approves the plans, and monitors the execution" [1975a:31]).

Most important, the process must be consciously elaborated through extensive decomposition. Ansoff, for example, drew a sharp distinction between "the two principal management regimes" of strategic management and operations management (183–184), and at one point in the text even proposed that upon the arrival of a strategic surprise, "the responsibilities of top management are partitioned" into one group concerned with control and maintenance of morale, another assuring business as usual, and a third dealing with the surprise (24). On the classic distinction between formulation and implementation, Ansoff bounced back and forth. At some points in the text it was naturally assumed (e.g., 242, 259); at others it was formally rejected, at least under certain conditions (e.g., 435, 466). But even this was not done consistently. For example, in managing surprises, where we might expect rejection, at one point Ansoff proposed that "the top management group formulates the overall strategy, assigns implementation responsibilities, and coordinates the implementation" (25).

Finally, above all, Ansoff remained firmly committed to the formalization, or institutionalization, of procedure, the chief characteristic of the planning approach. This he has done with absolute consistency, throughout his writings. Although he titled one chapter of his 1984 book, "Institutionalizing Strategic Responsiveness," he might just as well have given the same title to the entire book. As he wrote in that 1975 article, capturing the very essence of his approach: "If, as experience suggests, modern planning technology does not insure against surprises, the *technology* needs to be extended to provide such insurance" (1975a:21, italics added). Or, as he put it in his 1984 book: "If the firm expects its environmental turbulence to be around level five [surpriseful], it needs to invest in *yet another system*, a strategic surprise system" (24, italics in original). At the end of this book, Ansoff predicted "increased uses of systematic approaches in strategic management" (471), presumably in the face of what he believed to be the increased turbulence faced by contemporary organizations.

Thus Ansoff seemed to want to have his cake and eat it too. He recognized the need for organizations to be flexible and responsive to dynamic conditions. Yet he believed they could rely on the decomposition and formalization of procedure—essentially institutionalization in the tradition of planning—to achieve it. And this led to his curious position on planning itself.

Ansoff did not hesitate to note the problems of conventional planning. "Early efforts to use strategic planning ran into serious difficulties," he wrote in the 1984 book (460). And in places he did question comprehensiveness (461), in order to gain speed of responsiveness (without really addressing how management was supposed to pull it all together). But he was not about to embrace "intuitive managing" as the alternative. Instead, he proposed "an appropriate type of planning" that "does work when it is properly installed in the firm" (461), for which he claimed "empirical and practical proof" (without really providing any). This "planning" turned out to be "ad hoc issues management," really ad hoc strategy analysis, which "addresses strategic issues one at a time," executed promptly (462). Thus Ansoff's most contemporary form of planning became, however ad hoc, the formalized, institutionalized response to discontinuity—a rather generous interpretation of the word planning, to say the least.[17] In the final analysis, Ansoff identified planning more with formalization and institutionalization than with comprehensiveness per se. (This, however, does not mean that he rejected comprehensiveness. His favored response to what he saw as the problems of contemporary business—his ideal world, when possible—was to combine comprehensiveness with formalization and institutionalization.)

Ultimately, then, Ansoff's own response to the evidence on the failures of planning was to elaborate it, ever deepening the degree of formalization and ever widening the extent of comprehensiveness. When his corporate planning of 1965 did not work, he elaborated all kinds of procedures through the 1970s to deal with discontinuities, weak signals, and social forces in the environment, finally attempting to weld them all into a comprehensive system in the 1980s. As Dill wrote in 1979 of Ansoff's work (although he would have been even more correct in 1984): "Today, hundreds of charts and diagrams later, Ansoff has introduced many new elements into his master plan for management. Ansoff's answer to failure is always to make the strategy formulation effort more comprehensive" (1979:48).

If all of this sounds confusing, we would like to think it reflects Ansoff's 1984 book rather than our own misreading of it. Once again, Ansoff produced an important work based on premises that we believe to be questionable—a book that is stimulating and full of novel and interesting ideas (not the least of these being the

---

[17] To say a little more, in the "glossary of terms" at the back of his 1984 book, Ansoff defined "Ad Hoc Management" as "a management process in which response to challenges is systematic but without reference to an overall plan or strategy" (475), which takes his liberties with the word planning even further (planning being merely "systematic"). In this regard, I find it ironic that Ansoff criticized me (gently, I should add) in this section of his book for not being clear about different forms of planning: "One explanation for the disagreement [about the usefulness of planning under dynamic conditions] arises from the fact that Mintzberg does not make a clear differentiation between the various types of planning. Certainly, in the early days of planning when extrapolative long range planning was the only alternative to ad hoc management, Mintzberg's advice [on the need to rely on intuitive behavior] was well given. In those days, when environments turned turbulent, it was better to revert to unassisted, unstructured but flexible 'managing' than to assume (as is done in long range planning) that the future will be an extrapolation of the past" (466).

concepts of "strategic surprise" and the need to respond to "weak signals"). Taken *out* of his context—that is, away from the systems and technologies within which he sought to embed them—many of these ideas are useful. In other words, in our opinion Ansoff again identified important problems and supplied interesting concepts in the process of developing questionable procedures. We take his real contribution, perhaps to his chagrin, to be, not *prescriptive*, but *descriptive!*[18]

And to complete this discussion, the proposed elaborations of planning, even in the forms Ansoff developed, let alone through stakeholder or cultural or even scenario analysis (to be discussed later), did not address the negative evidence on planning at all. If anything, these likely aggravated the problem by offering more to what seems to be their cause—throwing oil on the fire, if you like. Thus Huff and Reger observed:

> Bresser and Bishop [1983:595], in a thoughtful theoretical piece, explored the possibility that formal planning may actually cause increased intraorganizational contradictions, contradictions partially responsible for the introduction of formal planning. Organizations, they suggested, may be trapping themselves in dysfunctional amplifying loops of more formal planning, leading to more contradictions, leading to more formal planning that ultimately may threaten the viability of the organization. (1987:221).

---

[18] Ansoff also reissued his original book *Corporate Strategy* as *The New Corporate Strategy* in 1988. The first two-thirds of this, labeled "Part 1: Strategy Formulation," is the original book with various changes, in examples and some conceptual material, etc., while the last third, labeled "Part 2: Strategy Implementation," was added, new to this particular book more than to Ansoff's existing portfolio of publications (see Fahey's review of it, where he referred to Part 2 as providing "little, if any, new material," seemingly "added on" with 'little attempt to directly link parts 1 and 2" [(1989:460]). In the Preface to the new edition, Ansoff noted that one "deficiency which dates *Corporate Strategy* is the almost exclusive focus on analytical reasoning" (p. v.) But later in the book, in a new passage within the old text, he wrote: "This book is focused on strategic management in difficult and turbulent environments. Therefore, we will now proceed to outline the method of comprehensive strategic planning" (1988:102). However, in a journal article published in 1987, Ansoff presented a more balanced case, arguing for the inclusion alongside the "systematic model," whose "results were frequently disappointing," of an "organic model ... based on a political-social optic," an "organizational inertia" model based on "social-anthropological" optics, and an "ad hoc management model" based on a "psycho-sociological" optic. "While the limited optic of systematic management was the furthest from reality, there is much evidence to suggest that all of the optics are relevant to all organizations ..." (1987:509, 510).

As Oakeshott noted, rationalism is "without the power to correct its own short-comings; it has no homeopathic quality; you cannot escape its errors by becoming more sincerely or more profoundly rationalistic" (quoted in van Gunsteren, 1976:20).

Reversion: "Back to Basics"

In May of 1986, at the first conference of The Planning Forum (formed by the merger of America's two largest planning societies), Michael Naylor, General Motors' Executive-in-Charge of Corporate Strategic Planning and one of the field's leading practitioner spokespeople, gave an address titled "Innovative Management and Global Competition." In our opinion, the speech was marked by exactly the opposite approach, in relation to the first issue at least. In criticizing conventional planning, Naylor rediscovered the old design school model—that is, the basic framework that underlaid strategic planning from the very beginning, minus planning's own characteristics of formalization and elaboration. He talked about establishing competitive position, assessing strengths and weaknesses, and finding sustainable competitive advantage, and he kept referring to "plan implementation." Thus, instead of providing innovation himself, Naylor offered a return to the status quo of the past.

In the face of all the complaints about strategic planning, this became another popular response of planners in the mid-1980s—to revert to the simpler model of the design school. For example, the *Planning Review* interviewed Michael Carpenter, another chief planner at General Electric, this time in 1985 after planning's fall from grace at the company. He was quoted as follows:

> I make a distinction between planning and strategy—they're two different things. Strategy means thinking through a company's basis of competitive advantage—the way the economics work; where the competitors are going; how to nail the other guy and end up with the highest rate of return and the highest gross in the industry. Planning, on the other hand, focuses on making the strategy work—adding capacity, for instance, or increasing the sales force. Historically, GE's strategic approach emphasized planning more

than strategy. . . . If you think about strategy the way I've defined it, strategy is a thought process, a conceptual process. It's a thinking harder, not trying harder, process. (in Allio 1985:18)[19]

Consultants also rediscovered the model about the same time. Walker Lewis, founder of Strategic Planning Associates, argued in a 1984 article that "the CEO must be an informed generalist"; "he must foster the building of comparative advantage," doing so by "knowing how to integrate or synthesize" the relevant information about "internal operations" and "external forces" to produce "comprehensively developed strategy"; and "he must prod the corporation along the path to implementation" (1984:1, 2, 6). Like Naylor, Lewis's claim that "coming to terms with these changes requires more than the old answers" (6) is belied by his words, which offered just that.

Reverting to a purer rendition of the design school model may ameliorate some of the worst excesses of the formalized planning one. But that does not resolve any fundamental problem, since most of the premises of the two approaches are identical (especially in the way they ignore strategic learning). We must, therefore, look elsewhere to explain the evidence of the problems of planning.

Pitfalls: "Them, not us"

Most planners have done just that. But not constructively, in our view. By far, the most popular response of planners to critical evidence about their practice has been to acknowledge it and immediately attribute it to a set of so-called "pitfalls."

---

[19] As suggested in the title, "GE = Giant Entrepreneur?", here the design school model was associated with entrepreneurship. Ansoff did the same thing in a 1977 article, referring to "entrepreneurial planning" as a new type of planning system, capable of coping with discontinuities (1977:14; see especially his graphic rendition of it on p. 15 for similarities with the design school model). There is a certain irony in this, given the efforts of the design school's leading spokesman Kenneth Andrews to distance the model from entrepreneurial behavior (though the ground he tried to seize for it between entrepreneurship and planning can be narrow). Coming at the design school model from the perspective of planning, however, with its own emphasis on formalization of procedure, it may look like entrepreneurship!

Pitfalls are to planning what sins are to religion: impediments to be brushed aside, perfectly understandable cosmetic blemishes to be removed, so that the nobler work of serving the almighty can proceed. Except for one fundamental difference: pitfalls are mostly committed by "them," not "us," by managers or by organizations, not by planners or their systems. The fault may not lie in the stars, but neither can it be found in planning. Thus in Gray's survey, where 87 percent of the respondents expressed disappointment and frustration with their planning systems, 59 percent attributed this "discontent mainly to difficulties encountered in the implementation of plans," not to the plans themselves or the process of planning (1986:90). To quote one respondent, in this case a senior line manager: "We actually used to tell ourselves our planning system was OK, even though we admitted it fell apart in implementation. That was our way of telling ourselves that the trouble was not at the top" (93). Nor was this particular trouble new. Here is what Emmanuel Kant had to say about planning two hundred years ago:

> The making of plans is mostly an uppish, presumptuous mental exercise in so far as the planner claims some creative genius when he demands of others what he cannot himself deliver, or blames others for what he could not do himself. . . . (in Spender, 1989:12)

Abell and Hammond have commented that "The underlying causes of [the] problems [of making planning work] are seldom technical deficiencies with the planning process or the analytical approaches. Instead they are human and administrative problems," and "have as their source the nature of human beings" (1979:432, 434). What this seems to mean is that the systems would work fine if it weren't for all those darn people. This, of course, easily explains every problem that planning has had, since it has been tried only in organizations composed of people! But until we are willing to get rid of the people for the sake of the planning, we had better look elsewhere to explain planning's problems.

Steiner wrote extensively on the pitfalls of planning. In a survey he conducted among several hundred, mostly larger companies, he asked for responses to 50 listed pitfalls. The fact that any additions made to the list "were either modifications [of the 50 pitfalls] or subsets of them . . . confirmed my conviction that [the list] includes the most important traps, both conceptually and operationally, that must be avoided if a formal planning system is to be effective" (1979:288). Confirmed *his conviction* maybe, but certainly did not confirm the conclusion. If Steiner did not think beyond the pitfalls, what could he expect of his respondents? Faced with a list of 50 items, which bounded the issue, which busy managers would be inclined to add more, let alone rethink the whole framework? That was Steiner's responsibility, not their's. So the survey did not necessarily uncover the most important traps at all; it delineated only the ones Steiner thought about when he mailed the questionnaire. (There is an appropriate similarity in the ritualized filling-out of research survey questionnaires and planning documents themselves, each with their own preconceived categories.)

In any event, Steiner concentrated his analysis on the ten pitfalls that received the most frequent mention, which we list in our Table 3–1.[20] Other lists of planning pitfalls—either from surveys or the authors' own—look very similar to these (e.g., Ringbakk, 1971, the first of these surveys; Lorange, 1980a:133ff; see also the latter's review of other pitfall studies, 1979:231–235). Heading almost every list, in one form or another, is the absence of senior management support or commitment to planning, while a common second theme has to do with the attitude or "climate" in the organization toward planning. In Steiner's survey, in fact, six or seven of the ten pitfalls seem to fall into these two categories (numbers 1, 2, 4, 7, 10, and perhaps 9 for the first, and number 6 for the second). In one case, the management is ostensibly at fault, in the other, the entire organization.

The "Top Management Support" Pitfall. Since the voice of Ringbakk first appeared on this pitfall in 1968 ("neither corporate nor

---

[20] Repetitions of the same survey in Japan, Canada, England, Italy, and Australia produced similar results (298). Steiner also asked his American respondents to express their degree of satisfaction with their planning systems. His claim that "they reported much more satisfaction than dissatisfaction" (289) is belied by his own figures, which show barely a tilt to satisfaction: 10.0 percent reported highly satisfied, 8.5 percent highly dissatisfied, 34.1 percent above average and 15.2 percent below average satisfaction, with 32.2 percent at the average (295). Bear in mind that this mediocre level of satisfaction was expressed largely by planners themselves, who made up 75 percent of the respondents.

Table 3–1: **"The Ten Most Important Pitfalls to be Avoided as Rated by Respondents (N=159)"**
(From: Steiner, 1979:294)

Description
1. Top management's assumption that it can delegate the planning function to a planner.
2. Top management becomes so engrossed in current problems that it spends insufficient time on long-range planning, and the process becomes discredited among other managers and staff.
3. Failure to develop company goals suitable as a basis for formulating long-range plans.
4. Failure to assume the necessary involvement in the planning process of major line personnel.
5. Failing to use plans as standards for measuring managerial performance.
6. Failure to create a climate in the company which is congenial and not resistant to planning.
7. Assuming that corporate comprehensive planning is something separate from the entire management process.
8. Injecting so much formality into the system that it lacks flexibility, looseness, and simplicity, and restrains creativity.
9. Failure of top management to review with departmental and divisional heads the long-range plans which they have developed.
10. Top management's consistently rejecting the formal planning mechanism by making intuitive decisions which conflict with the formal plans.

divisional managers have fully accepted formal planning as part of their responsibility"; they "have usually delegated planning tasks to staff personnel" [1968:354]), a virtual chorus of complaints developed, accompanied by an orchestration of platitudes, always with the same refrain. Eleven years later, Steiner informed us that "there can and will be no effective formal strategic planning in an organization in which the chief executive does not give it firm support and make sure that others in the organization understand his depth of commitment" (1979:80). In that same year, Abell and Hammond claimed that "the support of senior management is an absolute must" (1979:434), and a year later Lorange added that the chief executive "will get only as much out of the system as he puts into it" (1980a:258). By 1989, after two decades of this, Reid added that "without the commitment of the chief executive to the objectives, as well as to the process of planning, the process will cease to be effective" (1989:557).

But might chief executives not sometimes get less from planning than they put into it? And can they sometimes have good reason to be not committed, even to actively resist planning? Might they know something that the perpetrators of the pitfalls do not? Jacques Sarrazin (1981), who quoted some of the passages reproduced above, pointed out thoughtfully that "it is really astonishing that such a discrepancy between theory and practice with respect to the role of top management in corporate planning still exists ten years after having been brought to light for the first time." He offered two choices: continue to try to convince managers to "fit their practice to the theory" or else "attempt first to understand the causes of the discrepancy" (10).

Writers on planning almost inevitably concentrated on the former. If only top managers would listen—would change their attitude, see the light—all would be well with planning. But planning is not alone in this: every new technique, system, or function vies for top management support. In the final analysis, some succeed and some don't, not because they have top management support per se but because they provide something of value (and so get that support). Public relations has become well established at General Motors, but there is (presumably) no program for executive ballet classes. All the top management support in the world would not have helped the latter, while public relations may well have succeeded without such support. What the experience of planning over the past two decades does tell us is that top management support may be a necessary condition for success, but it is certainly not a sufficient one. Indeed, as Pennington pointed out, "formal planning has, in general, received the kind of attention and support from top management that most emerging techniques can only dream of" (1972:2). Clearly, something else must have been wrong.

Ringbakk was one of the few who addressed Sarrazin's second choice—after a fashion. He offered several explanations for the discrepancy between the theory and the practice, a particularly pretentious one being that managers exhibit "a lack of understanding of the different dimensions of planning" (1971:19). Later some others agreed. "A surprisingly large number of those who are expected to plan simply don't understand how to" (Abell and Hammond, 1979:433). Ansoff pushed this argument further, in tone as well as implication: "Some managers fear that planning will expose their incompetence" (1977:20). He also suggested that managers "fear the uncertainty and ambiguity which planning brings into their lives" (20). Saunders and Tuggle commented in the same vein that a lack of stringent competition allows managers to "satisfice at a more comfortable level" instead of having to optimize, as planning supposedly does (1977:21).

Later we shall seek to show that all of these statements can be precisely false, that it is planning that often satisfices, that planning may artificially reduce uncertainty and ambiguity, and especially that it may be planners—at least those sympathetic to the above sorts of arguments, the *conventional* planners we have been referring to—who do not understand management. Among other things, their pretensions get in the way.

Writing in 1980, just before strategic planning was dethroned at General Electric, one of its senior planners attributed its acceptance "first and foremost" to "the commitment and involvement of the executive office" (Rothschild, 1980:13). Reginald Jones, CEO at the time, no doubt understood the process. But can we say that his successor, Jack Welch, who soon after decimated formal planning at GE, understood it any less? Indeed, Welch probably understood it more, since as a division manager he had to do it himself, not just force others to do so. If planning is so good, why did the American firm most experienced with the process turn against it? Why was GE "first out" after being "first in"? Did Welch know too much?

We believe so and will develop the substance of our argument in Chapter 4. Among the points we shall make is that planning, in its own pitfall, can undermine the very commitment it so urgently demands.

The "Climate Congenial to Planning" Pitfall. In what often sounds like a tautology, planning writers referred to a climate "congenial" to planning (Steiner, as noted; also Steiner and Kunin, 1983:14–15). In responding to "questions about the usefulness of [his] original prescription" fourteen years later, Ansoff replied:

My own belief continues to be that the prescription was and remains valid, provided that it is applied in an appropriate organizational climate: and, contrariwise, that strategic planning is going
to be rejected when the climate in which it is implanted is wrong.
(1979a:6)

That would be fine if we were told what the right climate is (besides being supportive of planning). It really doesn't help at all to
claim, as Steiner did, that "It must engender a certain amount of
enthusiasm for planning and avoid blind resistance to planning.
There must be no serious anti-planning biases" (1983:15). Steiner
did add that the climate "must foster creative rather than pedes-
trian thinking" and that "managers must be capable of conceptual
thinking" (15). But what evidence did he and others offer that such
climates are in fact congenial to planning?

Again, the point we wish to develop in Chapter 4 is exactly the
opposite, namely that conventional planning tends to be a conservative process, sometimes encouraging behavior that undermines both creativity and strategic thinking. It can be inflexible,
breeding resistance to major strategic change and discouraging
truly novel ideas in favor of extrapolation of the status quo or
marginal adaptation, ultimately, therefore, focusing attention on
the short term rather than the long term. We shall also provide
evidence of how planning can impede the conceptual thinking of
managers. Moreover, we shall show how the internal political climate considered so antithetical to planning can sometimes help to
foster necessary strategic change in organizations, while planning
itself can sometimes foster dysfunctional political activity. Ultimately, then, we shall conclude that a climate congenial to planning can *sometimes* be antithetical to effective strategy making, and
so the "right" climate can sometimes be hostile to planning.

In effect, planning's own pitfalls serve inadvertently as foils to
help us uncover some of the serious problems with the process, by
allowing us to probe into some of its basic characteristics. As we
consider these real pitfalls in Chapter 4, followed by Chapter 5 on
the more serious fallacies of planning, we enter fully into our critique of the process.

4

Some Real Pitfalls of Planning

Our critique of planning proceeds on two levels. The first, discussed in this chapter, considers some of the general characteristics of planning that help to explain its difficulties. The tone of this discussion and even the actual set of issues discussed correspond to that of the literature on the pitfalls of planning, except that here we turn the conventional pitfalls back on themselves. That is to say, this chapter considers some of the more evident characteristics that impede the successful practice of planning in general. In Chapter 5 we shall look more deeply into more fundamental causes of the failures of strategic planning in particular.

The present chapter reverses the two main "pitfalls" of planning, seeking to show that not only do they miss the point, but that the point may often be the opposite of what is claimed. Planning may, in other words, impede *itself* from functioning as its proponents claim it should. Certainly planning cannot work effectively without the *support* of the people who hold senior positions in organizations, nor can it survive in *climates* hostile to its practice. The real questions are, however, why such support is so often eventually withheld and why such climates do arise.

In suggesting some answers, we introduce a number of problematic characteristics of planning. These include an "objective" detachment that often undermines commitment and evokes politics, and a tendency toward conservatism as well as an obsession with control that can breed a climate of conformity and inflexibility that favors incremental, generic change focused on the short run. These may be the real pitfalls of planning.

Planning and Commitment

The most popularly claimed pitfall of planning concerns commitment. The assumption is that with the support and participation of the top management, all will be well. But the questions must be asked: well with what and well for whom? For planners? To be sure. But for the organization?

This assumption is rooted in the notion of the "one best way," to return to Frederick Taylor's favorite phrase. Planning is assumed to be the one best way to formulate and implement strategy. That it is not—not only that there are other ways to do so but that these can be superior—is a theme that pervades this entire book and need not be addressed specifically here. What does need to be questioned and elaborated on here are the naïve assumptions in the literature about the relationship between planning and commitment, first that the commitment of top management automatically fosters the acceptance of planning, and second that planning itself automatically engenders commitment within the organization (e.g., in the introduction to David Hussey's book entitled *The Truth About Corporate Planning:* "A corporate planning process will assist companies to obtain a higher level of involvement of managers in the development of the organization" [1983:5]).

To be more specific, the issue is not simply whether management is committed to planning. It is also (a) whether planning is committed to management, (b) whether commitment to planning engenders commitment to the process of strategy making, to the strategies that result from that process, and ultimately to the taking of effective actions by the organization, and (c) whether the very nature of planning actually fosters managerial commitment to itself. The discussion that follows will put into question each of these beliefs.

Commitment at the Top

Planning has always had a curious relationship with top management. On one hand, it has deferred to the power of authority, at least formally, over the process itself. Planning has assumed, in other words, an all-powerful and centralized top management that must pull things together and make things happen (especially planning itself). Even Ansoff referred to this as a "strangely, naive presumption": "If managers [at lower levels] do not plan willingly, threaten them with the displeasure of the big boss and tell them he loves planning" (1977:19).

On the other hand, whether implicitly or explicitly, by its very nature planning is designed to reduce a good deal of top management's power over strategy making. No matter how much lip service is paid to the top management's ultimate control over the process, it is an undeniable fact that, through formalization, planning seeks to put some of that power into its own systems, and specifically at the expense of managerial intuition. Thus Lorange argued that the "CEO should typically not be the one who is deeply involved with the detailed carrying out of the strategic planning and control process," since that person could not "normally have the time or temperament to do this." Rather, "he is the designer of the system in a general sense" (1980b:2). *Remote control* seems to be Lorange's preferred posture for the CEO.

Of course, no one has wanted to eliminate top management entirely. Planning models have always been careful to leave a role for the top managers. In Steiner's illustrative "time schedule for a corporate five-year plan," for example, of the 31 steps delineated from August to December, top management was allowed involvement in eight:

• In August:

1. Corporate Planning Staff (CPS) meets with corporate officers, and checks with division planning staff, concerning a timetable for planning.
2. CPS confers with corporate officers concerning changes in basic objectives, strategies, and policies that should serve as new guides for the planning program. . . .

• In November:

1. If chairman of CPC [Corporate Planning Council] is not Chief Executive, the chairman and the director of corporate planning discuss major issues with the chief executive. . . .

• And in December:

1. A two-day planning conference is held off site, attended by top executives of company and each division. Each division presents its plan and its problems, alternatives are discussed, and courses of action are determined. The chief executive is chairman of this conference.
2. At the end of the conference the chief executive, who is the de facto conference chairman, decides how each plan is to be modified as a result of the conference proceedings. . . .
3. An alternative procedure in many companies is for each division to present plan individually to top executives. . . .
4. An overview and selected parts of the plan are presented to the board of directors by the corporate planner.
5. Annual budget reviews and approvals for next year's operations are made by the chief executive. . . . (1969:133–134)

This reads almost as if the senior managers should be thankful for the roles they were allowed. After all, they got to be conferred with on changes in strategy at the outset, and the CEO got to chair the two-day planning conference at the end, indeed to "decide" how the plans were to be modified (even if he or she did not get to present the plan to the board!). Never mind that top management had no role to play in the five steps in September, the four in October, or the other seven of the eight in November; the process was in the capable hands of the CPS who met with the division managers "to discuss completely their plans in conformance with CPS manual," who decided "on areas for study to aid in evaluating plans when received [and] modifying existing strategies," and who "aggregate[d] and review[ed]" divisional plans.

In a column entitled "How to implement strategic plans," published by a widely circulated strategy journal, the author commented in a section on "a committed CEO" that the chief executive "must make and carry out the corporate decisions that are indicated by the strategic plans" (Collier, 1984:92, who did not add, "whether he or she likes them or not"). If this is what commitment means, even in Steiner's slightly more subtle form, then how in the world is anyone to expect the support of top management?

Leaving senior managers out of the essence of the process is one thing, but insulting the way they work is another. To quote Steiner again: "If an organization is managed by intuitive geniuses there is no need for formal strategic planning. But how many organizations are so blessed? And, if they are, how many times are intuitives correct in their judgments?" (1979:9).

Later, when we address the more deeply rooted problems of planning directly, we shall challenge Steiner's assumptions that good intuition is a rare commodity in management and that, even when present, it is generally unreliable (or at least less reliable than planning). Here we wish to ask only how planning hopes to engender top management commitment when it puts down the most human side of management. If planning is not committed to management—even to the extent of respecting what may be its very essence—then how can management be committed to planning?

Commitment Lower Down

At least the attitudes expressed above were soft-pedaled; when it came to dealing with managers of lesser authority, the writings of planning became less circumscribed. This is clear in Steiner's own illustration, where, for example, in September "Division planning staffs meet with division managers to discuss completing their plans in conformance with CPS manual" and "corporate functional officers meet with CPS to discuss nature and relationship of their plans and division plans" (1969:133). No wonder the head of General Electric's Major Appliance Group spoke so vehemently about "grabbing hold" of his business from "an isolated bureaucracy" of planners. All he wanted was personal commitment to his own strategy, for which he had to fight the planners!

If planners own the process, if they take charge of the integration of the different subunit plans, in effect they remove control over strategy from the very people who are supposed to think it through. With the planners sequestered in their own offices pulling it all together for top management, everyone else gets reduced to a mere implementor. And that undermines commitment to the strategy making process as well as to its resulting strategies, "stifl[ing] the initiative of individual operators and supervisors" (Newman, 1951:67). Bass showed this in experiments conducted in various parts of the world. People were more productive and more satisfied when they operated their own plans instead of other people's. He suggested a number of reasons for this.

> Productivity and satisfaction are lower when planning for others because (1) sense of accomplishment is less when executing someone else's plan; (2) there is less tendency to try to confirm the validity of another's plan by executing it successfully—less confidence that it can be done; (3) there is less commitment to see that the plan works well; (4) there is less flexibility and less room for modification and initiative to make improvements in an assigned plan; (5) there is less understanding of an assigned plan; (6) human resources are not so well utilized; (7) there are more communications problems and consequent errors and distortions in following instructions; (8) there are competitive feelings aroused between planners and doers, to such an extent that it appears that if the former "win" the latter "lose." (1970:159)

"Decentralized" Planning

Of course, no self-respecting planner today would support any of the positions attributed to planning above. Strategic planning is the job of line managers; planners only provide support—they "facilitate." But what if the line managers don't want to make strategy that way; what if they insist on using their intuition; what if they refuse to coordinate with their colleagues? Do planners simply sit back and shrug their shoulders? Not in the experience of this observer.

"Decentralization" of the planning process is one supposed approach. But what does that mean if the very purpose of planning is to ensure coordination among different units? As Durand concluded in his survey of planning in France, "decentralized planning does not mean decentralized decision making" (1984:14). So long as decentralized planning requires the lower-level managers to carry out set procedures on set schedules under premises set by others in the hierarchy above them, no one should expect a great deal of commitment. Sucking in the grain from below does not provide the goose with any more autonomy than forcing it down from above, especially for geese who don't need that much grain.

The call for decentralized planning avoids an obvious dilemma. In the words of Erich Jantsch, the "planning process should be . . . democratic, i.e., based on decentralized initiative and centralized synthesis" (1969:473). That sounds fine. Except that centralized synthesis has a tendency to undermine decentralized initiative, as was clear in so much of the evidence presented in Chapter 3: by Sarrazin, Gomer, and Koch, and in General Electric, Air Canada, and the PPBS experience in the American government (which had "an extreme centralizing bias" [Wildavsky, 1974:188]). To quote what we wrote in an earlier publication about analysis in general: "In its search for *the* objective function, analysis ignores conflict and coalition in favor of *the* word from *the* boss . . . ; in its call for the support of top management to implement its solutions, it assumes centralized control; in its search for the optimal solution— *the* logical answer, 'the one best way' . . . —it discourages pluralism in the organizational structure" (Mintzberg, 1979b:131).

The essence of the problem is coordination—somehow pulling the whole planning exercise together. As usual, Wildavsky did not mince his words, labeling coordination "another term for coercion":

> Since actors A and B disagree with goal C, they can only be coordinated by being told what to do and doing it. The German word, Gleichschaltung, used by the Nazis in the sense of enforcing a rigid conformity, can give us some insight into this particular usage of coordination. To coordinate one must be able to get others to do things they do not want to do. (1973:143)

Planners need not, of course, impose the plan per se; they may instead call for all kinds of participation by those to be affected by it. But unless all those people can informally reach their own consensus, on goals and strategies and action programs and budget allocations—no simple feat in any substantial organization—then some central group has to do the coordinating for them and impose the result on them. A leader can, of course, do this through a personal vision. But that is rooted in intuition, a taboo process for those who subscribe to the planning school. Coordination has to be formalized, and that means planned. And so, while participation may be fostered in gathering inputs to the process, it tends to be precluded in the determination of the final result. Here is how Meyerson and Banfield characterized an urban planning experience in the City of Chicago:

> The best that such an agency as the Authority could do . . . was to gather up what information it could about the intentions of others, use this information to bring about as much voluntary coordination as possible, and then to choose its course of action in such a way as to achieve its ends without interfering with (perhaps even while complementing) the activity of the agencies and individuals whose ends it wished to further. (1955:275)

Our conclusion is that planning is a centralizing process, discouraging the very commitment it claims so earnestly to require. Anyone who doubts this might like to consider the response of planners themselves subjected to planning, as described by Ely Devons in his lucid account of the process in the World War II British military:

> On the highest level there was a conflict between the central co-ordinators in the Cabinet Office and Ministry of Production and the planners in the individual departments. The supreme co-ordinators struggled for more centralization, the planners in each department for more to be left to their discretion. But inside each department, the planners, who argued for delegation when dealing with the central organs of Government, argued for centralization of decisions inside their own department. (1950:14)

The honest response, then, when different activities must be tightly and formally coordinated, would seem to be to forget about participation and commitment and simply impose central planning. As Bass put it, "if the actions of doers are fully programmed by the planners, the gain in predictability of performance may be offset by the loss in doer interest" (1970:167). And when commitment is crucial, the appropriate response may be to forget about planning, at least as conventionally practiced.

Planning and Freedom

This issue has been most vigorously argued in the public sector, where it is not only the public employee but also the general citizen who is affected. In particular, some years ago a whole debate erupted about "planning and freedom," obviously with strong ideological overtones.[1] One side argued that the two are fundamentally antithetical, the other that freedom itself requires some degree of planning.

Reduced to pure ideology, where planning becomes almost synonymous with any kind of government intervention in the "free" market, the debate loses its meaning, at least for anyone who believes in collective rights alongside individual ones. But seen as the "obvious conflict between system efficiency, which is based on order, and spontaneity, which arises from the autonomy of the individual," it is difficult to dispute Chamberlain's conclusions that "planned order is not the antithesis of individual freedom but is necessary to it," at least up to a point, so that "the issue is not plan *or* individualism but how much of each" (1968:154–155).

But accepting that *plans* themselves are necessary to function in a free society does not lead to the conclusion that the *process of planning* is itself fundamentally democratic. (Recall Koch's characterization of state planning in France as a "façade" of democracy and participation.) Lewis stated the case well:

> On account of its complexity, planning by direction does not increase, but on the contrary diminishes democratic control. A plan cannot be made by "the people" or by parliament or by the cabinet; it has to be made by officials, because it consists of thousands of details fitted together. Its results are embodied in thousands of administrative orders and decisions, of which parliament and ministers can have only the briefest knowledge. . . (1969:19)

Of course, even a rather centralized planning process can reflect the democratic will of the people, so long as it takes its lead from

---

[1] See, for example, Frederick Hayek's book, *The Road to Serfdom* (1944), Barbara Wootton's response, *Freedom Under Planning* (1945), and Chester Barnard's review of the latter (1948:176–193).

popular consensus or from democratically elected officials. Indeed, Richard French has pointed out that in a democratic society, it has to be. "Planning cannot create political conviction. . . . Without political conviction based on popular perceptions, the planning enterprise is like a hothouse plant, with bright flowers and no roots" (1980:153).

In effect, as citizens we have to forfeit certain freedoms of choice in order to gain other benefits. This is much as we concluded about organizations themselves, which sometime have to forfeit participation for performance. Giving up all freedom of choice for the sake of planning clearly makes no sense. But no more so does giving up all formal coordination for the sake of unobstructed individual choice. We simply have to recognize the costs of the trade-offs necessary to achieve the right balance. And we must also be sensitive to the fact that planning itself is not neutral; as we shall see later in this chapter, there are biases in the process of planning that affect the outcomes.

The experiences of the Communist states stand as dramatic examples of the suspension of individual freedoms for the sake of unimpeded planning, with its own biases so evident that today hardly anyone is seriously proposing extensive government planning of the economy. How ironic, then, that the large corporations of the West—the central institutions in the unplanned, so-called free market economy—should have been the very ones to lead Western efforts to institutionalize formal planning! What was so terribly bad for the state, because of its effects on participation, commitment, and flexibility, became so awfully good for business, despite producing the very same effects. Indeed, those effects extended beyond the employees to the general citizens, if we accept John Kenneth Galbraith's arguments about the "new industrial states." Here we are reminded of those planners who so resisted being the objects of planning while they themselves insisted on subjecting everyone else to their planning.

In this regard, we cannot resist the temptation to quote Lorange and Vancil about formal planning as a means of catering to the objective of improving strategy making:

> An explicit, highly visible formal system was one way to meet the objective, even if it also involved a certain amount of bureaucratic documentation and red tape. In many companies, that objective

has now been achieved, and some of the trappings of the formal
apparatus can be allowed to wither. (1977:xiv)

Their choice of words is intriguing, since one cannot help but be
reminded of the Bolsheviks' promises about the "withering" of the
state bureaucracy once the Communist revolution had been consolidated. Indeed, the voluntary withering of planning groups
seems to have been about as common in American corporations as
it was in Communist governments!

As corporations grow large, of course, state and private planning grow closer. To quote Galbraith: "the modern large corporation and the modern apparatus of socialist planning are variant
accommodations to the same need" (1967:33). Or as Lewis put it
more simply, "the truth is that we are all planners now" (1969:4,
and, we might add, the destruction of Communism notwithstanding).

Back in 1959, James Worthy articulated this same point, comparing especially the planning of the East with the scientific management of the West (which Jelinek claimed to be the precursor of
corporate planning):

There are interesting parallels between communism and scientific
management. In both cases workers are seen as means rather than
ends, doers rather than planners or initiators; to be manipulated—by persuasion is possible, by coercion if necessary—in other
interests and for other needs than their own. (1959:78)

Indeed, Worthy pointed out that Soviet Russia was where "Scientific management has had its fullest flowering. . . . And Russia's
planning has been characterized as 'an attempt to do on a national
scale what scientific management was doing within the individual
plant' " (77, quoting Filipetti). Worthy, in fact, recalled efforts by
early American followers of Taylor to impose just such planning
on American society. For example, he quoted Henry Gantt that
"finance and industry must be socialized somehow," proposing
"The New Machine," which Worthy referred to as "a fantastic
organization" to create the "Planned Society" (76). This may sound
extreme, but Worthy's warning of 1959 sounds awfully contemporary:

Today it is unfashionable to speak of planning outside the particular enterprise—for that involves government, and all "right-minded people" want less, not more, government interference in economic affairs. But let there be a serious downturn in business, let the present smooth functioning of markets collapse under the blows of economic adversity, and the habit of mind that thinks in terms of mechanistic organization of the enterprise will make it easy to think in terms of mechanistic organization of the economy. (1959:79)

Commitment Versus Calculation

In choosing to plan formally, as noted above organizations sometimes have to give up participation for performance. But as Allaire and Firsirotu pointed out, sometimes they in fact adopt planning to make up for the absence of such commitment in the first place. These authors found that more and more Western corporations "are peopled by mobile, calculative managers and technicians who will not buy (and are not offered) the traditional psychological contract of life-long employment and secure promotions in exchange for loyalty and devotion to the corporation's aims" (1990:106). This tends to "irredeemably cut" the "bond of legitimacy and credibility" between senior managers and others, "with nothing to replace it but control by numbers or by corporate staff enforcement" (12).

What this suggests is that culture and planning may be alternate ways to manage an organization, one more concerned with commitment, the other with calculation.

That planning is more concerned with the calculation of things than the commitment of people is reflected in its emphasis on formalization. This can be seen in the treatment of strategy formation as a detached, analytical process, to be executed by systems rather than people. Consider how Ansoff summarized his own model:

The underlying methodology is a succession of difference reduction steps: a set of objectives is identified for the firm, the current position with respect to the objectives is diagnosed, and a difference between these (or what we called the "gap") is determined. Then a search is instituted for an operator (strategy) which can reduce the gap. The operator is tested for its "gap reducing" properties. If the properties are satisfactory (the gap is essentially closed) the operator is accepted; if the gap is partially closed the operator is provisionally accepted and an additional operator is sought; if the operator is marginal or negative in its ability to close the gap, it is rejected and a new one is sought. (1964:73)

In today's jargon, Ansoff might be accused of "neutron bombing" the strategy making process: eliminating the people so that the procedures can get on with the process! The problem, unfortunately, is that analytical detachment on the front end, in formulation, tends to impede personal commitment on the back end, in implementation.

Some years ago, Air Canada embarked on "Rapidair," an experimental shuttle service between Montreal and Toronto. But it failed to guarantee a seat on the airplane. When customers continued to book seats, the airline backed off the shuttle nature of the service—after only a few *days*. The attitude was not one of commitment—"Let's make this thing work"—but of calculation—"Oh well, we tried, didn't we" (in Mintzberg, Brunet, and Waters, 1986). Contrast this with IBM's development of the 360 computer system in the 1960s (in Wise, 1966, a, b). The project was initiated as an act of faith: the company executives decided to reconceive their entire product line with only a very general set of guidelines concerning a form of technology, the linking of different models, and so on. No serious calculation was even possible. And so, in place of detailed planning at the outset, there was enough firm commitment to see it through. This change was sustained by inspiration, while the other was subverted by calculation.

Brunsson has been one of the few to address this issue on a conceptual level. He contrasted a "commitment building type" of behavior—more an act of will than a cognitive process, which tends to produce a high rate of acceptance—with a "critically scrutinizing type" of behavior, of which he wrote:

> personal risk is avoided mainly by refraining from responsibility and commitment. The evaluators try to cope with the uncertainty in the situation by cognitive processes. One tries to take all important variables into account in calculating what decision is best. The emotional involvement in the accepted projects is disregarded. This type is more apt to reject than to accept . . . In addition, acceptances are not very committing. (1976:172)

We do not wish to push this distinction too far—clearly organizations need both calculation and commitment. But we do wish to point out that by so tilting its priorities to one side, the planning school may have had a negative effect on the sustainment of personal commitment in organizations.

Analytical staff people, including planners, have sometimes accused managers of being too emotional, too involved in their pet projects, lacking the detachment needed to assess proposals objectively. This can certainly be a valid criticism. But the other side of the coin—clear in the IBM 360 story and in the incredible popularity of Peters and Waterman's 1982 book, *In Search of Excellence*—is that deep commitment, all-out support, is a necessary prerequisite to the successful pursuit of difficult courses of action. And that commitment seems to grow out of personal control, a sense of ownership of a project (hence the popularity of the word "champion"), not deeply constrained by the specifics of formal plans or the detachment of so-called objective calculations. When a British planning manager recently volunteered the comment to an interviewer that "Through the control process, we can stop managers falling in love with their businesses" (Goold, 1990), he may have had overly enthusiastic line managers in mind. But considered on its own, the statement is astonishing.

What is sometimes not appreciated is that there is no such thing as an "optimal" strategy, calculated via some formal process. Intended strategies have no value in and of themselves; they take on value only as committed people infuse them with energy (to paraphrase Selznick, 1957). That is why every problem of implementation is also one of formulation—not only for the actual strategies conceived but also for the process by which conception occurs. And that is why the planning pitfall of lacking top management support ultimately explained nothing.

Planning and Change

We now turn to the pitfall of a climate congenial to planning. Again, we wish to turn this around, suggesting that a climate congenial to planning may not always be congenial to effective strategy making, while a climate hostile to planning may sometimes prove effective for strategy making.

The Inflexibility of Plans

In the first chapter of this book, several reasons were delineated as to why planners believe organizations should plan. Planning is proposed to ensure that organizations coordinate and control their activities, take the future into account, and act "rationally." For some reason, these characteristics are implicitly linked to claims about planning stimulating creativity as well as providing a means to deal with change in general and "turbulent" conditions in particular. Thus, *The Journal of Business Strategy* (November-December, 1990:4) introduced an article with the claim that "Because the planning process is where change originates, planners are in a unique position to provide leadership." And Lorange, Gordon, and Smith proposed that "one measure of planning's effectiveness . . . will be the degree of frequency of major organizational and other systems changes" (1979:32). In fact, there is no systematic evidence that planning does any of these things, and no shortage of anecdotal (as well as some systematic) evidence that it can do exactly the opposite.

Almost a century ago Henri Fayol, one of planning's earliest and best-known proponents, noted that the very purpose of planning is not to encourage flexibility but to reduce it, that is, to establish clear direction within which resources can be committed in a coordinated way. In the ensuing years, Fayol's message was lost on all but a few writers. One of the latter was William Newman, who wrote back in 1951: "The establishment of advanced plans tends to make administration inflexible; the more detailed and widespread the plans the greater the inflexibility" (63). Or as Ramanujam and Ventakraman put it later, "planning systems need to be more rigid than conventional wisdom currently advocates. . . . Concrete isn't such a bad material in which to cast a plan—compared to clay or putty" (1985:23, 24)!

Newman attributed the inflexibility of planning to several psychological factors: making "the executive feel too secure and thus inattentive to changes"; "a tendency, having once prepared a plan, to 'make it work' "; and "psychological resistance" due to the establishment of "mind-set" and fear of "loss of face" if plans are changed (1951:63). His points did, in fact, receive support in the psychology laboratory. Of even the informal "plans" we develop in our heads, Miller, Galanter, and Pribram found:

> the realization that an enduring Plan must be changed at a strategic level can cause a considerable upheaval in the person's Image as well as in his Plans. A rule that most people seem to learn, probably when they are very young, is: When in the execution of a Plan it is discovered that an intended subplan is not relevant or is not feasible, the smallest possible substitutions of alternative tactical subplans are to be attempted first, and the change in strategy is to be postponed as long as possible. (1960:114)

These researchers in fact suggested that the abandonment of personal plans could produce psychological problems, the change being "accompanied by a great deal of emotional excitement" possibly followed by "anxiety"; the individual (much like some organizations we all know) "may then develop Plans to cope with the anxiety (defense mechanisms) instead of developing new Plans to cope with the reality"! (116).

This research pertains only to individuals. Imagine, then, having to change the formal plans of an entire organization—of the hundreds or thousands of individuals already directed to behave in a particular way. As Lewis noted:

> planning by direction has to be inflexible. Once the planners have made the thousands of calculations that are necessary to fit the plan together, and have issued their directions, any demand that any of the figures be revised is bound to be resisted. That plan once made must be adhered to simply because you cannot alter any part of it without altering the whole, and altering the whole is too elaborate a job to be done frequently. (1969:17)

Planning, as noted, is meant for coordination. And the more tightly coordinated the plan, the less flexible it must be. Change one serious part of an integrated plan and it *dis*integrates.

The planning literature expresses clearly the need to make strategy explicit. But the more clearly articulated the strategy, the greater the resistance to its change—due to the development of both psychological and organizational momentum. Indeed, Kiesler (1971) found that having people in a psychology laboratory merely articulate a strategy that they were about to apply anyway stiffened their resistance to changing it later. As for bureaucratic momentum, we saw in our own study of U.S. government strategies in the Vietnam conflict (Mintzberg, 1978) that when Lyndon Johnson formally articulated the strategy of escalation that had been emerging over the previous four years, the bureaucracy ran with it far beyond his expectations—they *over*realized the explicated strategy—and it subsequently became that much more difficult to stop.

A strategy is formulated to direct energies in a certain direction; momentum is, therefore, not only the inevitable result but the desired one. And the more clearly the strategy is articulated, the more deeply embedded it becomes, in both the habits of the organization and the minds of its people. Thus the greater becomes its momentum. The price, of course, is the organization's ability to change when it must, sooner or later. If later, articulation may have proved to be a good thing. But eventually that price must be paid. Even if planners may be sure for now, they cannot be sure forever.

The Inflexibility of Planning

So far our argument about inflexibility has focused mostly on the plans themselves, which, especially when clearly articulated, tend to breed a resistance to change. But what about the planning process? In what may be a more controversial, but ultimately more important point, we wish to argue that planning itself breeds a basic inflexibility in organizations, and so a resistance to significant change. Unterman, for example, after reviewing the popular "Stanford method" of strategic planning, concluded from his own consulting experience that "he has yet to see any drastic or major corporate revisions resulting from it" (1974:41).

Planning is fundamentally a conservative process: it acts to conserve the basic orientation of the organization, specifically its existing categories. Thus, planning may promote change in the organization, but of a particular kind: change within the context of the organization's overall orientation, change at best in strategic positions within the overall strategic perspective. Expressed differently, in our view planning works best when the broad outlines of a strategy are already in place, not when significant strategic change is required from the process itself.

Formally planned change of the kind we are suggesting tends to have three essential characteristics: (a) it is incremental rather than quantum, (b) it is generic rather than creative, and (c) it is oriented to the short term rather than the long term. Let us consider each in turn.

Planned Change as Incremental

As we noted in our review of the Quinn study (1980a), the practice of planning "usually institutionalized a form of incrementalism" (see also Burgelman, 1983c:1359 and Brunsson, 1982:43). This likely happens because incremental change—change at the margin, of limited scope—is consistent with the established orientation of the organization, as is planning itself. In contrast, quantum change—which means comprehensive reorientation (Miller and Friesen, 1984)—disrupts all the established categories of the organization, on which planning depends. As a result, such change tends to be resisted, or more commonly, ignored, in the planning process.

Recall that planning depends on decomposition, which provides sharply defined sets of categories. These almost always reflect what already exists in the organization. In other words, planning maps onto the currently used categories, strategic as well as structural; it does not tend to invent new ones. For example, planning tends to proceed in terms of the existing product-market strategies (sometimes defined as strategic business units). Earlier we discussed planning at Air Canada in terms of five little airlines, one of which was labelled "thin" southern routes. As we noted, how could the company consider thickening them when its planning process proceeded on the assumption that they were thin? As Tregoe and Zimmerman commented:

> Without a clear strategic framework to define what the organization wants to be, long-range planning is forced to build a composite

picture of the organization by projecting every detail of the business forward. . . . Such effort acts as a deterrent to change; it transforms most long-range plans into Gothic structures of inflexibility. (1980:26)

Note a key implication of this: that rather than creating new strategies, planning cannot proceed without their prior existence. Freeman offers a useful analogy here, to the manager whose filing system breaks down because the old categories do not fit the new documents, and so everything ends up under "Miscellaneous." "Cross referencing becomes such a nightmare that you and your secretary finally give up. Planning imposes a fixed filing system on the organization, good only so long as old categories are relevant" (1984:7).

Perhaps more important is that planning almost inevitably overlays these existing strategies as well as its own procedures on the existing structure of the organization. In other words, organizations develop their plans in terms of the subunits they already have—be they functions, divisions, or departments. As Durand noted in his survey of planning in French business, ". . . in most firms, the Strategic Planning Procedures have been designed according to the organizational structure. Actually, to be able to present their planning procedures, most interviewees first outlined the structure of their firm" (1984:11).

The problem, here again, is that planning in terms of the existing categories discourages the reordering of things, which is generally a prerequisite to major change—strategic as well as structural.[2] As Gray noted:

When strategic planning is newly installed, it is often assumed that the organizational units already in place should handle the planning. These units, however, may owe their boundaries to many factors that make them inappropriate to use as a basis for planning: geography, administrative convenience, the terms of old acquisition deals, product lines, traditional profit centers, a belief in

---

[2] This may explain why the planning school seems to have given much less attention to the design of structure, in the implementation phase, than did the design school. Structure, too, is less mutable when it serves as the framework for planning.

healthy internal competition, or old ideas about centralization and decentralization. (1986:93)

Moreover, as Tregoe and Zimmerman pointed out, there is the problem of effecting change when planning consists of integrating the existing unit plans into a comprehensive one. "Long-range plans are built up from the lowest levels, where information exists to make projections. These projections from various parts of the organization are consolidated and, in total, become the recommended plan. By the time these accumulated and detailed plans reach the top, there is virtually no opportunity for injecting fresh insight about the future" (1980:25).[3]

Planning exhibits other characteristics that encourage incremental change at the expense of more quantum change. One is its "lockstep" schedule, which leaves "little or no slack" and puts "great time pressures on managers to keep the system on schedule" (deVillafranca, 1983b:1). This hardly encourages them to consider disruptive alternatives. Besides, "problems, opportunities, and 'bright ideas' do not arise according to some set timetable;

---

[3] Organizations have tied themselves into all kinds of knots attempting to avoid these problems. For example, under PPBS, McNamara tried to separate the "operating" categories of structure (Army, Navy, Air Force, Marines, Coast Guard) from the "mission" categories of strategy (deterrence, limited warfare, etc.). But "this split created conflicts and a lack of coordination" (Ansoff, 1984:40). And so General Electric "used a different solution": trying to make the strategic business units responsible for both strategy and operations. "But as [it] and other companies have found, the historical organizational structure does not map simply on to the newly identified [Strategic Business Area] and the resulting responsibilities are not clear cut and unambiguous" (40). As Gluck et al. noted:

> You can only really know the proper definition of an SBU when you have an agreed strategy: different strategic thrusts require the inclusion of different product-market units and functional capabilities within the SBU. But one purpose of the SBU strategy is to provide a framework for planning. Which came first, strategy or structure?
> Second, in most companies, the planning structure is force-fitted into the current organizational structure, or the other way around. Both are equally unsatisfactory. The planning structure should be shaped around tomorrow's concepts of the business. An organizational structure is responsible for implementing today's strategies as well; when the two are different, conflict is inevitable.
> It should not be surprising, therefore, that no one has been able to prescribe an entirely acceptable definition of an SBU, or describe satisfactorily how to derive an SBU structure. SBU definition remains something of a black art . . . (in Hax and Majluf, 1984:37)

they have to be dealt with whenever they happen to be perceived" (Anthony, 1965:38; Gomer [1974] made this especially clear in his study of the Swedish firms' responses to the energy crisis). As we have argued elsewhere, the repetitive nature of the annual planning process "can easily become a mechanical extrapolation of information. That kind of exercise, like 'crying wolf too often,' may actually desensitize top managers to strategic issues, so that the need for substantive change may not be recognized when it does arise" (Mintzberg and Waters, 1982:494). Managers may be so busy discussing strategies and budgets on schedule year after year that when real change becomes necessary, they miss it.

As Quinn remarked, the "mechanics often begin to overwhelm thought processes" (1980a:169). When that happens, organizations get not even incremental change but straight extrapolation of the status quo. "What passes for planning is frequently the projection of the familiar into the future," claimed Henry Kissinger (1969:20). Or to quote another famous political figure: "Planning is deciding to put one foot in front of the other" (Winston Churchill, in Rogers, 1975:56).

In fact, efforts to tie strategic planning to operational budgeting—which received great attention in the planning literature, at least in principle—also encourage change that is incremental, for just as the strategy is supposed to drive the budget, so too does the budget constrain the strategy. Operational budgeting is a device for short-term control, not long-term change ("the figures have to conform to the next year's budget, which is traditionally a method of restraint and control" [Rossotti, n.d., circa 1965:6]). Moreover, such budgeting is also mapped onto the existing organizational structure, in its case usually down to the smallest subunit. So the tendency again is to preserve the established direction.

Thus, in the context of the business firm, even Ansoff has commented that "planning has been most successful when it dealt with extrapolation of the past dynamics of the firm and least successful to non-incremental major departures from the historical growth trends of the firm" (1975b:75). In the context of big government, Lindblom noted about the Eastern European nations, which dedicated such enormous resources to the process, that "economic planning ... consists of remedial, sequential, incremental alterations of the production scheduled for the previous period"

(1977:325). And even in the context of the single mind, Miller, Galanter, and Pribram have noted that "Probably the major source of new Plans is old Plans. We change them around a little bit each time we use them, but they are basically the same old Plans with minor variations. Sometimes we may borrow a new Plan from someone else. But we do not often create a completely new Plan" (1960:117). No matter what the context, then, planning seems to become another "aspect of what de Jouvenel calls 'modern fatalism,' i.e., the conception of the future as mostly linear derivations of the present" (in Gluntz, 1971:11). Ironically then, given our current propensities, in order to take our destiny into our own hands—to become truly proactive—we would seem to need not more planning but less!

Planned Change as Generic

Creativity, by definition, rearranges established categories. Planning, by its very nature, preserves them. That is one reason why planning does not easily handle truly creative ideas. It should, therefore, have come as no surprise to Michael Allen, ex-head of planning for General Electric, that "despite all [its] gains, the development of creative strategy . . . remains the Achilles' heel of business planning" (1985:6). In a survey published in 1985, Javidan found that 60 percent of the CEOs, 50 percent of the division managers, and even 40 percent of the chief planning officers themselves responded that the planning department had "a somewhat negative impact" on managerial innovativeness (1985:91). To quote David Hurst:

> [Strategic planning] is helpful for looking *backward* rather than *forward*, for what it *excludes* rather than what it *contains*. [Strategic planning] cannot tell managers where they are going, only where they have been. It is useful for managing today's business, the business that already exists. (1986:15)

Being subjected to planning means being locked into set categories that generally discourage real creativity. As Newman wrote back in 1951, the rise of planning departments and plans tend to circumscribe the discretion of the man on the firing line. Thus, it usually is true that with more extensive planning a large group of employees have less freedom in the exercise of their own judgement. Conformity, rather than originality, is expected of them. This restriction on initiative tends to snuff out the creative spark that is so essential in successful enterprise, and it also has a bad effect on morale. (1951:68)

"Creativity," to quote yet another of those GE planners, "diminishes under the weight of big, thick leather binders" (Carpenter, in Potts, 1984). In effect, plans are blinders put in place to block out peripheral vision—to keep their subjects focused clearly on the established direction. And to tie back to our earlier discussion, creativity depends above all on the wholehearted commitment of the originator, which the calculations of planning can discourage. "Creative thought requires an act of faith" (George Gilder quoted in Peters and Waterman, 1982:47).

Sawyer commented eloquently that "a plan, as a snapshot of a process, is a closed analysis of an open system" (1983:180). But when he went on to characterize "planning as a creative process" (the title of the last section and, with the adjective "corporate," of his entire monograph), arguing that the process as well as the function "logically become the center of the creative, innovative activity in the firm" (174), we part company with him, concluding that their effect is more often exactly the opposite. At 3M, for example, a company noted for its creativity, the planning system was described by one executive as "exceptionally good . . . for the analysis and direction of existing businesses," but " 'pretty low' on identifying opportunities" (in Kennedy, 1988:16).

Generic means well-defined, belonging to a class, which implies that the categories of change have already been worked out, perhaps by some other organization that did the innovating (as when Burger King "McDonaldized" its strategy years ago). This seems to be more compatible with formalized planning. In fact, we suspect that the proliferation of "mainline," or generic, strategies in American business in recent years (and of the concept of "generic strategies" itself in the literature, dating primarily from Porter, 1980) corresponds to the rise to popularity of formal procedures of planning. Thus Quinn found in the "formalities" of decision making "an important reason why most revolutionary innovations originate outside the industries they upset" (1980a:174).

Planned Change as Short Term

Planning, of course, is supposed to look far ahead. "The faster one drives, then the further one's headlights must throw their beams," argued Godet (1987:xiv, quoting Berger), in a homily he presented in support of planning.[4] But headlights throw their beams only straight ahead (with decreasingly effective illumination over distance, it should be added), while roads tend to have dips and curves; driving fast enough in this way might be a sure way to kill yourself.

Another problem with planning, therefore, is precisely this: it can look into the future only in the way headlights look down a road. That is, to say (as we shall discuss at length in Chapter 5), planning relies on formal techniques of forecasting to look into the future, and the evidence is that none of these can predict discontinuous changes in the environment. So planning, again always in the formal sense, cannot do much more than extrapolate the known trends of the present.

That is why Weick concluded that "Plans seem to exist in a context of justification more than in a context of anticipation. They refer more to what has been accomplished than to what is yet to be accomplished" (1969:102). When "far ahead" means straight ahead, planning can be long term only if the environment cooperates—either remains unchanged, or is easily predictable (in terms of known trends or cycles), or else acquiesces to whatever strategies the organization chooses to impose on it. Otherwise the perspective becomes short term.

Moreover, to the extent that planning links to budgeting (or becomes synonymous with it), the attention of the managers lower down gets riveted on the short term. As Quinn noted, "These operating managers know that their long-term plans will soon be

---

[4] Another he offered was "the longer a tree takes to grow, then the less time there is to lose in planting it," without bothering to explain why a few days spent finding the right site will make such a difference over the decades the tree will grow.

converted into tight operating budgets, one- to six-month program commitments, and financial performance measurement systems that emphasize the present, the current month, or the current quarter" (1980a:175). So why should they worry about the long term when they do their planning?

Flexible Planning: Wanting Things Both Ways

George Steiner once acknowledged the inflexibility of planning: "Plans are commitments, or should be, and thus they limit choice. They tend to reduce initiative in a range of alternatives beyond the plans." Then he added, "This should not be a serious limitation, but should be noted" (1979:46). But why isn't it? Because he says so. Indeed, it is a profound limitation.

Steiner reflects here a widespread tendency in this literature: wanting to have things both ways. Earlier in our discussion, it was the desire for decentralized planning—engendering participation while maintaining tight coordination. And before that it was Ansoff wanting to formalize the planning process while allowing the organization to retain its entrepreneurial character. Ackoff characterized planning as a continuous process that somehow manages to cough up strategies on schedule (1970:3). But that is no problem (to him at least) because the plan is only "an interim report" (5). But what about those expected to implement it? Ansoff as well as Ackoff (who promoted the "systems" approach) argued that planning can somehow be made ever more comprehensive while never losing control over programming the details. It has been as if dilemmas don't exist in this field, which may just reflect how far the rhetoric has gotten ahead of the practice. As Wildavsky put it, "planning stands for unresolved conflicts" (1973:146).

Chief among these is the "be flexible but do not alter your course" presumption, again in Wildavsky's words (146). In the first issue of the *Academy of Management Journal*, in 1958, Harold Koontz wrote that "effective planning requires that the need for flexibility be a major consideration in the selection of plans" (55). And in the third decade after that, Gluck et al. added that "while planning as comprehensively and thoroughly as possible, [the most advanced] companies also try to keep their planning process flexible and creative" (1980:159). The man who held what was one of America's most prestigious planning positions, heading it for General Motors, must have been listening because in his speech on "Innovative Management" to the 1986 Planning Forum Conference he kept talking about "managing our business to stay on that trajectory" or "preplanned flight path" alongside reminders that "change is a way of life," without ever addressing the obvious contradiction.[5]

Somehow, planners want to retain the stability that planning brings to an organization—planning's main contribution—while enabling it to respond quickly to external changes in the environment—planning's main nemesis. Amazingly, the contradiction is hardly ever addressed by anyone. Like a progressive conservative, flexible planning remains just another oxymoron, a reflection of vain hopes rather than practical realities.

What the writers on planning failed to address was the strategists' fundamental dilemma of having to reconcile the concurrent but conflicting needs for change and stability. On one hand, the world is always changing—more *or* less—and so organizations must adapt. On the other hand, most organizations need a basic stability in order to function efficiently. Weick captured the dilemma well, contrasting the sacrificing of "future adaptability for current good fit," or else being perpetually ready to respond to everything in principle but nothing in practice (1979:247).

As we have already argued, planning by its very nature generally opts for stability over adaptability. Lorange et al. (1979), for example, contrasted in four airlines "adaptive" with "integrative" types of planning, one concerned with the development of strategy, the other with control and implementation, and found that while the latter tended to be well established and formalized, the former received less attention and was generally carried out only informally by management itself. Indeed, as we noted in our study of another airline, Air Canada, during a crisis provoked by a reorganization, planning saved the day by ensuring operating continuity while the senior managers struggled with the changes.

---

[5] Michael Naylor's oral comments were recorded by the author at The Planning Forum's Montreal conference, May 5, 1986.

Reflecting this orientation to stability, Marks, a planning practitioner, railed against the "particularly dangerous" habit of "ad hoc reactions" in times of rapid change; what the firm needs, he argued, is "consistent action" (1977:5). But how in the world can a management be consistent when it has to respond to a world unfolding in an unexpected way? Planning may provide "consistent action" all right, but rooted in a lost stability.

What seems to be forgotten in much of the rhetoric of planning is that organizations must function not only *with* strategy but *during* periods of the formation of strategy, when the world is changing in ways not yet well understood. The danger during such periods is *premature closure*, settling too early on that "consistent action," especially when it is the one already in place for previous conditions. At such points, questions may be better than answers.

A danger inherent in all analytical approaches, planning included, is the tendency to close on strategies prematurely: to skip past the creative but uncomfortable stage of inventing new models or strategies, in order to get down to the more settled job of programming the consequences of the ones readily at hand. Thus, management cannot turn to conventional planning practice when faced with uncertain change (although it may be able to find help from unconventional planners, as we shall discuss in Chapter 6).

"Flexible planning" thus reduces the process to sheer confusion, or else, if recognized for what it is, simply folds into another process commonly known as management.[6] The very reason organizations use planning is to be inflexible—to set direction—"even though," as Kepner and Tregoe put it, the plans "are usually presented in three-ring binders as evidence of their flexibility" (1980:26). Thus, Lenz and Lyles reported that "When queried about his firm's strategic plan, [one planning officer they interviewed] placed before us a three-inch-thick ring binder containing, in seemingly endless detail, the annual plan. He dubbed it 'the beast'!" (1985:69). Some flexibility!

---

[6] "When planning is placed in the context of continuous adjustment it becomes hard to distinguish from any other process of decision," or, more to the point, "by making planning reasonable, we render it inseparable from the techniques of decision it was designed to supplant" (Wildavsky, 1973:135 and 1979:128).

The untenability of planning's view of change is reflected in Henri Fayol's turn-of-the-century use of the analogy of a ship at sail to emphasize planning's role in maintaining stability:

> unwarranted changes of course are dangers constantly threatening businesses without a plan. The slightest contrary wind can turn from its course a boat which is unfitted to resist. . . . regrettable changes of course may be decided upon under the influence of profound but transitory disturbance . . . [compared with] a program carefully pondered at an undisturbed time. . . . the plan protects the business not only against undesirable changes of course which may be produced by grave events, but also against those arising simply from changes on the part of higher authority. Also, it protects against deviations imperceptible at first, which end by deflecting it from its objective. (1949:49)

The assumptions underlying these comments are intriguing: that change of course is a bad thing, "contrary winds" being threats and organizational responses to them being "undesirable" and "regrettable." Courses should be set in "undisturbed" times, namely before the winds begin to blow. Above all, the organization must never be deflected from its set course. A good way to deal with the occasional gust perhaps, but a heck of a way to cope with hurricanes (let alone icebergs, or news of the discovery of gold on a different island).

Of course, Fayol had gusts in mind—minor perturbations rather than major discontinuities. And he assumed the organization knew a great deal about the waters in question. These are, of course, the conditions where planning makes the most sense, where the price of inflexibility is relatively low (assuming the ability to forecast accurately). As Makridakis pointed out,

> Strategy . . . should not change at the first sign of difficulty. A fair amount of persistence will be required to get beyond difficulties and problems. On the other hand, if substantial environmental changes are occurring, if competitors' reactions have been misjudged, or if the future is turning out contrary to expectations, strategy must be modified to take such changes into account. In other words, strategy must adapt: It is better to follow a side alley that leads somewhere than to finish at a dead end. (1990:173)

And in that case, the organization may well be advised to discard its plans as well as its formal process of planning. A common problem is that it does not.

The "disturbance" at the infamous World War I battle of Passchendaele was not the wind but the rain. According to Feld, it was sunny when the plans were made at corps headquarters; as a result, 250,000 British troops fell:

> The critics argued that the planning of Passchendaele was carried out in almost total ignorance of the conditions under which the battle had to be fought. No senior officer from the Operations Branch of the General Headquarters, it was claimed, ever set foot (or eyes) on the Passchendaele battlefield during the four months that battle was in progress. Daily reports on the condition of the battlefield were first ignored, then ordered discontinued. Only after the battle did the Army chief of staff learn that he had been directing men to advance through a sea of mud. (1959:21)

To quote Stokesbury's account in his history of World War I, the "great plan" was implemented despite the effect of the steady, drenching rain on the battlefield—despite the fact that the guns clogged, that soldiers carrying heavy ammunition slipped off their paths into muddy shell holes and drowned, that the guns could not be moved forward and the wounded could not be brought backward. "Still the attack went on; they slept between sheets at corps headquarters and lamented that the infantry did not show more offensive spirit."

> [A] staff officer . . . came up to see the battlefield after it was all quiet again. He gazed out over the sea of mud, then said half to himself, "My God, did we send men to advance in that?" after which he broke down weeping and his escort led him away. Staff officers . . . complained that infantrymen failed to salute them. (1981:241, 242)

What causes human beings to behave in this way? The story is extreme, but anyone who has spent time in the world of organizations knows that similar behaviors are all too common. What is it about planning that causes us to close down our minds, to block out perceptions? Are we that afraid of uncertainty? Or that enamored of our own formal powers of reason?

To conclude this discussion of planning and change: for one thing, it suggests various reasons, besides the obvious ones, why organizations plan, some having to do with our psychological makeup as human beings, a point we shall return to shortly. For another, we learn that planning seems more suited to the sustenance of stable operations for purposes of efficiency than to the creation of new ones for purposes of change. We shall eventually return to this point as well. Finally, we find that people may resist planning, not because of their "fear of change" (to quote Taylor, 1976:67), but for exactly the opposite reason: some people may resist planning because of their fear of *stability,* while others may *embrace* planning because of their fear of change!

Planning and Politics

The implication in the pitfall literature is that political activity interferes with planning, that planning is an apolitical, objective exercise that is undermined by the pursuit of self-interest through confrontation and conflict. Here we wish to take this argument apart, showing first that planning is not as objective as its proponents claim, second that sometimes it may in fact breed certain kinds of political activity, and third that other kinds of political activity can sometimes prove more functional for organizations than planning.

The Biases of Objectivity

What kind of climate does planning itself foster? What are its own values? Planners are apt to respond that their own processes are value-free, that they respond to the situation at hand with an objectivity and a rationality designed to ensure that the organization pursues *its own* values as efficiently as possible. In other words, they depict themselves as hired guns, with techniques in their holsters. But let us consider the planners' own rationality, and *its* rationality—that is, whether the objectivity of planning is all that objective.

To begin, conventional planners are biased about objectivity, at least their own form of it. To borrow a quotation used for another group of analysts (operations researchers), they "exhibit a passionate attachment to dispassion" (Corpio et al., 1972:B-621). Or as Orlans put it, "the brain is not a bloodless organ" (1975:107). As we have already seen, processes that are not *verifiably* objective—intuition being one good example—tend to get dismissed by planners. Alternatively, processes that *seem* to be formally rational—planning itself being the best example—are embraced as exemplary. Typical of this sentiment (if rather more blatantly expressed) is the comment by Collier that companies yet to see the light of planning are "immature," unlike the "large, well-established companies . . . with a clear pattern of management system, understood at all levels of management" (1968:79). Planners like this are not objective at all—not about planning or technique or analysis or even about the organizations that use them (since, for example, they tend to favor large organizations, namely those most inclined to use formal planning).

In his book about *The Art and Craft of Policy Analysis,* Aaron Wildavsky addressed this issue in some depth, especially the concept of "rationality." His comments are worth quoting at length:

> In reality, planning is not defended for what it accomplishes but for what it symbolizes—rationality. Planning is conceived to be the way in which intelligence is applied to social problems. . . . Key words appear over and over: planning is good because it is *systematic* rather than random, *efficient* rather than wasteful, *coordinated* rather than helter-skelter, *consistent* rather than contradictory, and above all, *rational* rather than unreasonable. (1979:129)

Wildavsky then proceeded to take these words apart, one by one:

> • What does it mean to say that decisions should be made in a systematic manner? A word like "careful" will not do because planners cannot be presumed to be more careful than other people. Perhaps "orderly" is better; it implies a checklist of items to be taken into account, but anyone can make a list. "Systematic" as a designation implies further that one knows the right variables in the correct order to put into the list, and

can specify their relationships. The essential meaning of systematic, therefore, is having qualities of a system—that is, a series of variables whose interactions are known and whose outputs can be predicted from knowledge of their inputs. . . . To say that one is being systematic, consequently, implies that one has causal knowledge, whether one does or does not. (131)

• Coordination is one of the golden words of our time. Offhand I can think of no way in which the word is used that implies disapproval. Policies should be coordinated; they should not run every which way. No one wants his child described as uncoordinated. Many of the world's ills are attributed to lack of coordination in government. But what does it mean? Policies should be mutually supportive rather than contradictory. People should not work at cross-purposes . . . Coordination means achieving efficiency and reliability, consent and coercion. Telling other people to achieve coordination, therefore, does not tell them whether to coerce or bargain or stipulate what mixture of efficiency and reliability to attempt. (131, 133)

• Consistency may be conceived of as vertical (over a series of periods extending into the future) or horizontal (at a moment in time). Vertical consistency requires that the same policy be pursued for a time, horizontal consistency that it mesh with others at the same time . . . One requires rigidity to ensure continuity, the other, flexibility to achieve accommodation with other policies. Be firm, be pliant, are hard directions to follow simultaneously. (133)

• By "rational" . . . we mean something like intended, designed, or purposeful. Something happens because it is supposed to. Rational behavior is action appropriately calculated to achieve a desired state of affairs. . . . So-called norms of rationality . . . are devoid of content in that they do not tell anyone what to choose. (135)

Let us consider the objectivity of focusing on specific means to achieve any ends. As "hired guns," ostensibly there to help managers pursue whatever goals they think best for the organization, the planners merely provide the means. As Majone put it, planners "are more set upon deciding rightly than upon right decisions" (1976–77:204). It is the process that counts. But what if the process biases the results, the means influencing the ends (as it did with those real hired guns)? Consider the following. Ringbakk has written that "experience has shown that 'if you cannot write it down, you have not thought it through'" (1971:18). Here he is merely expressing the belief long-held in planning about the value of formalization and articulation. But experience has never shown anything of the kind. Nor has experience shown that "If you *have* written it down, you *have* thought it through." (One need only read much of the planning literature itself, let alone many of the corporate plans!)

The unfortunate fact is that some things are more easily written down than others—numbers for example, as opposed to impressions. As a result, planning systematically favors those kinds of information. We shall return to this important point later in our discussion. Here we simply wish to note, quoting Wildavsky, that "seemingly rational procedures [can] produce irrational results." Planning "sacrifices the rationality of ends to the rationality of means" (1979:207).

Another problem with objectivity is that it can be biased against people. As someone once quipped, to be objective all too often means to treat people as objects. Earlier we saw how the calculation built into planning can discourage the commitment of those subjected to it. Victor Thompson has referred to planners and other staff analysts as the "new Taylorites," to whom "human motivation is not problematic; it can be assumed" (1968:53).

This bias also helps to explain why conventional planners are so suspicious of intuition. It cannot be explicated—formally written down—and so it cannot be decomposed, ordered, controlled. The process is a mysterious one, hidden deep in the mind's subconscious, and subjected to the most human of feelings. But because intuition is not *formally* rational, that does not necessarily make it *irrational*.

The Goals Implicit in Planning

Planners may claim to work for the goals expressed by management. But their processes can have a profound effect on what those goals turn out to be. In other words, there are goals implicit in the use of planning itself that are, in part at least, forced on any organization that relies on the process. Like the rest of us, planners favor whatever goals favor them.

For one thing, as we have already noted, planning exhibits a bias toward a particular type of change in organizations—not quantum change, with which its procedures have difficulty coping, but incremental. Quantum change has to be controlled by senior line managers, if it is controlled at all, or else it may emerge through the actions of many people at the operating levels (see, for example, Mintzberg and McHugh, 1985).

As for the pace of change, the organization that never changes hardly needs planners (at least, after the first plan is made), while the one that changes sporadically may call on its planners only irregularly. So planners who wish to maximize their influence, and maintain regular employment, would naturally favor incremental change that is steady, ideally following the schedule built into the planning cycle (see Mintzberg, 1979b:126).

A preference for steady incremental change translates itself into conservative goals that preserve existing perspectives and avoid major risks. Thus Sheehan found that the firms with the greater involvement in planning experienced less variability in performance than the others (and in fact lower growth rates overall), resulting, in his words, in "greater firm stability and security" (1975:182). Likewise, Hamermesh found in his study of portfolio planning at General Electric that "planning activities that were focused on SBUs more often resulted in divestiture recommendations than in bold business initiatives" (1986:198).

Planning further influences organizational goals by its insistence on the articulation of these goals into quantifiable targets, which are necessary for the planning models, especially the setting of objectives at the front end and budgeting at the back end.[7] Conventional planners naturally assume that such goals are readily available and nothing gets lost in the process of quantification.

To elicit the goals they need, planners do not generally try to elicit consensus from all those who have a legitimate claim on the behavior of the organization—to use that so-called "stakeholder analysis." That these people would be willing to articulate their own goals, let alone be able to reach collective consensus on their

---

[7] Bourgeois (1980b:230) cited as emphasizing the need for operational goals at the start of the planning process a virtual who's who of the writers of the planning school, including Ackoff (1970), Ansoff (1965), Hofer and Schendel (1978), Steiner (1969), Anthony (1965), and Lorange and Vancil (1977).

different ones, is hardly evident, to say the least. Besides, the planners are hired by the senior managers, not the other stakeholders. So to elicit goals, they generally turn to these managers, assuming they will somehow reconcile all the differing interests. And that, of course, fosters a certain centralization in the organization, implicitly focusing influence at the top of its internal hierarchy.

The expectation of formal goals assumes not only that each of the different value dimensions of the organization can be articulated, but so too can all of the trade-offs between them. In other words, all goals are assumed to be reconcilable in a single statement of objectives. As Wildavsky expressed this in the public sector, these goals "exist somehow 'out there,'" as we quoted him earlier, each one "labeled as if they came out of a great national sausage machine in the sky" (1973:134). The further assumption is made that the objective function, and therefore the goals, will remain stable over the planning period, influenced neither by changes in external conditions nor realignment of the power coalitions.

Where all of those assumptions hold up least—most obviously in government but similarly in any complex power system, which must include a good deal of big business—planning has experienced its most dramatic failures. But success here may sometimes be more onerous, because it generally means that the values of top management take precedence over those of other influencers. To ask senior managers to reflect broad values for the organization sounds reasonable enough, but it has to be recognized that these people have their personal axes to grind as well, for example, a preference for the growth of the organization over the maximization of shareholder value per se (e.g., Berle and Means, 1968). Thus, van Gunsteren has argued that planners are led to "respect existing inequalities of power," or to "reproduce or reinforce existing power configurations" (1976:10):

> The planner does more than reformulate given goals. He participates in the setting of goals and thereby involves himself in politics. Moreover, the planner will design only plans that are politically feasible, and thereby sides with some people against others. (9)

Charles Lindblom, who has spent a career studying policy making in government, found the whole process of goal articulation to be artificial. He considered it rooted in the economic concept of the utility or welfare function, of which he wrote: "The fundamental reason why analysts do not employ a rational-deductive system or a welfare function in policy analysis is simply that no one has even been able actually to construct either" (in Braybrooke and Lindblom, 1963:22). Lindblom offered a variety of reasons for this, including the "multiplicity of values" that enter into policy making and the conflicts among them, as well as "the instability or fluidity of values" that "change with time and experience" (23, 26).

Government is, of course, among the most complex of human systems. But even in the simplest—decision making by the single individual—Soelberg found in a study of MBA students choosing their first job (as they were graduating from the MIT Sloan School of Management and so heavily steeped in analytical techniques) that:

> scalar utility theory is a poor way of representing the structure of human values. Decision value attributes are usually multidimensional; they are not compared or substituted for each other during choice. No stable utility weighting function can be elicited from a decision maker prior to his selection of a preferred alternative nor do such weights appear to enter into each person's decision processing. (1967:22)

If individuals cannot do this, how then can collections of individuals called organizations?

Cyert and March offered a suggestion as to how organizations reconcile different goals (say short-term and long-term profit, growth, and risk). They called it "sequential attention to goals" (1963:118). Different goals are favored for a time (or even for a decision), so that, over time rather than at any one time, some sort of rough balance is maintained. But that sort of adaptation is incompatible with conventional planning, which requires consistency of action.

Far more serious than the problem of who expresses the goals or how they are expressed are the very consequences of the expression process itself, which, in our view, produce one major systematic bias. Planning, as noted, is concerned with means, not ends. But its own preferred means is articulation, ideally quantification, and some goals lend themselves to it more easily than others.

Planning therefore favors those goals. As Marsh et al. found in their study of capital budgeting, "typically, hard-to quantify costs and benefits were excluded from the financial analysis" (1988:26).

Ackerman (1975) and others have shown that, in business at least, it is the economic goals, especially the shorter-term ones (such as immediate profit and growth in sales) that are most easily quantified. Other goals, longer-term and in some cases social (ranging from product quality to worker commitment), which may in fact foster profit on a more sustained basis, are less easily quantified. Thus organizations that favor planning may be driven toward a short-run economic focus that can impede not only social, but ironically, also long-run economic performance.[8]

The consequences of this in business may be a tendency to favor "cost leadership" strategies (that is, ones that emphasize internal operating efficiencies, which are generally measurable) over product leadership strategies (which emphasize innovative designs or higher quality, which tend to be less measurable), also to ignore strategies that cater to external stakeholders other than shareholders (since their needs are often less easily expressed as qualitative targets). Overall, the effect may be to reduce strategies to their basest elements, away from a rich and integrated perception of what an organization can do. As Bernard Taylor, a proponent of the planning school and editor of *Long Range Planning*, one of its best-known journals, wrote:

> Up to this point at least, formal planning systems have over-emphasized certain aspects of management, i.e., the economic, and the quantitative, and they have undervalued or omitted other considerations—e.g., the socio-political, the entrepreneurial and the creative aspects of strategy. In formal planning, strategy is all too often reduced to a game in resource allocation rather than a dialogue about the character of the enterprise and its future. (1975:29)

Thus, we find all kinds of systematic biases possible in planning: toward planning as an end in itself ("it's the process that

---

[8] Hayes argued that a short-term economic focus does not promote "truly sustainable competitive advantage," which takes time to develop. "Goals that can be achieved within five years are usually either too easy or based on buying and selling something. Anything that a company can buy or sell, however, is probably available for purchase or sale by its competitors as well" (1985:113).

counts") and the narrow form of rationality that it represents; away from intuition, creativity, and other forms of human expression; toward steady incremental change rather than periodic quantum change and therefore away from risk and boldness; toward centralized power in the organization and status quo interests and away from the needs of influencers whose stake in the organization is not formally economic; toward short-run economic goals and away from longer-run ones related to quality, innovation, social need, and even long-run economic performance; and toward simpler, impoverished forms of strategies themselves.

The Politics of Planning

The "climate congenial to planning" pitfalls inevitably cites political activity as detrimental to planning. Because planning is objective and comprehensive, the argument goes, politics, which is subjective and parochial, threatens it. For example, Wildavsky has commented that "McKean and Anshen speak of politics in terms of 'pressure and expedient adjustments,' 'haphazard acts . . . unresponsive to a planned analysis of the needs of efficient decision design.' From the political structure they expect only 'resistance and opposition' . . ." (1966:309).

But as we consider some of planning's real effects—the promotion of stability in the name of change, reification in the name of flexibility, detachment in the name of commitment, etc.—we might also begin to wonder if planning itself doesn't promote conflict in the name of harmony. Here again, therefore, we wish to turn the pitfall around, to suggest that planning's own particular type of objectivity, among other things, can be subjective and parochial, encouraging the very climate it considers uncongenial to its own practice.

We all know that issues are often more easily resolved in specific contexts than on general principles. For example, to get managers in marketing and manufacturing to agree on the relative importance of maximizing sales as opposed to minimizing costs may be impossible. But these people readily agree every day on sales and costs targets for specific products (perhaps through Cyert and March's sequential attention to their respective goals). The point comes out even more sharply in the political arena: parties on the left and the right may never agree in principle on the effort that should be put into stimulating the economy as opposed to enhancing social welfare programs, but they reach ad hoc compromises on these issues all the time.

By forcing managers to decide on goal trade-offs in the abstract rather than on choices in context, planning "can have the effect of sharpening the differences participants perceive between themselves and others, thereby increasing the conflict in the organization" (Whitehead, 1967:164). For example, this can bring to light "a lot of currently repressed conflicts" (Gluntz, 1971:7). In other words, just the act of setting objectives in a planning process can increase political activity among managers.

Perhaps this is why Bourgeois, in a study of twelve firms, found that agreement on strategies was a "significantly more important" factor in explaining performance than agreement on goals (1980b). To be specific, the firms whose managers agreed on strategies but disagreed on goals exhibited the best performance by far, while those whose agreements were the opposite (on goals but *not* on strategies) exhibited negative performance![9] The implication seems to be that the journey is more important than the destination: organizations may be better off agreeing on how they are traveling, so that everyone can pull together, rather than on where they will eventually end up.

There are also more direct ways in which planning, through its own practice, can produce political activity in organizations, as we have already seen at a number of points in our discussion. When planners put down the intuition of senior managers, when they pit their centralized systems against the decision making responsibility of middle line managers, when they act as watchdogs for top management, they create high potential for conflict in the organization. (Recall the comment by Rothschild of General Electric that "we tell the CEO when a manager is not on plan," also the re-

---

[9] Agreement as well as disagreement on both was associated with intermediate performance levels. These findings were reinforced by those of Grinyer and Norburn (1977/78). There remains, of course, the problem of inferring causation in these correlational studies. As Bourgeois himself pointed out, poor performance might cause managers to disagree on what strategies would rejuvenate the organization (1980b); likewise, everyone might agree on the goals required for turnaround.

sponse of the GE Appliance Group head to such planners, and Sarrazin's description of how the top managers of the French firm he studied used planning as a political tool to wrest power from managers at lower points in the hierarchy.) Indeed, all the fuss in the first pitfall about needing the support of top management can also be interpreted as a political ploy to lord the power of authority over junior managers who may resist planning. (Recall also Ansoff's critical comment that "If managers do not plan willingly, threaten them with the displeasure of the big boss and tell them that he loves planning.")

Allaire and Firsirotu pointed out that "the planning process may turn into a cat-and-mouse chase between staff planners and line managers" (1990:110). Part of the problem is that "planning drifts so easily to a staff-driven mode":

> [Planners] proximity and access to the ultimate source of power, their knowledge of corporate wide strategic information, their cognitive superiority at the games of planning and analysis, provide many opportunities for them to play, and be seen, as surrogate CEOs. Some line managers will cozy up to them, defer to their judgements; other will try to coopt them and manage the numbers and processes which appear important and relevant to them. This taste of power and authority has inebriated many a staff planner . . . (1990:113).

In effect, planning means control, at the very least over the processes by which decisions are made and interrelated, but more commonly over the premises that underlie those decisions if not over the actual decisions themselves. Now if it could be demonstrated empirically that planning is superior to other methods of making decisions and strategies, then planners could use logical arguments to wrest control from the line managers. But because, as we have seen, there is no such systematic evidence, planners have sometimes fallen back on arguments that, when not based on pure faith, ultimately turn out to be political in nature. We have already seen numerous examples of this, for example, in arbitrarily pronouncing planning's superiority, dismissing intuition, and using objectivity as a club against those who resist planning.

Ringbakk's comments, however polite, illustrate the point. "If the general management style is based on *last-minute* decisions, *hastily* arrived at by intuition, planning will not fit in. It results *naturally* when management uses *sound* analysis" (1971:17, italics added). "Would you like this nice thin meat, or that thick crappy stuff?" is how a friend used to react to such statements. Less polite are the words of Chakraborty and David in a *Planning Review* article, about managers who "jump to simplistic, naive solutions," who "resort to taking the path of least resistance to cover themselves," who "concentrate on staying busy," all of this to avoid a planning process that "exposes intuitive inconsistencies" (1979:19, 18—no italics necessary!). Or those of Kyogoku, who claims that strategy making "can no longer be left to the chance outcome of some vague, unstructured or ego-controlled process" (in Heirs and Pehrson, 1982, xxi). And planners accuse managers of provoking political conflict!

When battle lines are drawn between analysis and intuition, political conflict inevitably occurs because both sides rest on shaky ground. There can be no logical arguments to dismiss or support intuition because it does not work according to conventional logic. It is a subconscious process, which no one really understands, except by certain of its characteristics (such as the speed with which it can sometimes produce answers). Thus, the dismissal of intuition as an irrational process is itself irrational, just as embracing it as a process superior to formal logic is itself illogical.

When analysis and intuition do not find a natural balance in an organization, based on mutual appreciation of their respective strengths and weaknesses, supporters of each are drawn into political arguments, as each side uses whatever bases of power it can muster to proclaim its own superiority. Those favoring intuition generally rely on the power of authority, while those favoring planning tend to fall back on the use of rationality as a club. "The relationship between the [General Electric] Appliance Group's operating managers and strategic planners was 'us vs. them' from the start" (*Business Week*, 1984a:64). The battle is, in fact, an old one, begun at least a century ago in the factories that Frederick Taylor studied, but later finding its key manifestation in executive offices:

> With some entrances barred to them, the scientific managers are marching in through another. The coat of arms is different. No stop watches or meshing gears or broken heads. A new status has been achieved under the title of "planners." The tools are basically the

same, but now they are much more powerful and the stakes much higher. (Wrapp, 1963:102)

Politics over Planning

There is one last point to be made about planning and politics. Just as planning can evoke the very climate that it considers uncongenial to itself, so too can a climate of politics, which may be uncongenial to planning, sometimes prove congenial to the effectiveness of the organization. In other words, politics has functional roles to play in organizations too (as well as no shortage of dysfunctional ones), sometimes over the resistance of planning.

As we have argued elsewhere (Mintzberg, 1983:229–230), the system of politics in an organization can promote necessary strategic change blocked by the more legitimate systems of influence. The prime legitimate system is, of course, that of formal authority. A major flaw in this system is that by concentrating power up a unitary hierarchy, it tends to promote only a single point of view, usually the one believed to be favored at the top. In other words, a single individual at the apex of the hierarchy—the chief executive—can block necessary strategic change, consciously or not. As we have already seen, planning depends on that system of authority—both for the goals that feed into its process and for support of its process as well as its resulting plans—and so it defers (albeit sometimes reluctantly) to a central power at its apex. Thus does planning reinforce the notion of a unitary, centralized hierarchy.

Now true strategic reorientation—a major shift in perspective, quantum in nature—usually requires the championing of a novel point of view and the challenging of established assumptions, including set categories of strategy and of structure. So it must often take place outside the formal procedures of planning as well as the formal channels of authority. The arena where it sometimes must take place is the one appropriately labeled politics, a name for the system of influence that is technically illegitimate (or more exactly *a*legitimate, meaning beyond formally sanctioned influence). But that nonlegitimacy refers to the *means* of politics, because when it is used to challenge formal authority that is itself resisting change necessary for the organization, then its *ends* have to be considered legitimate.

A common example of this occurs when a management blind to shifts in the marketplace is challenged politically by a group of "young Turks." They may, for example, go over the head of the chief executive and take their case directly to the board of directors or to the public at large. Or they may simply take it upon themselves to shift the organization's strategy in a clandestine (and emergent) way. Indeed, it is surprising how much important strategic change in large organizations is initiated by political activity. Our conclusion is that politics, like intuition, can be a viable and, in some circumstances, preferable alternative to formal planning in promoting change. (Of course, planners can be—and often have been—those young Turks too, but not because of their formal procedures. We shall return to "unconventional" planners in Chapter 6.)

To conclude this discussion, we are not arguing that planning be eliminated in favor of politics. But to argue that politics interferes with the practice of planning is to ignore the political effects of planning on the one hand and the positive effects of politics on the other.

Planning and Control

Earlier we alluded to planning's interest in control. Here, in concluding this discussion of the pitfalls of planning, we wish to develop the point further, as it brings together much that we have noted about the characteristics of planning.

Obsession with Control

George Bernard Shaw once claimed that "To be in hell is to drift; to be in heaven is to steer." This might be designated the conventional planner's motto.

Perhaps the clearest theme in the planning literature is its obsession with control—of decisions and strategies, of the present and the future, of thoughts and actions, of workers and managers, of markets and customers. Thus Dror wrote (citing Friedman) that "Planning is an activity by which man in society endeavors to gain mastery over himself and to shape his collective future by power of his reason" (1971:105).[10]

Most indicative of this, perhaps, are the comments of a chief of planning for AT&T, who asked himself, "if corporate planning is so important," why did it "not surface anywhere in the Bible?" He concluded that "the elements of good planning" did, in fact, appear there because Moses "was so well acquainted with the environment that he could predict it with ease and change it on command (Exodus 7–14, 14:2)" (Blass, 1983:6-3). Is it any wonder that Kets de Vries and Miller, in their analysis of "the neurotic organization," characterized what they called the "compulsive firm" as having a "substantial planning department," which ensures that "every move is very carefully planned" (1984:29–30).

An obsession with control generally seems to reflect a fear of uncertainty. Of course, planners are not basically different from anyone else in this regard.[11] We all fear uncertainty to some degree, and one way to deal with a felt lack of control, to ensure no surprises, is to flip it over—to seek control over anything that might surprise us. At the limit, of course, that means everything—behaviors as well as events—and some planners at least give the impression of wanting to approach that limit. In a sense, reducing

---

[10] Planning would seem to come by this honestly, given Jelinek's description of Frederick Taylor as the real father of planning. Of Taylor, J. C. Worthy wrote:

> Taylor's personality emerges with great clarity from his writings. His virtual obsession to control the environment around him was expressed in everything he did; in his home life, his gardening, his golfing; even his afternoon stroll was not a casual affair but something to be carefully planned and rigidly followed. Nothing was left to chance if in any way chance could be avoided. Every personal action was thought through carefully, all contingencies considered, and steps taken to guard against extraneous developments. And when, despite all precautions, something did occur to upset his plans he gave evidence of great internal distress—distress that sometimes expressed itself in blazing anger and sometimes in black brooding. (1959:74)

[11] Although Worthy did distinguish Taylor:

> From his writings and his biography one gets the impression of a rigid, insecure personality, desperately afraid of the unknown and the unforeseen, able to face the world with reasonable equanimity only if everything possible has been done to keep the world in its place and to guard against anything that might upset his careful, painstaking plans. (1959:75)

uncertainty is (or at least has become) *their* profession. Thus, C. West Churchman noted that "planning enthusiasts," when asked the reason for planning, "point out the absolute need to prepare for all contingencies," to "minimize surprise, because for the planners surprise is an unsatisfactory state of affairs" (1968:147). Or to quote Wildavsky's (as usual) more emphatic words:

> Planning concerns man's efforts to make the future in his own image. If he loses control of his own destiny, he fears being cast into the abyss. Alone and afraid, man is at the mercy of strange and unpredictable forces, so he takes whatever comfort he can by challenging the fates. He shouts his plans into the storm of life. Even if all he hears is the echo of his own voice, he is no longer alone. To abandon his faith in planning would unleash the terror locked in him. (1973:151–152)

An obsession with control leads to all kinds of behaviors, as we have seen throughout our discussion. One is aversion to risk, which means a reluctance to consider truly creative ideas and truly quantum changes, both of whose effects are unpredictable and so beyond formal planning. Another is conflict with the subjects of the planning, who don't appreciate their own loss of control. Planners may see their procedures as merely bringing order and rationality—in effect, coordination—to decision making. But coordination *is* control, as Worthy noted:

> The obsession for control springs from the failure to recognize or appreciate the value of spontaneity, either in everyday work or in economic processes. Hence the need for *planning*. Hence the machine as the idea for human organization. For the machine has no will of its own. Its parts have no urge to independent action. Thinking, direction—even purpose—must be provided from outside or above. (1959:79)

"Our age is turbulent, Chicken Little"

An obsession with control can also lead to some curious behaviors, none more so than planning's attitude toward so-called "turbulence" in the environment. The planning literature has long made a terrible fuss about such turbulence; it is almost as if every writer in the field had to pay lip service to the idea at some time or other. "The Age of Discontinuity had just dawned when General Electric started its strategic planning process in 1970," wrote its chief planner, Michael Allen (1977:3). In the mid-1980s, two consultants wrote about "today's turbulent business environment" (Benningson and Schwartz, 1985:1). And toward the end of that decade, an academic introduced his book on planning with a comment about the "increasingly turbulent" environments of public and nonprofit organizations (Bryson, 1988:1). It was, of course, Alvin Toffler, in his 1970 book, *Future Shock,* and Igor Ansoff, in his host of writings during the 1970s and 1980s, who popularized this notion of turbulence. But the initial idea really stemmed from two articles of the 1960s, one by Emery and Trist in 1965 and the other by Terreberry in 1968.

Reading this literature one decade at a time may give the impression that the world of planning has always been turbulent. Of course, the question naturally arises: How could we ever have survived so much turbulence? But reading all of this literature in retrospect provides an answer. For much as planning writers have been inclined to describe *their* own age as turbulent, so too have they been equally inclined to dismiss the previous one as stable (the same one their predecessors found turbulent). "Gone are the 'good old days,' " wrote Freeman in 1984 of the business and service organizations "experiencing turbulence" (4); "times have changed," wrote Leff in the same year (1984:88). Schon and Nutt, who tracked "consensuality and turbulence in American public planning" in 1974 (183), showed consensuality up to 1963 and "a zone of turbulence" from that year to the time of their publication (ironically, just as the energy crisis was hitting—how then to characterize the following years?).

Why is it always our own age that is so turbulent? In the 1960s, organizations were implored to plan because the stable 1950s were gone; in the 1970s they were told how comparatively stable were the 1960s; in the 1980s there were writers who claimed that techniques such as the Boston Consulting Group's growth share matrix worked in the 1970s because, unlike the 1980s, these were stable years.

Ansoff was part of this too. Remember his comments on "the new conditions of turbulence" when he wrote, "Today, c. 1977, this problem is significantly different from ten years ago, when my first book on [the strategic problem] made its appearance" (1979b:5). But in that first book, published in 1965, Ansoff referred to strategic change as being "so rapid that firms must continually survey the product-market environment in search for investment opportunities," and he contrasted "highly dynamic" industries with "the remaining ones which have enjoyed relative stability in the past" (125, 126).

Of course, there was a way out, and Ansoff recognized it. "During the twentieth century the level of turbulence has progressively escalated in most industries" (1984:57). In other words, the curve of change has been exponential (a condition presumably akin to what Schon and Nutt [1974] termed "endemic turbulence"). But then again, if true, the first differential of that curve would be a straight line, would it not, and the second exponential flat? That means turbulence would have become stability, steady state, normalcy. "Plus ça change, plus c'est la même chose, non?" We quote from *Scientific American* without comment:

> Few phenomena are more remarkable yet few have been less re-
> marked than the degree in which material civilization, the progress
> of mankind in all those contrivances which oil the wheels and
> promote the comforts of daily life have been concentrated in the
> last half century. It is not too much to say that in these respects
> more has been done, richer and more prolific discoveries have been
> made, grander achievements have been realized in the course of
> the 50 years of our own lifetime than in the previous lifetime of the
> race. (This appeared in the issue of September 1868.)

In fact, the argument about escalating or endemic turbulence is as silly as are all the claims about today's turbulence. Toffler was writing *Future Shock* in the 1960s, when Terreberry and Emery and Trist were also publishing their articles on turbulence. With regard to this period, Makridakis, a leading authority on forecasting, commented "it is not an exaggeration to say that the 1960s was *the most* stable period in the history of Western Industrialized countries" (1979:18). He pointed out that America experienced "the longest period of uninterrupted growth—i.e., 105 months—of any country since historical records have been kept" (18).

Go tell the tales of the turbulence of the 1960s or even those of the 1970s (when oil price increases caused certain disruptions) to the people who experienced the Great Depression of the 1930s or the ones who lived through the siege of Leningrad during World War II, or even those soldiers subjected to that planning at Passchendaele. (Perhaps the most astounding comment in this regard was that of Katz and Kahn: "Even before turbulence characterized many environmental sectors, organizations frequently faced new problems, for example, those created by war or economic depression" [1978:132].) In 1986, when Toffler spoke at The Planning Forum Conference about "third wave planning" being "marked by rapid, dramatic, and often erratic discontinuity,"[12] we wondered how everyone had been able to cope with the sixteen years of turbulence since the publication of his initial book, indeed with the "hyperturbulence" that suddenly appeared in 1984 (at least in the title of an article by McCann and Selsky). How in the world did Toffler ever fly to Montreal under such conditions? And how did McCann and Selsky ever get to publish their article?

In fact, few of us have known anything resembling real turbulence (whatever that means) in our lifetimes. After all, the day after the oil prices increased in 1973, and every day thereafter, planners rose at more or less the same time, got into more or less the same cars with more or less the same four-cycle engines they had driven for half a century (perhaps occasionally having to line up to fill them with gasoline), turned on their radios to more or less the same stations, and took themselves to work in more or less the same kinds of places (unless, of course, they were fired by managers who felt planning would be of less help rather than more under such "turbulent" conditions).

The fact is that "environments" vary, across sectors and over time. Some organizations may occasionally experience severe disruption. But at the same time, many others are experiencing relative stability. (When did the Harvard Business School last change its strategic perspective? Indeed, Toffler himself has been pursuing the same theme for decades.) Toffler published his book about the shock of the future in 1970 much as books have been published for

---

[12] From a one-page handout at The Planning Forum Conference, Montreal, May 5, 1986.

years, indeed centuries. And Ansoff lived comfortably in the 1970s with little bother from that turbulence all around.

Thus, to call the entire context of organizations turbulent, and especially to claim that we have been experiencing much turbulence at any time since World War II, is ridiculous. Such conditions would have undermined all organizational activity, dissolving every bureaucracy and rendering every strategy (which by any definition imposes a stability on an organization) useless. To pronounce any environment permanently turbulent is as silly as to call it permanently stable: environments are always changing in some dimensions and always remaining stable in others; rarely do they change all at once, let alone continuously (and, in any event, rarely are those who experience them the best judges of the degree of their change).

More important for our purposes here, planning has generally garnered its greatest support when conditions have been relatively stable. The process gained popularity initially during those 1960s that Makridakis described as years of such steady economic growth. And it had its greatest setbacks when conditions changed unpredictably (notably after the energy price increases of the 1970s). But this should come as no surprise, because it is consistent with the conclusions that we have drawn in this chapter: planning works best when it extrapolates the present or deals with incremental change within the existing strategic perspective; it deals less well with unstable, unpredictable situations or quantum change in the organization. Thus when conditions became unpredictable (a word that Emery and Trist themselves used for their "turbulent fields," due to "gross increase" in "relevant uncertainty" [1965:26]), planning departments tended to be the first to go.

Why, then, does the planning school make such a fuss about turbulence, the very thing it cannot handle? Let us try some explanations. One might be that it believes it *can* handle it, or at least can convince management that it can. When the environment goes "turbulent," "plan or else" becomes its prescription. And this may be a compelling argument. For if the sky is really falling, as Chicken Little warned, then someone had better do something about it. And who better than the planners?

In one restricted sense, this argument may have been right. If all firms in an industry accept the prescription and thus plan diligently, then all strategies will be stable and no one will get any nasty surprises. "Turbulence" will magically disappear, thanks to planning. That, in fact, is the point underlying Galbraith's (1967) "new industrial states," giant oligopolies that controlled their markets (and each other) by planning. For a time, it seemed to work marvelously in certain situations, such as the American automobile industry. But only so long as no competitor appeared that refused to play by the same rules. When some did—ones that, for example, preferred rapid response to stable planning—we all know full well from the experiences of the automobile and other industries what happened. The magic of planning disappeared. And again Chicken Little began to brood.

Let us try another explanation for all those claims of turbulence, this one more cynical. It is simply that we glorify ourselves by describing our own age as turbulent. We live where it's at, as the saying goes, or at least we like to think we do (because that makes us feel important). One is reminded here of those people who, in categorizing periods of history, always reserve one for their own time (say, the total quality management movement of the 1990s alongside the eras of the dinosaurs and the Ming dynasty). In other words, what we really face are not turbulent times but overinflated egos.

In the final analysis, however, while we do believe in the above explanation, we prefer a third one, which contradicts the first. Planning is so oriented to stability, so obsessed with having everything under control, that any perturbation at all sets off a wave of panic and perceptions of turbulence. Thus when American industry was faced with some serious competition from abroad (much like Chicken Little getting hit on the head by an acorn), likely due in good part to all those years spent with its collective head buried in the sands of "rational" planning, its planners ran around like Chicken Little, crying, "The environment's turbulent! The environment's turbulent!"

And what was that turbulence? Nothing more than change that planning could not handle—conditions beyond the comprehension of *its* procedures.[13] And ones that played havoc with its care-

---

[13] "turbulence is the perception (both personally and generally) of the absence of clear and stable paths, guideposts by which to make sense of issues in order to propose and achieve resolutions" (Schon and Nutt, 1974:181).

fully designed plans. The world was imposing "discontinuities" which (as we shall see at the start of the next chapter), planning has no formal means to predict. But what was the source of these discontinuities? Not some malevolent deity, but other organizations, themselves in control, thank you, and with no thanks to strategic planning. That turbulence in America was simply opportunity in Japan.

One might conclude, therefore, that the Western planners were spoiled by the munificent conditions of the 1960s, when planning first cut its teeth. Every time the sheiks raised the price of oil or the Japanese introduced a better product at a lower price, the planners ran around crying "turbulence." Ironically, though, while it was *planning* that experienced the turbulence, it was the *environment* that got labeled turbulent! In other words, while the world of some other people was unfolding according to their wishes, the planners' sky really was falling, Chicken Little!

Strategic Vision and Strategic Learning

We have alluded in several places to ways to create strategy other than by formal planning. At the outset of this book we outlined nine other schools of thought on strategy formation. For our purposes here, we can focus on two approaches in particular, one labeled *visionary*, the other *learning*, the former dependent on a single creative strategist, the latter on a variety of actors capable of experimenting and then integrating.

While, in our view, all three processes can, and in fact must, work in concert for any organization to be effective, an overemphasis on planning—in fact, a belief that strategies can be created through formal procedures—tends to drive out the other two. And with the disappearance of the visionary approach goes vision itself, as broad, integrated strategic perspectives get reduced to narrow, decomposed strategic positions.

The visionary approach is a more flexible way to deal with an uncertain world. Vision sets the broad outlines of a strategy, while leaving the specific details to be worked out. In other words, the broad perspective may be deliberate but the specific positions can emerge. So when the unexpected happens, assuming the vision is sufficiently robust, the organization can adapt—it learns. Certain change is thus easily accommodated. Of course, when even vision cannot cope, then the organization may have to revert to a pure learning approach—to experiment in the hope of capturing some basic messages and converging behaviors on them. With a specified plan, in contrast, serious adaptation becomes much more difficult, as discussed earlier.

Thus, changes that appear turbulent to organizations that rely heavily on planning may appear normal to, even welcomed by, those that prefer more of a visionary or learning approach. Put more boldly, if you have no vision but only formal plans, then every unpredicted change in the environment makes you feel like your sky is falling. It comes as a fitting lesson, therefore, that the Japanese have been able to impose so much of that "turbulence" on American business in good part because they have been informal strategic learners more than formal strategic planners.[14]

Illusion of Control?

In Saint-Exupéry's *The Little Prince* (1943), the King claims that he has the power to order the sun to rise and set. But only at a certain time of the day. Is the power of planning equivalent? Does the *obsession with* control merely reflect an *illusion of* control?

An ironic side of this obsession with control is that planning manifests it collectively, not individually. In other words, planners prefer to gain control, not by struggling for it individually (as does the entrepreneur), but through the collective will of the organization. (Thus Koch has referred to planning as "collective voluntarism": People "want to shape their destiny . . . yet they also want to avoid the Darwinian consequences of individual competition"

---

[14] Which is not meant to imply that the Japanese are not good *operational* planners. (See Pascale, 1984, for a particularly striking example of this, in the case of Honda's initial success in the American motorcycle market.) Some informal evidence of the Japanese propensity to favor strategic learning over strategic planning comes from my own coding of all the articles I collect on strategy making into one or more of the ten schools (based on a reading of their abstracts, or else a scanning of their contents). In sorting recently the piles I had collected over several years, I realized that I had coded almost every single one by a Japanese author in the learning school!

[1976:371].) And this they seek to do not through the tangible actions of the organization so much as through the abstractions of its plans, its statements of intention. Is this just an illusion of control?

In their paper titled "Forecasting and Planning: An Evaluation," Hogarth and Makridakis found an "uncanny similarity between the history of [forecasting and planning] and formal psychological experiments concerning the 'illusion of control'" (1981:127). In one set of these, for example:

> Langer ... has documented how even in chance determined situations (e.g., lotteries), observing an early sequence of "successes" can lead people to believe they have some control over outcomes. Similarly, if people are allowed to engage in cognitive activity about the outcome prior to its occurrence (e.g., by choosing a ticket number), they are also inclined to believe they gain some control. These findings are entirely consistent with the need *to master and control the environment.* (121)

These authors saw such illusions of control in the success of planning in the 1960s: when things went well, and there was a good deal of formal planning, that is what must have done it. ". . . people have a tendency to attribute success to their own efforts and failure to external factors" (127), which is, in fact, exactly what the conventional "pitfalls" of planning are all about.

Gimpl and Dakin pursued this point to its logical conclusion in a paper they titled "Management and Magic." "Experts in the techniques of forecasting and planning perform the function of magicians in primitive society. They provide a basis for a decision when there is no rational method" (1984:130). These techniques are "not far removed from the ancient techniques" that we now scoff at, such as reading the entrails of slaughtered animals or gazing into crystal balls (126). The point seems terribly overstated, until one considers the comments of an individual in a leading forecasting position (Vice-President of Economic Research at the Conference Board): "The history of forecasters is that we've always been wrong. But a wrong forecast is better than none." To plan, "you need some kind of a forecast, whether you're preparing the federal government's budget or a civic association's" (in McGinley, 1983:1).

Why? Maybe only for the same reason magical rites were practiced by so-called primitive societies. As discussed by Gimpl and
Dakin, ritualized forecasting might encourage necessary random
action.

> O.K. Moore tells of the use of caribou bones among the Labrador
> Indians. When food is short because of poor hunting, the Indians
> consult an oracle to determine the direction the hunt should take.
> The shoulder blade of a caribou is put over the hot coals of a fire;
> cracks in the bones caused by the heat are then interpreted as a
> map. The directions indicated by this oracle are basically random.
> Moore points out that this is a highly efficacious method because if
> the Indians did not use a random number generator they would
> fall prey to their previous biases and tend to over-hunt certain
> areas. Furthermore, any regular pattern of the hunt would give the
> animals a chance to develop avoidance techniques. By randomiz-
> ing their hunting patterns the Indians' chances of reaching game
> are enhanced. (1984:133)

Competitors can, of course, be similarly fooled when companies so
randomize their actions, perhaps a part of what is becoming known
in strategic management as "signaling." The point, however, may
be stretched when it is realized (as we shall discuss shortly) that
much of business forecasting is based on extrapolation, in other
words, on smoothing established trends rather than randomizing
arbitrary ones.

But Gimpl and Dakin offered another reason for such planning,
which may be closer to the thinking of that person at the Conference Board. It "boost[s] confidence," "reduces anxiety," affirms
managerial action, makes the "managerial group . . . more cohesive" (133, 134). "When people feel out of control there is a tendency toward inactivity"; when they have even the illusion of
control, they can act (133). In the words of Hofstede, having a
planning system "allows the managers to sleep more peacefully,
even if it does not really work" (1980:160). Likewise, Huff attributes the popularity of the "rational model" to the "lure of
simplifying structures that make our diverse world more understandable" (1980:33).

This may help to explain some of the planning in the very
largest organizations, especially highly diversified ones that at
times seem to have little idea of how to manage themselves. But at

what price? "Don't expect the plans to be accurate," warned Gimpl and Dakin (134). But what happens when they are not?

Furthermore, while plans can stimulate action, they can also paralyze it, investing so much energy in concocting the future on paper (or simply playing the numbers game), and draining so much commitment from those who are supposed to act, that necessary actions just do not get taken (leading to the popular phrase, "paralysis by analysis"). Then, problems are assumed to be solved, not because viable solutions to them have been implemented, but simply because they have been approached in systematic ways. In other words, to have it on paper is to have it under control. ". . . reality itself doesn't matter . . . Problems are removed from consciousness, by putting other people and money to work on them (Slater calls this the Toilet Assumption)" (van Gunsteren, 1976:142). Thus we have a possible explanation for the claim that "it's the process that counts": "Since he can only create the future he desires on paper, [man] transfers his loyalties to the plan. Since the end is never in sight he sanctifies the journey; the process of planning becomes holy" (Wildavsky, 1973:152). Planning thus becomes the end, and "a lot of planning activities consist of making the world safe for planning" (van Gunsteren, 1976:20).

Planning can likewise serve influencers outside the organization who share the same obsession with, and illusion of, control. If only the organization plans formally, then all will be well. Governments often behave this way, imposing planning processes on their own agencies as well as on other organizations to which they give money (such as schools and hospitals). Nothing much ever happens, except that the plans are duly deposited, and so the planners and the technocrats in government are duly satisfied. But the problem is hardly restricted to the public sector. All kinds of influencers around businesses—shareholders, bankers, stock market analysts, directors, even headquarters executives with respect to the business divisions they oversee—alleviate their anxieties about lack of knowledge by ensuring that the managers engage in formal planning. The businesses must be properly managed if their managers plan formally.

> Security analysts say that they place a relatively high value on a company's strategic planning, both the soundness of strategic plans as well as the soundness of a strategic planning system. . . . If the survey responses are a reliable indicator, one would conclude that

not only security analysts consider corporate strategy to be important in rating stocks, but even more important than quarterly performance. (Higgins and Diffenbach, 1985:67, 65)

We saw this kind of behavior in our study of the Steinberg supermarket chain (Mintzberg and Waters, 1982). The first time the company went to capital markets, it had to issue long-range plans. As we noted earlier, the founding president of the company could hardly say, "Listen, I'm Sam Steinberg and I've done awfully well. So kindly give me $5,000,000." No, he had to issue plans for the money, to show that he managed systematically, even though the company had achieved all of its success to that date by managing entreprenurially—and with hardly any of that planning at all![15] And so it goes in board meetings, annual reports, statements to the press, dealings with financial houses, government regulators, and on and on. No plans, no support.

In fact, the more distant are external influencers from the specifics of the organization's operations, the more they seem to believe that planning will provide that necessary but elusive control. Of course, in this regard, they are not different from those chiefs of giant corporations perched atop remote hierarchies, detached from the real world of making and selling products, who believe that planning will somehow produce the strategies that they themselves cannot. Such beliefs may be illusory, yet they drive a great deal of behavior, giving rise to one particular role played by planning.

Planning as Public Relations

Some organizations take advantage of these demands, turning them around to use planning as a tool, not because anyone necessarily believes in the value of the process per se but because influential outsiders do. Once again, planning becomes a game. This time it's called "public relations."

This view of planning as a facade to impress outsiders is sup-

---

[15] Gupta noted exactly the same thing for another supermarket chain (1980:IV:32).

ported by no shortage of evidence. As an example of what he called planning as a "gesture process" to suggest the "trappings of objectivity," Nutt cited those "city governments [that] hire consultants to do 'strategic planning' to impress bond rating agencies," and "firms [that] posture with each other and the marketplace with their claims of long-range planning" (1984a:72). In universities, Cohen and March described plans that "become symbols": for example, "an organization that is failing can announce a plan to succeed," one that lacks a piece of equipment can announce a plan to get it. They also discussed plans that "become advertisements," noting that "what is frequently called a 'plan' by a university is really an investment brochure," one "characterized by pictures, by ex cathedra pronouncements of excellence, and by the absence of most relevant information" (1976:195). Langley found this to be true of the public sector in general, where public relations was "probably a very common motivation for 'strategic planning,' " although "the same kind of role is played by subsidiaries and/or autonomous divisions who have to produce 'strategic plans' for their parent firms" (1988:48).

Wildavsky has pointed out that national leaders who "wish to be thought modern . . . have a document with which to dazzle their visitors," one that "no one who matters attends to." In fact, it "need not be a means of surmounting the nation's difficulties, but rather may become a mode of covering them up" (1973:140). And why shouldn't they do this? After all, "capitalist America insisted upon a plan" in return for its foreign aid to poor countries: "It did not matter whether the plan worked; what did count was the ability to produce a document which looked like a plan" (151).

Presumably to be able to plan is tantamount to being able to spend money responsibly. To repeat the Lorange and Vancil quotation from earlier in our discussion:

> Announcing that his organization would undertake a formal program of strategic planning was almost like a public announcement that he was going to quit smoking. It forced the Chief Executive to attempt to change his own behavior in a way that he knew was desirable. (1977:16)

But did he? Maybe Henry Kissinger put it more accurately when he referred to planning as "a sop to administrative theory" (1969:264).

To continue with Wildavsky's metaphor about "A mode of covering up," if planning is fashionable, then it appears that every well-dressed organization must wear it. But then again, as Norburn and Grinyer pointed out, "the fable of 'the king who wore no clothes' ... seems remarkably pertinent to the adaption of planning systems" (1973/74:37).

In a narrow sense, of course, some planning for the purposes of public relations seems to be justified. After all, supermarkets need their capital, the developing nations their aid, universities their support. In the poorer nations, national planning "may be justified on a strictly cash basis: planners may bring in more money from abroad than it costs to support them at home" (Wildavsky, 1973:151).

But in a broader sense, is this kind of planning justified at all? Leaving aside the obvious waste of resources on a collective basis—the money that could be saved if everyone stopped playing the game—public relations planning probably distorts priorities in the organization itself. In poor nations, for example, it misallocates skills that are in very short supply, capabilities that could be devoted to solving real problems (or doing useful planning!). Even in more developed countries, think of how much time and talent has been wasted over the years. Especially if Dirsmith et al.'s claim is true that "PPB, MBO and ZBB may have been used more as political strategies and ritualistic symbols for controlling and directing controversy ... [than] as management tools for improving decision making within the U.S. Federal bureaucracy" (1980:303). Worse, what is intended as public relations can be taken seriously when it should not be. That may have happened at the Steinberg supermarket chain, where the formal planning began to displace the entrepreneurial initiative of its leader, which had been the very basis of its success.

Organizations that are forced to articulate strategies that are not really there—because their managements lack the necessary vision, or because they are still engaged in a complex learning process in order to create their strategies—get caught up in all kinds of wasteful behaviors. One is the pronouncement of platitudes— ostensible strategies that no one has any intention of implementing, even if that were possible. As Taylor found in one study of four small organizations, "if the organization was in the process of changing its strategy, these [public] announcements were so general, or incomplete, as to be next to useless in understanding what the organization was actually doing" (1982:305). Another wasteful behavior is to reiterate existing strategies, perhaps in revised language, even though new strategies may be emerging. To return to Taylor's study, "A second point is that when specific public announcements of intended strategy were made, they were made well after the fact, when the announced changes were well on the way to being implemented" (305). Indeed, in reading Colonel Summers's (1981) account of the articulation of U.S. military strategy since World War II, one gets the impression of pronouncements racing like mad to keep up with the emerging reality. For example, after the Korean War, the Field Service Regulations acknowledged "wars of limited objective" and removed "victory" as a necessary aim of war (41); by 1962, cold war was acknowledged! (42)

Some of the more dysfunctional side effects of public relations planning are suggested in Benveniste's discussion of what he called "trivial planning."

1. There is a tendency to use past trends to predict future developments, i.e., predict "more of the same." . . . the experts are not asking any difficult questions. They take the status quo for granted. They raise no policy options. . . .

2. Trivial planning exercises are well-publicized. . . . Everyone is encouraged to participate and have his or her say. The plan is published and widely distributed. The document is beautifully printed, and the less content it has, the longer it becomes.

3. Trivial planning is sequential. . . . No sooner has one set of experts made its bland recommendations than another set is studying the same problem or some appropriate variant. . . . Most trivial planning is undertaken by ephemeral bodies: task forces, presidential commissions, and the like. These bodies have the dual advantage of relying on prestigious outsiders, thus adding to the body's visibility, and providing these experts with insufficient time to find out how they might effect changes. . . .

4. Trivial planning tends to be used by conservatives. . . . Since the planning movements espouse a mild reformist ideology, and since planning is perceived as an attempt to bring about change, providing technocratic legitimacy is more useful to policies that preserve a conservative stance. (1972:107–109).[16]

In his book on the French national planning experience, Cohen concluded that "planning is either political or it is decorative" (1977:xv). But decorative (i.e., public relations) planning can easily become political, pitting outsiders in search of control against insiders seeking protection. The same can happen internally when planning becomes a device to impress the senior management, which Cohen and March referred to as "an administrative test of will":

> If a department wants a new program badly enough, it will spend a substantial amount of effort in "justifying" the expenditure by fitting it into a "plan." If an administrator wishes to avoid saying "yes" to everything, but has no basis for saying "no" to anything, he tests the commitment of the department by asking for a plan. (1976:195–196)

Add all this together, and public relations planning becomes a device by which almost everyone, no matter how obsessed with gaining control, loses it. Outsiders get useless pronouncements, and junior managers waste time filling out forms while senior managers get distracted from the more important issues. Only the planners come out on top in some perverse way, not for how they benefit the organization so much as themselves. And that makes such planning for them fundamentally political. Thus, in the final analysis, much as in the experiences of the Communist states, planning that is used artificially, for image instead of substance, does not help managers or outside influencers to control organizations or even the environments of those organizations. Nor does it en-

---

[16] Benveniste also discussed "utopian planning," similar in that the "plans do not affect anyone's behavior or decisions because no one takes them seriously." They too were "well-publicized" (109), and could be even better for public relations because of their glorified nature: "Since [the plan] does not have to be coherent, there can be something in it for everyone" (110).

able planners to do so. Rather, that inanimate system called planning ties everyone in knots and so ends up controlling everybody!

To conclude this discussion of the pitfalls of planning, we find the conventional planners' most common explanations for the failures of planning wanting. Managers sometimes do not support planning for very good reasons, and climates conducive to effective planning are sometimes not conducive to effective strategy formation, and vice versa. The face validity of these pitfalls conceals the fact that they are only skin-deep. What these pitfalls really reveal is a number of dysfunctions of planning itself—its discouragement of commitment in organizations, its essentially conservative nature, its own biases and capacities to breed political activity, its obsession with and illusion of control.

But in our opinion even these characteristics do not get to the root of the problem. They are based on the pitfalls, which reflect only difficulties of planning that are closer to its surface. To find out why strategic planning in particular really has gone wrong, and why reasonable people have devoted so much effort to a process that never produced the desired results, we need to look beyond the pitfalls—beyond the symptoms.

5

Fundamental Fallacies of Strategic Planning

An expert has been defined as someone who knows enough about a subject to avoid all the many pitfalls on his or her way to the grand fallacy (Edelman, 1972:14). We have already discussed the concerted efforts in planning to avoid all those many pitfalls. In this chapter we address what we believe to be the fundamental fallacies of strategic planning, which, in conclusion, we reduce to that one grand fallacy.

"How can this be," asked Wildavsky, that "planning fails everywhere it has been tried?" After all, "the reasonable man plans ahead. . . . Nothing seems more reasonable than planning. . . . Suppose . . . that the failures of planning are not peripheral or accidental but integral to its very nature" (1973:128). This is the theme we pursue here. We shall first consider some basic assumptions that underlie planning, in order to develop arguments contrary to each, in effect concluding that the rationality assumed in strategic planning can be irrational when judged against the needs of strategy making.

Some Basic Assumptions Behind Strategic Planning

As we saw earlier, particularly in Jelinek's book, *Institutionalizing Innovation*, first and foremost underlying planning are the **assump-**

tions of formalization—initially that **the strategy making process can be programmed by the use of systems.** It is not people so much as systems that create the strategies, much as Frederick Taylor's systems were considered to program the manual work in factories a century ago.

No one, of course, makes such a blatant claim. But as the words are written, this is a message. As we saw earlier, the planning literature depicts people as idiosyncratic. Especially when they rely on intuition, they cannot be trusted. Systems, in contrast, are reliable and consistent. To Allaire and Firsirotu who wrote about what they called "staff driven" planning, there "is the rational impulse to fight complexity with analysis and stamp out every inconsistency with policies and procedures" (1990:114). Thus, formal planning is not considered a stage in the process of strategy formation, nor a support to it, so much as the very process itself, at least when executed properly. Strategic planning *is* proper strategy making. The system does the thinking: "planning is the key to various components. *It* directs the process, generates policy alternatives, and manages them to form an approved plan" (Albert, 1974:249, italics added). Or, to quote Michael Porter in *The Economist:* "As firms grew and became more complex . . . they needed a systematic approach to setting strategy. Strategic planning emerged as the answer" (1987:17). Even in 1990, the head of planning for a major American corporation (Bell & Howell) could claim that "It is the responsibility of strategic planning to make sure that the entire organization knows very well what its customers' requirements are, what is the direction in which customer needs and customer expectations are changing, how technology is moving, and how competitors serve their customers" (Marquardt, 1990:4). The responsibility is, not of the people, even of the planners, but of *planning!*

Indeed, some of the claims in the mainline literature took a major step beyond this. In the words of George Steiner, "In a fundamental sense, formal strategic planning is an effort to duplicate what goes on in the mind of a brilliant intuitive [manager]" (1979:10).[1] Or to quote a Stanford Research Institute economist,

---

[1] Steiner ended the sentence with the word "planner," but in the context of the text immediately preceding and following the quote, he was clearly referring to the manager.

"by analyzing the attributes and state of mind of the 'genius entrepreneur,' " its people have designed a framework to "recreate" that person's processes for execution by the "management team" (McConnell, 1971:2).

And how is this recreation accomplished? By reducing that intuition to a series of carefully delineated steps, to be executed in sequential order. In other words, the essence of informal intuition can be captured by a process that is basically analytical. Or, to express it differently—and this is planning's grandest assumption of all—**analysis can provide synthesis.** As Porter expressed it: "I favor a set of analytical techniques for developing strategy . . ." (1987:21). Later we shall see that this assumption has had some powerful proponents, including at least one Nobel prizewinner. But that does not make it right and, indeed, we shall see him diametrically opposed by another Nobel prizewinner. Planning's biggest assumption of all, as we shall discuss, may be contemporary society's trickiest problem.

Following from these first assumptions of formalization are the *assumptions of detachment.* If the system does the thinking, to produce the strategies to be implemented, then **thought must be detached from action, strategy from operations, ostensible thinkers from real doers, and, therefore, "strategists" from the objects of their strategies.** In other words, managers are to manage by *remote* control, using processes that are essentially cerebral. Again Jelinek said it most clearly in her 1979 book, positioning senior managers (the acknowledged strategists, but like Taylor's laborers, stripped of much of their control over their process) together with the planners on a hierarchical pedestal, sufficiently removed from the daily pressures of running the business so that they can think the big thoughts (or get their systems to do so), while everyone down below scurries around handling the implementational details. Citing Taylor's experiences as a model for strategic planning, Jelinek wrote about "the large-scale coordination of details—planning and policy-level thinking, above and beyond the details of the task itself" (1979:136).

The trick, of course, is to get the relevant information up to that pedestal, so that its occupants and their systems can be informed about those details without having to enmesh themselves in them. And here is where the *assumption of quantification,* a corollary to that of detachment, comes in: **the strategy making process is**

driven by "hard data," comprising quantitative aggregates of the detailed "facts" about the organization and its environment. Having to probe into the messy world of details would force senior managers off their pedestals and, even worse, force the planners to leave the comforts of the staff for the pressures of the line. Unless, of course, all the necessary data could be collected and combined, packaged conveniently and delivered regularly. Thus, enter the so-called management information system (MIS), or in its latest rendition, a "Strategic Information System." To quote Jelinek's rendition of Taylor's experiences once again, "The systemic relationship among quantitative measures of performance and environmental indicators—substantially abstracted, be it noted, from details of task performance—is what permits control at [the senior manager's] level" (140); the *"systems* generalize knowledge far beyond its original discoverer or discovery situation" (139, italics added).

Corresponding to this flow of hard data up the hierarchy is the assumption of the flow of explicit strategies down it, likewise on schedule. Planning systems, in the words of two planning consultants, one the former head of strategic planning at General Electric, "set up an orderly agenda for consideration" (Roach and Allen, 1983:7–38). And by so doing, the world is made to conform to the plans, through a process called "implementation." The good thoughts have emanated from on high; there remains merely the need for everyone else to enact them. As van Gunsteren puts it for the public sector, "Policy exists fully defined prior to implementation. Invention and adaptation stop before implementation begins. Policy remains stable during implementation. It can only be changed by the centre" (1976:19).

Part of this grew out of the belief that different decisions have to be taken, not on the spot or on some ad hoc basis, but well in advance, in conjunction with each other: "Management needs action laid out in advance in order that it choose its actions wisely." The plan is designed "so that [the organization] will remain on the course defined by its goals and strategy" (Sawyer, 1983:6, 82). This constitutes the *assumption of predetermination*: that **because the context for strategy making is stable, or at least predictable, the process itself as well as its consequence (strategies) can be predetermined.** The world of organizations thus unfolds in a manner convenient to planning . . . and to planners.

First, [planners] assumed that the world of competition is predictable and that clear paths can be charted across it much like a highway system across a road map. . . . The managerial logic of ends-ways-means also attributes a certain stability to the company itself. There is an expectation that the company's values and needs will not change over the planning horizon . . . Managers can, therefore, concern themselves with "static optimization"—that is, with making a few key decisions and then holding to them. (Hayes, 1985:117)

Our intention in this chapter is quite simple: to demonstrate the fallaciousness of all of these assumptions—of formalization, detachment, and predetermination—and thereby to explain the failures of strategic planning.

Missing Taylor's Message

Frederick Taylor was quite clear about one particular point of great importance here: work processes that are not fully understood cannot be effectively programmed. Accounts of his own efforts dwelt at length on this (see, for example, those on machine tool cutting and coal shoveling [Taylor, 1913]).

Here is how Taylor outlined in 1911 his own approach to improving factory work:

First.	Find, say 10 or 15 different men (preferably in as many separate establishments and different parts of the country) who are especially skillful in doing the particular work to be analyzed.
Second.	Study the exact series of elementary operations or motions which each of these men use in doing the work [that] is being investigated, as well as the implements each man uses.
Third.	Study with a stop-watch the time required to make each of these elementary movements and then select the quickest way of doing each element of the work.
Fourth.	Eliminate all false movements, slow movements, and useless movements.

Fifth.   After doing away with all unnecessary move-
                   ments, collect into one series the quickest and
                   best movements as well as the best implements.
                   (1913:117–118)

Thus, at the same time as it embraced Taylor's notion of programming, the planning school missed what might have been his
most important message. For nowhere in the planning literature
has there been any indication whatsoever that efforts were made to
understand how the strategy making process really does work in
organizations. Nowhere in the cited writings of Steiner, Ansoff,
Ackoff, Lorange, or in the Jelinek book of 1979 was there a shred of
evidence that they had tried to understand how effective strategists really think or how effective strategies really do form in organizations. Instead they merely assumed a correspondence
between strategic planning, strategic thinking, and strategy making, at least in best practice. The CEO "can seriously jeopardize or
even destroy the prospects of strategic thinking by not consistently
following the discipline of strategic planning..." wrote Lorange
(1980b:12) with no support whatever.

In effect, a kind of *normative naivete* has pervaded the literature
of planning—confident beliefs in what is best, grounded in an
ignorance of what really does work. The claims by Steiner and
people at the Stanford Research Institute that they were able to
"duplicate" or "replicate" the intuitive processes of managers (let
alone "brilliant" or "genius" forms of it) were sheer nonsense,
since even today we have no real understanding of how intuition
works and certainly no indication that it proceeds in any stepwise
fashion. All these writers did, therefore, was what Taylor never
dared to do: leap straight into prescription. In just plain ignorance
of the strategy making process, they proposed a simplistic set of
steps as their "one best way" to create strategy, claiming at their
most naïve that it simulated intuition and at their most arrogant
that it was superior.

While we now understand little about intuition, or the creation
of strategy in a single head (presumably a related process), we do
know a certain amount about how the process tends to unfold in
the collectivity that is an organization. And none of this supports
these planning theorists' view of that process. Research by Quinn
(1980a), Burgelman (1983c, 1988), Pascale (1984), as well as our

own work (Mintzberg, 1978, 1987; see also earlier references in Chapter 3), among others, paints a very different picture of the process, as different as is a Cubist abstraction from a Renaissance rendition. This research tells us that strategy making is an immensely complex process involving the most sophisticated, subtle, and at times subconscious of human cognitive and social processes. We know that it must draw on all kinds of informational inputs, many of them nonquantifiable and accessible only to strategists who are connected to the details rather than detached from them. We know that the dynamics of the context have repeatedly defied any efforts to force the process into a predetermined schedule or onto a predetermined track. Strategies inevitably exhibit some emergent qualities, and even when largely deliberate, often appear less formally planned than informally visionary. And learning, in the form of fits and starts as well as discoveries based on serendipitous events and the recognition of unexpected patterns, inevitably plays a key role, if not *the* key role in the development of all strategies that are novel. Accordingly, we know that the process requires insight, creativity, and synthesis, the very things that formalization discourages. As our discussion proceeds, we shall detail some of these aspects of the process.

It is interesting, therefore, that if the planning theorists had heeded Taylor's message, they would not have had any more success at programming the strategy making process, but at least they would have realized the futility of trying to do so. With this indication of our final conclusion in mind, let us reconsider the basic assumptions of planning, under the headings of the fallacy of predetermination, the fallacy of detachment, and the fallacy of formalization, drawing them all together in conclusion under the grand fallacy.

The Fallacy of Predetermination

Planning assumes predetermination in a number of respects: the prediction of the environment through forecasting or its enactment through organizational action, the unfolding of the strategy formation process on schedule ("strategies on demand"), and the imposition of the resulting strategies on an acquiescent environment, again on schedule, with the organization stabilized to do so through programming. As Allaire and Firsirotu noted, "Uncertainty is the Achilles' heel of strategic planning. Strategic planning, as it is still practised, is heavily slanted toward the 'predict-and-prepare' mode of coping with the future. The strategic plan is a 'road map' with a fixed and well-defined target, as well as the steps to reach that target" (1989:7).[2] Let us, therefore, take a close look at these aspects of predetermination.

William Dimma, CEO of a major Canadian financial institution, stated simply: "there are only four ways I know of to deal with the future. 1. You can ignore it. 2. You can predict it. 3. You can control it. 4. You can respond to it" (1985:22). The first and last of these (at least in the absence of the middle two) are not planning by almost any stretch of the imagination. Most planning seems to be concerned with the second, prediction, although we shall argue later that planning by the third may be more prevalent. We turn, therefore, to a discussion of forecasting as planning's means of prediction.

The Performance of Forecasting

Almost everything written about planning stresses the importance of accurate forecasting. Short of being able to control the environment, planning depends on an ability to predict where that environment will be during the execution of the plans. Of course, if the environment does not change, and planners react accordingly— forecasting by extrapolating—then there will be no problem. If, however, the environment does change, then those changes must be predicted. They may be *regular*, or cyclical, as in the annual pattern of seasons, or *discontinuous*, which means they happen on a one-time, ad hoc basis. This, as we shall see, makes a huge difference.

---

[2] "A strategy is a road map to the goals; that is, an assembly of the elements which, when linked together effectively, permit a plan which moves the business towards the specific accomplishments it has chosen to attempt" (Sawyer, 1983:37).

Part of the problem, of course, is predicting *what* kind of change will come, let alone predicting the changes themselves. As we enter this discussion, therefore, it would be well to bear in mind Schumacher's disarmingly simple point that "the future does not exist; how could there be knowledge about something non-existent"? (1974:190) It is a point Ansoff might have considered when he wrote in his original *Corporate Strategy:* "We shall refer to the period for which the firm is able to construct forecasts with an accuracy of, say, plus or minus 20 percent as the *planning horizon* of the firm" (1965:44). But how in the world can any firm forecast the accuracy of its forecasts (let alone just do the forecasting itself)?! How, in other words, can predictability be predicted?

Spyros Makridakis is a leading scholar in the field of forecasting, author of several popular textbooks on the subject (e.g., Makridakis, Wheelwright, and McGee, 1983; Makridakis and Wheelwright, 1989; Makridakis, 1990). In his 1990 book, Makridakis commented:

> The ability to forecast accurately is central to effective planning strategies. If the forecasts turn out to be wrong, the real costs and opportunity costs . . . can be considerable. On the other hand, if they are correct they can provide a great deal of benefit—if the competitors have not followed similar planning strategies. (170)

His evidence on the ability to forecast, therefore, articulated especially in a review article with Robin Hogarth, a psychologist, entitled, "Forecasting and Planning: An Evaluation," should be of considerable interest. In a nutshell, "Long-range forecasting (two years or longer) is notoriously inaccurate" (1981:122).

Hogarth and Makridakis cited one review of the predictive accuracy of forecasting in the fields of population, economics, energy, transportation, and technology—fields "characterized by much experience and expertise in making forecasts as well as readily available data." Its "conclusions are pessimistic." Errors varied "from a few to a few hundred percentage points," biases were systematic, and the author "could not specify beforehand which forecasting approach, or forecaster, would have been right or wrong." Thus, " 'choosing' a forecast can be as difficult as making one's own." In another paper, Makridakis and Hibon (1979) used a large number of time series to examine the accuracy of various methods of forecasting: in general, the simpler methods—straight extrapolation, simple moving averages, etc.—did as well as the most statistically sophisticated ones. As Pant and Starbuck put it in their recent review of "Forecasting and Research Methods": "In forecasting, simplicity usually works better than complexity. Complex forecasting methods mistake random noise for information. Moderate expertise proves as effective as great expertise" (1990:433).

Hogarth and Makridakis concluded that "planning activities must accept the inaccuracies inherent in long-term forecasts" (122). But how can organizations do so and still plan with confidence? The Gomer and Dubé studies discussed in Chapter 3 indicated how an inability to predict can undermine planning, as did our discussion of the evidence on capital budgeting, which showed how this opens the door to biases in estimating costs and benefits. (Indeed, Marsh et al., in their study of capital budgeting, "found that the extent of forecasting was quite limited" [1988:25].) Perhaps heeding Dimma's advice would make the most sense:

> *Be sceptical, though not cynical, about all forecasts.* Distrust extrapolations intensely because they're usually based on simplistic assumptions. Distrust econometric models and elaborate simulations. In particular, distrust computer-driven models which convey a spurious air of authenticity to the exercise but are based on no-less-suspect assumptions than any more mundane approach. Distrust elegance and complexity. Prefer judgment to technique. (1985:25)

The Forecasting of Discontinuities

George Sawyer has written:

> Changes rarely or never occur abruptly or without a supporting context. The challenge to the foresight group is to define the relevant context, learn to read its evolution, and then to anticipate and suggest changes which will avoid adverse impacts on corporate programs as external changes occur. (1983:85)

While the claim about the rarity of abruptness may be disputed, that about the presence of a supporting context seems reasonable, and the need to understand it is certainly a challenge. The question is whether that challenge can reasonably be met.

Makridakis expressed some faith in our ability to forecast repeating patterns.

> Humans can predict the future by observing regularities (patterns) in certain phenomena (the daily sunrise or the seasons) or causal relationships (cultivating seeds and growing crops, or intercourse and pregnancy). A prerequisite of any form of forecasting, whether judgemental or statistical, is that a pattern or relationship exists concerning the event of interest. (1990:56)

But when it comes to one-time events—changes that never occurred before, so-called discontinuities, such as technological innovations, price increases, shifts in consumer attitudes, government legislation—Makridakis argued that forecasting becomes "practically impossible." In his opinion, "very little, or nothing" can be done, "other than to be prepared, in a general way, to . . . react quickly once a discontinuity has occurred" (1979:115).

Herbert Simon has written that "forecasts are likely to be reliable only when made within the context of a good structural model" (1973:2)—in Makridakis and Wheelwright's terms (1981:122), the "causal" method of forecasting, based on a good understanding of cause-effect relationships. The problem with one-time events is that such understanding is usually absent—the model can't be built. As Rhenman (1973:79) pointed out, unless the supporting context is "more or less closed," too many factors can intervene to throw off the prediction. "Retrospection often errs partly because history makes a sample of size one" (Pant and Starbuck, 1990:435). Or as Kundera pointed out in his novel, *The Unbearable Lightness of Being* (1984), the trouble is that we only get to live life once: as soon as we have experienced something, and finally understand it, it tends not to happen again!

As discussed earlier, Ansoff devoted a good deal of his 1984 book to the premise that systems can be devised to detect strategic surprises through weak signals. But can they? In 1952, the Steinberg company received an invitation to bid on the supermarket that was to go into Montreal's first shopping center. Sam Steinberg, the founder and chief executive, immediately decided that this was unacceptable to him: he could not sustain his desired rate of growth if he had to bid for stores in all the new shopping centers. He had to control those shopping centers himself. So, quite suddenly, he launched his business into shopping centers and, for the first time, had to enter the capital markets to get the necessary funds (see Mintzberg and Waters, 1982). In retrospect, it all seems very logical. But in 1952 the signal was weak: who knew if shopping centers would succeed? Sam Steinberg seemed to know. But could any formal system of forecasting have known?

Contrast this story with Ansoff's discussion of his system of "weak signal management":

> Knowledge about each T/O {threat/opportunity} will progress through typical stages: first there is a sense of turbulence in the environment, then the probable source of T/O's is identified, then a particular T/O becomes concrete enough to describe but not sufficiently concrete to estimate its full consequences for the firm. At the next stage of development it becomes possible to develop responses to the T/O ... Profit consequences can be estimated at the next stage of development, but the estimates are still uncertain, which means that a probability must be assigned to each. Eventually certainty is reached ... (1984:369)

Quite a difference from what may have happened in an instant in the mind of one human entrepreneur! Ansoff went on to claim that: "The choice of whether and how to respond should be determined, first, by comparing the timing of the T/O with the time required for the response and, second, by comparing the gain to the firm responding to the cost of making the response" (369). It all sounds like those complex formulae mathematicians need to describe how to keep a bicycle upright, something any five-year-old can do with ease, thank you. Ansoff commented further that "When strong signal issue management becomes too slow, it should be replaced by weak signals," as if it is all a question of the formal selection of formal systems. Go tell that to Sam Steinberg!

Of course, the perception of a subtle discontinuity is hardly in the class of riding a bicycle. It is a complex process of pattern recognition, based on a deep understanding of an industry and its context (in the Steinberg example, the shopping habits of consumers, their moves to the suburbs and their new-found uses of the automobile, etc.). That takes a very sophisticated causal model indeed. What system, what technique has even been able to build one of these? Certainly there has been a great deal of research on "artificial intelligence" and, of late, some on so-called "expert systems." And a number of rather ambitious claims have been made about our abilities to program such processes. But the conclusion we reach, to be discussed toward the end of this chapter, is that nowhere is there convincing evidence that such a sophisticated form of pattern recognition for discontinuities is amenable to formalization—or ever will be, for that matter. Even the systems Ansoff calls "quasi-analytic," by at least partially trying to program the process, may possibly reduce its effectiveness by interfering with the informal exercise of human judgment.

Thus, Ansoff is wrong to expect systems to detect weak signals (other than the simplest, most repetitive kinds, such as downturns in the growth of a country's GNP). To quote Makridakis and his colleagues:

> Monitoring weak signals (Ansoff, 1975a) and surprise-management still remain an academic idea of little practical value. It is obvious that an almost infinite number of weak signals constantly exist in the environment. To pick up those signals whose influence on the organization is critical, requires considerable abilities which are far beyond present technological capabilities. (1982:5–6)

And yet, people like Sam Steinberg, using nothing more than their processes of informal thought (intuition?), sometimes get it right. Are they just lucky? Or do they have very sophisticated causal models, built up in their minds over the years? How can anyone know for sure? Indeed, even the great visionaries sometimes got wrong the very things that eventually made them famous. "I think there is a world market for about five computers," Thomas J. Watson reportedly said in 1948! "Not within a thousand years will man ever fly," was apparently Wilbur Wright's opinion in 1901! (in Coffey, 1983). So the key to managing discontinuities may not necessarily be to see them immediately, or even first—although the story of a Sam Steinberg is that it certainly doesn't hurt—but to see them soon enough to act, and to do so earlier or at least better than anyone else. To quote the quip of a researcher in the British Foreign Office from 1903 to 1950 on the opposite sort of behavior: "Year after year, the worriers and fretters would come to me with awful predictions of the outbreak of war. I denied it each time. I was only wrong twice!" Twice in half a century can be much too often!

Our conclusions about forecasting should really come as no surprise to anyone, since they have long been recognized. In the first article we could find on business strategy as now conceived, published in 1951, William Newman wrote that "The reliability of most forecasts diminishes rapidly as they are projected further into the future," and he didn't mean long: "two or three months" may be "reasonable" for wage rates, but "three or four years" was "hazardous" (58). Three decades later, in a survey of the "state of the art" of strategic planning in twelve firms, Fahey et al. found that "all of the practitioners admitted they presently do a highly inadequate job [of forecasting]. Most were involved in, or preoccupied with, the short-term implications of events which have already come to pass" (1981:37). As Makridakis summarized the "paradox":

> Although forecasts can and will be inaccurate [since "the future can be predicted only by extrapolating from the past, yet it is fairly certain that the future will be different from the past"] and the future will always be uncertain, no planning . . . is possible without forecasting and without estimating uncertainty. (1990:66)[3]

Why, then, has all the effort been invested in forecasting?

Forecasting as Magic

Leonard Sayles has written that "Apparently our society, not unlike the Greeks with their Delphic oracles, takes great comfort in believing that very talented 'seers' removed from the hurly-burly world of reality, can foretell coming events." Indeed this has even been formalized into what has been labeled the Delphi technique, in which the subjective estimates of a panel of experts are shared and repeated until a consensus is reached. Van Gunsteren has

---

[3] The deleted words after planning are "or strategy." But strategy must surely be possible without forecasting, at the very least strategy of an emergent nature.

referred to its result as "pseudo information," used when real information is lacking. The Delphi technique "provides us with the average 'guesstimate' of ignorant experts, which is then used as the best available scientific forecasting. Planners forget that pseudo-scientific knowledge is much more dangerous than plain ignorance or common sense" (1976:24).

In their article on "Management and Magic," discussed earlier, Gimpl and Dakin gave special attention to forecasting. They opened with an item from the *Natal Daily News:* "A long range weather forecast should be obtained before leaving, as weather conditions are extremely unpredictable"! (1984:125) We hope the writer meant "variable," but the comment does stand for a good deal of the forecasting associated with strategic planning. To quote another of those GE planners: "Basic change is so rapid" that "planning must be more far seeing, operating with a more distant time horizon than previously" (Wilson, 1974:2).

Gimpl and Dakin noted the "fundamental paradox in human behavior—the more unpredictable the world becomes, the more we seek out and rely upon forecasts and predictions to determine what we should do" (125). The explanation they offered was that a good deal of forecasting is simply akin to magic, done for superstitious reasons and because of an obsession with control that becomes the illusion of control. In their words:

It is our contention that management's enchantment with the magical rites of long-range planning, forecasting, and several other future-oriented techniques is a manifestation of anxiety-relieving superstitious behavior, and that forecasting and planning have the same function that magical rites have. . . . they make the world seem more deterministic and give us confidence in our ability to cope, they unite the managerial tribe, and they induce us to take action, at least when the omens are favorable. In addition, these rites may act to preserve the status quo. (125)

To suggest that putting forecasters in today's organizations is akin to putting young girls in the caves of ancient Delphi may sound outlandish. But some of the evidence we have seen does little to refute that assertion.

Forecasting as Extrapolation

There is, of course, one condition under which all of these difficulties disappear: stability. If the world holds still, or at least continues to change exactly as it did in the past, then forecasting can work fine. It has, after all, only the evidence of the past to work from ("projecting past performance patterns into the future" is how Ansoff put it when he teamed up with Eppink and Gomer [1975:13]). That is presumably why the simple extrapolative techniques do so well against the more sophisticated ones. To produce an accurate forecast under conditions of stability, the forecaster has merely to conclude that the future will be just like the past.[4] Forecasting may also come out reasonably well if trends change in a way favorable to the organization, for example, if markets grow faster than predicted. Then at least extrapolation does little harm. Typically it is *over*estimation that causes the problems, for example, by projecting a higher demand for a company's products than actually materializes.

This may help to explain why the 1960s were such good times for forecasters and planners—not because their techniques were any better, but because the trends at that time were more stable or at least more favorable to business. (Recall Makridakis's comment, cited in Chapter 4, about 105 straight months of income growth in GNP.) Thus, in an article entitled "The Accuracy of Long Range Planning," Vancil reported on 16 companies whose five-year forecasts of 1964 "turned out to be only 84 percent of the volume actually generated in 1969" (1983:308). "Long range planning," as a result, "grew and flourished in the sixties" (Hogarth and Makridakis, 1981:122).

As the 1970s progressed, however, especially after the jolt in oil prices in 1973 was followed by new kinds of recessions, forecasting ran into increasing difficulties. Indeed, one type of dysfunctional behavior became so prevalent in the field that it merited a label: the "hockey stick" forecast. Downward trends were extrapolated for a short time, followed by sharp upward predictions, the former be-

---

[4] One subtle problem remains with this, however. Brumbaugh may claim that "there are no past possibilities, and there are no future facts" (in Bolan, 1974:16), but as Chester Barnard has pointed out in a critique of formal planning as a "delusory exercise" (1948:164), the past is uncertain too: "the significance of history and experience" (168) must be interpreted, and that may not be an easy matter.

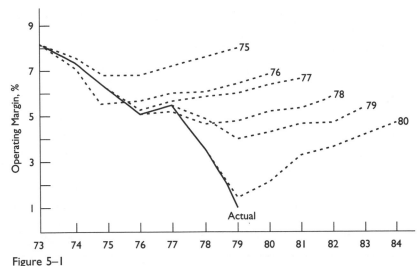

Figure 5–1
The "Hockey Stick" Forecasts
(From "a top fifty U.S. Multinational" in Roach and Allen, 1983:7–13)

ing forecasts, the latter hopes. Things had to get better eventually (or should we say magically)! Figure 5–1 shows the hockey stick forecasts of operating margins for one multinational company: for six years running they predicted the upturn while conditions mostly continued to decline. Unfortunately, the magic had gone out of their forecasting!

Forecasting and "Turbulence"

There is an interesting irony in the ability of forecasting to extrapolate known trends as opposed to predicting new discontinuities, because the very condition that the planning literature has made the most fuss about—turbulence in the environment—is the one characterized by such discontinuities, and therefore the very one that planning can do least about.[5]

---

[5] Godet has written in his book, *Scenarios and Strategic Management:*

> The profound crisis throughout the industrialized world has only just begun. That is the striking fact that sweeps away one's remaining illusions about official forecasts. This crisis was not only unforeseen, but is going to last and grow, contrary to what has been (and continues to be) proclaimed. (1987:3)

An amazing feat of logic: discontinuities form the pattern, which then become predictable themselves. Hence Godet's own "official forecast": turbulence!

Earlier we argued that all this fuss about turbulence really belies the conventional planners' preference for stability, if not actual worries about uncertainty (as well as loss of control). Now we can see why. Organizations may need planning for conditions of stability, to program the consequences of their current strategies into their future operations. But they certainly do not need planning for conditions of instability. Quite the contrary, as we saw most clearly in the Gomer study, or in Koch's comment: "the planners could only sit hopelessly by while phenomena such as the energy crisis wreaked havoc with their predictions" (1976:381). In effect, planners had cried wolf for so long about turbulent environments that when something faintly resembling that condition finally came along, it consumed planning, leaving only the entrails of budgeting behind. They tried to reconstitute planning, through even fancier methods of forecasting—procedures to deal with surprises, analyses of stakeholders, etc.—but all these did was to make the process of planning that much fatter, providing even more delectable meals for the turbulence wolf.

As we argued earlier, the turbulent environment is generally a figment of the conventional planners' imagination. Conditions meriting a label so extreme are rare, at least in Western business. But unexpected changes do occur. An environment may be stable for years, even decades, and then suddenly go all to hell; then planners have to stop extrapolating.

As we noted in Chapter 4, these conditions of so-called turbulence may be nothing more than some serious competition, in recent years from Far Eastern companies less enamored of planning. In other words, an aggressive competitor can waylay the best of plans. Witness the number of wars that were lost by sticking to plan. In business, Rhenman noted the reluctance of companies to take the "idea of 'opponents' " into their planning (1973:139). As one ex-employee of Texas Instruments said of its famous OST planning system: "They've created a paperwork mill that makes it absolutely impossible to respond to anything that moves quickly" (in *Business Week*, 1983:57). Even in so constrained an environment as a game of chess, Alexander Kotov wrote in his book, *Think Like a Grandmaster:*

> There is probably no other strategic concept which a student of the game has dinned into him as much as the concept of conceiving a plan . . .

I tried to play in a planned fashion, working out a plan right after the opening to take me into the ending, but for all my efforts and deep thought on the subject, I got precisely nowhere . . . When you meet a strong inventive opponent and he counters every one of your intentions not only by defensive but also by counter-attacking measures, it is far from simple to carry out a single plan. (1971:147, 150)

Of course, far simpler and less exigent forces than competition can undermine planning too. Like that "unpredictable" weather. The Soviets found out about it when they controlled everything in their plans except the weather. Nature intervened, the crops failed, and the plan was thrown into turmoil. But states don't have to be Communist to suffer the consequences of weather. As we described earlier, the British suffered enormous casualties at the infamous World War I Battle of Passchendaele because when the weather changed, the plans did not.

The Dynamics of Strategy Formation

Part of the assumption of predetermination in strategic planning is the notion of holding still. While the planning is done, and historical data are analyzed, the world sits patiently by. After that, it remains stable, or at least unfolds as predicted, so that the plans can be conveniently implemented. Here we wish to show that all this too is fallacious, that the process of strategy making usually takes place precisely *because* the world does not hold still.

Because planning, in the absence of an ability to control the environment, must rely on forecasting, and because forecasting amounts to extrapolation of known states, existing trends, or recurring patterns, planning typically works best under conditions of relative stability. Now, it turns out that strategy itself, by any definition, is associated with this same condition of stability. Intended strategy refers to the effort to impose a *stable* course of action on the organization, while realized strategy refers to the achievement of a *stable* pattern in the behavior of an organization. Thus, whether deliberate or emergent, strategy is always about stability in an organization's behavior. And so is planning, as a vehicle to help stabilize that behavior. Thus, strategy and planning may sometimes fit quite naturally together. But not planning and strategy *making*.

Bear in mind what strategic planning has been promoted to be: a formalized process that is designed, not to deal with strategy, but to create it. The problem, however, is that while strategy may be associated with conditions of stability, strategy making is generally associated with times of change, and often discontinuous change at that. Organizations do sometimes develop new strategies in times of stability, perhaps because their people have come up with new ideas or simply because they failed earlier to understand previous changes. But more often, it appears, strategies are changed because conditions change, not cyclically or regularly so much as discontinuously. In other words, strategy typically gets changed because something fundamental has changed in the environment, on a one-time basis. And the very fact of changing the strategy creates its own discontinuity in both the organization and the environment on which it is imposed.

No one has ever seen or touched a strategy. Strategies, in other words, do not exist as tangible entities. They are abstract concepts, in the minds of people. And the best of them seem to be *gestalt* in nature, tightly integrated, whether intended strategies as synthesized patterns of preferences prior to the taking of actions[6] or realized strategies as synthesized patterns already formed among actions. Thus, serious change in strategy generally means shift in gestalt—the *conception* of a new worldview, generally based on a permanent change in conditions, or at least the *perception* of such a change. On both sides, therefore—in the mind and out—serious change in strategy tends to be associated with discontinuity, the very thing that planning is least able to handle.

The important consequence is that no matter how compatible planning may be with strategy, it tends to be incompatible with strategy making. As we saw in the Steinberg study in Chapter 3, strategic planning did not create the strategy so much as pursue

---

[6] Andrews, for example, used the word pattern in his definition of strategy as intended: "For us strategy is the pattern of objectives, purposes, or goals and major policies and plans for achieving these goals, stated in such a way as to define what business the company is in or is to be in and the kind of company it is or is to be" (in Learned et al., 1965:17).

the strategy created by other means: it programmed the consequences of the given strategy, in terms of funds to raise, facilities
to build, workers to hire, budgets to prepare, and so on. We can
call this *deterministic planning:* specifying a determined course of
action for the organization. (Ackoff called it "commitment planning" [1970:16].)

The conditions surrounding the strategy making process may
be dynamic, but a general assumption behind much of the planning literature is that the process itself is not dynamic: it is an
unhurried process, that unfolds on a predetermined schedule,
with carefully considered formulation followed by tightly controlled implementation. For the sake of the long-range intentions
of planning (or perhaps the short-range pretensions of conventional planners), organizations are supposed to sit back and work
out their futures at a leisurely pace but on schedule. Strategies
thus appear at predetermined times, popping out when expected,
full-blown, all ready for implementation, with that process too on
schedule. It is almost as if strategies have to be immaculately
conceived. Except that here, ironically, a form of bureaucratic
birth control seems to be firmly in place. We get those "strategies
on demand!"

Well, all of this is fiction. If the empirical research has taught us
anything at all about strategy formation, it is that the process is a
fundamentally dynamic one, corresponding to the dynamic conditions that drive it. It proceeds at its own pace, through what is
best described as a form of learning (e.g., Quinn, 1980a; Pascale,
1984; Mintzberg, 1978; Mintzberg and McHugh, 1985; see also our
critique of the design school in Mintzberg, 1990a). If strategies
represent stability, then strategy formation is interference: it tends
to occur irregularly and unexpectedly, upsetting stable patterns
because of unanticipated discontinuities, whether these originate
from threats in the external environment or opportunities in a
managerial mind. "New ideas do not originate according to a timetable," Anthony wrote in 1965 (39).

In this regard, it is ironic that one of the most appealing concepts concerning strategic response—the *strategic window,* namely
the brief time an organization may have to exploit a fleeting opportunity—came from the pen of an enthusiastic supporter of the
planning school (Abell, 1978). The concept is a good one, but not
for planning, which prefers to keep the windows tightly shut until

the time for spring cleaning arrives.[7] Thus, on a fateful weekend in 1933, after Sam Steinberg discovered that one of his eight stores was losing money, he closed it on a Friday night, shifted it to self-service, slashed its prices by about 25 percent, changed its name, printed and circulated handbills in the area, and reopened Monday morning. That's strategic change! After that, in his words, "We grew like Topsy" (Mintzberg and Waters, 1982:482–483). Good thing Sam Steinberg had no planning system to contend with!

Conventional planners are quick to condemn "management by crisis." They prefer to picture managers as orchestra conductors, standing up there on the podium directing the whole system in controlled and organized harmony. The image is certainly conducive to formal planning. But not to real managing. To quote Len Sayles, a man who has dedicated much of his career to researching managerial work:

> The achievement of . . . stability, which is the manager's objective, is a never-to-be-attained ideal. He is like a symphony orchestra conductor, endeavoring to maintain a melodious performance in which the contributions of the various instruments are coordinated and sequenced, patterned and paced, while the orchestra members are having various personal difficulties, stage hands are moving music stands, alternating excessive heat and cold are creating audience and instrument problems, and the sponsor of the concert is insisting on irrational changes in the program. (1964:162)

Our own research on managerial work (Mintzberg, 1973) indicated that managers spend a good deal of their time responding to high-pressure disturbances. These seem to arise, not only because poor managers let problems deteriorate but also because good managers promote changes that are necessarily disruptive. The effective managers are not the ones who avoid all crises, but those who exploit in opportunistic ways the crises they know they can-

---

[7] Abell tried to reconcile the problem by claiming that "investment in a product line should be timed to coincide with periods in which such a strategic window is open" (21). But how can anyone know in advance when that will be?

not avoid, much as Sam Steinberg did in 1933. (He could, after all, simply have closed that one problematic store. That would certainly have been more compatible with plans for the seven other stores, had such plans existed.)

What this throws into question is the accepted distinction in planning between issues that are long-range strategic and short-range tactical. Decisions made for immediate purposes under short run pressures—whether to handle a crisis or seize an opportunity—can have the most long-range and strategic of consequences (as in the Steinberg example). Likewise, seemingly momentous "strategic" decisions can sometimes fizzle like a punctured balloon. The trouble with the strategy-tactics distinction is that one can never be sure which is which until all the dust has settled. Yet planning has to assume this is known even before the dust begins to blow.

It is this dynamic characteristic of strategy making that helps to explain why managerial work itself has been found to be so dynamic: so hectic in its pace ("one damn thing after another"), so characterized by interruption (rarely half an hour without interruption [Stewart, 1967]), so predisposed to current, oral information; so brief in the duration of its activities and so disorderly in their patterns (Mintzberg, 1973:Chapter 3). As we concluded in our study of the work of five chief executives:

> The pressure of the managerial environment does not encourage the development of reflective planners, the classical literature notwithstanding. The job breeds adaptive information-manipulators who prefer the live, concrete situation. The manager works in an environment of stimulus-response, and he develops in his work a clear preference for live action. (Mintzberg, 1973:38)

All of this is anathema to conventional planners, whose response is to try to "correct" such behavior, for example, by scheduling lengthy long-range planning sessions, perhaps as retreats off in the country. Thus Blass called for a "general change in management style," so as "to schedule deliberately significant amounts of time away from the in-basket and the telephone so that thinking and anticipation would replace rushing and reaction" (1983:6–7). Failing that—finding that "many managers are ill-equipped and

ill-disposed to plan," as Abell and Hammond put it (1979:434)—
some planners try to bypass the managers, doing as much of the
"strategic planning" as possible themselves. That way, as we have
seen, the senior managers need only to review the resulting documents (in summarized doses) for an occasional day or two. And
then the planners pretend that they have created the strategy (until
the president runs off and makes a major acquisition).[8]

The problem with all this is that managers work in "calculated
chaos" (F. Andrews, 1976). They do so not because they are dis-
organized, or do not know how to make use of their secretaries to
screen interruptions, or even because they fail to recognize the
importance of reflective planning, but for quite the opposite reason: because they know that only by working in this way can they
hope to be able to develop strategies in a dynamic setting. (And if
they cannot, the problem is not an absence of formal planning but
of managerial ability, or, as we shall see, of the detachment of
managers from context.) For example, struck during our own study
of chief executives by the frequency of interruptions in their work,
we began to notice that they positively encouraged it. In part they
were no doubt caught up in the pressures and pace of their work
(for example, their inevitable backlog of obligations). But in part
they were also sensitive to the unpredictable nature of the situations around them, the need to remain responsive to the changes
that were always unfolding. Likewise, we found that oral information was favored because it was faster, more current, and richer
in content (as we shall discuss).

Thus, while strategies themselves are by definition stable, and

---

[8] As, in fact, did Reginald Jones, who, as chief executive of General Electric, may
have been planning's greatest supporter ever. In complete disregard of his firm's
own plans, he up and made "at the time . . . the largest acquisition ever to take
place in the United States":

> . . . Reg Jones' most significant strategic move, the 1976 acquisition of Utah
> International, was not made because of analysis provided by GE's portfolio
> approach to strategic planning. Jones explained: "This was sort of an ad hoc
> decision that came about because of a fortuitous opportunity developing. . . . It
> is true that when our strategic planning was put in place and we began to look
> for areas of growth and diversification that mining was not one that came to us
> from our own strategic planning exercises. It did develop because Ed Littlefield
> (Utah's chairman) was a valued member of the Board of Directors . . ." (Hamer-
> mesh, 1986:195).

environments may be more or less stable, the process of strategy making must always be dynamic, precisely because it is about change and one can never know when or how environments will change. (In our own studies, situations sometimes remained roughly stable for decades, only to collapse in a period of weeks.) This is another reason why planning fails at strategy making.

Forecasting as Control (and Planning as Enactment)

There is one condition under which all of these arguments would seem to fall away and those of planning to hold up. That is when the organization has the power to impose its own plans on its environment. To repeat Karl Weick's favorite word, it can "enact" its environment (1979). Then it can plan at its leisure, and implement the plans on schedule, after that even remaining consistent, ignoring signals from the outside if it so wishes. Indeed, such an organization need not even worry about forecasting, since its plans are its forecasts! What they specify determines what the environment does.[9] Also, by the same token, planning reverts to its preferred condition of stability, but here by virtue of its own efforts: it defines the form of stability desired and then imposes it on a benevolent environment. Under what we might call *enactment planning*, the obsession with control finds its perfect home.

Nice work if you can get it. Some do try, and even succeed for a time. The Soviet Union tried to control everything through planning and had some degree of success (in realizing its plans if not in enhancing its productivity by using them), so long as the weather and the populace acquiesced. Enactment planning requires some kind of closed system, at least in one direction: the organization may be able to influence the environment but the environment cannot seriously affect the organization. Weather has to be controllable (or not relevant), citizens or employees have to work diligently, competitors have to cooperate (i.e., there must be no

---

[9] Makridakis and Wheelwright preferred to call this "normative" or "teleological" forecasting, which "assumes that people are not passive agents, but rather can, and should, take an active role in formulating the future" (1981:122). This, however, seems to take excessive liberties with the word forecasting.

real competitors), and so on. In "modern planning theory . . . government is seen as a 'closed system' which can be organized in cybernetic terms" (Dyson, 1975:170).[10]

Unfortunately, perfectly closed systems just do not exist. When the weather changes unpredictably, or the economy suddenly falters, or those workers or citizens or competitors develop ideas of their own, the careful planning can collapse, as it did, ironically, in the Communist states and American corporations alike.

These experiences notwithstanding, enactment planning has always had its supporters, even for the private sector. For example, Ackoff wrote in an article entitled "Beyond Prediction and Preparation" that "control is obviously more desirable than prediction of and preparation for, what we do not control": "the future is largely subject to creation; it can be prepared. The more of it we can create, the less of it we need to forecast or predict" (1983:62, 61). In fact, Eric Rhenman, an astute observer of business behavior, argued that only enactment planning, not deterministic planning, can succeed, because having to rely on forecasting is unacceptable: "Corporations," by which he meant organizations that set their own strategic directions

> must dominate their environment if they are to be able to fulfill their own internal (strategic) planning. Only thus can the corporation compensate for the inevitable uncertainty of all environmental forecasting. . . . An organization that cannot thus dominate its environment, but which behaves as though it could predict environmental developments and designs long-range operational plans accordingly, is almost sure to run into serious difficulties. (1973:79–80)

Or as Eric Hofer, the popular philosopher, put it more succinctly: "The only way to predict the future is to have power over the future" (in Ansoff, 1979a:196).

But even when it works, we must ask: What price enactment? What price planning? What kind of society do we create when we promote such planning?

---

[10] See also our discussion of the closed system power configuration (in Mintzberg, 1983:Chapter 19), the form of machine-type bureaucracy that seeks to seal itself off from external influence.

The Communist states provided us with an answer for the public sector (see also our discussion of "planning and freedom" on pages 167–170). And the answer for the private sector is not so different. John Kenneth Galbraith wrote an entire book, referred to earlier, to make the point that giant corporations—which he considered to be oligopolies, relatively free of serious competition—engaged in planning in order to enact their environments. Referring to them as the "new industrial states," he argued that they were what made planning so popular in America.

> in addition to deciding what the consumer will want and will pay, the firm must take every feasible step to see that what it decides to produce is wanted by the consumer at a remunerative price. And it must see that the labor, materials and equipment that it needs will be available at a cost consistent with the price it will receive. It must exercise control over what is sold. It must exercise control over what is supplied. It must replace the market with planning. (1967:23–24)[11]

Note the year of Galbraith's publication: 1967. It was the ideal time for enactment planning in America. Things have not been quite so good since, however, what with the energy crises, the advent of Japanese competition, a certain amount of deregulation, and the loss of buoyancy in the Western economies. This is not to say that enactment planning has disappeared: there remain organizations in comfortable niches (for example, with patent protection), some utilities with monopolistic powers, certain government departments that can impose their strategies on the citizenry, and so on.[12] But for the rest, likely the vast majority, that can neither enact their environments nor predict them, life has not been so

---

[11] Steiner provides us with a perfect example of this way of thinking, although his vocabulary is somewhat euphemistic: "The Franklin Mint . . . found an unfulfilled demand for coins and metals produced specifically to be collected, but it took a substantial marketing effort to convince collectors that they had this need" (1979:185–186).

[12] Hydro Quebec, a powerful state-owned electricity utility in Canada, provided a marvelous example in early 1987. It asked the government for a guarantee of regular 5 percent rate increases over the next twenty years! (And that on the claim of needing to run itself in a businesslike way! Which real—read competitive—business can control its prices in 20 months, let alone 20 years?)

easy in the planning department. Rather than give up, however, many chose instead to elaborate: to replace straight forecasting with more sophisticated "scenario" building, and simple deterministic planning with more complex "contingency planning."

Scenarios Instead of Forecasts

Scenario building, another "tool" in the "strategist's arsenal," to quote Michael Porter (1985:481), is predicated on the assumption that if you cannot predict *the* future, then by speculating upon a variety of them, you might just hit upon the right one. Porter devoted a chapter of his 1985 book to the subject, describing a scenario as "not a forecast but one possible future structure," involving the identification of uncertainties, the determination of causal factors that drive them, and the formation of a range of possible assumptions about each combined into the scenario (448, 449).

There has been a good deal of interest in scenario building in recent years, stimulated in part by Pierre Wack's article about development of a scenario for Royal Dutch Shell that described the nature (if not the timing) of the shift in the world petroleum market that occurred in 1973. In Wack's account of the Shell experience, the reader learns how complex and subtle such an exercise can be, dependent on judgment no less than formal analysis. Compared with traditional planning, "the scenarios focused less on predicting outcomes and more on understanding the forces that would eventually compel an outcome; less on figures and more on insight" (1985a:84).

This is no simple business, however. For one thing, there is the problem of deciding how many scenarios to build. The more there are, the better chance that one will hit it right. But planners' time is not limitless, neither is the manager's mental capacity to consider all the possibilities. The planners, in other words, need enough scenarios to cover not only the probable but also the important possible contingencies, yet few enough to be manageable (quite literally). In a footnote, Wack claimed that "six are far too many" (82). But what is the number of possible configurations that an environment can throw at an organization? Can anyone know?

Another problem is what to do once several scenarios have been built. Porter suggested five possibilities: bet on the most probable one, bet on the best one for the firm, hedge so as to get satisfactory results no matter which one results, preserve flexibility, or go out and exert influence to make the most desirable scenario a reality. Short of being able to do the last (enactment), the choice is not easy. Hedging or remaining flexible has its own costs, primarily in lack of commitment to a clear strategy. But betting incurs risks. Who is to know whether any of the scenarios will occur? And as Wack pointed out at some length, even when the planners are quite sure that one of their scenarios is on the right track—as he claimed they were at Shell—there remains the problem of convincing the management to do something about it.

The scenario favored by the Wack group "varied sharply from the implicit worldview then prevailing at Shell," which he "characterized loosely as 'explore and drill, build refineries, order tankers, and expand markets' " (82). Under the scenario he believed most likely, upstream managers, in charge of exploration and production, had to accept the possible loss of their traditional profit base and had to develop new relationships with the producing nations, while downstream managers, in charge of refining, transporting, and marketing, had to face lower growth. Changing the managerial worldview proved to be a "much more demanding task" (84) than actually building the scenario. Among other things, they had to build "challenge" and "phantom" scenarios (82, 86). His group eventually succeeded, as he reported it, so that managerial behaviors changed. But perhaps more important, the shift in worldview, in Wack's opinion, enabled the managers of this decentralized company to deal more effectively with the crisis when it did occur, in 1973.

> Strategies are the product of a worldview. When the world changes, managers need to share some common view of the new world. Otherwise, decentralized strategic decisions will result in management anarchy. Scenarios express and communicate this common view, a shared understanding of the new realities to all parts of the organization. (89)

Shell, as Wack described its experience, was a fortunate organization, perhaps an unusual one, given the sophistication of the scenario builders and their ability to convince a management of the need for change. Perhaps we can conclude that this is an example of *planners* at their best—but not *planning* because the exercise produced analytical (really what Ansoff would call quasi-analytical) inputs to managers, but did not constitute an attempt to formalize the process of making strategy per se. (Indeed, it is not clear that it even constituted scenario building per se, because by Wack's own account, in the course of the exercise the group seized on one particular view of the future and promoted it heavily: "now we saw the discontinuity as predetermined" [84].)

The Wack account does not point out how commonly such exercises fail, either in the scenarios built or the behaviors avoided. On one hand, few groups seem to be as adept as Wack and his colleagues at hitting things so right, especially in such a complex set of circumstances. (Perhaps its exceptional character is why the *Harvard Business Review* chose to publish Wack's article in the first place and why it subsequently became so well-known.) Other groups are sometimes less astute, more reliant on hard data to the exclusion of soft judgment, or perhaps just less well-informed. Or else they simply face environments subjected to more random disturbances (unexpected technological breakthroughs, chance wars, replacement of key actors, etc.). To Wildavsky the future "is an infinity of branching possibilities" (1971:104). Or as March put it:

> Because there are so many very unlikely future events that can be imagined, and each is so improbable, we ordinarily exclude them from our more careful forecasts, though we know that some very unlikely events will certainly occur. As a result, our plans are based on a future that we know, with certainty, will not be realized. (1981:572)

On the other hand, there are the groups that do it well in conditions where it can be done, like that of Wack, but then fail because they cannot influence the necessary behavior, namely to convince management to agree with the prediction and act accordingly. Wack, in fact, had trouble with Shell's second-echelon managers. At one point, "the scenario package had sparked some intellectual interest but had failed to change behavior in much of the Shell organization" (84). Wack may have overcome this eventually but there are famous stories of planners who did not:

As far back as 1936 war games and drills in the Hawaiian Islands had been planned on the basis of a surprise attack on Pearl Harbor ... defined as a surprise air raid by Japan. G-2 had a plan known as "Orange," to provide for defense against such an attack. The general and admiral in command of air units in Hawaii had approved the requirements for that defense. But the actual organizational routines proceeded without reference to that planning exercise. ... [D]espite two alerts in July and October 1941, "before December 7 Short [the Army Commander] held no drill or alert in which the boxes of ammunition were opened. (Allison, 1971:92, quoting Wholstetter)

Ansoff remarked in his 1984 book that "observation, as well as some recent studies of the responses to the petroleum crisis, both show that many firms which do forecasting exhibit the same procrastinating behavior as the reactive firms," even those that use "scenarios" and other techniques "specifically addressed to ... strategic discontinuities" (317). He attributed the problem to delays of four types: those due to systems, to awaiting verification, to politics, and to rejection of the unfamiliar. A systems delay involves "the time consumed in observing, interpreting, collating, and transmitting information to the responsible managers" (316). The other delays result because management may consider "the triggering information ... conjectural," it being "imprudent and foolish to respond to 'mere speculations' about the future"; because the management may feel politically threatened by the information; and because psychologically, the managers "may refuse to take seriously a vague threat which has no precedent in prior experience" (318). All things considered, the probabilities of getting everything right in scenario building do not seem to be high, thus perhaps explaining why "scenario planning has been scarcely developed" (Wack, 1985b:139).

Contingency Planning Instead of Deterministic Planning

Scenario building is, of course, just the first step. If strategic planning is to prevail, then the scenarios must be formally factored into the organization's plans. To turn a set of scenarios into a deterministic plan would obviously not make a lot of sense unless there is overwhelming confidence in one of them (as in the Shell experience). What corresponds to scenario building, therefore, is *contingency planning*, the creation of alternate plans to deal with different scenarios.[13] Then the organization can be prepared for whichever scenario may be borne out.

It all sounds good in theory. Practice, however, presents several problems. Contingency planning may work when the possibilities are circumscribed and each is well structured, based on long experience—as in the occurrence of snowstorms in northern cities or government interest rate changes affecting a bank. But contingency planning poses several problems in more open-ended contexts, where knowledge about possible contingencies is limited. As already noted, no matter how much is invested in such planning, the contingency that does arise may never have been contemplated, or at least planned for. To quote Makridakis, "practical considerations prohibit the consideration of all but a small number of [the "innumerable" possibilities that can arise]" (1979:106). And even those considered may turn out to have been "precapsuled programs to respond in precise ways to stimuli that never quite occurred as expected" (Quinn, 1980a:122). Of course, in some cases the consequences are so important that the effort must be made anyway, as in contingency planning for the sudden death of a key executive.

The less obvious problems concern commitment, with which contingency planning can play havoc, in two very different ways. Porter's suggestion of hedging notwithstanding, it is difficult to act in the face of several scenarios. Organizations function on the basis of commitment and mind-set. In other words, it is determined and inspired people who get things done. Being faced with an "on the one hand, on the other hand" possibility hardly engenders such spirit. That, presumably, is one reason why, as Wack noted, managers "yearn for some kind of 'definiteness' " (1985b:139). Contingency planning risks causing "paralysis by analysis," since managers are encouraged, not to act but to wait. As Weick put it, people who "cultivat[e] future adaptability, and sacrific[e] current

---

[13] This might be added as a sixth to Porter's list of possible responses, although he did mention it as a lead into his discussion of scenario building, dismissing it as "rare in practice" because firms "facing considerable uncertainty . . . tend to select strategies that preserve flexibility . . ." (1985:446).

adaptation . . . live in an eternal state of readiness and loneliness and are able to handle everything except the next customer who walks through the door" (1979:247). This is reminiscent of Dubé's (1973) finding that the Canadian military planned when it had nothing else to do, then scrapped its plans when it had to act.

More subtle, but oftentimes more serious, is the opposite problem of commitment: the organization executes a contingency plan not because it needs it but because it has it. We all carry a spare tire in our car in case of a flat tire, as Ackoff (1983:63) noted as an example of contingency planning. But we do not puncture a good tire so that we can use it. The same is not always true of organizations, whose equivalent of a spare tire can be a department committed to the execution of the contingency plan. Thus some years ago (December 17, 1971), *Time* magazine reported the story of some firemen in Texas who set fire to abandoned buildings because they were bored. Less frivolous was the story of the Green Berets, set up as "special forces" to fight a guerrilla war just in case they were needed. Unfortunately, in Vietnam they made themselves needed: the contingency plan became self-fulfilling. To quote Halberstam on the broader story:

> It was an odd year 1964, the calm before the storm; the bureaucracy was, in a phrase which the Vietnam war would help create, doing its own thing, planning away, storing up options. The military were beginning to check out bombing sites, and deep in the bowels of the Pentagon, trained professional staff men who knew something about contingency plans were working on what might be needed if we decided to go to war, and if we needed ground troops, and if so, which units would go and which reserve units might be called up. All ifs, of course, but the Pentagon was ready. (1972:398)[14]

Of course, given pressures to act and a superficial understanding of a new situation, what more convenient response than to pull out the contingency plans at hand? They at least satisfy the leaders'

---

[14] The same phenomenon in Britain appears to have helped set World War I on its unfortunate course: "despite a great deal of reluctance in the British cabinet . . . the plans determined the action which the British did in fact take" (Steinbruner, 1974:133).

need to do *something* and the planners' need to have been useful. Even if the plans don't quite fit. Again, the abstract myth provides a convenient substitute for the messy reality.

To conclude discussion of this first fallacy, predetermination works fine when the world of planning is stable, or at least the trends are favorable, so that the organization can extrapolate forecasts as well as the existing strategies themselves. It also works fine (for the organization at least) when the world is under the control of the organization and its plans, so that strategies can be imposed on a benevolent environment, in effect enacting whatever "forecasts" are made. Scenario building followed by contingency planning may work fine when the uncertainties of the world are few and certain, in other words, when they reduce to an inability to predict only which of several well-defined options will in fact happen (assuming that such planning promotes neither inaction nor the invocation of a plan just because it exists). It also works, perhaps, when it can be done with the sophistication that Wack described—probably not all that common. Otherwise—and this encompasses a great deal of behavior—the predetermination assumption of planning proves to be a fallacy.

The Fallacy of Detachment

As we have seen, a key assumption in planning is that of detachment, particularly of strategy from operations, and, as a result, of what is called strategic management from operating management. Earlier we quoted Jelinek on the benefits of "abstracting" management from the day-to-day operations: "true planning direction" becomes "possible solely because management is no longer wholly immersed in the details of the task itself" (1979:139). Instead it can concentrate on the really important, long-range, "strategic" issues.

No small number of advisors to management have picked up this torch. "One consulting firm ... informed its client that the officers of the company should give up day-to-day operational management to their subordinates and devote the majority of their time to planning for the future" (Blass, 1983:6–7). Or better still, "some companies have seriously considered coding their data banks so that upon inquiry from a senior executive on a question of detail, it would point out: 'You are above the level in this company authorized to have this information'" (Tilles, 1972:68). Perhaps most blatant of all was this comment reported by a British executive:

> ... the Chief Executive of a world famous group of management consultants tried hard to convince me [in the early 1960s] that it is ideal that top level management executives should have as little knowledge as possible relative to the product. This great man really believed that this qualification enabled them to deal efficiently with all business matters in a detached and uninhibited way.[15]

In fact, this view is built right into the strategic planning model itself, in the sharp distinction it makes between formulation of strategy—a task restricted to the important people in the organization, ostensibly senior management, but also including the strategic planners—and the implementation of strategy, the job of everyone else.

The justification for this amounts to what March and Simon years ago labeled a "Gresham's Law of planning: Daily routine drives out planning" (1958:185). Accordingly, conventional planners have seen it as their duty to try to drive out the daily pressures ("routine" being hardly the right word for managerial work), so that the managers could concentrate on the planning.[16] They establish timetables and schedule retreats to make sure it happenes, or, failing that, as we have seen, take over as much of the process as possible themselves. (A more recent rendition of this has been to establish the post of "strategic manager," a kind of hybrid line

---

[15] Hopwood (1981:173).

[16] Given the parenthetical point, there is an interesting irony to how March and Simon restated their law: An individual "faced both with highly programmed and highly unprogrammed tasks" will tend to allow the former to "take precedence" over the latter (195). The problem, therefore, is to preserve the capacity to do the necessary unprogrammed work. But planning, as we have seen, is predicated on programming, while managerial work is, by its very nature, largely unprogrammed. Are managers, therefore, doing well for March and Simon by resisting planning?

manager and staff planner, with formal responsibility for strategy itself, nothing more.)

But did any of this resolve the problem? Indeed, was the problem correctly defined in the first place? Was the amount of time devoted to planning, or to "strategy," really the problem? We think not, believing the real problem has not been the lack of strategic *planning*, perhaps not even the lack of strategic *thinking* per se, but a lack of strategic *acting*. Some organizations have failed to adapt. Far from solving this problem, formal strategic planning may have aggravated it where it did exist, or created it where it did not.

Seeing the Forest And the Trees

There is no doubt that organizations need good strategic thinkers, sometimes at least. There is no doubt too that good strategic thinkers are reflective, the kind of people who, in the popular metaphor, can rise above the trees to see the forest—can take the broad, long-term perspective. But to claim that effective strategic response depends on those kinds of people being perched permanently in the air (presumably on the platform of a formal system) is, in our view, a fallacy that has proved terribly costly to many organizations. To quote one sober planning executive, "the notion that an effective strategy can be constructed by someone in an ivory tower is totally bankrupt" (in *Business Week,* 1984a:64). Or, as Dean Acheson responded to President Eisenhower's presumed need for more time in isolation to think:

> This absorption with the Executive as Emerson's "Man Thinking" surrounded by a Cabinet of Rodin statues, bound in an oblivion of thought . . . seemed to me unnatural. Surely thinking is not so difficult, so hard to come by, so solemn as all this. (in Sayles, 1964:209)

Effective strategists are not people who abstract themselves from the daily detail but quite the opposite: they are the ones who *immerse* themselves in it, while being able to abstract the *strategic messages* from it. Perceiving the forest from the trees is not the right metaphor at all, therefore, because opportunities tend to be hidden under the leaves. A better one may be to detect a diamond in the rough in a seam of ore. Or to mix the metaphors, no one ever found a diamond by flying over a forest. From the air, a forest looks like a simple carpet of green, not the complex living system it really is.

Our discussion so far in this book has been laced with reasons why detachment works against strategic management. In the pitfalls, we pointed out how detachment can discourage the very commitment that may prove so crucial to the effective realization of an intended strategy. In this chapter, we have already noted the problems of trying to distinguish strategy from tactics a priori, since what may have appeared tactical at the outset (such as the weather at Passchendaele) may turn out to be strategic in the final analysis. By distancing managers who are expected to make strategy from what has been predesignated tactical, planning reduces their chances of recognizing the tactical that ultimately proves strategic. As we quoted when discussing Passchendaele, while the battle may have been "strategically desirable," it was "tactically impossible." But the detached strategists never knew that, and so a quarter of a million British troops fell.

Here we shall discuss several concerns we have with the assumption of detachment, the most significant being the artificiality of separating thinking from action. We shall consider this in its own terms after discussing its manifestation in two places in the basic model—the assessment of strengths and weaknesses and the dichotomy between formulation and implementation. But first we wish to take the assumption of detachment at face value and consider instead the validity of one of its key corollaries—that managers and planners detached from the operating details can be properly informed by so-called "hard data." If this proves to be a fallacy, then so too must be the assumption of detachment.

The Soft Underbelly of Hard Data

The belief that strategic managers and their planning systems can be detached from the subject of their efforts is predicated on one fundamental assumption: that they can be informed in a formal way. To be more specific, detachment is possible only if the information they need can be provided conveniently. The messy world of random noise, gossip, inference, impression, and fact must thus be reduced to firm data, hardened and aggregated so that they can be supplied regularly in digestible form. "It is not until the senior management learns to content itself with more aggregate reporting, leaving the middle management to cope with the details, that effective planning can be considered" (Tilles, 1963:111–121). Perhaps all too true.

The message in the planning literature has been that such data are not only valid substitutes for the softer, more qualitative data, but that they are, in fact, superior to them. This message was as evident in the early years of the planning literature, which emphasized numerical forecasting and analyses of costs and benefits, as it is today, with the current interests in competitor analysis and shareholder value (which assumes measurable relations between strategies and stock prices).

For data to be "hard" means that they can be documented unambiguously, which usually means that they have already been quantified. That way planners and managers can sit in their offices and be informed. No need to go out and meet the troops, or the customers, to find out how the products get bought or the wars get fought or what connects those strategies to that stock price; all that just wastes valuable time. This is, after all, the age of the computer. Systems will do it, whether they go by the names of (reading back over the years) "information technology," "strategic information systems," "expert systems," "total systems," or just plain so-called "management information systems" (MIS).

We have already considered some of the problems of hard data in our discussion of the planning pitfalls, for example, how calculation can impede commitment and how a bias toward the quantitative can allow the economic to displace the social and the financial to displace the creative. The conventional planners' emphasis on "objectivity" reflects itself not only in biases in the goals favored but also in the data processed. But here we wish to go beyond these points, to suggest that hard data can seriously bias and so distort any strategy making process that relies on it excessively.

Study after study has demonstrated that managers of every sort rely primarily on oral forms of communication, on the order of about 80 percent of their time (see Mintzberg, 1973:38–44; our favorite statistic in this regard is that even managers of information systems proved to be no less dependent on oral communication, at 76 percent of their time [Ives and Olson, 1981]; they also made almost no use of computers in their own offices!). What makes speaking and listening so important to managers? We believe the primary answer lies not in bad habits or gregarious personalities but in the kind of information conveyed by the oral media. Several years ago, in a monograph for the National Association of Accountants entitled "Impediments to the Use of Management Information" (Mintzberg, 1975b), we drew a number of conclusions about the limitations of information provided by formal management systems. We summarize them here:

1. Hard information is often limited in scope, lacking richness and often failing to encompass important noneconomic and non-quantitative factors. Formal information tends to provide the basis for description but not explanation, for example, revealing that sales were lost but not what drove the buyers away. That is why a conversation with a single disgruntled customer can sometimes be worth more than a major marketing research report.[17] Moreover, the emphasis on quantification tends to discourage the consideration of a whole range of factors, softer but no less critical for strategy making. That is why Marsh et al. found in their study of capital budgeting that the costs and benefits most difficult to quantify tended to be excluded from the financial analyses (1988:26). And, more generally, Pfeffner has contrasted "economic rationality" with "administrative rationality," the latter "taking into account an additional spectrum of facts. These are the facts relative to emotions, politics, power, group dynamics, personality and mental health" (1960:126). The point is that much information important for strategy making never does become hard fact. The expression on a customer's face, the mood in the factory, the tone

---

[17] In academia, the equivalent is the quantitative course evaluations that (in our view) prove effective at gauging the sentiments of the class but are useless for understanding successes or diagnosing failures. Again, a conversation with a candid student or two can often supply the needed explanation. Bryson, raising the problem of measuring performance in schools—"how 'educated' [the] students are"—commented: "The recent movement toward standardized testing of school graduates is an attempt to measure outcomes in order to remedy this shortcoming . . . " (1988:55). Remedy the situation or force the problem (and the teaching) to conform to the measures?

of voice of a government official, all of this can be information for the manager but not for the MIS.

These dangers of excessive reliance on hard information were nowhere better illustrated than in what Wilensky referred to as the "ghoulish statistics" of the war in Vietnam:

> analysis of the easy-to-measure variables (casualties suffered by the Viet Cong and the South Vietnamese) was driving out consideration of the hard-to-measure variables and long-run costs (the nature of popular support for a South Vietnam government, the effect of the war on the Western Alliance and on domestic civility, the effect of bombing on the will to resist) . . . kill ratios and the like represent a touch of spurious certainty in a highly uncertain world . . . (1967:188–189)

Halberstam commented in his book, *The Best and the Brightest,* on the first of these variables, popular support:

> When [civilian advisors] said the Diem government was losing popularity with the peasants because of the Buddhist crisis, [Secretary of Defense] McNamara asked, well, what percentage was dropping off, what percentage did the government have and what percentage was it losing? He asked for facts, some statistics, something he could run through the data bank, not just this poetry they were spouting. (1972:56)

The oral channels of communication, especially face-to-face contact, are favored by many managers (if not McNamara) because these enable them to "read" this indispensable poetry. Hard information is often sterile in comparison and so, when relied upon, tends to encourage the development of less flexible strategies, lacking nuance (as in the Vietnam experience).

Managers, of course, have natural access to such soft information within their own organizations, so long as they do not detach themselves from it. They can read the faces of their colleagues, walk around the factories, listen for tone of voice in meetings. The same type of information may be accessible from the external environment as well, although less conveniently. But that does not make it any less critical (as McNamara eventually found out). That is why managers generally spend a great deal of time developing their own *personal* information systems, comprising networks of contacts and informers of all kinds, including customers, suppliers, trade organization members, government officials, and competitors (Aguilar, 1967; Mintzberg, 1973). In his study of the external information that managers use, Aguilar found that personal sources exceeded impersonal sources in perceived importance by 70 percent to 29 percent. He illustrated this with the comment of a senior partner in an investment banking firm:

> Probably the most important source of external information for any successful executive in a large corporation is the informal network of contacts which he has outside the company. . . . These are the people on whom the executive will rely for information, advice, and reactions. You could think of them as constituting a kitchen cabinet for the executive. (76)

2. Much hard information is too aggregated for effective use in strategy making. The obvious solution for a manager overloaded with information and pressed for the time necessary to process it is to have the information aggregated. And as the organization gets larger, and the managerial level higher, more and more information must be aggregated. Back to the forest instead of the trees. After all, how can you manage a large forest if all you see are single trees? General Electric before 1980 provided an excellent example of this type of thinking. First it introduced the "Strategic Business Units" (SBUs) over the divisions and departments, and then the "Sectors" over the SBUs, in each case seeking to increase the level of aggregation to enable top management to comprehend the necessary information quickly. Hamermesh tells the story. He quotes CEO Reginald Jones:

> Right from the start of SBU planning in 1972, the vice chairmen and I tried to review each plan in great detail. This effort took untold hours and placed tremendous burden on the Corporate Executive office. After a while I began to realize that no matter how hard we would work, we could not achieve the necessary in-depth understanding of the forty-odd SBU plans. Somehow the review burden had to be carried on more shoulders. (1986:197)

Hamermesh wrote that "creating the sector structure was Jones' way to spread the review load." This was "a new level of management that represented a macro-business or industry area," which would integrate the SBU strategies into a single plan, six in all. "The Corporate Executive would thereafter focus its review on the strategic plans of the six sectors," thereby "reducing the review burden on the CEO" (197). Jones was enthusiastic:

> The Sector approach turned out to be very successful. It even exceeded my expectations. I could look at some planning books and understand them well enough to ask the right questions. I could not do that before. (202)

It was very convenient for Jones, especially as he spent more and more of his time in Washington serving as the elder statesman of American business, which "limited his time for internal GE matters" (198). The only problem was that the more aggregated became the information, the more detached became the CEO. Eventually the situation was reversed when Jack Welch replaced Jones as CEO, with a more "hands-on" approach to management (and, presumably, fewer illusions about being able to run the corporation by remote control).

The fallacy of relying on hard information lies in the assumption that nothing is lost in the process of aggregation. The reality is that a great deal is lost, often the essence of the information, sometimes to the point where management loses control of the strategy making process. How much could aggregated data on six sectors really tell Jones about the complex organization he headed? It may be fine to see forests, but only so long as nothing is going on among the trees. Even lumber companies cannot make strategy by looking only at the forests. They need to study the wood and the terrain, and many other details. Consider the comments of Richard Neustadt, who studied the information-collecting habits of three Presidents of the United States:

> It is not information of a general sort that helps a President see personal stakes; not summaries, not surveys, not the *bland amalgams*. Rather . . . it is the odds and ends of *tangible detail* that pieced together in his mind illuminate the underside of issues put before him. To help himself he must reach out as widely as he can for every scrap of fact, opinion, gossip, bearing on his interests and

relationships as President. He must become his own director of his own central intelligence. (1960:153–154, italics added)

Managers need such tangible detail for two reasons. First, they require triggers to action—tangible stimuli that will encourage them to evoke decision-making activity (Mintzberg, Raisinghani and Théorêt, 1976). As one executive commented: "The many tidbits of information that an executive picks up through informal conversations with other businessmen serve . . . in alerting the businessman that *something* has changed . . . that there is something more to be learned" (quoted in Aguilar, 1967:103). Second, managers describe their worlds in terms of conceptual models that they develop in their heads (Allison, 1971; Holsti, 1962). As Neustadt suggested, such models are built from tangible scraps of identifiable information, not from bland aggregations.

3. Much hard information arrives too late to be of use in strategy making. Information takes time to "harden." Time is required for trends and events and performance to become recorded as "facts," more time for these facts to be aggregated into reports, even more time if these reports are to be presented on a predetermined schedule. Thus hard information is fundamentally historical: it reflects things that happened in the past. But strategy making, as described earlier, is an active, dynamic process, often unfolding quickly in reaction to immediate stimuli. As a result, oftentimes managers cannot wait for information to harden. While that is happening, competitors may be running off with valued customers, workers may be staging wildcat strikes, and new technologies may be undermining existing product lines. The world is hardly prepared to wait for information to get itself into a form acceptable to the planners and their systems. For example, while McNamara's "best and brightest" were processing the body counts—statistics that were dead in more ways than one—the Vietcong were moving live bodies down the jungle paths.

A military commander has to know about enemy movements as they take place, not later in terms of official statistics. Likewise, a politician has to understand the mood of the people, not some sterile polling of voter preference. And a business manager has to know the real customers, not just their historical buying habits.

These are the reasons why managers bypass formal systems to create their own informal ones, and why gossip, hearsay, and speculation form such a large part of every effective manager's informational diet (Mintzberg, 1973). Such information may not be precise, but it is timely; Davis (1953) who conducted extensive research on grapevine communication, found it to be fast and selective.

4. Finally, a surprising amount of hard information is unreliable. Soft information is supposed to be unreliable, subject to all kinds of biases. Hard information, in contrast, is supposed to be tangible and precise; it is, after all, transmitted and stored electronically. In fact, hard information can be no better and is oftentimes far worse than soft information.

Something is always lost in the process of quantification—before those electrons are activated—not just in the rounding-out of numbers but in the conversion of confusing events into numerical tabulations in the first place. Quantitative measures, noted Ijiri, Jaedicke, and Knight (1970), who wrote from within the accounting field, are only "surrogates" for reality. And some are rather crude. The body counts in Vietnam were precise but hardly reliable. How were the counters to distinguish enemy guerrillas from innocent bystanders? Indeed, what incentive did they have to do so, given their understanding of what the planners in Washington wanted to read?[18] Anyone who has ever produced a quantitative measure—whether a reject count in a factory as a surrogate for product quality, a publication count in a university as a surrogate for research performance, or estimates of costs and benefits in a capital budgeting exercise—knows just how much distortion is possible, intentional as well as unintentional.

---

[18] In the mid-1980s, William Westmoreland, who had commanded the U.S. forces in Vietnam, sued CBS for the implication in a television documentary that he had deliberately deceived his superiors in Washington in presenting data on troop strengths. His suit suggested that the distortions may have occurred below his level of command, that he too was detached from the real facts. But of interest here in the court trial was that, while "elite officials who set American policy and managed the war in Vietnam," such as Robert McNamara and Walter Rostow, testified on Westmoreland's behalf, "lower-ranking officers and intelligence analysts" testified for CBS (Glynn, 1985:48). What, one is tempted to ask, did McNamara and Rostow really know about these distortions?

In this regard, Devons's account of "statistics and planning" (1950:Chapter 7) in the Air Ministry of the British government during World War II makes fascinating reading. "Without statistics there can be no planning," he began, since "planning is mainly based on the examination of past trends and their extrapolation into the future." He noted that "The first stage in planning a production program must, therefore, be the collection of records of actual production in the past." But "elementary and fundamental though this point may appear, the collection ["of the production statistics"] led to untold difficulties" (133).

Devons then proceeded through a litany of horror stories. The collection of such data was extremely difficult and subtle, demanding "a high degree of skill," yet "was treated . . . as inferior, degrading and routine work on which the most inefficient clerical staff could best be employed" (134). Errors entered the data in all kinds of ways, even just treating months as normal although almost all included some holiday or other. "Figures were often merely a useful way of summing up judgement and guesswork," and were sometimes based on "quite arbitrary assumptions," even developed through "statistical bargaining," in which officials compromised their estimates (155). A guess "hazarded" in the past "quite rashly" was sometimes seized on and perpetuated (156). But "once a figure was put forward . . . it soon became accepted as the 'agreed figure,' since no one was able by rational argument to demonstrate that it was wrong and suggest a better figure to replace it" (155). And when these figures were portrayed in charts and used by people who did not understand them, all kinds of strange behaviors resulted, including one case where an official eyeballed a line, reflected that it was "too steep at the end," and asked that 10 percent be "knock[ed] off" the later months: that "became the official aircraft programme"! (163)

The problem was the strong tendency "to assume that anything expressed in figures must necessarily be precise":

> It was a common error to impute to figures a greater accuracy and reliability than the basis on which they were arrived at could warrant on the most generous interpretation. And once the figures were called 'statistics', they acquired the authority and sanctity of Holy Writ. (155)

"Figures," Devons argued "gave the processes by which decisions were reached, an apparent air of scientific rationality. A document which contained statistics was nearly always considered superior to one which was mere words" (156). And this, despite the inadequacy of the statistics. "For to have recognized the inadequacy of the figures would have meant admitting that policy decisions were not being taken on a rational basis" (158).

Of course, soft information has problems too. Much of it is speculative; it relies on human memory, which can be fuzzy; it is subject to all kinds of psychological distortions. Ideally, strategy making draws on both kinds of information, hard and soft. But there are also times when managers have to rely on the soft kind. For example, what marketing manager faced with a choice between today's rumor that a major customer was seen lunching with a competitor and tomorrow's fact that the business was lost would hesitate to act initially on the former? Or as suggested earlier, a single story from one disgruntled customer may be worth more than all those reams of market research data simply because, while the latter may identify a problem, it is the former that can suggest the solution.

Thus, given that hard information tends to be limited, aggregated, late, and sometimes unreliable, it should come as no surprise that managers generally exhibit a bias toward soft information. At the very least, it enables them to test the hard information. But more important, it helps explain and resolve the problems that arise, provides the basis for the construction of their mental models of the world, and facilitates early response to unfolding events. Overall, in our opinion, while hard data may inform the intellect, it is largely soft data that generate wisdom. They may be difficult to "analyze," but they are indispensable for "synthesis"—the key to strategy making.

A number of popularly used words imply that such mental processes are based on soft information: hunch, judgment, intuition itself, as well as wisdom. Each suggests that there exists a form of knowing deeper than analysis, deeper than what is offered by the mechanical manipulation of hard data. That is why the planning school's assumption about hard data is a fallacy, and why, as a consequence, so is the assumption that strategists should be detached from the details of their context.

The Detachment of Planners from Strategy Making

Rather than needing to detach "strategic managers" from the operations, we should now like to argue something quite different: that strategic planning detaches planners, and (in the next section) the managers who rely on it, from the strategy making process.

While hard information may be equally available to every trusted party (assuming access to a computer or photocopier), soft information, much of it critical for strategy making, is available only to those directly exposed to it—"in touch," so to speak. And planners are not generally in touch in that way. For example, "Washington is an *oral* rather than a *written*-driven community. In the last analysis, the telephone and the small meeting are the operative instruments, and these effectively exclude the planner" (Cooper, 1975:229).

Being in touch means having personal access to the sources of the information—the customers, the factories, the government officials. In general, it is the line managers who have that access, by virtue of their formal authority. As we have argued elsewhere (Mintzberg, 1973:56–57, 65–72), such authority renders each manager the "nerve center" of his or her own unit. Having personal access to each subordinate provides the manager with the broadest information base about the unit itself, while having the highest formal status in the unit provides informational access to peers at equivalent levels in other organizations, themselves nerve centers. Thus, the President of the United States should know more about the government as a whole than any other individual, by virtue of his ability to access every one of its departments. Moreover, his access to the Prime Minister of Great Britain can provide him with a level of understanding (by virtue of that person's equivalent nerve-center knowledge of the British government) unavailable even to his Secretary of State. Indeed, a similar conclusion can be drawn about that Secretary of State vis-à-vis any of the deputies, and so on down the line. Thus, any manager who knows how to play this information game should emerge as a highly informed individual, far ahead of any subordinate or staff specialist (in breadth about all issues if not in depth about any single one).

This is a crucial factor in managerial work, and a key to the managers' capacity to make strategy, which we believe many planners fail to appreciate. Many planners, in turn, tend to be restricted largely to hard data—market research figures, analyses of competitors, statistics on economic cycles, performance reports, etc.—data often necessary for effective strategy making, to be sure, but seldom sufficient. So these planners necessarily become detached from the strategy making process, or, in those organizations that believe strategies can be planned formally, the process becomes detached from reality.[19]

Of course, the planners naturally promote their own comparative advantage, namely that they alone have the time and the technique to analyze the hard data. But their problem is that while line managers can easily gain access to those data (or, at least, to the results of their analyses), the planners cannot easily gain access to the managers' soft data, which tend to be stored only in natural memory (i.e., human brains). Hard data can be shared through a photocopier; soft data cannot. At best they can be written out as a report, or shared orally in some kind of debriefing session. But managers often hesitate to do such things because they can be terribly time-consuming.

Moreover, much of the knowledge of managers seems to be "tacit," to use Polyani's term (1966). In other words, managers (like the rest of us) know more than they can tell. They seem able to use that knowledge in their decision making (that is presumably what "intuition" is all about), but they cannot easily transmit it directly to others—including planners and their processes. Thus, when Keane wrote, in his article on "the external planning facilitator," that such a job may be "inappropriate" when, "on occasion, strategic planning requires familiarity with unusually complicated knowledge" (1985:153, 157), we would respond that except for the most trivial organizations, or ones willing to accept the most trivial strategies, the requisite knowledge for strategy making must always be "unusually complicated" for the outsider.

And so we conclude that, given (i) that strategy making requires soft information as well as hard, and (ii) that while both

---

[19] This problem would not appear to be restricted to planners, but should be common to any specialists whose beliefs about being "professional" extend to a detachment from the subject of their work, for example, doctors who lose "touch" with their patients and teachers who "know better" than their students.

planners and managers have access to hard information, it is generally only the managers who have effective access to soft information, it follows that (a) managers must take active charge of the strategy making process; (b) in so doing, they must be able to make use of their tacit knowledge; (c) which means that their intuitive processes must be allowed liberal rein; and (d) for that to happen, they must have intimate contact with, rather than detachment from, their organization's operations and its external context.

Staff planners, by virtue of their staff role and the data they *cannot* access, must necessarily be relegated to a true support role in strategy making, particularly concerning the analysis and use of hard data. Even if formal planning were a viable approach to strategy making—a point we shall dispute under the fallacy of formalization—it would quickly falter for lack of the right kind of data, much as the fanciest refinery would come to a halt without the petroleum necessary to fire it. As Cooper has written about the breakdown of planning in the foreign policy process:

> decision makers, by design or oversight, rarely inform planners of their current or likely future interests. Thus, planning staffs tend to be insulated from the real world. Much of the planning effort is consequently self-generated, based on what planners, in their innocence, assume the decisionmakers want, or based on what they think they ought to have. (1975:229)

When planning departments are staffed with analytical people who lack operating experience—financial experts, young MBAs, recently hired consultants, etc.—it is easy to dismiss the problem as a lack of knowledge of the business. But the problem goes deeper than that. People removed from the daily details of running an organization can never gain the requisite knowledge. As for those who come into the planning process with it—for example, line managers transferred into the planning staff—they tend eventually to lose it (as we shall discuss). That is perhaps why companies like Alcan, the Canadian aluminum giant, have been inclined to rotate line managers into the planning function for about three years—long enough to use their knowledge before it dries up.

The Detachment of Managers Who Rely on Planning from Strategy Making

Our discussion has assumed that while the nature of their staff function necessarily disconnects planners from strategy making, managers, by virtue of being on the line, need not be disconnected. Here, however, we wish to argue that those who take seriously strategic planning, and especially its assumption about hard data, do become disconnected. While the former point has gained some currency in perhaps the last decade, the latter—concerning the detachment of managers—seems to be less widely recognized. But, in our view, it is far more serious.

Why should a senior manager take strategic planning seriously? In the light of decades of literature on the subject, the appropriate answer seems to be: how could he or she *not* do so? We feel we have already given an adequate reply to this too-obvious answer. Learning and visionary approaches appear to be superior to planning as means for creating strategy. But for an increasing number of senior managers, unfortunately, these approaches become precluded. Cut-off from soft data, as a result of being perched atop overgrown hierarchies and overdiversified operations, such managers find themselves unable to use these other approaches. Strategic learning is an inductive process; it cannot take place in the absence of detailed, intimate knowledge of the situation. And strategic *vision* depends on an ability to *see* and to *feel*; it cannot be developed by people who deal with little more than words and numbers on pieces of paper. Amidst anxious calls for "some vision around here," therefore, detached managers turn to planning, as if the formal systems will do what their brains starved for information cannot (Rice, 1983:59; Brunsson, 1976:214). Thus Porter's solution for his claimed problem that "strategic thinking rarely occurs spontaneously," especially in the large, complex organization, is strategic planning: "Formal *planning* provided the discipline to pause occasionally to *think* about strategic issues" (1987:17, italics added).

But in our opinion it has done exactly the opposite. Such reliance on planning has only aggravated the very problem it was intended to solve, further detaching the managers from the contexts they desperately needed to understand. By seeking to mute the calculated chaos of managerial work and by emphasizing the hard data, formal planning has impeded rather than aided managers in being in touch in order to create viable strategies. Thus, we conclude that managers who rely on formal strategic planning cannot be effective strategists. To quote Langley in her intensive study of planning and analysis in three organizations:

> The call for strategic planning is really a plea for leadership and direction. Because strategic planning is universally viewed primarily as a means of making strategic decisions, people imagine that a mere formal process can generate a strategy. . . . But this is the wrong solution to the problem. The CEO may agree to do it, but this will not transform him or her into a person capable of taking strategic decisions. Strategic vision from above was crucial to the planning process in all three organizations. Strategic planning cannot provide this strategic vision on its own, and is totally useless without it. (1988:48)

In fact, we have already seen a good deal of evidence of this. There was Robert McNamara, who believed he could run the U.S. Department of Defense on the basis of planning (namely PPBS), hard data, and short, case-like reports. There was Reginald Jones, who ceded much of the responsibility for strategy to the staff planners and their systems at General Electric. As we noted earlier, the more "bureaucratic" the process of planning became at GE, the more "managers begin to confuse strategy with planning and implementation." *Business Week* (1984a) provided an example of a "bad" strategy that resulted from GE planners' miscalculation about the market for small home appliances, "because they relied on data, not market instincts" and drew their conclusions "somewhat in isolation." Yet the "top management, which also lacked contact with the market, did not see that the planners' data failed to tell the true story" (65). All this while CEO Jones was expressing his pleasure at having only six small strategy binders to review![20]

---

[20] In 1976, the UPI circulated a story about a survey of the workloads of company presidents: "The increased working load in the president's office these days does not involve more attention to detail, the executive recruiters discovered. On the contrary, the average corporation president is paying less attention to detail, delegating it to his subordinates, while he devotes his time to planning" (in the *Montreal Gazette*, January 17, 1976:22). The article also provided a new and interesting definition of planning: "Planning is a vague word that means hunting for money and trying to figure out how to deal with the bureaucrats and with the various problems created by inflation"!

Worse still is when planning becomes a numbers game, so that managers pretend they are making strategy when all they are really doing is manipulating figures. Here, "financial management supersedes strategic management" and financial strategy, rather than being "reconciled with other strategies," instead "preempts them as the final arbiters of corporate resource allocation" (Gray, 1986:95). The hard data drive out the soft, while that holy 'bottom line' destroys people's ability to think strategically. *The Economist* (June 11, 1988:71) described this as playing tennis by watching the scoreboard instead of the ball!

Many of the great strategies are simply great visions, "big pictures." But the big picture is not there for the seeing, in three-ring binders or MIS reports or financial statements. It must be constructed, in fertile minds. And like all big pictures, these are created from myriads of little details. Fed only abstractions, managers can construct nothing but hazy images, poorly focused snapshots that clarify nothing. As we noted in our Steinberg study:

> A striking aspect of Sam Steinberg and many key managers in the firm was their apparent ability to invest themselves in a question about the quality of a shipment of strawberries with the same passion and commitment as in a question about opening a chain of restaurants. The strategy analyst explicitly downgrades the importance of the former questions to focus on the latter, the "big" questions. Somehow, that distinction seems less clear-cut for the managers of this study. Indeed, their thorough involvement in the day-to-day issues (such as the quality of strawberries) provided the very intimate knowledge that informed their more global vision. That is why analysts may develop plans, but they are unlikely to come up with visions. (Mintzberg and Waters, 1982:494–495)

Or, in the more direct words of Konosuke Matsushita (the founder of the company that bears his name), "Big things and little things are my job. Middle-level arrangements can be delegated"!

Of course, to create a new vision requires more than just soft data and commitment: it requires a mental capacity for synthesis, with imagination. Some managers simply lack these capabilities—in our experience, often the very ones most inclined to rely on planning, as if the formal process will somehow make up for their own inadequacies. Planners, of course, have long encouraged this behavior: witness the earlier Steiner and Stanford Research Institute quotations about planning being necessary in the absence of brilliant intuition. If a manager could not or would not think strategically, then the planners stood ready to have their procedures do so instead. Of course, it was all a fallacy. Formal planning never provided strategic thinking at all, never offered a viable alternative to ordinary managerial judgment, let alone brilliant intuition. It was all based on hope, never on fact, simply because *systems do not think,* even when people cannot (a point to which we shall soon return).

When the necessary strategic thinking is not forthcoming in an organization, more fundamental questions have to be raised— about the structure of the organization, the expectations of who is supposed to make its strategy, the capabilities of those people, and the status of the organization itself.

If the senior managers cannot think strategically—and the organization at that point really does need such thinking (not always a foregone conclusion, since strategies are often fine just the way they are)—then there is but one viable alternative, and that is to find other people who can think in that way.[21] Either the managers must be replaced, or else others with that capability must be found in the organization, perhaps lower down where people are in closer touch with the operations.

Sometimes, of course, the senior managers do have the capacity to think strategically but are too detached from the details of the organization's operations. Then they had better find ways to get themselves back in touch, or else (again) ensure that the power over strategy making is decentralized to those who are. As we shall soon discuss, effective strategy making under difficult circumstances requires either that the formulator be the implementor or else that the implementors take personal charge of the formulation. In other words, the power over the process must rest with people

[21] In its March 19, 1984 issue, *Fortune* magazine reported that Roger "Smith didn't seem a likely revolutionist when he took over [General Motors] in 1981" (Fisher, 1984:106). One wonders how the board of America's largest firm could have made such a choice at that particular time, when the firm was facing such severe international competition. The article went on to say that happily, if inadvertently, Smith turned out to be a strategic thinker. But the mixture of disjointed strategies attributed to him in that article must surely have given the reader cause to wonder, leaving aside subsequent events.

who have an intimate sense of the context in which the strategies have to work. Either the leaders must be able to probe deeply into the organization or else people deep inside the organization must be able to influence the strategies that are formed.

Finally there is the situation where no one can hope to think strategically: the organization is simply too complex to develop viable strategies. In other words, the problem lies neither with the people nor the structure, but with the organization itself. Some organizations are simply too big and/or too diversified. The people in close touch with particular operations are necessarily restricted to small fragments, and cannot get together, while the leaders at the top can never hope to know enough of the detail to create viable strategies (or even to reconcile and integrate the disjointed strategies that came up from below).

> as the firm grew bigger without investing sufficiently in creating a common culture throughout the organization, as it became diversified in weakly related areas, as corporate management became more professional with corporate officers and staff recruited for their generic management expertise from other industries and from business schools, the corporation moved inexorably towards numbers-driven or staff-driven planning. The bond of legitimacy and credibility between [corporate managers and divisional managers] had been irremediably cut, with nothing to replace it but control by numbers or by corporate staff enforcement. (Allaire and Firsirotu, 1990:107)

In our view, this is no small problem but one that is common to a great many of the most significant businesses and governments of our day. Certainly the waves of consolidation in diversified businesses reflect one effort to deal with this. But we still have to realize that society would be better off without many of its largest and most widespread organizations (see Mintzberg, 1989: Chapter 17).

Gray wrote of "senior managers" who, when "invited to try their hands at action detailing . . . often find it an uncomfortable exercise." He therefore proposed the participation of people lower down: "top management knows the direction, those below know the terrain" (1986:94). But can society afford to have organizations led by people who set the direction but do not know the terrain? To put this another way, what kind of strategy does one get from someone who knows what a forest looks like from a helicopter but has never seen a tree?

Learning About Strengths and Weaknesses

So far we have criticized the assumption of detachment rather directly and generally. But the root of the problem goes beyond simply the paucity of the data and the detachment of the actors, whether staff planners or line managers. It goes right inside the basic "design" model (see Figure 2–1 on page 37) that underlies almost all prescriptive approaches to strategy making. Here we address two basic parts of that model, first the assessment of strengths and weaknesses and second the dichotomy between formulation and implementation. In both cases, the fundamental problem concerns the separation of thinking from acting.

Whether manifested in its looser rendition in the design school, or in the more formalized version of the planning school, the assessment of strengths and weaknesses is inevitably depicted as thought independent of action, strategy making as a process of conception rather than one of learning. In other words, on the question of how does an organization *know* its strengths and weaknesses, the model is quite clear—by consideration, assessment, analysis if not judgment, in other words, by a conscious process of thought. One gains the image of managers and planners sitting around a table listing the strengths, weaknesses, and distinctive competencies of an organization, much as do students in an MBA case study class. Having decided what these are, they are then ready to develop their strategies. Some writers (such as Ansoff, 1965:98–99 and Porter, 1980:64–67) offered exhaustive lists of potential strengths and weaknesses, for all organizations. Others, while not offering such lists per se, nonetheless appeared to assume that strengths and weaknesses do exist *in general*. And some (such as Andrews, 1971, 1987) tended to associate strengths and weaknesses with particular organizations—to draw on the traditional phrase, their competencies are *distinctive* to themselves (Selznick, 1957), or, in the more recent literature, these exist in their very *cores* (Prahalad and Hamel, 1990).

But does this constitute sufficient specification? Might competencies also be distinctive to time, even to application? Indeed, can an organization be sure what its competencies are even in the narrowest context of a single application?

In an article on "strategic capability," Lenz (1980a) pointed out the difficulties of an "organizational frame of reference," which focuses on some abstract ideal or a comparison with the past situation. Lenz believed there is the need for an *external* frame of reference as well, for example, a comparison with other organizations. In other words, strengths and weaknesses are situational: internal capability can be assessed only with respect to external context—markets, political forces, competitors, and so on. As Radosevich noted, "a strength in one strategic alternative may well be a weakness in another," with the result that "generic statements" of strengths are "rarely done well" (1974:360). Thus, Hofer and Schendel pointed out that "one cannot tell whether it is a strength or a weakness to be seven feet tall until one specifies what the tall individual is supposed to do"—for example, "play basketball" as opposed to "ride a race horse" (1978:150).

But even this may not go far enough. Even with respect to a particular context, organizations may not be able to know themselves generally, in advance. Expressed differently, how can we *know* that a strength is a strength without acting in a specific situation to find out?

This point came out most clearly, if inadvertently, in a study carried out by Howard Stevenson (1976), and reported in an article titled "Defining Corporate Strengths and Weaknesses." Starting out with a conventional design school view of these (53), Stevenson asked managers to assess their companies' strengths and weaknesses *in general*. Overall, "the results of the study brought into serious question the value of formal assessment approaches." In general, "few members of management agreed precisely on the strengths and weaknesses exhibited by their companies." "Objective reality," whatever that means, "tended to be overwhelmed" by individual factors, such as the managers' positions in their organizations (55). In particular, while higher-level managers perceived organizational factors as strengths, lower-level ones focused on marketing and financial factors. "Overall a pattern of greater optimism exists at higher organizational levels" (61), which might reflect either the kind of people who move up the hierarchy in the first place, or else a detachment of senior managers from the operating details. Also, strengths tended to be judged primarily on historical and competitive grounds, whereas weaknesses were judged on normative grounds (consultants' opinions, rules of thumb, etc.), which suggests that managers may be more realistic in assessing strengths, while engaging in more wishful thinking when considering weaknesses.[22]

The overall impression left by this study is that the detached assessment of strengths and weaknesses may be unreliable, all bound up with aspirations, biases, and hopes. More seriously, these distortions seem to be greatest at the senior managerial levels, where strategies are supposed to be formulated. In fact, the managers Stevenson studied seemed to understand well the message of his study:

> The most common single complaint of managers who did not feel that the definition of strengths and weaknesses was meaningful was that they had to be defined in the context of a problem. One manager stated his opinion succinctly.

> As I see it, the only real value in making an appraisal of the organization's capabilities comes in the light of a specific deal—the rest of the time it is just an academic exercise. (65)

The message seems to be that the assessment of organizational strengths and weaknesses cannot be just a detached cerebral ex-

---

[22] A bias toward strengths over weaknesses, as well as opportunities over threats, has been evident in the literature too. For example, Learned and Sproat commented in 1966 that Ansoff, in his book, *Corporate Strategy* (1965), had "shown a more exclusive interest in strategies reflecting company strengths and opportunities, and a correspondingly less developed interest in strategies responsive to weaknesses and risks," which they attributed to "his own experience with large expanding firms during a boom era," in contrast to "Harvard's thinking [which] reflects its inheritance of a long tradition of interest in strategy, extending back through hard times as well as good . . ." (1966:38). Yet, the mainline Harvard textbook has reflected over the years the same biases (see, for example, Christensen et al., [1982:181–187], where sections entitled "opportunity as a determinant of strategy," "identifying corporate competence and resources," "sources of capabilities," "identifying strengths," and "matching opportunity and competence" were not paralleled by sections related to weaknesses and risks).

ercise.[23] It must be above all an *empirical* one, in which these things are *learned* by being tested in context.[24]

Every strategic change involves some new experience, a step into the unknown, the taking of some new kind of risk. No organization can, therefore, ever be sure in advance whether an established capability will prove to be a strength or a weakness—ultimately a help or a hindrance in making that change.[25]

Thus, the supermarket chain we studied (Mintzberg and Waters, 1982) discovered that discount stores, which looked so similar to its existing operations, did not work for it, while fast-food restaurants, which looked so different, did. Appearances notwithstanding, the former seemed to turn up serious differences in fashion and obsolescence, while the latter demonstrated that the company's skills lay in merchandising perishable, commodity-like products. An even more surprising example involved the film company we studied (Mintzberg and McHugh, 1985), which failed in its initial efforts to produce films for television, where the only evident difference was the size of the screen! Less evident, however, was that its efforts to produce *regularly* for television proved incompatible with its highly creative and most decidedly *ad hoc* skills of filmmaking. It, too, learned the hard way (the only way?), and eventually settled down to doing only specials for television. As we noted in the supermarket study, the company's "search for what business should we be in could not be undertaken on paper. To discover its strengths and weaknesses . . . the firm had

---

[23] This message was perhaps not appreciated by Stevenson himself, who followed this quotation with a number of the usual prescriptions to managers carrying out internal assessments—develop lists, make measures explicit, and so on (66).

[24] This probably explains what appears to be a propensity of planners (especially of late, heavily influenced by Porter's work) to give more attention to the external appraisal of the environment and competitors than to the internal appraisal of the organization's strengths and weaknesses. The former is out there, objective, in principle unaffected by what is inside.

[25] As Perutz pointed out, being small and lacking natural resources are considered weaknesses for states, yet Switzerland has transformed these into strengths. In contrast with the prevalent idea that "one wants to improve on what one does already" is the view that "weaknesses frequently trigger off greater efforts" (1980:14, 15).

to undertake an empirical exploration that spanned decades" (489).[26]

Organizations turn out to be highly specialized instruments, whose capabilities for lateral extension often prove narrow indeed. Strategic changes must build on evident strengths, to be sure, but because they necessarily break new ground, must inevitably tread into areas of weakness as well. Who can tell, without actually trying, if the strength will carry the organization through or the weakness will undermine its efforts? How, then, can any organization rely on some abstract conceptual exercise in an executive suite? Competencies have to be "core," no doubt; they have to be "distinctive" too; and they must also be "in demand." But above all, competencies have to be applicable, and that can never be known for sure without trying. We conclude, therefore, that strengths and weaknesses can be detached neither from each other, nor from specific contexts, or from the actions to which they are directed. Thought must take place in the context of action.

"Marketing Myopia" Myopia

A theme in the literature of some years ago brings out well the points we are making here—sometimes with bizarre consequences. Launched in a celebrated article entitled "Marketing Myopia" by Theodore Levitt (1960), a marketing professor at the Harvard Business School, it was taken up enthusiastically by planners and managers alike.

The basic argument was that firms should define themselves in terms of broad industry orientation—"underlying generic need" in the words of Kotler and Singh (1981:39)—rather than narrow product or technology. To take Levitt's favorite examples, railroad companies were to see themselves in the transportation business, oil refiners in the energy business.

Companies had a field day with the idea, rushing to redefine

---

[26] See Miles for a detailed account of the diversification experiences of the American tobacco companies and his conclusion about why diversification must be a learning process (1982, especially 186–189).

themselves in all kinds of fancy ways—for example, the articulated mission of one ball bearing company became "reducing friction," and "a simple publishing company" (McGraw-Hill), having "made the strategic decision of who we are" according to its chief executive (Dionne, 1988:24), became "an 'information turbine' " (apparently with the help of Porter, according to *Forbes* magazine [Oliver, 1990:37]). It was even better for the business schools. What better way to stimulate the students than to get them dreaming about how the chicken factory could be in the business of providing human energy or garbage collection could become beautification? Unfortunately, it was all too easy, again a cerebral exercise that, while opening vistas, could also detach people from the mundane world of plucking and compacting. (According to *Forbes* magazine [Oliver, 1990:37], the "information turbine" blew $172 million finding out who it really was.)

Coming back to the assessment of strengths and weaknesses, the problem is that while the new definition of the business might sound wonderful, it could make some awfully ambitious assumptions about the strategic capabilities of the organization—namely that these are almost limitless, or at least very adaptable. (It should be remembered that Levitt's article was written at the height of enthusiasm for conglomerate diversification and "professional" management.) Thus we have the example from George Steiner, planning's most prolific writer, presented in apparent seriousness, that "buggy whip manufacturers might still be around if they had said their business was not making buggy whips but self-starters for carriages" (1979:156). But what in the world would make them capable of doing that? These products shared nothing in common—no material supply, no technology, no production process, no distribution channel—save a thought in somebody's head about making vehicles move. Why should starters have been any more of a logical product diversification for them than, say, fan belts, or horns, or the pumping of gas? As Heller suggested, with just a touch of sarcasm, "instead of being in transportation accessories or guidance systems," why could they not have defined their business as "flagellation"?! (quoted in Normann, 1977:34)

Why should a few clever words on a piece of paper enable a railroad company to fly airplanes, or for that matter, run taxicabs? Levitt wrote that "once it genuinely *thinks* of its business as taking care of people's transportation needs, nothing can stop it from creating its own extravagantly profitable growth" (1960:53, italics added). Nothing, of course, except the limitations of its own distinctive competences. What proved extravagant was the marketing myopia concept itself, a lovely thought disconnected from the world of action. As two other marketing professors wrote: "any astute organization can spot a market need; but only a minority can deliver a sound product for a particular need" (Bennett and Cooper, 1981:58). What we have here is the assumption that an organization can transform itself through words—that "a new 'business' can be forged as a result of the intellectual exercise of a management group" (Normann, 1977:34). It can all be worked out on paper—on that "flat surface" of planning.

Levitt's intention was to broaden the vision of managers. At that he may have succeeded—only too well. As Kotler and Singh, also from marketing, argued: "very little in the world . . . is not potentially the energy business" (1981:34). Ironically, by in effect redefining strategy from position to perspective, Levitt really *reduced* its breadth. Internal capability got lost; only the market opportunity mattered. Products did not count (railroad executives defined their industry "wrong" because "they were product-oriented instead of customer-oriented" [45]), neither did production ("the particular form of manufacturing, processing, or what-have-you cannot be considered as a vital aspect of the industry" [55]). But what makes market intrinsically more important than product or production, or, for that matter, a contact in the Pentagon, or Werner in the laboratory? The fact is that organizations have to build on whatever strengths they can make use of, while they must avoid being submerged by weaknesses that they may never have considered, marketing ones included. And that means they must go beyond mere words on paper—beyond the verbal tricks—to find out what these things really are, by connecting their thinking to their acting.

Critics of Levitt's article have had their own field day with the terminology, pointing out the dangers of "marketing hyperopia," where "vision is better for distant than for near objects" (Kotler and Singh, 39), or of "marketing macropia," in which "previously constrained market segmentations and product definitions [are] escalated beyond experience or prudence" (Baughman, 1974:65). We prefer to conclude simply that Levitt's notion of marketing myopia itself proved myopic.

Attaching Formulation to Implementation

Thinking and acting are most obviously separated in the dichotomy between formulation and implementation, central to all the prescriptive schools of strategy making—design and positioning as well as planning. In other words, the ultimate prescription is that organizations should complete their thinking before they begin to act.[27] Even when not stated so blatantly, the very fact of identifying only certain people as strategists, notably the senior managers together with the planners, forces a perceived separation between those who think first, and those who do afterward.

But how can anyone possibly question this assumption? Like motherhood, it is so deeply rooted in the very philosophical basis of Western society that it seems indisputable. Is it not true, after all, that organizations, like people, have heads with which to think and bodies with which to act? Is not such thinking what managers are paid for, politicians elected for, generals appointed for? Do they not make the strategies so that everyone else can deal with the tactics?

Recall the story of the Battle of Passchendaele. There the generals formulated the strategy for everyone else to implement, and all those troops fell to gain four and a half miles. Who should be blamed for such a tragedy? General Haig, the British commander in charge? No doubt. But not solely. Behind him was a long tradition, especially but not only in the military, of separating strategy from tactics, formulation from implementation, thinking from acting. The ultimate enemy, once again, proves to be ourselves—not just how we behave but how we *think* about behaving. As Feld noted in his article on the dysfunctions of traditional military organization, a sharp distinction is made between the officers in the rear, who have the power to formulate the plans and direct their execution, and the troops at the front, who, despite their first-hand experience, can implement only the plans that are given to them. One decides while the other salutes. The "organizations place a higher value on the exercise of reason than on the acquisition of

---

[27] Although it should be noted that implementation as conceived in this literature is not about real acting at all but about thinking in detail—about budgets, schedules, programs, and the like.

experience, and endow officers engaged in the first activity with authority over those occupied by the second" (1959:15):

> The superiority of planners is based on the assumption that their position serves to keep them informed about what is happening to the army as a whole, while that of the executor limits knowledge to personal experience. This assumption is supported by the hierarchical structure of military organization which establishes in specific detail the stages and the direction of the flow of information. In terms of this hierarchy, the man who receives information is superior to the man who transmits it . . . (22)

We have already discussed the fallaciousness of this assumption so critical to the formulation-implementation dichotomy, that data can be hardened and sent up the hierarchy with no significant loss or distortion. Passchendaele simply represents one of its most dramatic failures. The critical data never did get back up the hierarchy (any more than they did from McNamara's advisors in Vietnam), nor did the intended strategy get its necessary revisions. Unfortunately, "the conditions most favorable to rational activity, calm and detachment, stand in direct antithesis to the confusion and involvement of combat. Conditions entering into the drawing up of plans, therefore, are of a different order than those determining their execution . . . " (Feld, 15). Thus, as noted earlier, the Battle of Passchendaele was "strategically desirable"; it just happened to prove "tactically impossible." In other words, it worked wonderfully well, but only in theory. But the formulators never allowed themselves to find out—until it was too late. "The deadlock enforced by barbed wire and automatic weapons brought about an almost complete disassociation of strategic and tactical thought." But while neither "was in a position to guide the other," strategic thought had "outright dominance" (21). Hence the tragedy.

The Passchendaele example may be extreme, but the story it tells is all too common. In how many contemporary organizations do "the conditions most favorable to rational activity, calm and detachment, stand in direct antithesis to the confusion and involvement" of the factory floor, the sales office, the hospital ward? In how many does detached formulation render the organization ineffective? In how many is critical information ignored because it is deemed "tactical"? Speaking from Japan, Kenichi Ohmae went so far as to suggest that the "separation of muscle from brain may well be a root cause of the vicious cycle of the decline in productivity and loss of international competitiveness in which U.S. industry seems to be caught" (1982:226).

What we really seem to be caught in is a misguided metaphor. This is the machine, or "cybernetic," model of the organization, comprising a top and a bottom, a head that thinks and a body that acts, with regulated flows between them of downward command and upward results. Bear in mind what this orderly abstraction really looks like in reality: a bunch of buildings, not stacked up vertically, but spread out horizontally, across the land, with labels such as factory, sales office, and warehouse, each inhabited by people with their own heads and bodies, also one building somewhere or other called headquarters, the ostensible "top," whose people, in fact, look just like all the others. Is it not strange, then, that whenever someone asks about an organization, the first thing shown them is an organization chart—in effect, a listing of management, by status. How can anyone tell from one of these charts what the organization really does, what products it makes, what customers it serves? It would be as if the program at a baseball game were to list only the coaches and the managers. Thus, the cybernetic model is just a metaphor, and judging from what really goes on in the collective systems we call organizations, a rather dangerously misguided one at that.

Recall Kiechel's (1984:8) comment about the ten percent success rate in implementing strategies (which Peters called "wildly inflated"). The popular way to address this problem has been to try to improve the implementation. "Manage culture," executives have been advised, or "tighten up on your control systems." A whole segment of the consulting industry has grown up to help organizations become better at implementation.

But all of this may well be wrongheaded, based on a false diagnosis of the problem. It may also reflect who has done that diagnosis—the thinkers, whether senior managers or central planners or the consultants who advise them, people who may have used their "outright dominance" not only to create the problem in the first place but then to attribute the blame for it. Seeing themselves "atop" that metaphorical hierarchy, they point the finger at everyone else, "down below." "If only you dumbbells had appreciated our brilliant strategies, all would be well." But the clever dumbbells might well respond: "If you are so smart, why didn't you formulate strategies that we dumbbells could implement? You knew who we are: why didn't you factor our incompetences into your thinking?" In other words, *every failure of implementation is, by definition, also a failure of formulation.*

But in our view, this does not get it right either, because it still assumes the traditional dichotomy: that a failure to think it through at the center could be corrected by even better thinking at that center—even more comprehensive and rational thought. This may be asking too much of brains that cannot even handle just plain formulation. In our view, therefore, most often the real blame has to be laid, neither on formulation nor on implementation, but on *the very separation of the two.* It is the disassociation of thinking from acting that lies closer to the root of the problem.[28]

Sometimes the environment simply changes in ways that were not predicted, and the formulators resist making changes, perhaps because they are stubborn—enamored of their own strategies—or perhaps because they are not even aware of the external changes (as at Passchendaele). Other times, it is the implementors who resist, in this case the formulated changes, perhaps because they are too narrow-minded to break with their traditional ways, too small-minded to recognize a good strategy when it is placed before them, or too bloody-minded to pursue anyone's agenda but their own. But often they resist because they are right-minded: informed enough to recognize the limitations of the strategies imposed upon them. Indeed, to some extent, this is always an appropriate posture. Even the best of intended strategies have to be tailored to all kinds of circumstances inconceivable in their initial formulation. In other words, every intended strategy must be interpreted by a great many people facing a wide range of realities (Rein and Rabinovitz, 1979:327–328). As Majone and Wildavsky put it, "literal implementation is literally impossible" (1978:116). That is why no

---

[28] Thus Majone and Wildavsky referred to this dichotomy as the "planning-and-control model of implementation," with its notion that "the perfectly pre-formed policy idea . . . only requires execution, and the only problems it raises are ones of control" (1978:114).

firm dichotomy can be delineated between the heads on top and the bodies down below, nor can any correspondingly sharp line be drawn between formulation and implementation.

The so-called implementors are not robots, nor are the systems that control them airtight. Each so-called implementor must inevitably retain some discretion, to interpret intended strategies in his or her own way (Wildavsky, 1979:223). Furthermore, as we argued above concerning the assessment of strengths and weaknesses, some of the real limitations of any intended strategy can be discovered only when actions are finally taken (Majone and Wildavsky, 106). To quote a rather different Jelinek when she later reviewed the "vexing theoretical issues . . . ignored or dismissed" in a book titled *Implementing Strategy* (by Hrebiniak and Joyce, 1984):

> Although there is some mention that it is possible to adjust strategic plans, the overwhelming emphasis is on inducing and controlling action through plans imposed in a top-down strategy. Yes, subordinates' operational knowledge is required, but only to flesh out directives from above into operating objectives. There is little recognition that input from lower levels might suggest a strategic thrust, improve on overall strategy, or change it fundamentally. Such bottom-up input is seen to enter the process only after the direction is set and to operate only within the limits set by top management. (1984:463).

The result is not simply that intended strategies "slip" and "drift," to borrow terms popular in the public sector (Majone and Wildavsky, 1978:105; Kress, Koehler, and Springer, 1980; Lipsky, 1978), which mean that strategic intentions get distorted or deflected on their way to implementation. Rather it means that the whole process of how strategies are created in the first place has to be reconceived. Instead of the formulation-implementation dichotomy so long promoted in the prescriptive literature, we believe the strategy making process is better characterized as a process of learning—formation in place of formulation, if you like. People act in order to think, and they think in order to act. The two proceed in tandem, like two feet walking, eventually converging in viable patterns of behavior (that is, realized strategies).

In such a learning process, the formulation-implementation dichotomy collapses in one of two ways—one centralized, the other decentralized. In the first, the formulator implements. That is, a leader monitors the impact of his or her decisions closely and personally, so that a formulated strategy can be continuously assessed and reformulated during implementation. Here the leader remains in intimate ("soft") touch with the operations, following events closely so as to be able to respond quickly to unanticipated changes. We call this a centralized approach, "entrepreneurial" or "visionary," because it tends to be associated with strong leaders who have clear visions.

Where situations are rather complex, however—say, a research laboratory as opposed to a supermarket chain—strategic thinking cannot be concentrated at one center. Therefore, the dichotomy has to be collapsed in the opposite way: the implementors have to become formulators. To quote Lipsky, implementation is "turned on [its] head," so that strategy is "effectively made by the people who implement it" (1978:397). They champion proposals that may prove strategic and thus shift the direction of the organization. At the limit, the organization can pursue what we have called a grass-roots model of strategy formation:

1. *Strategies grow initially like weeds in a garden, they are not cultivated like tomatoes in a hothouse.* In other words, the process of strategy formation can be overmanaged; sometimes it is more important to let patterns emerge than to force an artificial consistency upon an organization prematurely. The hothouse, if needed, can come later.

2. *These strategies can take root in all kinds of places, virtually anywhere people have the capacity to learn and the resources to support that capacity.* Sometimes an individual or unit in touch with a particular opportunity creates his, her, or its own pattern. This may happen inadvertently, when an initial action sets a precedent. Even senior managers can fall into strategies by experimenting with ideas until they converge on something that works (though the final result may appear to the observer to have been deliberately designed). At other times, a variety of actions converge on a strategic theme through the mutual adjustment of various people, whether gradually or spontaneously. And then the external environment can impose a

pattern on an unsuspecting organization. The point is that organizations cannot always plan when their strategies will emerge, let alone plan the strategies themselves.

3. *Such strategies become organizational when they become collective, that is when the patterns proliferate to pervade the behavior of the organization at large.* Weeds can proliferate and encompass a whole garden; then the conventional plants may look out of place. Likewise, emergent strategies can sometimes displace the existing deliberate ones. But, of course, what is a weed but a plant that wasn't expected? With a change of perspective, the emergent strategy, like the weed, can become what is valued (just as Europeans enjoy salads of the leaves of America's most notorious weed, the dandelion!).

4. *The processes of proliferation may be conscious but need not be; likewise they may be managed but need not be.* The processes by which the initial patterns work their way through the organization need not be consciously intended, by formal leaders or even informal ones. Patterns may simply spread by collective action, much as plants proliferate themselves. Of course, once strategies are recognized as valuable, the processes by which they proliferate can be managed, just as plants can be selectively propagated.

5. *New strategies, which may be emerging continuously, tend to pervade the organization during periods of change, which punctuate periods of more integrated continuity.* Put more simply, organizations, like gardens, may accept the biblical maxim of a time to sow and a time to reap (even though they can sometimes reap what they did not mean to sow). Periods of convergence, during which the organization exploits its prevalent, established strategies, tend to be interrupted periodically by periods of divergence, during which the organization experiments with and subsequently accepts new strategic themes. The blurring of the separation between these two types of periods may have the same effect on an organization that the blurring of the separation between sowing and reaping has on a garden—the destruction of the system's productive capacity.

6. *To manage this process is not to preconceive strategies but to recognize their emergence and intervene when appropriate.* A destructive weed, once noticed, is best uprooted immediately. But one that seems capable of bearing fruit is worth watching, indeed sometimes even worth building a hothouse around. To manage in this context is to create the climate within which a wide variety of strategies can grow (to establish flexible structures, develop appropriate processes, encourage supporting cultures, and define guiding "umbrella" strategies) and then to watch what does in fact come up. The strategic initiatives that do come up may in fact originate anywhere, although often they do so low down in the organization, where the detailed knowledge of products and markets resides. (In fact, to be successful in some organizations, these initiatives must be recognized by middle-level managers and "championed" by combining them with each other or with existing strategies before promoting them to the senior management.) In effect, the management encourages those initiatives that appear to have potential, otherwise it discourages them. But it must not be too quick to cut off the un-expected: sometimes it is better to pretend not to notice an emerging pattern to allow it more time to unfold. Likewise, there are times when it makes sense to shift or enlarge an um-brella to encompass a new pattern—in other words, to let the organization adapt to the initiative rather than vice versa. More-over, a management must know when to resist change for the sake of internal efficiency and when to promote it for the sake of external adaptation. In other words, it must sense when to exploit an established crop of strategies and when to encourage new strains to displace them. It is the excesses of either—failure to focus (running blind) or failure to change (bureaucratic momentum)—that most harms organizations. (Mintzberg, 1989:214–216)

This model may seem extreme, but it is certainly no more ex-treme than the pure planning model (perhaps best labeled "hot-house"). The two define the end points of a continuum along which real-world strategy making behavior must lie. Sometimes organizations have to tilt toward the more deliberate end, where clear thought has to proceed action, because the future seems roughly predictable and the requisite learning has already taken place. Formulation, in other words, may precede implementation. But even so, there has to be "implementation as evolution," as Majone and Wildavsky titled one article (1978)—because prior thought can never specify all subsequent action. But in times of difficult change, when new strategies have to be worked out in processes of learning, the tilting has to be toward the emergent end. Then the dichotomy between formulation and implementation has to collapse, whether the formulators implement in a more centralized way or the implementors formulate in a more decentralized, grass-roots way. Either way, thinking gets reconnected directly to acting.[29]

Connecting Thinking and Acting

To conclude this discussion of the fallacy of detachment, let us take a close and direct, if brief, look at the underlying issue, the disconnection of thinking from acting.

A student of ours who had been working in an engineering department of a manufacturing company once recounted a personal story in class. Involved in the operations, he came up with certain ideas that the head of the department appreciated. To encourage him further, the department head asked him to set aside his operating duties so that he could focus on these ideas. Accordingly, he was named to the position of planner, in that very small department. He subsequently recorded what he had said in class:

> I was, therefore, separated from the everyday pressures and put in an office all by myself and asked to write reports on anything relevant. I kept myself busy for about three months. I formulated most of the ideas I had collected on the job. However, by the end of three months I "dried up." It became more and more difficult for me to identify problem areas. The communication network I had established and maintained between myself and the various operating people was becoming more and more rusty. As far as I am concerned this particular approach had failed. (S. K. Darkazanli, in personal correspondence with the author)

Being "free to think," as planners supposedly are and as they urge managers to be, may prove to be its own prison. Ansoff wrote

---

[29] For more details on the centralized visionary and decentralized learning approaches to strategy making, see Mintzberg (1973, 1987, 1989:121–130 and 210–217, and 1990b:137–141 and 146–159).

later of strategic planning as an "off line process compared with the real time character" of what he called "strategic issues management" (1975:32). We prefer to call the latter *strategic thinking* and to emphasize that it is predicated on involvement rather than detachment. Apparently, such thinking must not only be informed by the moving details of action but be driven by the very presence of that action. That may be a main reason why managerial work demonstrates such a strong "action orientation" (Mintzberg, 1973:35–38).

Conventional planners may believe that managers are too involved in the details to reflect. But effective managers may know that only by being so involved can they reflect. To think strategically, in other words, they must be active, involved, connected, committed, alert, stimulated. It is the "calculated chaos" of their work that drives their thinking, enabling them to build reflection on action in an interactive process. That is what prompted Dean Acheson to write of that "unnatural" process we quoted earlier, of " 'man thinking' surrounded by a cabinet of Rodin statues."

Peter Drucker claimed that "long-range planning does not deal with future decisions. It deals with the futurity of present decisions." (1959:239). This may be true but it is redundant. That is because all decision making is fundamentally about the future, not the present. A decision is a commitment to future action—whether in ten minutes or ten years. Planning, likewise, is about the future, not the present. But the future is always an abstraction, "out yonder," as the expression goes. It never arrives. So the survival of every organization depends on its actions in the moving present. Thus future planning disconnected from present acting is futile. Alone, therefore, planning is useless. The plans become "wish lists"—the expression of vague hopes. At the limit, as we noted in discussing the illusion of control, reality ceases to matter; things are under control because they are down on paper. To quote that famous line (variously attributed to William Gaddis and John Lennon), "life is what happens while you're making other plans." Only when these processes—planning as well as deciding, thinking, *and* managing—connect intimately and interactively with operating activities taking place in the present (a customer being served, a product being produced, etc.) do they come alive.

Peters and Waterman (1982:119) made famous the "Ready. Fire. Aim." comment of a Cadbury's executive. In fact, this makes a great deal of sense, as long as one gets to fire more than once, which is normally the case. Extend the phrase and you have strategy formation as a learning process: "Ready-fire-aim-fire-aim-fire-aim," etc. Just as structure must always follow strategy, the way the left foot must follow the right foot walking, so too must firing always follow aiming, and preceed it too, in order to make the necessary corrections. Action and thought must interact. Planners may be rightfully concerned about Rambo-type behavior in management—"fire-fire-fire" in every direction, with no aiming. But managers must be equally wary of planning behavior that amounts to "Ready. Aim. Aim."

This leads us to an intriguing point developed by Karl Weick on the relationship between the taking of action and the generation of meaning. In the "truly novel situation," the crux of true strategy making, Weick argued that all one "can do is act." *Then* the act is "made sensible"—appearing "to be under the control of the plan" (1979:102). In other words, planning does not promote significant change in the organization so much as deal with it when it is introduced by other means (as we concluded in our discussion of the pitfalls).

But in the absence of these other means, "postponing action while planning continues could prove dangerous. If action is postponed, meaning will be postponed, and any chance of clarifying the situation will decrease, simply because there is nothing available to be clarified or made meaningful." In these circumstances, planning "could spiral larger and larger, becoming an end rather than a means . . . [The planners] can lose sight of what they were originally planning for" (103). Then planning can become a ritual.

Of course, where there is no action to take, as Dubé concluded in his study of the Canadian military, planning may be a way to keep busy. But the danger is that too much detailed planning in the busy organization can kill the incentive to act (that paralysis from analysis). "I plan therefore I do" wrote a more cynical Ansoff in 1975 (with Hayes, 11), in criticizing its "cartesian" approach. He might have written instead, "I plan because I don't" or "I don't because I plan"!

Ironically, however, Weick also argued that a *plan* could sometimes be a necessary spur to action. We saw this earlier, in our discussion of the illusion of control, for example, in Gimpl and Dakin's comment in their 1984 paper on "Management and Magic" that in ambiguous situations, planning boosts confidence, tightens up the management group, and reduces anxiety. In this regard, Weick (1990:4) likes to tell the story of the army squad lost in the wintry Alps, about to give up when a map was discovered. Stimulated to action, they found their way out, only to discover back at base camp that it was a map of the Pyrénées! It is a cute story (and a dangerously misleading one, as anyone who has tried to maneuver in the wilderness with the wrong map knows well), but his basic point is fair. Having no sense of direction can sometimes be worse than having a precisely determined one. Both preclude choice. Having a broad orientation allows people, in a sense, to dismiss the future and get on with the present. In other words, if the orientation is a good one, one can feel secure in the belief that whatever occurs will be manageable.

But this does not make a case for planning, for again we must point out the difference between having a plan and engaging in planning. A plan does not necessarily result from formal planning (as in that map the army squad happened to find). Indeed, a plan as vision—expressed even in imagery, or metaphorically—may prove a greater incentive to action than a plan that is formally detailed, simply because it may be more attractive and less constraining. That is presumably why there has been so much attention to strategic vision over the past decade. Moreover, vision as a stimulant to action may be easier to come by, since it emerges from the head of a single leader instead of having to be agreed upon collectively by a group of senior managers and planners. As discussed in the previous chapter, having to get such agreement *in principle* (rather than on specific actions), may, in fact, paralyze action.

Thus, we conclude that while thinking must certainly precede action, it must also follow action, close behind, or else run the risk of impeding it! Formal planning poses the danger of distancing that connection and therefore discouraging action. That is why, at least under difficult conditions, planning may be better conceived as an interpreter of action than a driver of it,[30] and why action itself

---

[30] Note that Weick offered his conclusion under conditions of novelty, or uncertainty. Under conditions of assumed stability or certainty, when the future seems to be known, planning might seem to be able to proceed effectively. But make no mistake: this assumed stability is nothing more than the extrapolation of past conditions.

may better be driven by thinking of a less formalized and more involved nature.

The Fallacy of Formalization

Gradually we are converging on the essence of the problem, planning's grand fallacy. Closer to its core, really a compendium of the points made so far, is the fallacy that the strategy formation process can be formalized, in Jelinek's words of 1979, that innovation can be institutionalized. The prime assumption behind this is that systems can do it—can detect discontinuities, comprehend stakeholders, provide creativity, program intuition. As Jelinek herself put it in a later, reconsidered article with David Amar: "If managers follow the check-lists, they'll generate the needed plan" (1983:1). Or recall the Stanford Research Institute (SRI) economist's claim (quoted at the beginning of this chapter) about being able to "recreate" the thought process of the "genius entrepreneur."

The Failure of Formalization

The evidence repeated throughout this discussion provides not a shred of support for this assumption: neither SRI nor any other organization or individual has ever succeeded in recreating any such intuitive process, genius or otherwise. In our discussion of forecasting, we saw how systems are incapable of detecting discontinuities, although some people seem quite able to do so; earlier we saw how formal planning discourages creativity, although some people are obviously highly creative; in the last section, we saw how managers easily internalize soft data while hard data lose much of their richness, and how the dynamic needs of strategy making, so naturally accommodated informally, seem to get violated when the process is formalized.

Somehow, formalization never felt quite right for strategy making, whether in the formalized articulation of goals (or stakeholder needs), the formalized assessment of strengths and weaknesses, the formal determination of business portfolios through the manipulation of the Boston Consulting Group's stable of cows, dogs, and the like, or Ansoff's "quasi-analytic" systems to deal with weak signals and the like. Even the simple act of formally isolating someone in a planning function, as in the Darkazanli experience described above, or of calling an official meeting to discuss strategy—in effect, merely formalizing the time for strategic thinking—sometimes has the same effect:

> In fact, the meetings to reflect on strategy organized as part of planning are often dull for the participants: they have the impression of repeating what has already been said and decided upon in previous strategic studies. Or else, the discussion goes nowhere because the studies that would provide the data are not available. (Sarrazin, 1975:89, our translation from the French)

The more elaborated the planning procedures became—in response to the failures of the simpler ones—the greater seemed to be their failures. This was especially evident in the area of forecasting and the heroic efforts to apply PPBS in government. Indeed, even Texas Instruments' highly touted OST system—on which Jelinek based her conclusion about institutionalizing innovation—failed no less than did the famous systems of General Electric. *Business Week,* in an article entitled "TI: Shot Full of Holes and Trying to Recover" (1984b), reported that in 1982 (just three years after Jelinek published her book), the top management "scrapped TI's matrix management system and returned control of products to their managers" (83). (An earlier *Business Week* article [1983:56] had referred to OST as "the creaking management system.") The article pointed out that:

> It was Haggerty who introduced strict financial controls and strategic planning to control TI's rapid growth and increasingly complex business mix. But Haggerty also championed TI's stable of entrepreneurs, understanding that people, not rigid systems, produce innovation. (83)

The implication is that Jelinek falsely attributed the firm's innovative capacity to its planning system. It seems to have been

designed for control, not for creating strategy. "An overly complex management system—including matrix management and
numbers-dominated strategic planning—tended to smother entrepreneurship" (82). Indeed, who better to quote on this than Jelinek
herself, who in her book with Schoonhoven in 1990, noted that
under the managers who followed Haggerty, "somehow the focus
seemed to be on the system itself, rather than the innovation it was
expected to generate. The OST was *thoroughly institutionalized*" and
that, together with other aspects of formalization "seemed to cost
TI its innovative spark" (1990:410, italics added!).[31] Jelinek and
Schoonhoven concluded in an earlier chapter that:

> A strategy of innovation is contained not in 'plans', but in the
> pattern of commitments, decisions, approaches, and persistent be-
> haviors that facilitate doing new things. . . . Consequently, while
> the material of this chapter has little to do with formal plans or
> planning procedures, it has everything to do with enacting a strat-
> egy of innovation. (203, 204).

And later, "Formal systems operate most explicitly after strategy
has been developed, to monitor its achievement, assess its continued fit with reality, and signal major new intentions. . . . they are
not expected to substitute for creativity or management attention,
which must come first" (212). Finally, at the close of this particular
chapter, they comment: "Reality frequently intrudes, to 'keep managers humble' " (215). Not only managers![32]

Thus, we have no evidence that any of the strategic planning
systems—no matter how elaborate, or how famous—succeeded in
capturing (let alone improving on) the messy informal processes

---

[31] They noted that the system did come back in the late 1980s, but as a tool to
facilitate rather than to control.

[32] Jelinek actually recanted in that earlier paper with David Amar, a consultant
on strategy, where she critiqued "bureaucratic planning systems"—"corporate
strategy by laundry lists," which suggest that strategy is "a clean, pristine and
definitive plan for future action, with the details specified and the future insured.
. . . often managers are encouraged to stay within functional boundaries . . . [They]
are often blind to key 'soft data' that spells success or failure for strategy: creativity,
intuition, collective managers' experience, gut feelings are often perceived as 'irrational' " (Jelinek and Amar, 1983:1).

by which strategies really do get developed. All the efforts at programming seemed to prove no better at imitating intuition than did the techniques of psychoanalysis at imitating empathy. Something has clearly been wrong with formalization. It may have worked wonders on the highly structured, repetitive tasks of the factory and clerical pool, but whatever that was got lost on its way to the executive suite.

Was Formalization Ever Even Tried?

Of course, one could argue—with a good deal of support—that the whole strategic planning effort failed because it never seriously tried to formalize the behavior in question. Putting boxes on charts labeled "be creative" or "think boldly" (only the worst examples of a practice common in planning) hardly amounted to programming anything. Take apart any model of strategic planning, box by box, and at the heart of the process where strategies are supposed to be created, you will find only a set of empty platitudes, not any simulation of complex managerial processes. That is the "missing detail" we wrote about in Chapter 2. "At best, planners offered checklists: 'analyze the problem', 'select the preferred course of action', etc.," wrote Ansoff and Brandenburg in 1967 (B224), although they were hardly innocent of the practice. As we noted earlier, the proponents of the planning school, unlike Frederick Taylor, never did their basic homework—never tried to get inside the strategy formation process to find out how it really does work. Again we can cite Ansoff and Brandenburg on what they said, if not what they did: "Much of the planning literature has concerned itself with programming of the firm's activities and not with the manner in which the underlying decisions are arrived at" (B224). As a result, the prescriptions never reflected an understanding of the reality and so remained essentially devoid of real content.

Earlier we quoted Wildavsky on the presumption that all you really need do to answer a question is to ask it. Planning may have tried to ask a question. But did planning ever really try to answer it?

The Analytical Nature of Planning

Even if planning did give it a try—or will do so in the future—
could it work? This is another way of asking if the conventional
planning people asked the *right* question, let alone answered it. We
think not. Accordingly, we conclude that the serious efforts to
formalize strategy making may have proved more damaging than
the frivolous ones, because they were taken more seriously. We
believe there is something fundamentally wrong with formalization applied to processes like strategy making, which constitutes
the grand fallacy. It has to do with the reductionist, analytical
nature of planning.

Formalization is achieved through decomposition, in which a
process is reduced to a procedure, a series of steps, each of which
is specified. That is essentially analytical: the breaking down of the
whole into its component parts. "... the word analysis itself ...
comes from a Greek root meaning subdivide" (Wildavsky,
1979:8).[33] It is analysis, therefore, that is the basis for strategic
planning. Recall Porter's comment that "I favor a set of analytical
techniques for developing strategy." Whenever organizations were
too large, managers too detached, or businesses too diverse, then
strategic planning (meaning analysis) became the proposed solution: strategic processes were to be decomposed into categories of
specified steps composed of formalized procedures.

But it never worked, producing, as we saw in Chapter 3, the
"conspicuous failure" of massive urban renewal, the "nondemocratic nonplanning" of the French government, the dramatic rejection of planning at General Electric, and the PPBS burlesque, which
"failed everywhere and at all times" according to Wildavsky. Even
the subsequent promises of salvation—"just you wait"—led to
nothing more than the wasting of more time and more money. At
one point, the "systems approach" became popular. Ackoff wrote
of attacking problems "holistically, with a comprehensive systems
approach" (1973:670). Forrester proposed ever grander models:
first he wrote *Industrial Dynamics* (1961), then *Urban Dynamics*
(1969), finally *World Dynamics* (1973). Somehow the analytical techniques were going to synthesize all the dimensions into even larger

---

[33] The Greek root "also means to undo or unloose"! (402)

and more elaborate systems. But something had to give. As the breadth of the procedures increased, they became shallower in depth. Extending the bounds of the context meant aggregating the content (Sharp, 1977:491). Dror claimed that "good comprehensive planning limits the degree of comprehensiveness within the boundaries of manageability" (1971:122). But because neither he nor anyone else ever suggested how that could be done, these words became another empty platitude.

Eventually, it became clear that the systems offered no improved means to deal with the information overload of human brains; indeed, they often made matters worse. The mechanical combination of the information did not solve any fundamental problem that existed with human intuition. And all those promises about the benefits of "artificial intelligence," "expert systems," and the like, never materialized at the strategy level. The formal systems could certainly process more information, at least hard information; they could consolidate it, aggregate it, move it about. But they could never *internalize* it, *comprehend* it, *synthesize* it. Analysis was never up to the job set for it. In a literal sense, planning never learned.

Consider creativity. In our chapter on the pitfalls of planning, we discussed how creativity can be impeded by planning. Let us elaborate on that conclusion here. Planning by its very nature defines and preserves categories. Creativity, by its very nature, creates categories, or rearranges established ones. That is why formal planning can neither provide creativity nor deal with it when it emerges by other means. And that is why the entrepreneurial types fought the systems at TI and GE, why innovation was never institutionalized.

Indeed, the imperative "be creative" or "think boldly" reflects exactly the same problem: creativity becomes an isolated step, another box on a chart. Imagine managers sitting around a table having to "think boldly." What better way to suppress it![34] If we have learned anything at all about creativity, it is that it cannot

---

[34] Mitroff et al. recounted a "strategic planning" exercise in which members of a large government agency were implored to "think boldly" in creating scenarios for the long-term future. But they did not take "seriously enough the injunction," instead producing reports that were "too contemporary-bound . . . too timid" (1977:47).

happen in isolation or on schedule, let alone on demand (any more than can strategy formation, the best of it being just a form of creativity in any event). "Creativity is compromised by squeezing the peregrinations of the mind into one sequence" (Wildavsky, 1979:8). Or to return to Weick's notion of the relationship between thinking and acting with a critically important point:

> Scientific thinking is probably a poor model for managerial thinking, yet, with few exceptions . . . theorists encourage this myth by providing steplike analytical formats . . . which require that managers take time away from what they are doing to think more as scientists do. . . . The problem is basically that we treat *thinking* as a verb of doing when in fact it [is] an adverbial verb that requires that some *other* activity must be underway if thinking is to occur. Thinking is a qualification of an activity, not an activity itself. (1983:225)

Reinforcing this conclusion are studies of people oriented to the analytical approach. They tend to favor convergent, deductive thinking, to search for similarities among problems rather than differences, to decompose rather than to design (Leavitt, 1975a and b). One study reported "that people who tend to specialize in analytic thinking (convergers) are less likely to recall dreams than those with the opposite bias (divergers), whom [the researcher] characterized as more imaginative and more able to deal with the non-rational" (in Ornstein, 1972:65).

A particular weakness of the "analytical mind," mentioned in Chapter 4, is its tendency toward "premature closure": problems are structured early, the alternatives delineated prematurely, so that attention can be concentrated on assessing them (McKenney and Keen, 1974:83). In other words, the analyst tends to want to get on with the more structured step of evaluating alternatives and so tends to give scant attention to the less structured, more difficult, but generally more important step of diagnosing the issue and generating possible alternatives in the first place.[35] The result tends

---

[35] The same problem is reflected in the formal literature of decision making: "substantive discussion of [the diagnosis] routine is almost totally absent in both the descriptive and normative literature" (Mintzberg, Raisinghani, and Théorêt, 1976:254).

to be conservative problem solving, heavily biased towards the status quo: problems are approached as they have always been conceived, in terms of the alternatives already available.

Is this not exactly what we have been seeing in the conventional planning approach, which has always appeared more intent on proceeding within a well-defined framework of categories and steps than developing its framework in the first place? In the early days of planning, Meyerson and Banfield noted in the public context that:

> Some people are temperamentally incapable of reflection, of dealing with the larger aspects of matters, of seeing the elements of a situation in their mutual relations, or of viewing affairs in a long perspective of time. . . . There is, in fact, a natural selection which tends to fill top planning posts with such people. (1955:277)

This seems terribly ironic, does it not? In fact, as we shall discuss later, the point is overstated, because various kinds of people populate the planning field, some less formally analytical than others. But this tendency that was noted in 1955 clearly took hold, dominating much of planning practice as well as its mainline literature to the present day. It is with regard to this tendency that we have used the label "conventional" planner. Later we shall discuss another type of planner, who takes analysis, decomposition, and formalization—indeed the prescriptions of the planning school in general—less seriously. But the many who do, in our opinion, discourage the very needs that are essential to effective strategy making.

Let us return to the Texas Instruments experience, because it so clearly illustrates these problems of planning. Its OST system took things apart analytically, establishing a priori categories for everything. The overall corporate objective was factored into nine subobjectives, each in turn giving rise to several strategies. Then, "for each objective, there [was] an objective manager. . . . For each strategy, there [was] a strategy manager" (Galbraith and Nathanson, 1978:129). Strategy managers reported in matrix fashion to "one boss for operations . . . and one for strategy." The strategies in turn "consist[ed] of several tactics," on which progress was reported monthly (130). And so on through two-day reviews by the board of directors three times a year "to establish overall direction" (130–

131). As a sobered-up head of planning was to comment later, "One of our errors was we had the tendency to substitute mechanics for thought . . . People would fill out forms thinking they were doing strategies. It was strategy by cookbook" (quoted in *Business Week*, 1983:57).

Note that the problem in such planning systems is not any specific category so much as the process of categorization itself. No amount of rearranging of boxes could resolve the problem of the very existence of boxes (a conclusion that could well be extended to structural reorganizations). Strategy formation, like creativity (or as creativity), needs to function beyond boxes, to create new perspectives as well as new combinations. As someone once quipped, "life is larger than our categories." Planning has not felt right because, as Weick put it, "everyday thinking almost never presents a series of steps. . . . Even if people tried to implement [linear and step models], they would find them foreign to what they are trying to do" (1983:240).

Hax and Majluf (1984:37) have commented on a "chicken and egg" problem of planning, that it needs categories to proceed but that the categories only make sense once the strategies are established. But that is a problem only if planning tries to establish those strategies. Their point makes clear that planning has no business trying to do so. When planning and strategy making are perceived as different, the problem disappears. Strategy formation (by other processes) establishes the categories; then planning might take over to operationalize them, when necessary.

Thus we conclude that Jelinek's contention of 1979, that managerial work can be programmed now the way production work was programmed a century ago, is fundamentally wrong. "Thought-Taylorism" is not the same as "Thing-Taylorism" (de Monthoux, 1989). Taylor sought to squeeze out whatever creative potential remained in the jobs he programmed. His concern was for mechanical efficiency in repetitive production, not for creative effectiveness in ad hoc thought. By *pre*scribing the workers' procedures, he *pro*scribed their discretion. As he put it, "All possible brain work should be removed from the shop and centered in the planning or laying-out department" (1947). Strategic planning set out to do the same thing (its claims notwithstanding), and when it succeeded, the results were devastating. The process of strategy formation simply has different needs—for creativity and synthesis, which depends on the discretion of informed actors. The work of creating strategy cannot be programmed like that of shoveling coal. Taylor's engineers could put the steps back together into an efficient job; Texas Instruments' planners never could. Nor could the capital budgeters, whose process proved not only disjointed but also disjointing, an explicit deterrent to synergy. (How ironic that "synergy"—the word Ansoff gave to management in his 1965 book—should be impeded by the very planning procedures he himself popularized in that same book!) Humpty Dumpty taught us that not everything that comes apart can be put back together. Of all forms of reductionism in planning, therefore, this one above all amounted to *reductio ad absurdum*!

Intuition Distinguished

Herbert Simon was awarded the Nobel Prize in Economics in 1978; in 1965 (and again in 1977) he wrote: "We now know a great deal about what goes on in the human head when a person is exercising judgement or having an intuition, to the point where many of these processes can be simulated on a computer" (1965:81–82; 1977:81). Roger Sperry was awarded the Nobel Prize in Physiology in 1981; in 1974 he wrote: "The right [hemisphere of the human brain], by contrast [with the left] is spatial, mute, and performs with a synthetic spatio-perceptual and mechanical kind of information processing not yet simulatable in computers" (1974:30).

This striking contradiction between these two intellectual giants defines one of the most significant issues we face today: whether intuition exists as a distinct process of thought, different from rational analysis. Its consequences strike at the heart of some of our most pressing concerns—for example, the role of experts (such as psychiatrists, policy advisors, and scientists in general) in guiding the lives of lay people, the basis by which we are educated (for example, the assumption widely held that languages can be learned consciously, and more broadly, that formal knowledge should always supersede tacit knowledge), and the design of our institutions (organizations, systems of justice, etc.) to promote formal rationality in place of "gut feel." The field of planning, of course, commits itself to strong stands on the first and last of these, with not insignificant consequences over the past several decades. It has assumed, alongside Simon, that there are not two discrete, equally important forms of human thinking but rather one that is superior, and, in fact, able to encompass the second. Specifically, so-called intuitive processes can be rendered explicit and so improved by systematic analysis. Put most simply, the bridge between analysis and intuition can easily be spanned by the simple act of writing programs (at least as boxes on charts when not actually in computers).

In one way or another, this issue has been hotly debated over centuries, without resolution. That may be because debate, rooted in logical and rational thought, is itself an analytical process that unfolds step by step. How then, could it be used to disprove the discreteness, or prove the inferiority, of a thought process that is itself subconscious and so inaccessible to direct methods of decomposition. "Proof," in other words, loads the dice in favor of the contention of programmability, a little like trying to analyze color through the use of black-and-white photography.

Lacking real proof does not, however, mean that we have no suggestive evidence on this issue. Let us consider some of this, first from research in physiology and then from the study of organizations, looking at Simon's arguments in between.

Do the Hemispheres Have Minds of Their Own?

It has long been known that the human brain has two distinct hemispheres, one of which (on the left side) appears to be the seat of language (in most right-handed people). But more recent research has revealed much else. An article in *The New York Times* summarized this well, going back to the time when Roger Sperry became interested in a veteran who had suffered brain damage during World War II:

> A few years after his injury, W.J. [the veteran] had begun to have epileptic fits; these became so frequent and so severe that nothing could control them. He would fall down, unconscious and foaming at the mouth, often hurting himself as he fell. For more

than five years, doctors at the White Memorial Medical Center in Los Angeles tried every conceivable remedy, without success. Finally Drs. Philip Vogel and Joseph Bogen cut through his corpus callosum [the tissue that joins the brain's two hemispheres], and the seizures stopped, as if by magic. There was a rocky period of recovery, during which W.J., a man of above-average intelligence, could not speak, but within a month he announced that he felt better than he had in years. He appeared unchanged in personality. He seemed perfectly normal.

Meanwhile, Sperry had interested a graduate student, Michael Gazzaniga, in performing a series of tests on W.J. together with him and Dr. Bogen. Gazzaniga soon discovered some extremely odd things about his subject. To begin with, W.J. could carry out verbal commands ("raise your hand," or "bend your knee") only with the right side of his body. He could not respond with his left side. Evidently the right hemisphere, which controls the left limbs, did not understand that kind of language. When W.J. was blindfolded he couldn't even tell what part of his body was touched, if it happened to be on the left side.

In fact, as the tests proceeded, it became increasingly difficult to think of W.J. as a single person. His left hand kept doing things that his right hand deplored, if it was aware of them at all. Sometimes he would try to pull his pants down with one hand, while pulling them up with the other. Once he threatened his wife with his left hand while his right hand tried to come to his wife's rescue and bring the belligerent hand under control . . .

Only the left half-brain could speak. The right one remained forever mute, unable to do any tasks that required judgement or interpretation based on language. Of course, it was also unable to read. This meant that whenever he was faced with a page of printed matter, W.J. could read only the words in the right half of his visual field, which projected to his left hemisphere. His right hemisphere seemed blind. Reading thus became very difficult and tiring for him. He also found it impossible to write any words with his left hand, although he had been able to do so with a little effort before his operation. (He was thoroughly right-handed.)

Indeed, from the early tests on W.J. it appeared at first that his right hemisphere was nearly imbecilic. But then came the day when W.J. with a pencil in his left hand, was shown the outline of a Greek cross. Swiftly and surely, he copied it, drawing the entire figure with one continuous line. When he was asked to copy the same cross with his clever right hand, however, he could not do it. He drew a few lines in a disconnected way, as if he could see only one small part of the cross at a time and was unable to finish the pattern. With six separate strokes, he had made only half of the cross. Urged to do more, he added a few lines but then stopped before completing it and said he was done. It was clearly not a lack of motor control, but a defect in conception—in striking contrast with the quick grasp of his nonverbal half.

Since then, a tantalizing picture of the brain's mute hemisphere has begun to emerge. Far from being stupid, the right half-brain is merely speechless and illiterate. It actually perceives, feels and thinks in ways all its own, which in some cases prove superior.[36]

Research has suggested that the right hemisphere is most active in processes associated with spatial perception, emotion, dreaming, the interpretation of facial and body movement and of tone of voice (Ornstein, 1972:59). In sharp contrast, the left seems to be associated especially with language, and various forms of logic and systematic thought processes in general. As these findings kept coming in, one central pattern appeared obvious: that (in most right-handed people at least) the left hemisphere appears to be the base for a mode of thinking that is linear, sequential, and orderly—in other words, analytic—while the right hemisphere seems to be specialized for a simultaneous, holistic, relational mode of thinking—in other words, synthetic. One seems to favor the explicit, the other the implicit; one seems oriented to argument, the other to experience; one seems to prefer to decompose, the other to design; one seeks to analyze, the other to synthesize.

Of course, all complex human activity combines these two in tandem. Any serious engineering design, for example, requires analysis as well as synthesis, even if the notion of design itself—the conception of something new—seems more closely associated with the description of the right hemisphere. But the important conclusion drawn by Sperry and others was that, while these two processes might productively combine, they do not blend into one nor

---

[36] From Maya Pines, "We Are Left-Brained or Right-Brained," *The New York Times*, September 9, 1973.

can they easily substitute for each other. In other words, the bridge in question is the corpus callosum, spanning the two hemispheres of the human brain, and their respective methods of processing information cannot cross it even if their outputs can.

This conclusion was, of course, an inference, which others were not willing to draw. Simon, for example, has accepted that the hemispheres of the brain are specialized as to verbal and spatial capabilities, but he saw no reason to extrapolate this to the processes of analysis on one side or creativity on the other.[37]

> The evidence for this romantic extrapolation does not derive from the physiological research. . . . that research has provided evidence only for some measure of specialization between the hemispheres. It does not in any way imply that either hemisphere (especially the right hemisphere) is capable of problem solving, decision making, or discovery independent of the other. The real evidence for two different forms of thought is essentially the observation that, in everyday affairs, men and women often make competent judgements or reach reasonable decisions rapidly—without evidence indicating that they have engaged in systematic reasoning, and without their being able to report the thought processes that took them to their conclusion. (1986:58)

One problem in sorting this out is that, to the people inclined to draw the inference, inference itself would seem to be a right-hemisphere process, while the analysis of the evidence relies largely on processes of the left hemisphere. So is one to trust Simon's analysis or Sperry's inference? Who, in fact, can be neutral in this battle of the hemispheres?

The word battle may not, in fact, be altogether inappropriate, for in his work, Sperry found evidence of conflict between the hemispheres, specifically of the left hemisphere deploring the behavior of the right. As Pines (1973) summarized it in her *New York Times* review of Sperry's work:

> . . . the [left] hemisphere clearly does not trust its twin, at least in split brain patients, and generally prefers to ignore it, if not put it

---

[37] See the reprinted correspondence on this between Simon and the author in Mintzberg, 1989 (58–61).

down. The left hemisphere will usually deny that the left hand can do anything like retrieving, out of a grab bag, some object previously felt by that hand. When asked to do this for the first time, Sperry's subjects generally complain that they cannot "work with that hand", that the hand is "numb", or that they "just can't feel anything" or "can't do anything with it". If the left hand then proceeds to do the job correctly, and this is pointed out to the patient, the speaking half will reply, "Well, I must have done it unconsciously". It never even acknowledges the existence of its twin.

To Ornstein, whose book, *The Psychology of Consciousness*, popularized Sperry's work, this reflected the age-old tendency of the verbal hemisphere to put down its mute twin, manifested socially in the negative connotations associated with the word "left" (bearing in mind that we perceive the sides of our body not the sides of our brains, each of which controls movements on the opposite side, e.g., the left arm by the right hemisphere). Across all kinds of cultures, our verbal apparatus has described left as "bad," "dark," "profane" (1972:51). Indeed, while the word "right" means correct in English and straight (as well as the law) in French ("droit"), the French and Italian words for "left" are, respectively, gauche and sinistra!

Simon's Analytical View of Intuition

Let us take a closer look at how Simon deals with intuition. Much of his research on decision making has dealt with game situations such as chess and cryptarithmetic in the psychology laboratory (see Newell and Simon, 1972). There Simon relied on "protocols," verbal articulations of the subjects as they made decisions. "The thinking-aloud technique . . . can now be used dependably to obtain data about subjects' behaviors in a wide range of settings" (in Simon et al., 1987:21). From this research, Simon drew the following conclusion:

> The first thing we have learned—and the evidence for this is by now substantial—is that these human processes [problem solving,

thinking, and learning] can be explained *without* postulating mechanisms at subconscious levels that are different from those that are partly conscious and partly verbalized. Much of the iceberg is, indeed, below the surface and inaccessible to verbalization, but its concealed bulk is made of the same kind of ice as the part we can see . . . The secret of problem solving is that there is no secret. It is accomplished through complex structures of familiar simple elements. The proof is that we have been able to simulate it, using no more than those simple elements as the building blocks of our programs. (1977:69)

The "proof" Simon claims is, in fact, open to dispute (see Mintzberg, 1977). Indeed, while he also claimed in the 1977 edition of his book, *New Science of Management Decision,* that "it is only in the past twenty years that we have begun to have a good scientific understanding of the information processes that humans use in problem solving and nonprogrammed decision making" (64), the first edition, of this book, seventeen years earlier, contained almost the same passage quoted above (Simon, 1960:26–27; the only substantive change in 1977 being the addition of the phrase, "and inaccessible to verbalization").

Of course, if the mysterious combinations of the subconscious mind are not relevant, then something else must explain the apparent complexity of decision processes, even those of an individual nature (such as the playing of chess). And for this Simon had a ready answer: "The whole man, like the ant, viewed as a behaving system, is quite simple. The apparent complexity of his behavior over time, is largely a reflection of the complexity of the environment in which he finds himself" (in Weizenbaum, 1976:260). In other words, "Man is the mirror of the universe in which he lives . . ." (Newell and Simon, 1972:866).

But is he? Does nothing come from the inside, from a place inaccessible to verbal articulation? Why study individual chessmasters if all chess players are simply mirrors of their universes?

Mario Bunge (1975) wrote a well-regarded book on *Intuition and Science* that described a variety of uses of the word intuition: as perception (quick identifications, clear understanding, interpretation ability); as imagination (representation ability, skill in forming metaphors, creative imagination); as reason (catalytic inference, power of synthesis, common sense); and as valuation (good judgment, phronesis, discernment, or insight). Simon, however, recognized only one of these as intuition, namely quick identification.[38]

In a 1987 paper titled "Making Management Decisions: The Role of Intuition and Emotion," Simon discussed the "expert's intuition," particularly the ability of chess grandmasters to glance at a chessboard and quickly size up the situation. He argued that the expert recognizes "familiar patterns, recognizable old friends," that "the secret of the grandmasters' intuition or judgement" is "previous learning that has stored the patterns and the information associated with them" (60). Simon concluded from this that "the experienced manager, too, has in his or her memory a large amount of knowledge, gained from training and experience and arranged in terms of recognizable chunks and associated information." Thus, the essence of intuition lies in the *organization* of knowledge for quick identification, and not in its rendering for inspired design. He cited, for example, one study in which experienced business people could identify the key features of a case far faster than MBA students could. And, of course, once the identification has been made and the chunks isolated, the process of programming can begin. As Simon wrote in another paper, "On the basis of . . . models and experiments, it would appear that the process named 'intuition' by Gestalt psychologists is none other than our familiar friend 'recognition,' and that recognition processes are readily modeled by computer programs" (1986:244).

The key word is "chunks," because the fundamental assumption is that continuous knowledge can be broken into discrete elements, that is, decomposed for purposes of analysis. This

---

[38] In personal correspondence (June 25, 1986), Simon replied to receipt of this passage of Bunge's book with following:

> Bunge is right in observing that "intuition" is used in many ways by English-speaking people. But sometimes the enrichment of a word is its impoverishment, and this is a good example. To turn "intuition" into a useful concept for psychology, we must distinguish the different processes that are sometimes bundled together under this label, and then use different terms to refer to them. Thus, I generally restrict "intuition" to Bunge's "quick identification." His second and third categories, I would call "understanding." The fourth, in my terms, is "representation" and sometimes "imagery." The fifth is "analogy." The sixth appears otiose as a separate category since a creative product is the result of problem solving using the processes already mentioned. The seventh relates to the first, but also to the possession of representations associated with strong inference operators. The eighth is also a mixture of all the previous categories especially the second and third. The ninth is "knowledge."

represents a long-held belief, or at least premise, in the field of cognitive psychology, best articulated by George Miller's (1956) celebrated article, "The Magic Number Seven Plus or Minus Two: Some Limits on our Capacity for Processing Information." Intrigued by why the number seven appears so often in our categorization schemes (the seven wonders of the world, the seven days of the week, etc.), Miller concluded that this is how many "bits" or "chunks" of information we can retain in our short- and intermediate-term memories. We create our categorization schemes accordingly. But this is only one sort of memory. We remember other things too, such as images, that cannot be reduced to discrete chunks.

Assuming, nevertheless, the reduction of knowledge to chunks, Simon concluded in his 1987 article that "intuition is not a process that operates independently of analysis" (61).

> It is a fallacy to contrast "analytic" and "intuitive" styles of management. Intuition and judgement—at least good judgement—are simply *analyses frozen into habit* and into the capacity for rapid response through recognition. (63, italics added)

Flipping Intuition Across to Analysis

So intuition gets reduced to analysis (just as strategy formation got reduced to planning). Again, without being able to analyze this conclusion, the reader may wish to reflect on it intuitively. Does it "feel right" for creativity, for insight, for higher forms of synthesis such as the construction of a novel strategic vision? Here is how Edwin Land explained his development of the Polaroid camera:

> One day when we were vacationing in Santa Fe in 1943 my daughter, Jennifer, who was then 3, asked me why she could not see the picture I has just taken of her. As I walked around that charming town, I undertook the task of solving the puzzle she had set for me. Within the hour the camera, the film and the physical chemistry became so clear that with a great sense of excitement I hurried to the place where a friend was staying to describe to him in detail a dry camera which would give a picture immediately after expo-

sure. In my mind it was so real that I spent several hours on the description. (quoted in *TIME* magazine, 1972, 84)

What analyses were frozen into what habits in that charming town? Indeed, what are we to make of the protocol method itself when Land tells us that during his periods of creative insight, "atavistic competencies seem to come welling up. You are handling so many variables at a barely conscious level that you can't afford to be interrupted" (in Bello, 1959:158), least of all presumably by a psychologist with a tape recorder! The technique may work for the proverbial college sophomore on a simple arithmetic problem. But can it work even in the structured game of chess, when played with inspiration by a grandmaster:

> Let us suppose that at one point in your game you have a choice between two moves, R-Q1 or N-KN5. Which should you play? You settle down comfortably in your chair and start your analysis silently saying to yourself the possible moves. "All right I could play R-Q1 and he would probably play B-QN2, or he could take my QRP which is now undefended. What then?" Do I like the look of the position then? You go one move further in your analysis and then you pull a long face—the rook move no longer appeals to you. Then you look at the knight move. "What if I go N-KN5? He can drive it away by P-KR3, I go N-K4, he captures it with his bishop. I recapture and he attacks my queen with his rook. That doesn't look very nice . . . so the knight move is no good. Let's look at the rook move again." [more analysis] "No, [that] is no good. I must check the knight move again. [more analysis] No good! So, I mustn't move the knight. Try the rook move again . . . " At this point you glance at the clock. "My goodness! Already 30 minutes gone on thinking whether to move the rook or the knight. If it goes on like this you'll really be in time trouble. And then suddenly you are struck by the happy idea—why move rook or knight? What about B-QN1?" And without any more ado, without any analysis at all you move the bishop. Just like that with hardly any consideration at all. (Kotov, 1971:15–16)

Kotov's book is entitled *Think Like a Grandmaster*. But when it really gets down to it, when that insight strikes, do we really know how grandmasters think?

"I'll see it when I believe it," quipped Karl Weick. Can people enamored of computers and analyses allow themselves to "see" other kinds of thought processes? The famous parable of Nasrudun, who looks for his lost key under the lamppost where there is light rather than in the darkness of the house where he lost it, has been used with regard to the research on the two hemispheres (Ornstein, 1972). We have long been searching for the lost key to intuition in the light of the articulate analysis of the left hemisphere. Is it any wonder that we are still looking?

Might the real problem perhaps not lie in the reductionist perspective itself, the insistence on considering knowledge as discrete "chunks" to the exclusion of continuous images? Simon has referred to the "bottleneck" of short-term memory through which "almost all the inputs and outputs" of human thinking must pass (1986:250). But people draw pictures and they also make eye contact, by which enormous amounts of mysterious information seem to pass. True, we communicate formally, through articulated words, one by one, as discrete chunks, as in the case of Edwin Land, who hurried to explain his discovery to his friend. But even that is the consequence of the thinking, not the process itself. Land, in fact, who conceived his extraordinary idea "within the hour," needed "several hours" to explain it in words. Behind these decomposed chunks are thought processes we have barely begun to comprehend. We call them "intuition" or "judgment" to "name" our ignorance, as Simon (1977) pointed out. But to dismiss that ignorance is not to explain the behavior.

Some processes naturally lend themselves to "chunking." Shoveling coal may be one, even playing chess—at least without inspiration. After all, chess pieces are as discrete as shovelfuls of coal. But other processes involve less easily decomposed information. Even the simple behavior of recognizing a face, which any baby can do, poses formidable problems for a computer. (Curious, therefore, is Simon's use of the phrase, "recognizable old friends," for the chessmaster's instant recognition of the configuration of a chessboard. Apparently, different people have different kinds of friends!)

Is the information of strategy making easily decomposed? Michael Porter, with his enthusiasm for generic strategies and checklists of all kinds, may be inclined to answer in the affirmative. That is presumably why he considered "strategic thinking" as synonymous with "strategic planning," why he has "favor[ed] a set of analytical techniques for developing strategy," and why he claimed that "strategic thinking rarely occurs spontaneously" (1987:17, 21). Again, in*sight* cannot be *seen* in analysis, because it is not believed. Nor can strategic *vision*. The categories of strategic planning may be useful aids, conceptual tools to help reduce the complexity of the reality. But they are not the reality itself. None can substitute for the synthesis that molds the various perceptions of that reality—continuous images as well as discrete facts—into an integrated strategic vision. Where that synthesis comes from we cannot be sure. But of one thing we can: the question facing strategic management is not only how much formalization do we need, but also how much conscious thinking of any kind.[39]

John Bryson (1988) opened one chapter of his book on public sector planning with the comment by hockey player Wayne Gretzky that "I skate to where I think the puck will be" (46). He then laid out a planning process of eight steps (e.g., Initial Agreement, Strategies, Major Proposals, Work Programs, etc., 50–51) and claimed that "one can easily imagine [Gretzky] zooming almost intuitively through the eight steps," which serve, in his view, "*merely* [to] make the process of strategic thinking and acting more orderly and allow more people to participate" (62, italics added). But do they?

It is a bit difficult to imagine Gretzky securing the initial agreement of his teammates after he gets the puck, or developing work programs, no matter how quickly. Indeed, would doing so make Gretzky's playmaking any more "orderly" (whatever that could possibly mean here), let alone allow his teammates to better "participate" in his magic? Simon and Bryson and many others in this literature tried to give the impression that intuition can be flipped across the corpus callosum to analysis the way Gretzky flips the puck across the ice to a teammate. But that has never "felt" right to intuition, no matter how much "proof" analysis has tried to marshall. Gretzky does indeed skate to where the puck will be—

---

[39] In other words, how much emphasis do we want to give to the perspective of the design school, let alone the planning school? See Pascale (1984) on the propensity of Americans to "get off on strategy like the French get off on good food" (1982:115).

where the action is—almost by magic. Planning, in contrast, has tended to skate the other way.

Planning on the Left Side and Managing on the Right

Management has no more Wayne Gretzkys than does hockey. But like hockey it has its share of competent performers, who not only know how to use their intuition but fully appreciate that they often have to. Formal analysis simply does not suffice for many aspects of managing an organization. As for our case in point, while no one has perhaps *proved* that strategic planning cannot program the intuitive processes of the "genius entrepreneur," or the ordinary manager for that matter, the evidence is unmistakable that planning has failed to do so thus far. The systems, whether at General Electric or Texas Instruments, or as PPBS in the government, never quite made it. They never crossed that delicate divide, whether in an executive office or the human brain.

Note that we include here all the efforts to formalize, including the so-called "quasi-analytic" approaches proposed by Ansoff. It is the fundamental assumption of the need to formalize, most evident in Ansoff's writings, that we are calling into question here. Systems can certainly facilitate informal processes, as was concluded eventually at Texas Instruments and by Jelinek, and as we shall discuss in Chapter 6. But they cannot substitute for it.

Some years ago, inspired by the findings of Sperry et al. in physiology, we published an article titled "Planning on the Left Side and Managing on the Right" (Mintzberg, 1976). Our point was that "there may be a fundamental difference between formal planning and informal managing, a difference akin to that between the two hemispheres of the human brain." While formal planning "seems to use processes akin to those identified with the brain's left hemisphere," we "hypothesize[d] . . . that the important policy processes of managing an organization rely to a considerable extent on the faculties identified with the brain's right hemisphere" (53). In other words, what this research has done is to provide physiological support for the argument we have been making all along in this book, that there is something fundamentally different bctween the informal, "inluitive" kinds of managerial processes on the one hand (so to speak), such as the internalization of soft information and the creation of a novel strategy, and the formally analytical ones on the other hand, such as planning, based on decomposition and formalization. Sperry's phrase, "not yet simulatable in computers," is key because it suggests that one process cannot be substituted for the other. As Ornstein noted in drawing on that old story of the blind men and the elephant:

> Each person standing at one part of the elephant can make his own limited, analytic assessment of the situation, but we do not obtain an elephant by adding "scaly [skin]", "long and soft [trunk]", "massive and cylindrical [legs]" together in any conceivable proportion. Without the development of an over-all perspective, we remain lost in our individual investigations. Such a perspective is a province of another mode of knowledge, and cannot be achieved in the same way that individual parts are explored. It does not arise out of a linear sum of independent observations. (1972:10)

Our article of 1976 may have been speculative, but at about the same time, Robert Doktor (1978; see also Doktor and Bloom, 1977) was wiring up to electroencephalograph (EEG) machines three people specialized in business analysis (in the fields of accounting and operations research, each with a Ph.D.) and seven general managers, chiefs of divisions (three of whom had prior training in analytical fields, accounting and finance, whom he labeled "executive/analyst"). He then read their brain waves as they performed two sets of tasks, one intuitive-spatial (to perceive a whole picture with parts of lines), the other analytic-verbal (syllogisms). The findings were rather startling: the four managers without analytic training showed a relative propensity to perform all of the intuitive-spatial tasks in their right hemispheres (as would be expected of almost all right-handed people), but *also* 75 percent of the analytic-verbal tests (which would not be expected). The analysts, in sharp contrast, showed a relative propensity to perform all of the analytic-verbal tasks in their left hemispheres (again, as would be expected) but 67 percent of the spatial tasks *as well* (as, again, would not be expected). The executive/analysts fell in between, with more balanced responses.

In the light of our arguments here, these findings are rather striking. They suggest that not only do the individual hemispheres of the human brain appear to be specialized, but so too do whole brains, apparently favoring one hemisphere over the other by virtue of their training and experience (or maybe their self-selection into a line of work in the first place).[40] As Sperry commented, "excellence in one [mode of thinking] tends to interfere with top-level performance in the other" (in Pines, 1973).

This provides a physiological basis for distinguishing intuitive managers from analytical planners (and indeed, as we shall soon do, analytical planners from intuitive ones). Planning processes may well favor the left side of the brain and managing the right. These findings also provide support for some of our earlier conclusions about analytical-type people—their predisposition to convergent, deductive processes of thought and their tendency to close on alternatives prematurely, etc. Indeed, these very traits might explain why analytic thinkers, in the planning literature and elsewhere, have been so inclined to dismiss intuitive thought processes.[41]

Harold Laski (1930) wrote of the trained incapacity of the expert, in an effort to explain why experts can sometimes be so narrow-minded. Here, perhaps, we have some explanation: those experts avoid the clearly delineated pitfalls while missing the more fundamental, if less tangible, fallacies. In other words, they can recognize only what can easily be "chunked." An expert has also been defined as someone who knows more and more about less and less until finally he or she knows everything about nothing. Perhaps this means that if you understand only certain discrete chunks, ultimately you understand nothing. (Of course, a manager may be someone who knows less and less about more and more until finally he or she knows nothing about everything!) Finally, an expert has been defined as someone with no elementary knowledge. Intuitive knowledge is certainly elementary. To quote an

---

[40] Leavitt (1975b:17–18) cited evidence from two doctoral dissertations that supported the former interpretation: creativity declined during undergraduate education in engineering while it increased in fine arts, at the cost of analytic skills.

[41] Indeed, the accusation by analysts that managers are irrational and emotional, and the countercharge that analysts are cold and detached, takes on physiological meaning with the suggestion in research that emotion is related to the right hemisphere (Restak, 1976).

ancient Greek saying, "The fox knows many things but the hedge-hog knows one big thing." So too may it be with analysis and intuition.

Of course, there are other kinds of experts too, less narrow or "conventional," just as there are managers expert enough to know what they don't know as well as what they do. Both naturally blend the analytic with the intuitive, each (to use a term we shall discuss later) exhibiting at least a "minor" in the mode of thinking of the other. Clearly, we are best off when such experts work cooperatively with such managers.

Among the more intriguing findings of the brain research is that when listening to music, lay people tend to favor the right hemi-sphere whereas musicians tend to favor the left (see Fincher, 1976:70–71). The implication seems to be that generalists listen to the gestalt—they absorb music as a whole in a sense—while the experts tend to decompose—they hear the individual notes. That too fits with much that has been discussed here. But surely the great musicians, and especially the great composers, must do both. That has to be one source of their greatness, the blending of anal-ysis with synthesis. Indeed, in a truly astonishing comment, here is how Mozart described his act of creative composing:

> First bits and crumbs of the piece come and gradually join together in my mind; then the soul getting warmed to the work, the thing grows more and more, and I spread it out broader and clearer, and at last it gets almost finished in my head, even when it is a long piece, so that I can see the whole of it at a single glance in my mind, as if it were a beautiful painting or a handsome human being; in which way I do not hear it in my imagination at all as a succession—the way it must come later—but all at once as it were. It is a rare feast. All the inventing and making goes on in me as in a beautiful strong dream. But the best of all is the hearing of it all at once.

The Image of Managing

Research on managerial work (see Mintzberg, 1973) provides fur-ther evidence of the distinctiveness of intuition and its impor-tance here. Characterized as "calculated chaos" and "controlled disorder" (Andrews, 1976), managerial work appears to be more simultaneous, holistic, and relational than linear, sequential, and orderly. Managers likely prefer oral forms of communication, not only because these tend to bring information earlier and easier, but also because they provide a sense of facial expression, gesture, and tone of voice—all inputs that have been associated with the brain's right hemisphere. If managers have to "see the big picture" and create strategic "visions"—clearly more than just metaphors—then their perceptions require the soft, speculative information they favor, which is better suited to synthesis than analysis. And, of course, much of this information is from oral sources and so must necessarily remain "tacit," as noted earlier. That makes it inaccessible, not only to others by way of verbal articulation, but often even to the manager's own conscious mind. Hence the need to process it subconsciously, which probably means intuitively.

Managers revel in ambiguity and exhibit few patterns in their work, presumably because they spend so much of their time operating in the mode of synthesis. Likewise, the mysteries surrounding such key aspects of their decision making and strategy making processes as diagnosis, design, timing, and bargaining (see Mintzberg, Raisinghani, and Théorêt, 1976) can perhaps likewise be explained by their reliance on the thinking processes of the brain's mute right hemisphere, which are inaccessible to the apparatus of language—in other words, lost to analysis. Indeed, the whole nature of strategy making—dynamic, irregular, discontinuous, calling for groping, interactive processes with an emphasis on learning and synthesis—compels managers to favor intuition. This is probably why all those analytical techniques of planning felt so wrong. "People may resist steplike structures because the procedure they prefer is basically holistic in the sense that all steps are considered simultaneously" (Weick, 1983:240).

In particular, strategies that are novel and compelling seem to be the products of single creative brains, those capable of synthesizing a vision. The key to this would seem to be integration rather than decomposition, based on holistic images rather than linear words. Westley captured this notion well with her "contention that a good deal of what happens in all policy meetings is concerned with image making," which she characterized as "a kind of bricolage, a piecing together of a group image from the bits and pieces of individual imagery." She cited Tom Peters who had pointed out that "when one company demanded that its staff talk prose instead of numbers at a planning meeting, they were rendered speechless"; Westley suggested that "imageless might have been the appropriate expression"! (1983:16, 25)

There is, therefore, a big difference between a formal plan and an informal vision. An image cannot simply be rendered into words and numbers. When organizations try to do that, integrated perspective tends to get reduced to decomposed positions, and much is lost. As the psychologist Bartlett commented long ago, "words are essentially more explicitly analytic than images; they are compelled to deal with situations in a piecemeal fashion" (1932:304). Thus a Texas Instruments manager commented that Haggerty's successors "didn't have obviously either the foresight or strategic mind that Haggerty did, certainly did not have the vision that Haggerty did. . . . we lost vision completely. The whole job became one of control, and that basically killed the whole semiconductor operation, and almost the corporation" (in Jelinek and Schoonhoven, 1990:413). In other words, by relying excessively on words and numbers, planning can kill vision. "Like myopia, categories make vision less sharp" (Pant and Starbuck, 1990:449). In more ways than one, planning may simply have counted too much.

The inability of the analytical mode to synthesize and to perceive spatially might explain why planning has had such trouble dealing with strategy making, why observers of business could write about "the confusion between strategic thinking and long-range planning" (Tregoe and Zimmerman, 1980:23), and why the chief planner at General Electric could end up making his "distinction between planning and strategy—they're two different things. . . . Historically, GE's approach emphasized planning more than strategy" (Carpenter, in Allio, 1985:18). By decomposing an integrated process into a sequence of steps, planning shifted that process from the realm of synthesis to that of analysis, and so rendered it incapable of executing its own mandate.

Thus formal planning has had no business putting down informal managing, no matter how ancient may be the battle between right and left. Viewing it as gauche if not actually sinister was descriptively false even if *literally* true: informal managerial processes have always been largely "left" and thus inaccessible to the formalities of planning. But it was planning that ultimately proved itself gauche by so dismissing them.

The Grand Fallacy

Thus we arrive at the planning school's grand fallacy: **Because analysis is not synthesis, strategic planning is not strategy formation.** Analysis may precede and support synthesis, by defining the parts that can be combined into wholes. Analysis may follow and elaborate synthesis, by decomposing and formalizing its consequences. But analysis cannot substitute for synthesis. No amount of elaboration will ever enable formal procedures to forecast discontinuities, to inform managers who are detached from their operations, to create novel strategies. Ultimately, the term "strategic planning" has proved to be an oxymoron.

6

Planning,
Plans,
Planners

We have been highly critical throughout this discussion, concerned that by trying to be everything, planning has risked being dismissed as nothing. In fact, we never had any intention of so dismissing planning, although the tone of our discussion may well have given that impression. Instead, by overstating our criticisms, we have tried to draw the debate on planning to a more viable middle ground, away from the conclusion that planning can do either everything or nothing. To draw from one extreme (where we believe planning has always been) toward the middle, one has to pull from the far end (much as in trying to balance a seesaw with all the weight on one end, one has to put weight on the other end, not the middle). Having (we hope) succeeded in drawing the reader toward that middle, we can now position ourselves there as well to consider the viable roles that planning as well as plans and planners can play in organizations. Hence the tone of our discussion changes at this point, from critical to constructive.

Coupling Analysis and Intuition

The Planning Dilemma

Some years ago, we wrote about a "planning dilemma" (Hekimian and Mintzberg, 1968; Mintzberg, 1973:153–155). Planners have certain techniques to do systematic analysis, and more important, they have the time to consider strategic issues at length. What they tend to lack is the authority to make strategy, and, of far greater consequence, critical soft information as well as the connections needed to get it. It is the line managers who have these things, as well as the flexibility to respond to strategic issues in a dynamic way. But they lack the time to focus intensively on these issues, and especially to absorb and perhaps sometimes also to process certain necessary hard information. The nature of managerial work favors action over reflection, the short run over the long run, soft data over hard, the oral over the written, getting information rapidly over getting it right. These tendencies are inevitable and even necessary in the manager's job, but they drive the manager to overlook analytic inputs, which also have an important role to play in the strategy process.

The result of all this is that the manager understands the need to adapt to what does go on, while the planner feels the need to analyze what should go on. The manager tends to chase opportunities when not being chased by crises, produces plans that exist only vaguely in his or her head, and exhibits an "occupational hazard" to be superficial in his or her work—"to overload [himself or herself] with work, to do things abruptly, to avoid wasting time, to participate only when the value of participation is tangible, to avoid too great an involvement with any one issue" (Mintzberg, 1973:35). But the planner promotes a process that seems overly simplified and sterile when compared with the complexities of strategy making. Moreover, as we saw in our discussion of the two hemispheres, in particular Robert Doktor's findings (1978), planners and managers may also be differentiated cognitively, one being more predisposed to the analysis associated with the left hemisphere, the other to the synthesis more closely associated with the right hemisphere. At the limit, we seem to have to choose between "extinction by instinct" and "paralysis by analysis" (Kast and Rosenweig, 1970:390). Put differently, "the [intuitive] people tend to act before they think, if they ever think; and the [analytic] people think before they act, if they ever act" (in Wade, 1975:9).

So a fundamental dilemma arises: how to couple the skills, time, and inclinations of the planner with the authority, information, and flexibility of the manager, to ensure a strategy making process that is informed, responsive, and integrative.

Comparing Analysis and Intuition

Of course, while both parties have their weaknesses, they also have their strengths. Consider first the cost and speed of using analysis versus intuition. Analysis would seem to be slower and costlier: a team often has to be assembled and it has to study all kinds of data before it can draw a conclusion. For better or for worse, the decisions of intuition are available immediately. But that considers only the *operating* cost. The *investment* cost of intuition is far higher, for (even by Simon's definition) one cannot be (effectively) intuitive unless one has intimate knowledge of the subject in question, which sometimes requires years to develop. Good analysis, in contrast, is available anywhere clever analysts can get their hands on good hard data.

Next consider the ability of both modes to deal with issues of complexity. In his paper on "The Counter-intuitive Behavior of Social Systems," discussed earlier, Jay Forrester (1975) argued that people develop their own mental models, but that unless these are articulated and formalized (as in a computer program), they can be inconsistent, "apt to draw the wrong conclusions" even though possibly "correct in structure and assumptions" (214). For certain kinds of complex social problems, intuitive approaches are inclined to "address symptoms rather than causes, and attempt to operate through points in the system that have little leverage for change." This may help in the short run but "cause deepening difficulties" after that, "so that suppressing one symptom only causes trouble to burst forth at another point" (227). In *Urban Dynamics* (1969), for example, Forrester showed how politicians' interventions in decaying cities acted through positive rather than negative feedback loops to cause further decay. Forrester's main point was that "the human mind is not adapted to interpreting how social systems behave. Our social systems belong to the class called multiple-loop nonlinear feedback systems. In the long history of human evolution it has not been necessary for man to understand these systems until very recent historic times" (211–212).

Forrester presents a strong argument, in support of which a good deal of unhappy evidence can be cited, in government and outside of it (see, for example, Hall, 1976). Other, similar arguments pertain to the inability of intuition to handle certain structured issues (Tversky and Kahneman, 1974:1130), for example, that only 23 people need be assembled before the probability of two of their birthdays falling on the same day reaches 50 percent. Intuition also seems ineffective at assessing the consequences of its decisions long after they are taken. Natural memory can forget quickly; documents fade only very slowly.

Forrester believed that effective systems dynamics models can be based on the "structure and assumptions" of the manager's own mental models, because these may be correct even if their interconnections may not be. He wrote that the two models "are derived from the same sources" but that the language of the computer is "unambiguous"—"clearer, simpler, more precise." He claimed that "any concept and relationship that can be clearly stated in ordinary language can be translated into computer model language" (1975:214), and that "assumptions [in the computer model] can be checked against all available information" (234).

But the arguments we presented in Chapter 5 put these claims into dispute on a number of grounds—namely that intuition is necessarily inadequate (i.e., the interconnections are not "correct"), and that all information can be explicated through "ordinary language." Thus, no matter how strong Forrester's argument, there is also room for an article entitled "The Counter-analytic Behavior of Social Systems," because when the key data are soft, and so cannot be made "machine readable," and when the model in the human brain is perhaps more in the form of image than alphanumeric characters, or at least cannot easily be decomposed into discrete elements (as in models used to judge the character of a person), then it is the analytic model that can become inconsistent and "apt to draw the wrong conclusions."

Now consider accuracy. Analysis, when done correctly with the right kind of data, gives answers that are precisely correct. Intuition, in contrast, when applied to problems with which it can deal, tends to be only approximately correct ("in the right ballpark" being the popular American expression). These respective advantages, and their corresponding disadvantages, were made quite clear in an experiment conducted by Peters et al. (1974). As can be seen in Figure 6–1, the analytic approach to problem solving produced the precise answer more often, but its distribution of errors was quite wide. Intuition, in contrast, was less frequently precise but more consistently close. In other words, informally, people get certain kinds of problems more or less right, while formally, their errors, however infrequent, can be bizarre. (Perhaps that is why an expert has been defined as someone with no elementary knowledge. To intuition, a bizarre answer "feels" wrong and is reconsidered. But analysis just doesn't feel in this way, so mistakes are more inclined to go undetected.)

Peters et al. thus described analysis as equivalent to the switching of trains on a track, involving a set of discrete and well-defined

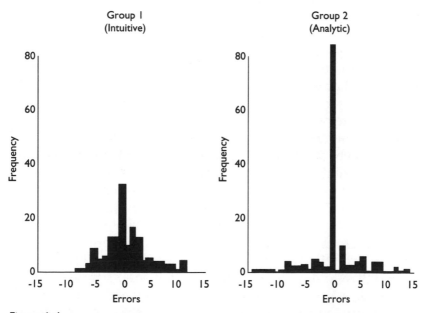

Figure 6–1
Distribution of Errors in an Experiment of Analytical and Intuitive Thinking (From Peters et al., 1974:128)

choices. Correct decisions all along the way lead to the right destination, while one simple error anywhere can take the train to an altogether different place. They concluded that "In situations where small departures from precision are tolerable—but where extreme error can lead to disaster—a compromise between the intuitive and analytic approaches may be the most appropriate" (131). Certainly one implication of this is that the decisions so quickly available from intuition must sometimes be checked for accuracy by formal analysis, while those produced by careful analysis must generally be confirmed intuitively for face validity ("eyeballing" the figures being the popular expression).

Next consider optimality. Intuition may seem superficial and suboptimal. As already noted, the characteristics of managerial work drive it to a form of superficiality—to get things done quickly, keep them moving. Incrementalism and opportunism can be major obstacles to sensible choices, as can a kind of "tunnel vision" by which the future is perceived through the narrow experiences of the past. Clearly, analysis can help here.

But analysis can be superficial too, for example, when it has to deal with soft data. It can likewise be opportunistic, as in its inability to cope with nonoperational goals. Merton (1968) has described this in terms of the confusion of knowledge with wisdom, which can lead to superficial studies by people who allow convenient data to substitute for in-depth understanding. To quote a seasoned airline operations researcher on his experience of loading baggage during a strike: ". . . you can sit in the Head Office, and work on systems, procedures and models all day, without really learning or understanding airline operations" (Davidson, 1977:33). Analysis can be suboptimal too, as we discussed in the last chapter, about the ambitious "systems approach" that tends to trade off breadth for depth. The obvious conclusion is that all brains—mechanical as well as biological—have their limits.

Finally, let us consider creativity. As discussed earlier, analysis does not seem to encourage creativity. It is a convergent process, in search of a solution, and a deductive one, oriented more to decomposition than to design. As noted, it often suffers from premature closure, locking onto alternatives to be evaluated before allowing full rein for their generation. "The systematics often preferred program-type problems while the intuitives liked open-ended ones, especially those that required ingenuity or opinion" (Mc-

Kenney and Keen, 1974:84). At best, analysis would thus seem to lead to marginal rather than radical innovation. But again we must look the other way. Intuition, presumably the seat of creative insight, can also be mightily constrained by experience and tradition, by that tunnel vision discussed earlier. Then it is analysis that may be used to break free, even if only partially (perhaps until intuition can open up anew). Thus, while analysis may produce only marginal innovation, intuition can lead either to dramatic forms of it or none at all.

Analysis and Intuition in Strategy Making

The obvious conclusion to this is that to be effective, any organization has to couple analysis and intuition in its strategy making as well as other processes. No matter how much we may disagree with Herbert Simon about the nature of intuition, we must agree wholeheartedly with his conclusion about its place alongside analysis:

> Every manager needs to be able to analyze problems systematically (and with the aid of the modern arsenal of analytical tools provided by management science and operations research). Every manager needs also to be able to respond to situations rapidly, a skill that requires cultivation of intuition and judgement over many years of experience and training. The effective manager does not have the luxury of choosing between "analytic" and "intuitive" approaches to problems. Behaving like a manager means having command of the whole range of management skills and applying them as they become appropriate. (1987:63)

The "planning dilemma" in fact suggests its own resolution, by identifying the comparative advantages of more analytical planners and more intuitive managers. In the terms of the grand fallacy, analysis may not be synthesis, and so planning may not be strategy formation, but effective strategy formation, especially in large organizations, does depend importantly on analysis, both as an input to the process and as a means of dealing with its outputs. Soft data may be indispensable, but hard data can hardly be ignored. Some issues depend on models locked deep inside the intuitive brains of managers, but other issues are better handled by models that have, in Forrester's sense, been made formally consistent. And, of course, while intuition may need to eyeball analysis, analysis must check out intuition.

Planners have the time and technique to engage in the necessary analysis; they have the inclination to find the important messages in the hard data and to apply the systematic models. Thus, the analyst able to develop a good rapport with managers can fill the important role of ensuring that they get these analytic inputs. Such inputs increase the managers' knowledge bases and extend the amount of material they can consider in strategy making. More important, the analyst can provide managers with new concepts and alternate ways to look at problems, sometimes freeing them from mind-sets imposed by years of experience.

It should be emphasized, however, that the analytic approach provides not a solution but a perspective—another way to look at problems. Analysts who expect to feed in formulations and then wait for implementation will have a long wait (unless they are dealing with managers disconnected from their contexts). But those who take a broad view are more likely to serve their organizations, for even the best of managers can benefit from planners (and other like-minded people) for this kind of support. The planning dilemma can, therefore, be resolved by combining these two modes of thinking, one largely represented by the manager, the other, the planner.

A Strategy for Planning

Put a little differently, the field of planning needs a strategy of its own, a viable niche that makes the best uses of its true comparative advantages. Here we wish to propose such a strategy in terms of a set of roles that can be played by planning, plans, and planners with regard to the process of strategy formation. (We do not consider roles for other purposes here, for example, those of a purely control, operating, or political nature, such as the numbers game of budgeting or various public relations exercises.)

We came to the conclusion in the previous chapter that formal planning does not create strategy so much as deal with the consequences of strategy created in other ways, likewise that while any creative and informed individual can be a strategist, there is nothing in the planners' comparative advantages that particularly predisposes them to this role. As Langley noted:

> formal strategic planning and strategic planners do not make strategic decisions. People and organizations make strategic decisions, and sometimes they use strategic planning as a discipline within which to do this, or to seem to do this. Strategic planning supplies a forum for announcing, selling, negotiating, rationalizing and legitimizing strategic decisions, and it also offers means for controlling their implementation. These roles are as important if not more important than the more usually noted role of providing information to improve the content of strategy. (1988:48)

In effect, the strategy making process, whether its strategies are formulated deliberately or just form emergently, must be seen as an impenetrable "black box" for planning as well as for planners, *around* which, rather than *inside* of which, they work. As shown in Figure 6–2, they may be involved in inputs *to* the process, support *for* the process, or consequences *of* the process. We shall describe roles for each of these in this chapter, after a brief comment on the nature of analysis for the strategy making process.

Figure 6–2
Planning, Plans, and Planners Around the Black Box of Strategy Formation

"Soft" Analysis

Admittedly, we have tended to stereotype planners so far in this book, using the adjective "conventional" to qualify the kinds of planners we have had in mind. But planners are, of course, no more monolithic in their cognitive predispositions than are managers. Particularly with regard to analytical orientation, planners range from the obsessively Cartesian to the playfully intuitive. We shall consider roles that fall along this whole range, but it is important to note that the planners who can best serve senior managers likely exhibit at least what Doktor and Hamilton (1973:887) referred to as a "minor" in intuitive thinking. They are, in other words, able to temper a predisposition to analysis with an appreciation for intuition, and even a certain use of it themselves. Theirs is a kind of *soft analysis*.

Soft analysis suggests an approach in which it is more important to pose the right question than to find the precise answer, to incorporate an appreciation for soft data alongside the necessary analysis of hard data. Judgment takes its place alongside formal procedures, and a mutual understanding is allowed to develop between staff planner and line manager, as analysis becomes "a continuing dialogue rather than a one-shot service" (Whitehead, 1967:57). Soft analysis forgets about optimization, accepts the absence of sharply defined goals, downplays elegance in technique. Each issue is approached as a unique, creative challenge. The approach is systematic but seldom rigorous, distinguishing between "analytic thinking" and "analytic technique" (Leavitt, 1975a:6). It depends on people comfortable with numbers but not obsessed with them, capable analytic types who also have intuitive skills and are not shy about using them, people from a range of backgrounds who can open up issues instead of closing them down prematurely. To quote Wildavsky, for once on a positive note: "The good systems analyst is a chochem, a Yiddish word meaning wise man, with overtones of wise guy. His forte is creativity" (1966:298).

In the spirit of such soft analysis, possible roles for planning, plans, and planners have been suggested at a number of points in our discussion, especially in the intensive studies discussed in Chapter 3. Some of these roles may have seemed trivial or even dysfunctional—for example, planning as a public relations exercise or as something to do for an organization that lacks a raison d'être. Our concerns here, however, are with the more substantial roles, ones that can have a major influence on the strategy formation process or on its consequences. These indicate, in the final analysis, why organizations really do have planners and planning, telling us not just what planners do but what planners *get done* that makes a difference. We delineate these roles here, first for planning, then for plans, finally for planners, drawing them into a single framework. We believe this framework constitutes an operational definition of planning that we claimed at the outset this field requires.

Role of Planning: Strategic Programming

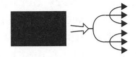

Why do organizations engage in formal planning? In other words, given all the difficulties, especially with regard to the formation of strategies, why do they persist in carrying out planning on a formal basis? The answer is evident, having been suggested many times in our discussion. **Organizations engage in formal planning, not to create strategies but to program the strategies they already have, that is, to elaborate and operationalize their consequences formally.** We should really say that *effective* organizations so engage in planning, at least when they require the formalized articulation of their intended strategies. Thus, strategy is not the consequence of planning but the opposite: its starting point. Planning helps to translate intended strategies into realized ones, by taking the first step that can lead to effective implementation. We present this not as our first role for planning but as the only one. All the other roles we shall discuss pertain to plans and planners but not to planning.

Planning as programming came out clearly in our strategy-tracking study of the Steinberg supermarket chain. That firm was run in a purely entrepreneurial fashion for decades, until it had to go to the financial markets for capital. Then it had to "plan"—that is, issue a document outlining where it intended to go, and how. As we noted in summary, however:

> . . . its planning did not give this company an intended strategy. It already had one, in the head of its entrepreneur, as his vision of its

future. That is what encouraged it to go to financial markets in the first place. Rather, planning was the articulation, justification, and elaboration of the intended strategy the company already had. Planning for it was not deciding to expand into shopping centers, but explicating to what extent and when—with how many stores and on what schedule, etc. In other words, planning was programming: it was used not to conceive an intended strategy, but to elaborate the consequences of an intended strategy already conceived. (Mintzberg, 1981:322)

Likewise we saw clear evidence of planning as programming at Air Canada, which engaged in very detailed programming of its aircraft and route structures as well as the scheduling of its regular operations. As in all major airlines, so many elements had to be executed in such a precisely coordinated manner, under the direction of a well-defined strategy, that the formalized procedures of planning were necessary for successful operation.

Note that all the definitions of planning discussed at the outset hold up here. Planning as programming is clearly systematic procedure to produce articulated result. It is clearly decision making, or more exactly a set of coordinated decision processes evoked by the dictates of strategy. And it clearly involves future thinking, and often controlling the future as well—specifically the enactment of desired end-points. But none of this requires that it be strategy formation.

This role of planning has long been recognized. Consider, for example, what Ansoff wrote in his 1967 paper with Brandenburg:

Programming is a management activity which translates decisions into specific action patterns for implementation. The primary management tasks in this phase are:

    a) Scheduling activities in support of decisions
    b) Assignment and scheduling of resources in support of decisions (commonly referred to as budgeting)
    c) Establishing patterns of work flows in the firm
    d) Establishing patterns of authority and responsibility
    e) Establishing communication flow networks

This area of management activity has traditionally been the focus of planners. This is where planning was born. Many planners can be found in the profession today who would argue that programming, as defined above, is the core and the substance of planning . . . (B225–B226)

Ansoff and Brandenburg went on, however, to refer to this as a "narrow context" in which to define planning and "predict[ed], therefore, that planners who refuse to take a broader view of their job [with respect to strategic decision making itself] are on their way to extinction" (B226). With a quarter-century of experience behind us, we can only conclude that the extinct ones are probably those planners who took these comments seriously!

Other writers, however, did recognize this as planning's pre-eminent role. Back in 1950, Devons wrote that "It would be more useful if 'planning' were confined to activity which seeks to lay down the full effects of any action which has been taken or it is proposed to take," with "the final and concrete expression of such activity" being "the drawing up of programs" (1950:12). A similar stand was taken by the writers we identified with the design school, who made a clear distinction between informal strategy formulation on one hand and more formal strategy implementation on the other, the latter carried out through the planning process. Newman, for example, in his 1982 text with Warren and Schnee, subtitled the section on planning, "The Execution of Strategy" (see also Andrews, 1987). And Tilles, back in 1972 considered it "unfortunate" that "many planners in U.S. companies have got off to a poor start by rejecting the validity of intuition. They viewed the planning process as a substitute for the judgement of the operating executive, rather than seeing it as a way of making such considerations explicit, and exploring its implications"(66).

Some practicing planners likewise came around to this interpretation eventually. In the aftermath of the General Electric experience, its chief planner could claim in an interview:

I make a distinction between planning and strategy—they're two different things. Strategy means thinking through a company's basis of competitive advantage. . . . Planning, on the other hand, focuses on making the strategy work—adding capacity, for instance, or increasing the sales force. Historically, GE's strategic approach emphasized planning more than strategy. (in Allio, 1985:18; for other related views of planning as programming, see Anthony, 1965, and Quinn, 1980a:38, 41, as well as Jelinek and Schoonhoven, 1990:212)

We should emphasize, however, that even this *strategic programming*, as it might properly be labeled, should not be viewed as a "one best way." It is not a mandatory process following strategy making, nor under certain circumstances even a desirable one. Only when an organization requires the clear articulation of its strategy—as in the example of the airline with the intricacies of activities to be precisely coordinated—does planning as programming make sense. At the end of this section, we shall consider the conditions under which this holds true.

Strategic programming can be considered to involve a series of steps. We consider below three in particular: the *codification* of given strategy, including its clarification and articulation; the *elaboration* of that strategy into substrategies, ad hoc programs, and action plans of various kinds; and the *conversion* of those substrategies, programs, and plans into routine budgets and objectives. (Two more steps might be added—the *identification* of the strategy before it is codified, and the *scrutinization* of the strategy after it is codified. But because these steps do not necessarily follow in the sequence of planning as programming, and the former at least is not even considered in the traditional planning model, we discuss them separately under the roles of the planner.) In these steps, we see planning taking over after strategy has been identified, so that the two elements of our planning dilemma combine in sequence. One creates the direction through synthesis, the other clarifies and orders that direction through analysis. Such a sequence of roles is, in fact, deeply rooted in our cognitive makeup, as Ornstein notes in his book on the research of the brain's two hemispheres:

> Our highest creative achievements are the products of the complementary functioning of the two modes. Our intuitive knowledge is never explicit, never precise in the scientific sense. It is only when the intellect can begin to process the intuitive leaps, to explain and "translate" the intuition into operational and functional knowledge that scientific understanding becomes complete. It is the function of the verbal-scientific intellect to fit the intuition into the

linear mode, so that ideas may be explicitly tested and communicated in the scientific manner. (1972:12)

Step 1: Codifying the Strategy

Assuming the existence of strategy in some form or other—whether as general perspective or specific positions, intended plan or evolved pattern—the first step in strategic programming is to "codify" that strategy, or "calibrate" it (the first word having been used by the chief planner of a major metal company in private conversation with the author, the second by Quinn in print [1980a:38]). In effect, the strategy is clarified and expressed in terms sufficiently clear to render it formally operational, so that its consequences can be worked out in detail. In the words of Hafsi and Thomas, planning makes "all the implicit assumptions . . . explicit," considers the "major hurdles," makes sure that "everything is taken into account" and that the inconsistencies and incoherences are uncovered and eliminated (1985:32, 7). Planning thus brings order to strategy, putting it into a form suitable for articulation to others in the organization.

In this regard, Quinn referred to one use of planning as "refining [the central strategic concepts of management] into a relatively few principal thrusts around which the organization can pattern its resource commitments and measure its managers' performance" (1980a:176).[1] He also referred to the planning role of "helping to crystallize or affirm consensus and commitment as they occur."

> Typically it was the chief planner who first drafted the broad goal statements used to guide subordinates' plans. It was the planner who first summarized understandings reached in more formal goal-setting meetings . . . It was the planners who helped subordinate groups . . . interpret the meaning of general enterprise goals from above. (200)

An image that comes to mind here is that of a planner sitting with a chief executive following an executive committee meeting.

---

[1] Accordingly, Yavitz and Newman wrote: "Failure to include thrusts in a strategic plan may leave the selected objectives floating; it is probably the major 'missing link,' in moving strategy from ideas to action" (1982:27).

The decisions just made are symbolically strewn about the table. The manager points to the mess and says to the planner, "There they are; clean them up, package them neatly together so that we can inform everyone else." Thus, Sawyer referred to the planner's role of "scribe"—"the one who tries to put [the] ideas on paper" (1983:159), also that of "documentor"—"someone [who summarizes] the conclusions and circulate[s] them, so the group will remember what they decided and can build from there the next time" (164). In their study of capital budgeting, Marsh et al. similarly referred to the planner as "clarifier" (1988:16), which resembles the comments of one manager in Langley's study:

> Ideas don't come out of planning . . . ideas are in the air. But the plan will force us to make an effort to group things together and to define these orientations more clearly. I don't think the plan will be a surprise. For most people, it's just a chance to articulate their ideas. (1988:48)

Obviously this is no mechanical task, but one that can require a good deal of interpretation. The codification of strategy can cause all kinds of problems if done poorly or inappropriately—or prematurely. Perhaps the greatest danger, besides premature closure, is what can be lost in articulation—nuance, subtlety, qualification. Converting from general thoughts to specific directives is much like going from broad goals to precise objectives, or from soft data to hard: something is inevitably lost in the translation.

Strategies can be rich visions, intricately woven images that can create deep-rooted perspectives. So long as they are articulated in their own terms—which often means images or metaphors rather than concrete labels—ideally by the people who know them best (notably their creators), they can maintain that richness. But decomposed and expressed formally, in precise words or, worse, numbers—which may be necessary for communication through a dense bureaucratic hierarchy—the rich imagery and intricate interconnections can be lost. The soul of strategy may thus be reduced to a skeleton, much as happens when a great painting is reduced by words to its categorical elements—size, color, texture. Thus, when Goold and Quinn claimed that "As far as possible, the objectives should be precise and measurable, otherwise there is a danger that plans will lack substance and specificity" (1990:44), the obvious response is that the quality of the plans do not matter so much as the quality of the organization's performance.

Accordingly, when codification *is* necessary, those who do it must be fully aware of its consequences. That way they can at least proceed carefully—with subtlety and nuance—when they must, and more important, can question the practice when they need not. There are times, in fact, when greater use can be made of images to convey strategies (as in the example of Jan Carlzon, who, as chief executive of SAS, made use of a "little red book" of cartoons to depict his turnaround strategy). Or at least some strategies can be conveyed figuratively, through the use of anecdotal stories and the like, perhaps conveyed orally. That is to say, strategies need not always be directly transmitted in formal documents with words and numbers; they can also be diffused through more osmotic processes.

Step 2: Elaborating the Strategy

Once codified, the strategy can be elaborated: its consequences decomposed into a hierarchy that begins with substrategies, proceeds through ad hoc programs of various kinds, and ends with specific actions plans—specifying what people must do to realize the strategy as intended. This constitutes what we referred to in our discussion of the four hierarchies (see Figure 2–10) as *action planning:* the organization pursues the connections down the strategy hierarchy and across to and down the program hierarchy.

The first step is the decomposition of strategy into substrategies of various kinds, whether at the corporate, business, or functional levels. Then the necessary capital programs are delineated, followed by the action programs and operating plans that detail the specific moves that must be made on an ad hoc (one-time) basis, including their sequencing and timing (or scheduling). Newman, Warren, and Schnee have commented on "establishing a hierarchy of plans":

> strategic thrusts call for a series of actions, such as opening an office in Sao Paulo or selling a public issue of company stock. Each thrust can be subdivided into steps and substeps that are assigned

> to individuals. This breakdown is continued until, to extend the Sao
> Paulo office example, one person finds the site, another determines
> the equipment and layout, and a third hires personnel. (1982:40)

The overall result is "a timed sequence of conditional moves in
resource deployment" (Katz, 1970:356).

When the circumstances require it, these plans may also be
elaborated on a contingency basis, so that they are evoked, not on
any predetermined schedule but only when the needs arise. Such
planning is costly, but perhaps relevant when, as we noted previously, the consequences of a few likely and significant contingencies can be delineated.

All of this no doubt sounds as though we have rediscovered the
conventional planning model that we seem to have just finished dismissing. But we sought to dismiss it only when out of context,
meaning that we accept it here with two key qualifications. First,
strategy formation is expressly precluded from the model. In other
words, we contend that the model is relevant for the programming
or implementing of strategy but not for the initial creation of it. And
second, strategic programming is presented here, not as some kind
of imperative but as a process that is appropriate only under certain
specific conditions (that we shall delineate shortly).

Step 3: Converting the Elaborated Strategy

From the conventional model as well comes the imperative to
determine the consequences of the *ad hoc* strategic (or programmatic) changes on the *routine* operations of the organization. This
is the crossing of what we referred to earlier as the great divide,
from the hierarchies of strategies and programs (action planning)
to those of budgets and objectives, namely *performance control*. Objectives are restated and budgets reworked, policies and standard
operating procedures reconsidered, to take into account the consequences of the specific changes in action.

As we noted in our discussion of the four hierarchies, this step
across the divide is not easily understood or conveniently executed. For its part, the literature is notoriously weak on how this
should be done, generally talking around the process as if it were

a foregone conclusion. Organizations do work it out somehow—after all, budgets eventually do get changed in response to changes in strategy—but how that does happen, or how it can be made to happen faster and more effectively, does not appear to be part of the published evidence of the planning school. One exception—and a model of the kind of research this school is in great need of—appears in Devons's (1950) classic discussion of wartime planning in the British Ministry of Aircraft Production. There he devoted considerable attention to the problems and ambiguities of strategic programming, illustrating how difficult it is to carry out what seems like such a simple process. Cairncross, in his introduction to the later publication of Devons' papers (1970), provided an apt summary: "he found that what was dignified as planning proved in practice to be little more than one step onwards from improvisation: muddle qualified by efforts to coordinate with imperfect foresight" (18).

To conclude, we have positioned the conventional model of "strategic planning" in the process of implementing, not formulating, strategy. But we wish to emphasize that we place it here only on a contingency basis: it makes sense to program strategy formally—to codify it, then elaborate it, and finally convert it into routine operations—only under particular circumstances. Strategic programming makes sense when viable strategies are available, in other words when the world is expected to hold still or change predictably while intended strategies unfold, so that formulation can logically precede implementation. Thus, it also makes sense only *after* any necessary strategic learning has been completed, and strategic thinking has converged on appropriate patterns. Strategic programming as premature closure can be costly indeed. It further makes sense only when the organization in fact requires clearly codified and elaborated strategies. This, we argue in the following discussion, pertains to a limited set of circumstances. In other circumstances, strategic programming can do organizations harm by preempting the flexibility that may be needed to react to a changing environment.[2] Thus, we conclude that the conventional model was not so much wrong as misapplied.

---

[2] See the discussion in the last chapter on the dangers of separating formulation from implementation.

Conditions of Strategic Programming

While it is clear that planning as strategic programming is not the "one best way" for all organizations in all circumstances, there has nonetheless been a notable reluctance in the practice and prescription of planning to specify such circumstances. Thus, Huff and Reger, in their review of the strategy process research, commented on having been "surprised that few articles discussing specific environments appeared in the planning prescriptions area" (1987:215), while Chakravarthy (1987), in a survey of senior executives, was likewise surprised to find that their planning systems often seemed to lack fit with both the external context and internal needs of the organization, and that furthermore these misfits seemed "inconsequential" to the executives themselves. Nevertheless, there are enough scraps of evidence to delineate the conditions that seem most favorable to strategic programming. We review them here.

Stability. In Chapter 3, we discussed the conditions of stability, controllability, and predictability at some length, concluding that these were necessary for effective planning. Here we focus on stability because, as concluded there, while controllability of the environment is even better, at the limit it amounts to a form of imposed stability, while the problem with predictability is that it cannot be predicted.

If planning, as strategic programming, is undertaken to reify strategy—"the plan is frozen at a point in time" is how Sawyer put it in his planning monograph (1983:2)—then conditions had better be stable. Thus Gomer (1974) and Murray (1978) found that planning systems were ill-suited to the dynamic aftermath of the 1973 oil crisis, while Frederickson (1984, see also Frederickson and Mitchell, 1984) found that the "comprehensiveness" of decision processes (linked to their integration and formalization in planning) was positively related to performance in stable environments, negatively in unstable ones.[3] And in an informal survey of 21 plan-

---

[3] Kukalis (1988, 1989) found a relationship between "environmental complexities" and various aspects of the planning process, namely its "extensiveness," shorter planning horizons, and more frequent plan reviews. But a number of his complex-

ners, Armstrong (1982) found only one who considered formal planning useful in "all situations," while 14 "cited environmental change as a big factor," and 11 of these "thought that formal planning was less appropriate when change was rapid" (202; see also Capon et al. whose respondents most commonly cited "substantial environmental uncertainty" as a factor "discouraging corporate planning" [1982:171]). But perhaps a Latin American executive made the point most clearly: "Planning is great. But how can you plan—let alone plan long term—if you don't know what kind of government you'll have next year?" (in Stieglitz, 1969:22).

Industry Maturity. Mature industries tend to be particularly stable ones: technology and product lines have settled down around "dominant designs" (Abernathy and Utterback, 1978); market growth has slowed and steadied; operating procedures have become standard, often to the point of having become "industry recipes" (Grinyer and Spender, 1979); even strategies have tended to become "generic" in segments of the industry (known as "strategic groups"). Likewise, competition tends to moderate with maturity, as surviving firms settle into more or less well-defined relationships, with leaders distinguished from followers, the former often able to exercise a good deal of market power. All of this obviously favors the categorization that planning itself favors. Thus, Khandwalla (1977) found a strong negative correlation between planning and the growth rate of the industry, with the high-growth industries favoring more entrepreneurial and adaptive modes of operating. He also found a tendency for firms that saw their environment as restrictive to use the planning approach to decision making.[4]

We saw all this clearly in our studies of Air Canada up to 1976, which became a heavy user of planning once its route structure, operating procedures, and relationships with other airlines were established. Air Canada settled into the dominant position in its domestic market, while joining the club of world class airlines in its

---

ity measures were, in fact, measures of stability (e.g., predictability of changes in demand, frequency of new product introductions). Shorter horizons and more frequent reviews could be consistent with our conclusion here, while greater extensiveness would presumably not be.

[4] Kukalis (1991) did not support this finding in his survey.

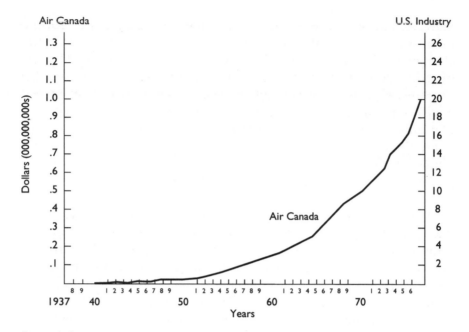

Figure 6–3
Air Canada Total Revenue (1937–1976)
(From Mintzberg et al., 1986:30)

international one, as Canada's flag carrier. To quote one of its executives, "we could forecast the future very accurately" (in Mintzberg et al, 1986:37). Indeed, in those days they could: as shown in Figure 6–3, the airline's revenue grew in almost perfectly exponential fashion for decades. Ironically, in order to free itself of government control, this state-owned airline locked itself ever more deeply into the structure of its industry, where the planning of the individual firms then combined implicitly to enact their collective environment.[5]

Capital Intensity. Heavy capital investment provides further incentive to engage in planning. The greater the commitment of

---

[5] Bear in mind that two highly controlled markets were involved here, the domestic one being very highly regulated (during our study period), the international one generally being viewed as a cartel (with an industry association setting rates, and the airlines themselves making pool arrangements with ostensibly competing carriers).

resources to a single program, the more carefully must these resources (as well as the context of their application) be controlled, and so the greater the need for strategic programming (Denning and Lehr, 1972:5; Kukalis, 1988, 1989; Al-Bazzaz and Grinyer, 1983), and as Channon (1976:54) noted, the longer the planning cycle. Given the irreversibility of these major commitments—the extremely high costs of exiting the industry—capital-intensive firms simply cannot afford the risks associated with dynamic environments. They must have a sense of what their markets will bring during the life of the investment; if they do not foresee that stability, they must try to impose it. Woodward (1965) expressed this point clearly in her description of manufacturing firms in "process" production, which is much more capital-intensive than "unit" or "mass" production: they have to ensure the markets for their products before they build their facilities.

Large Size. An organization need not be big to plan, but it certainly helps. As Newman noted back in 1951, "planning is expensive" (65).[6] Moreover, some of the factors already discussed—notably capital intensity and market control—tend to be associated with large organizations. Thus, studies by Sheehan (1975), Sapp (1980), Lorange (1979:234), Al-Bazzaz and Grinyer (1981, 1983), and Denning and Lehr (1972) all provided strong evidence for the relationship between the size of an organization and its propensity to engage in, or the degree of formality of its planning.

Formal planning generally requires elaborate administrative mechanisms, in the forms of budgets and procedures of various kinds, not to mention a planning staff that does not earn its keep by collecting receivables. And then there is the time that line managers must devote to the process. Moreover, "Planners tend to be big spenders"; they "have a vested interest in increasing the total amount of investment," being inclined "to seek the large and loud over the small and quiet. Their talents are better suited to the analysis of big projects that have a substantial impact . . . and that,

---

[6] Roach and Allen argued that "the 'smaller company' . . . must plan more formally, rigorously, analytically, and thus more strategically than the larger company—if only because it has fewer human and material resources to work with" (1983:7–26). These in fact sound like good reasons why small companies should *avoid* formal planning!

by their cost, justify expensive analytical attention" (Wildavsky, 1973:149–150). Hence, John Kenneth Galbraith made reference to planning's "unabashed alliance with size" (1967:31), which he believed may be especially true when planning is used to enact the environment:

> The size of General Motors is in the service not of monopoly or the economies of scale but of planning. And for this planning—control of supply, control of demand, provision of capital, minimization of risk—there is no clear upper limit to the desirable size. It could be that the bigger the better. (76)

Large organizations may not only be best able to afford planning, not only be best able to use it, but may in fact also be most in need of it. Small organizations can get away with informal means to achieve communication and control, but the evidence is clear that large ones have to place greater reliance on impersonal, formal means to do so, including systems of planning (see Mintzberg, 1979a:233–234).

Elaborated Structure. Strategic programming is undertaken to specify what has to be done to realize an intended strategy. This it does by decomposing the strategy, through programs, into specific activities of various kinds. But this presupposes an organization that itself can be decomposed—into a system of subunits and these into positions at different levels, and ultimately into specific tasks, over which can be laid the action plans. The same holds true for performance control: the budgets and objectives must be overlaid on specific subunits, ultimately perhaps on individuals whose labor has been clearly defined and differentiated. Thus, the ideal organization for both kinds of planning is the highly structured one. Loose organizations can make a mess of the highly ordered outputs of the planning process.

Tightly Coupled Operations. While highly structured activities may facilitate action planning, ones that are tightly coupled together, especially in the operating core, may demand it. Consider an organization with the first condition but not the second, say, a shop with a hundred barbers. Each works in a very structured way, but quite independently of all the others. The need for action planning—for formalized communication if not control—is hardly critical. But if we consider an assembly line of a hundred workers producing barber chairs—doing highly structured *and* tightly coupled work—the need for action planning becomes more evident: by standardizing the activities of each worker, such planning provides a means to coordinate and control their work tightly (Mintzberg, 1979a, 152–154). Thus we would expect to find a much higher intensity of planning in a General Motors (with its assembly lines and supplier networks) or an Air Canada (with its paramount need to achieve precise coordination among aircraft, routes, crews, and flight schedules) than in a 3M (with its multitude of independent products) or an MIT (with its agglomeration of independent academic departments).[7]

Note that, aside from internal operations, tight coupling can also apply to products ("bundling" being the currently popular term, as when a computer firm offers software with its hardware), also to external elements, such as the supplies of bauxite, carbon, and electricity to an aluminum smelter (Clark, 1980:7). As Rhenman put it, organizations that can regard "environmental changes as independent of each other" (1973:4) are able to survive successfully without action planning, although they may still have to use performance control (or even capital budgeting) to effect control if not coordination.

Simple Operations. As a means to effect tight coupling of activities, as discussed in Chapter 4 action planning becomes a force for centralization in the organization. It dictates the decisions associated with certain work, drawing discretion over that work away from those charged with doing it and sending it to those who

---

[7] Tita and Allio in fact described the 3M planning system as "bottom-up" to reinforce "the entrepreneurial spirit," with the manager of each of the firm's several hundred businesses being "allowed to plan as they like, to collect any amount of data" and to present the plans "at any time of the year." Moreover, "3M has never embraced 'staff' planning, with the few managers with the word 'planning' in their titles" belonging to a "planning services" group (1984:12). In a later article on the company, Carol Kennedy (1988) described a 3M that took strategic planning somewhat more seriously, rotating each of three executives vice-presidents into the leadership of the corporate strategic planning committee. But it sought to maintain a "pragmatic approach," with "constant questioning of planners' assumptions" (11), and the working out of plans "in true 3M 'bottom-up' style in conjunction with the key operating managers" (12). While acknowledging the value of the system "for the analysis and direction of existing businesses," Kennedy noted skepticism on the part of senior management about its capacity for "generating new ones" (16), thus raising a question about its label "strategic."

design it, namely the planners of the organization. But planning's capacity to effect such central coordination is not very sophisticated. As we have seen, its powers of synthesis are weak while those of analysis are not terribly sophisticated. Planning essentially remains what it has always been: a simple model (that of the design school) decomposed into simple steps elaborated by a variety of simple checklists and supported by the simple procedures of scheduling and budgeting.

Thus we must add a large, if controversial, qualification to the point about tight coupling: planning in that situation is feasible only where the operations are relatively simple to comprehend. The activities to be coupled may be many and their coordination intricate (as in airline operations), but those activities and the environment that surrounds them must be easily comprehended if they are to be accessible to the technology of planning (also to be executable by people who have no control over them).

Planning is "a means of reducing external complexity to 'manageable' forms," is how Zan has expressed it (1987:192). It is required, not because any one task is complex, but because the whole myriad of tasks that must be executed in precise concert is beyond the capability of a single brain or an *informal* procedure carried out in many brains. In other words, the whole system may seem complex, but decomposition necessarily renders each part of it simple, easily comprehended—even if not easily managed. For example, anyone can easily understand an automobile assembly line, each activity as well as the whole chain. But no one can informally organize all the details associated with running it. There are just too many of them. The same holds true for scheduling the activities of an airline. But not for conducting open-heart surgery, or even developing an innovative new product. So while the former *requires* action planning, the latter may be stifled by it (although limited amounts of scheduling, etc. may be appropriate—the where's and when's rather than the how's).[8]

In regard to this point, Normann and Rhenman cited Ashby's

---

[8] We should make clear here that the complexity of work is quite independent of its stability. Here we are discussing complex work, whether or not stable. Open-heart surgery is a complex but stable task; creative design is often complex and dynamic (i.e., unpredictable). For a discussion of the independence of these two dimensions, see Mintzberg (1979a:273, 285–287).

law of "requisite variety": that one system can only control another whose complexity or sophistication is inferior to its own. And for planning, that means simple systems, in the view of these authors:

> Application of the [planning] model generally depends on the possibility of making an exact definition of a problem ... In other words we have to be able to see quite clearly which factors we must take into account in solving the problem, and which we can ignore ... [This] approach is ... likely to be useful in the planning of simple operations in systems whose inputs and outputs are reasonably clear. (1975:44)

This may help to explain the difference between Huff, who described planning as facilitating action, and Weick, who suggested it could also paralyze action. Huff suspects that the endurance and spread of the planning model "may have to do in part with the lure of simplifying structures that make our diverse world more understandable," to repeat her words quoted earlier. What makes planning procedures "attractive" is their "simplistic" nature—"they are conceptually easy to grasp; they simplify, they structure information needs; they outline a series of next steps. In short, the belief system of goal based planning provides a vehicle for ordering (and sometimes ignoring) complexities that otherwise paralyze action" (1980:33). But while this may be true for a simple context, exactly the opposite may be the case in more difficult ones. Instead of acting, the organization engages in planning, which "could spiral larger and larger, becoming an end rather than a means" (Weick, 1979:103).[9]

External Control. Finally, another factor that encourages planning is an external influencer with the power and intent to control an organization from the outside. To succeed, such an influencer must find a pointed basis for control. And planning is one obvious candidate. This is especially so when the controlling

---

[9] But, as noted earlier, when there is *no* basis for action, formal or informal, Gimpl and Dakin claimed in their article on "Management and Magic," as did Weick in the story of finding the map in the Swiss Alps, that planning, or plans, at least get people to do something! (1984:133). But toward what end, we might ask?

influencer is an organization that itself uses planning systems—as in the case of a parent firm controlling a subsidiary. Performance control is the obvious means, but action planning can be enlisted too, especially when the external influencer wishes to control internal operations directly, whether because that is a functional thing to do or because it offers the illusion of control (as was probably the case with a good deal of the action planning imposed by the Communist governments, not to mention Western corporate headquarters).

The powerful effect of external control on the propensity for planning has come through clearly in a number of studies. For example, Denning and Lehr (1972) divided the 300 companies in their sample into six categories of structure. The one that most clearly reflected external ownership (subsidiaries of foreign multinationals) had the highest incidence of planning by far (64.7 percent), while the one that reflected it least (multiplant functional organizations) was close to the lowest in its use (11.1 percent). Likewise, Al-Bazzaz and Grinyer (1983) found "dependence on parent organizations" as well as "on major customers" to be one factor explaining planning activity. In another study they found "significantly more written plans" in the four nationalized companies in their sample than in the other firms they studied (1981:163), and somewhat more planning in subsidiaries than in parent organizations, "perhaps [because] higher organizations impose a level of formality on this lower level which they are not prepared to operate themselves" (165).

Clustering These Conditions. What are we to make of this whole set of conditions? One thing we can do is consider the importance of each, independently. Stability would seem to be a necessary (if not sufficient) condition, since without a reasonable degree of it, there can be no strategic programming. Internally, simple operations would likewise seem to be a necessary condition, since action planning cannot handle complex ones. When we add elaborate structure together with tightly coupled operations, we seem to have a set of conditions that leads to strategic programming, as illustrated in Figure 6–4. Large size, capital intensity, industry maturity, and external control, rather than being necessary conditions, would seem to encourage or facilitate the use of such planning, again as shown in Figure 6–4.

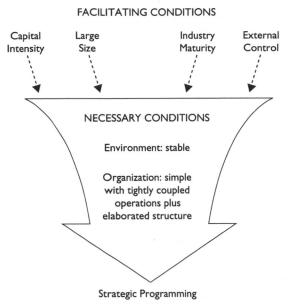

Figure 6–4
Conditions of Strategic Programming

Of course, as we have seen, these conditions are not independent of each other. For example, capital intensity tends to be related to large size, while elaborate structure would seem to require relatively simple operations (as in the automobile assembly line). Thus the conditions associated with strategic programming seem to cluster together. Toward the end of this chapter, we shall describe various types of organizations, one of which matches this cluster. We call it the *machine organization* and believe this is where strategic programming is most commonly found.

First Role of Plans: Communication Media

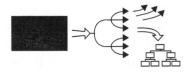

If planning is programming, then plans clearly serve in two capacities, or roles. They are media for communication and devices for control. (These "roles" for plans are, of course, "reasons" for planning.) Both roles draw on the analytical character of plans, namely their representation of strategies in decomposed and articulated form, if not quantified then often at least quantifiable.

Why program strategy? The most obvious reason is for coordination, to ensure that everyone in the organization pulls in the same direction, which may sometimes be facilitated by specifying that direction as precisely as possible. Plans, as they emerge from strategic programming as programs, schedules, budgets, and so on, can be prime media to communicate not just strategic intentions but also what each individual in the organization must do to realize them (insofar, of course, as common direction is more important than individual discretion). Thus Quinn referred to formal planning activities as fulfilling "certain vital functions in coordinating strategies," including "awareness building, consensus generating and commitment-affirming." Planning "forced managers to communicate systematically about strategic issues" (1980a:140).

"Improvements in communication and coordination" are not, as Hogarth and Makridakis (1981:128) claimed, just "functional side-effects" of planning, but the essential reasons to engage in it. As Langley described it in her intensive study of the use of analysis in three organizations, communication is "one of the most important, if not the most important role of strategic planning" (1986:324). Communication through planning provides "a means whereby management as a whole, on a regular basis, [can] talk about strategy" (Marks, 1977:2). It is planning's "conceptual tidiness" that "may provide a better vocabulary for communication within organizations" (Huff and Reger, 1987:216). More specifically, management can convey its intentions, ensure coherence across activities, and rationalize the allocation of resources (Barreyre, 1977/78:94).

Two papers on Air France emphasized this communication role in the company's extensive planning efforts of the mid-1980s. Hafsi and Thomas pointed out that a fifteen-page summary of "Le Plan" was circulated to each of the company's employees, 35,000 copies in all! (1985:27). This was supplemented by "a series of audio and visual documents, including a video discussion with the President," not to mention the several issues of the house magazine devoted to the plan and the 800 discussion meetings, averaging three hours and including 18,000 employees, which preceded all this documentation (28). Indeed, one gets the impression while reading Hafsi and Thomas's report that the exercise had more to do with communication per se—gaining commitment and understanding, overall consensus—than it did with attempting to program strategy through the system (though this is not Hafsi and Thomas's position[10]). In fact, in the second paper on Air France, written by two of its employees and entitled "Planning and Communication: the Experience of Air France," Guiriek and Thoreau emphasized the communication role above all. They referred to the plan as "a tool of internal and external communication" (1984:135):

> The plan of the firm thus presents itself . . . as a favored means of communication, providing the personnel with a statement of the firm's situation, an analysis of the ends and general objectives, and the expression of a clear policy, unblocking the way to concrete actions. (136, our translation from the French)

To return to the Hafsi and Thomas paper, the plan "forced [employees] to recognize the situation of the firm relative to its competitors. . . . the planning process allows them to understand better who they are and how they stand vis-à-vis comparable employees in other firms" (33).

But communication can be external as well as internal, with plans being used to seek the tangible as well as moral support of outside influencers (e.g., Langley, 1989:625). We are not referring here to what we earlier called planning as a public relations exercise—"planning for show" because it looks good rather than because it is good. Instead, we mean informing outsiders about the substance of the plans so they can help the organization realize them. Thus, in addition to the 35,000 short reports, the state-owned

---

[10] Those 800 discussion meetings were ostensibly designed to elicit feedback. But Hafsi and Thomas's statement that the "comments that justified important modifications to the plan" were "*surely* brought up" at these meetings "would not be taken into account in the current version of the plan, but would be formally written down and then included in the following year's version" leaves room for doubt about this (29, italics added). As the authors noted later, "in a sense the President is less concerned with what plan the process generates (what are the strategic decisions to make), and more with how committed are the key employees to the implementation of whatever strategic decisions are made" (34).

airline also distributed 10,000 copies of the complete 180-page document to, among others, "all key personnel in the agencies of government concerned with the activities of [the state-owned] Air France" (Hafsi and Thomas, 1985:27). The plan imposed "upon government decision-makers the firm's realities and even its rationality . . ." (32).

Second Role of Plans: Control Devices

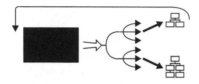

The last quotation on Air France ends, "leaving them little room to disagree with the managers' decisions" (32). This illustrates the point that communication can sometimes get rather close to control; at the limit the two emerge as opposite sides of the same coin.

The substantive purpose of strategic programming is to exercise deliberate control—to predetermine behavior, by dictating what people must do to realize a given intended strategy. Hafsi and Thomas referred to this (after Herbert Simon) as "setting . . . the decision premises" (1985:32), Devons as "control[ling] . . . the use of resources in real terms" (1950:1).

Plans, as communication media, inform people of intended strategy and its consequences. But as control devices they go further, specifying what behaviors are expected of particular units and individuals in order to realize strategy, and then being available to feed back into the strategy making process comparisons of these expectations with actual performance. It is perhaps this control role that prompted a chief planner at General Electric of the 1980s to characterize the planning department of earlier years as the "corporate policeman" (Carpenter, quoted in Potts, 1984).[11] Even in the context of individual cognition, psychologists Miller,

---

[11] Unless, of course, he was referring to the policing role of the planning process itself—ensuring that everyone planned in the way deemed desirable by the planning department.

Galanter, and Pribram used the word "plan" to "refer to a hierarchy of instructions," more specifically "any hierarchical process in the organism that can control the order in which a sequence of operations is to be performed," equivalent to "a program for a computer" (1960:16).[12]

Of course, we saw this role too in some of our earlier discussion, for example in Sarrazin's findings about how the top management of the French firm he studied used planning as a device to "regain control of strategic decision-making" (1977/78:56), and in our review of capital budgeting, which appeared to be less a means to interrelate decisions from below than simply a device to control capital spending from above.

In a brief, colorful discussion, Cyert and March "make four observations on plans within an organization":

> 1. *A plan is a goal.* . . . a planning prediction functions both as a prediction of sales, costs, profit level, and so forth, and also as a goal for such factors. Under some circumstances (and within limits) an organization can induce behavior designed to confirm its prediction (goal).
> 2. *A plan is a schedule.* It specifies intermediate steps to a predicted outcome. . . . the firm is forced by its plan (if for no other reason) into the specification of acceptable achievement levels for its subunits as well as for the organization as a whole. . . .
> 3. *A plan is a theory.* For example, the budget specifies a relationship between such factors as sales and costs on the one hand and profits on the other, and thereby permits the use of sales and cost data as guidepost to the achievement of a satisfactory level of profits. . . .
> 4. *A plan is a precedent.* It defines the decisions of one year and thereby establishes a prima facie case for continuing existing decisions. (1963:111–112)

Aside from the third point (which suggests another role, as simulations for analysis, which we shall discuss below), the others clearly specify the role of plans as devices for control.

---

[12] Indeed, they even claimed to be "reasonably confident that 'program' could be substituted everywhere for 'Plan' in the pages" of their own book (16).

Plans as controls serve not only top management wishing to control those below it in the hierarchy, but all sorts of influencers over each other. As Galbraith described the "new industrial state," large corporations also use plans to control their external environments—markets, competitors, suppliers, governments, even customers. (The distribution of those 10,000 copies of the Air France plan to government personnel was a case in point.) Much planning, in other words, exists for purposes of enactment: to impose strategies on the environment.

Similarly, outside influencers can impose plans on an organization as a means of external control. Most common are performance plans, as when a headquarters defines profit and growth targets for each of its divisions. But those plans can be strategic too, involving the imposition of specific courses of action. Indeed, it became popular in the 1970s for corporate headquarters to impose strategies such as harvesting or accelerating growth on divisions according to the Boston Consulting Group's (1973) growth share matrix (of cash cows, stars, dogs, and wildcats). Likewise, governments can impose specific intentions on their agencies through action plans. Firms with market power over their suppliers can do the same thing, as when they specify what quantities of supplies are to be produced on what schedule, in effect coupling the suppliers' actions plans with their own (a common occurrence in the relationship between retailers and their private-label producers).

In addition, as discussed earlier, there exists a whole set of games played around the exercise of planning itself as a device for control: investors who expect planning from companies going to public financial markets, governments that demand it of the public hospitals they fund, and so on. Here it is not the results of planning so much as the organization's very engagement in the process that becomes the form of control, or at least the illusion of control, and so the process risks being reduced to a public relations device, or simply another administrative "game":

> In an organization in which goals and technology are unclear, plans and the insistence on plans become an administrative test of will. If a department wants a new program badly enough, it will spend a substantial amount of effort in "justifying" the expenditure by fitting it into a "plan". If an administrator wishes to avoid saying "yes" to everything, but has no basis for saying "no" to anything,

he tests the commitment of the department by asking for a plan.
(Cohen and March, 1976:195–196)

Strategic Control

With regard to strategy, plans can help to effect control in a number
of ways. The most obvious is control of the strategy itself. Indeed,
what has long paraded under the label of strategic planning has
probably been more about strategic control. In the traditional view,
strategic control has had to do with keeping organizations on their
strategic tracks: to ensure the realization of intended strategies, their
implementation as expected, with resources appropriately allocated. This it supposedly does by subjecting intended strategy and
its consequences to strategic programming, which can then be used
as the standard against which to measure accomplishments. Plans,
as the most operational form of strategy, lend themselves naturally
to this type of control. Add a feedback loop at the end of the planning cycle to assess the results of the plans, and strategic programming becomes strategic control.

But there has to be more to strategic control than this. The
concept has been an elusive one in the field of strategic management, much discussed but never really clarified. We believe this is
because most writers have not thought it through on its own terms.
Instead, they have extrapolated the concept of control from its
traditional applications at the operating and administrative levels.
At worst, they allowed it to remain on the left side of our diagram
of four hierarchies, within the realm of routine budgeting and
objective-setting, by simply considering these at higher, more encompassing levels. This is presumably what encouraged Quinn to
comment that "formal planning has often become just another
aspect of controllership" (1980a:ix), much as we saw in our discussion of planning as a numbers game.

Slightly better, other writers have focused on the bottom-line
effectiveness of the organization's strategies—how well they have
performed in the organization's marketplaces. Rondinelli labeled
planners who perform this activity as "evaluative": "Evaluative
planners analyze previous . . . decisions to determine their results.
Evaluation includes performance auditing that leads to recommen-

dations for program reformulation, termination or continuation" (1976:81). Simons referred to this as the "cybernetic view"—"a system to keep strategies on track" (1988:2). It "equates strategy formation with planning, and strategy implementation with control," proceeding from the premise that "just as strategy formation must logically precede strategy implementation, so must planning precede control" (3).

Goold and Quinn (1990) took much this same approach in a recent article presented as a critique of strategic control. They identified a "paradox of strategic control" between a literature that "clearly advocates the establishment of some system of strategic controls to monitor strategic progress and ensure the implementation of strategic plans" and their evidence that "in practice . . . few companies . . . identify formal and explicit strategic control measures and build them into their control systems" (43). They discussed favorably the need for specification of "short-term goals (or milestones) which need to be achieved in order that the strategy ultimately be implemented" (45) and for a "broader conception of strategic control, such that differences between actual and planned outcomes lead not just to modification in the actions of individuals, but also to questioning of the assumptions of the plan itself" (46). Their own survey of the 200 largest companies in Great Britain "revealed that only a small number of companies (11 percent) would claim to employ a strategic control system of the type" they describe as "fully fledged" (47).

Goold and Quinn concluded that "the practice of strategic control is much more complex than most writers on the subject have acknowledged." Managers, therefore, "need to tread warily in implementing strategic control systems" (54), focusing particularly on conditions where "environmental turbulence" is "low" and the "ability to specify and measure precise strategic objectives" is "easy"(55).

Without being critical of Goold and Quinn's conclusions as far as they go, we must argue that these authors (and others) do not go nearly far enough. The reason they find so little use of strategic control, we believe, is that the concept of strategy formation has always been misconstrued, forcing strategic control to bypass one critical aspect—the possibility of emergent strategy. As shown in Figure 6–5, there is certainly the need to assess the performance of deliberate strategies (shown as B on the figure), and, stepping back (A), the need to assess the degree of realization of the strategies

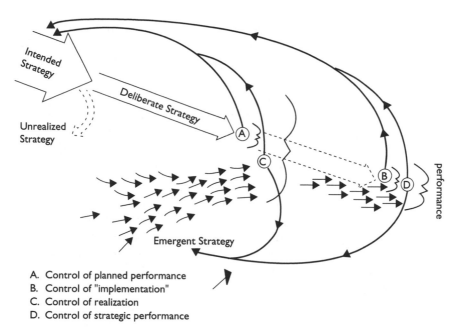

A. Control of planned performance
B. Control of "implementation"
C. Control of realization
D. Control of strategic performance

Figure 6–5
Strategic Control: Traditional (A and B); Enlarged (C and D)

that were formally intended in the first place (in the words of Schendel and Hofer's book on strategic management, "whether: (1) the strategy is being implemented as planned; and (2) the results produced by the strategy are those intended" [1979:18]). But before these must come another activity (C), namely the assessment of whatever strategies were, in fact, realized, whether intended or not. And the last activity must be enlarged (D) to encompass the assessment of the performance of all those strategies. In other words, strategic control must assess behavior as well as performance. Once again it must be appreciated that there is more to strategy formation than planning.

Thus we characterize strategic control as a two-step process. The first requires the tracking of realized strategies, as patterns in streams of actions, to consider the deliberate realization of intended strategies as well as the emergence of unintended ones. The second step then considers, in a more traditional control manner, how effective for the organization were the strategies that were actually realized.

Bear in mind an obvious point that is often overlooked. Strategies need not be deliberate to be effective (and vice versa)! There has certainly been extensive consideration of unrealized strategies in the literature of planning, virtually all of it under the guise of the failures of implementation. But deliberate strategies can be successfully implemented and then fail, just as unexpectedly emergent strategies can sometimes succeed. With regard to those "dumbbells" we discussed earlier, who weren't smart enough to implement their boss's clever intended strategies, failures of implementation are not just failures of formulation but also the failure to recognize the impossibility in many situations of clearly separating formulation and implementation, failure that has been built into the traditional conception of strategic control.

Put another way, strategies may fail, not only by being unsuccessfully implemented, but also by being successfully implemented and then proving inadequate. Likewise, strategies can succeed even though they were not initially intended. Planners can hardly dismiss successful strategies just because they were not deliberate. And more to the point here, strategic control must be concerned with the performance of the organization, not the performance of planning!

Thus, the person doing strategic control faces one of those two-by-two matrices: was the intended strategy successfully realized, and did the strategy that was in fact realized prove successful?

| | | Intended Strategy Realized? | |
		YES	NO
Realized Strategy Successful?	YES	Deliberate success (hurrah for rationality)	Emergent success (hurrah for learning)
	NO	Failure of deliberateness (efficient but not effective)	Failure of everything (try again)

As our matrix shows, all four yes-no combinations are possible. Two yes's mean that deliberate management was successful—the central managers set out to do something, they did it, and it worked. Rationality reigned supreme. A yes-no tells us that management successfully implemented a strategy that proved unsuccessful. Efficient but not effective. A no-yes means that intentions were not realized, but what was realized in fact worked. Strategic learning saved the day. Was the central management lucky—or clever? Whichever, they may not have been efficient, but whatever they did proved effective. And two no's, of course, means that nothing worked and no one was clever, effective, or efficient (except the strategic controllers, if they can sort out the problem!).

First Role of Planners: Finders of Strategy

Planners, of course, play key roles in the process of planning (namely strategic programming) and in the use of the resulting plans for purposes of communication and control. Here, however, we wish to focus on those roles of planners that are rather more independent of planning and of plans per se. Lorange claimed it is the central job of planners "to play the instrumental role in the design and implementation of the strategic planning system as well as to administer or manage the planning process" (1980a:265). Yet Javidan found in a survey that planning functions fell into two groups, one that had a "positive relative impact" and the other a "negative relative impact" on the perceived effectiveness of planning staffs (1987:307). In the latter group, alongside "encouragement of future thinking" was "co-ordination of planning process." In other words, attention to Lorange's central role—planning itself—may sometimes actually hamper the work of the planners!

Our contention is that many of the most important roles played by planners have nothing to do with planning or even plans per se. We discuss here three such nonplanning roles of planners: as finder of strategies, as analyst, and as catalyst, and in closing, we also consider a fourth, as strategist.

The first of these roles is perhaps the most novel—at least when compared with conventional conceptions of the planner's job[13]—

---

[13] Although it did get included in Javidan's list, on the positive side, as "identification of divisional strategies" which, curiously, he rendered in the text, together with "consolidation of divisional plans," as "to provide major assistance to divisional managers in their divisional strategic planning" (1987:307).

and perhaps the most interesting. Like strategic programming, this role takes place after the black box of strategy making, although it makes tentative probes into that box (as shown in the little figure), and tends to be ad hoc in nature as well as interpretative. It has already come up twice in this chapter, in the comments about finding strategies as a possible first step in strategic programming and about the uncovering of realized patterns as a way to effect broader strategic control. Both amount to the same role for planners, which we characterize as the *finders of strategy*, although "interpreters of action" or simply "pattern recognizers" might describe it equally well.

Logic in Action

The expression, "interpreters of action," was inspired by Karl Weick who, as we noted earlier, has pursued a major theme in his writing, namely that we make sense of our world by interpreting our own actions. Similar to the notion of strategy as the recognition of pattern in action, Weick suggested that "Plans seem to exist in a context of justification more than a context of anticipation. They refer more to what has been accomplished than to what is yet to be accomplished" (1969:102). His point was that actions in and of themselves have no meaning: "It is only when they are singled out reflectively that they become meaningful, coherent, and discrete" (102). To quote one corporate planner, "You plan to find out what it is you are doing."[14]

This suggests that a role for planners (ultimately, perhaps, also a purpose of planning) is to provide that logic in action of which Weick spoke so eloquently—to interpret behavior for purposes of understanding strategy. As March expressed it:

> Planning in organizations has many virtues, but a plan can often be more effective as an interpretation of past decisions than as a program for future ones. It can be used as a part of the efforts of the organization to develop a new consistent theory of itself that in-

---

[14] Personal communication from Robert Burgelman on a comment by one of his students at the Stanford Business School.

corporates the mix of recent actions into a moderately comprehensive structure of goals. . . . a manager needs to be relatively tolerant of the idea that he will discover the meaning of yesterday's action in the experiences and interpretations of today. (1976:80, see also Burgelman, 1984b:21)

In our terms, for purposes of strategic management, this means the tracking of patterns of action in the organization in order to identify strategies, whether emergent or deliberate. This can serve two purposes. First, it can be used to find fledgling strategies in unexpected pockets of the organization so that consideration can be given to making them more broadly and deliberately organizational (perhaps by strategic programming). Second, it can be used to effect strategic control by identifying the organization's realized strategies (as actual patterns in action) which can then be compared with its intended ones (as expressed in its formal plans or less formal statements of managerial intentions). In effect, what we are proposing here is that planners should be doing in their organizations what we at McGill University have been doing in our research (see pp. 109–115): tracking realized strategies across time, but in the planners' case to better understand the behaviors of their organizations for purposes of strategy identification, programming, and control.

We include this activity under the roles of planners, rather than of planning, simply because we do not see it as part of a systematic, regular process for the programming of strategy. Rather it provides ad hoc inputs to the processes of programming and control. Moreover, given its judgmental and interpretative nature, this role does not fit under the definition of planning as a formalized procedure. While such activity can, of course, become routine and regular, we suspect that such routinization may discourage the very creative and judgmental orientation that it so evidently requires.

Desperately Seeking Strategies

The first step that we noted in strategic programming is not to create the strategy but to take it from the strategy formation process and begin its operationalization through codification. The popular view in strategic management (especially the design school) is that such strategies come straight from the senior management, which offers them to the planners as sets of full-blown intentions all ready for programming. The evidence of all the careful research, however, is that strategies are not always forthcoming on silver platters, ready to be operationalized. There are often times when top management provides only the vaguest of intentions, and sometimes, in fact, none at all. It may do so deliberately, when conditions are unstable, to avoid the straitjackets of explicit strategy and strategic programming (Wrapp, 1967). But a management may also be incapable of producing the intended strategies its organization needs.

Our concern here is with a different situation, however (since in the first case, the organization needs no strategic programming, and in the second, staff analysis cannot substitute for the inadequacies of line management). This is the case, not uncommon, of the complex, decentralized, "learning" organization that must bubble up many of its strategies from below—for example, high-technology companies, professional service institutions, research laboratories. Here patterns that may prove strategic tend to form and reform continuously, in all kinds of curious ways, for example, as people in obscure corners work out big problems in little ways. The problem is that a dense hierarchy can fail to capture this kind of strategic learning systematically. Thus a crucial aspect of the strategy process is to find these emerging patterns so that they can be scrutinized for the benefit of the organization at large. That way, when appropriate, emergent strategies can be rendered deliberate and obscure ones pervasive, or, at the very least, the inconsistencies that tend to arise in emergent strategies can be cleared up (Sarrazin, 1975:137).

Clearly, the role of finding emerging strategies is an important responsibility of managers, and not just those at the top of the hierarchy, but especially the ones at middle levels who sit critically between the ideas bubbling up and the broader conceptions coming down (Nonaka, 1988). Line managers, after all, tend to be the intuitive pattern recognizers, and it is they who have the necessary nerve center information (in breadth as well as richness) and the authoritative access to operating activities. But they necessarily do this in informal and idiosyncratic ways, so that planners can help make the process a *little* more formal and systematic. They may not have the line authority, but they do have the time and, ideally, some of them have the creative spark to probe the organization in search of interesting emerging patterns. This can be accomplished partly through the study of hard data, for example, by analyzing figures on market segmentation of a firm's own products to discover newly developing types of customers. But much of this work will likely have to be done in far more flexible and unconventional ways.

For example, in discussion with the planners of a large energy multinational, concerned about ideas for diversification, we suggested that clues to future success might be uncovered deep within the firm itself. Perhaps the Malaysian subsidiary had hit upon a new market that worked for it and might serve as a model for subsidiaries in other countries. In recent years, planners have been inclined to search for clues to strategic success in reports of performance and analyses of industry trends. Important clues might also be found at their own doorsteps, hidden in experiments taking place in obscure corners of their own organizations, provided they are prepared to dig deep for them.

The planners, of course, might also turn some of those talents to tracking emerging patterns among competitors and other organizations that serve as frames of reference, seeking to infer their unannounced strategies (whether deliberate or emergent) as early as possible. This has to be at least as important a task as the formal competitor analysis that Porter has promoted so vigorously (e.g., 1980:Chapter 3), although clearly a trickier one.

As noted earlier, strategies found as emerging patterns in the organization's own behavior can also feed into the process of strategic control. In fact, this aspect of strategic control may have to depend largely on the planners, because the uncovering of realized strategies as patterns in action to compare with intended strategies likely has to be done comprehensively and systematically, which reflects the comparative advantage of the planners.

Unconventional Planners

References to being systematic, comprehensive, and somewhat more formal should not be interpreted to mean that this role of finding strategies fits into the conventional posture of planners. Quite the contrary, the approach here has to be quite different.

Conventional planners have tended to do what comes most naturally in this area: to close prematurely on the most readily accessible strategies. They have often extrapolated the organization's existing strategic orientation, or else copied in generic ways the strategies of the most obviously successful reference organizations (competitor or peer). Some conventional planners have also retreated into the most futile aspect of the catalyst role (to be discussed later), namely imploring sterile managements to come up with the missing strategies. Others have taken it upon themselves to produce the missing strategies, which in our view has usually been an equally futile exercise.

Finding strategies in the vagaries of the organization's own behavior (or that of reference organizations) is a kind of detective work, requiring planners to snoop around all kinds of places they might not normally visit, to finding patterning amid the noise of failed experiments, seemingly random activities, and messy learning. And then assessments have to be made as to the likely consequences of these patterns, which requires a good deal of interpretative judgment. Pattern recognition is an exercise in synthesis rather than analysis (although the analytic component of the actual tracking of action streams may loom larger). Likewise, any conclusion about rendering an emergent strategy formally deliberate has to be reached subtly, taking into account all kinds of soft factors. To return to our grass roots model of strategy making, the planners have to be looking for growths that, while seeming like weeds, are in fact capable of bearing fruit. These have to be watched carefully, sometimes without disturbing their emergent nature until their worth has become clear. Only then can they be propagated as valuable plants, or else cut down as worthless.

Thus the premature closure so common in analytical work is the last thing to be hoped for in the performance of this role. Planners who believe that all strategies (even uncovered emergent ones) must be made explicit and codified for immediate programming or else summarily discarded may do to organizations what gardeners inclined to pull up young shoots to inspect their roots would do to nurseries: put them out of business as soon as their current crop of strategies runs out. Put another way, this is a role best performed by planners with that minor in intuitive thinking we discussed earlier, those who are able to combine their analytical talents with a healthy dose of honed intuition. As we move from the more to the less conventional roles of planners, we shall find increasing need for this balance of the brain's two basic orientations.

The role of finding strategies may seem like a strange one to promote for planners, given that it is so far removed from conventional ideas about planning. But we consider it crucial because conventional planning itself has been too far removed from strategy formation. Planners who wish to call themselves "strategic" need to perform roles other than conventional strategic programming. Given that this is an important activity in the real process of strategy formation, and given that planners (unconventional ones at least) have the time and skills to perform a helping role in this process, it becomes logical that they do so. What matters is the importance of this role in strategy making and the fact that many planners have the time and skills to help perform it. Planners who restrict their work to deliberate strategies formulated systematically preclude themselves from contributing to the strategy process as it must often exist. Strategy formation cannot be helped by people blind to the richness of its reality.

Second Role of Planners: Analysts

Every one of the intense probes into what planners actually do suggests that the effective ones spend a good deal of time, not so much doing or even encouraging planning, as carrying out analyses of specific issues to be fed into the strategy making process on an ad hoc basis.[15] We shall refer to this as *strategic analysis*. Quinn,

---

[15] Surveys of what planners claim to do also bring this out. For example, in interviews conducted by Al-Bazzaz and Grinyer, "proposals, advice and recommendations" was acknowledged by 46 percent of the planners, second only to "design and administration of plans and initiation of planning process" at 58 percent;

for example, noted that "the most successful professional planners I have known essentially delegate running the annual planning process to someone else. Instead they concentrate on a series of almost ad hoc interventions . . ." (1980a:196). He elaborated from his more concentrated study as follows:

> in the companies observed, formal planning contributed most directly to significant change when it was set up as a "special study" on some important aspect of corporate strategy. . . . Such special strategic studies . . . represented a subsystem of strategy formulation distinct from . . . annual planning activities . . . (36)

Strategic Analysis for Managers

What we have here is a classic staff role: the analysis of the largely hard data that managers must take into consideration yet are not inclined to consider systematically themselves.

Effective managers, we noted earlier, have their fingers on the pulse of their organization and its external context through their privileged access to soft data. But as described in the planning dilemma, they lack the time and the inclination to study the hard data. The nature of their work favors action over reflection, quick response over long-term consideration, the oral over the written, getting information rapidly over getting it right. Someone has to take the time to study the hard facts—shifts in consumer buying habits, realignments of competitive positions, changes in product mixes, and so on—and ensure that their consequences are fed into the strategy making process (Quinn, 1980a:20).

Planners are obvious candidates for this job: they have the inclination to do analysis, the time it requires, the predisposition to consider the hard facts. They can thus analyze these data—drawing on whatever management science techniques seem appropriate (see, for example, Millett and Leppänen, 1991; Rutenberg, 1976; Steiner, 1979:Chapter 15)—to feed their summaries and conclusions to the managers for purposes of strategy making. As Ansoff noted:

"analysis and evaluation" garnered 44 percent, and "ad hoc work and special projects," 29 percent (1981:160).

The planner is the generator and analyst of data. He needs to forecast, to evaluate the present position, to generate action alternatives, to analyze their consequences to the firm, and to program the selected guidelines and constraints. In this process, the line executive plays the central role of receiving recommendations from the planner, adding his own perception of the problem, and making decisions, which almost invariably are risk decisions based on imperfect information. (1967:12)

We concur with Ansoff, except to make clear that these are not sequential steps in a planning process so much as ad hoc inputs to a managerial one.

We emphasize the ad hoc nature of these strategic studies because they feed into a strategy making process that itself is irregular, proceeding on no schedule and following no standard sequence of steps. To draw on our earlier conclusions, regularity in the planning process can interfere with strategic thinking, breeding a lethargy that can cause managers to miss important discontinuities. In contrast, ad hoc analytical inputs can stimulate reflection and so breed responsiveness. Indeed, in his article on long-range planning, Loasby came up with the provocative suggestion that planners might sometimes do well to use ad hoc analysis to *undermine* formal planning:

if, instead of asking how they can more accurately foresee future events and thus make better decisions further ahead, firms were to ask first what they can do to avoid the need to decide so far ahead, they might be led to discover important ways of improving their performance. (1967:307)

Of course, the fact that managers, if not continuously making strategy, must at least keep strategic issues under constant surveillance, means that there is always the need for such studies (especially when major strategic changes are under consideration). Thus there is merit in the claims of Sawyer (1983:100) and Allaire and Firsirotu (1990:114) that managers need systems to ensure a steady flow of the relevant hard information. But planners are challenged to provide it in ways that will not routinize its receipt and so dull its use.

Moreover, in our view the results of strategic analysis should not typically take the form of definitive recommendations, simply because a host of "soft" factors that may be known only to the managers must also be considered—personality and culture factors, questions of timing, and so on. Furthermore, analysis, as discussed earlier, is necessarily focused, tending to isolate one issue at a time, while managers generally have to consider the interplay of networks of issues. Thus, these analytic studies are more likely to conclude in the form of "notice this" or "consider that" than "do this" or "do that." Abraham Kaplan captured this spirit with the comment that "In general, planning aims at facilitating and rationalizing decisions. It facilitates them by making choices more clear-cut and alternatives more concrete. It rationalizes decisions by explicating values and by making decisions consistent" (1964:44–45).

In effect, strategic analysis can sometimes better provide a perspective than propose a position, because the insightful diagnosis of a problem can prove more important than the presentation of a solution. As technique is generally oriented to the latter—specifically to the evaluation of given alternatives (Mintzberg, Raisinghani, and Théorêt, 1976)—planners must be careful to avoid the "rule of the tool": that managerial issues look like nails just because planners have a hammer.

Furthermore, the ad hoc strategic analyses must come to the managers on their own terms, by which we mean be timely and to the point. What has been generally recognized as the first operations research study—"a quite elementary analysis [for the British Air Force] of fighter losses over France in May 1940, which helped in the momentous decision not to send any more British fighters to France" (Morse, 1970:23)—was, according to its leader, "an impromptu two-hour study" (Larder, quoted in de Montigny, 1972:5). Years later, one survey found that studies of the by-then established field of operations research were taking an average of 10.1 months! (Turban, 1972) But even for the military in peacetime or business at any time, managers cannot usually wait nearly that long. Perhaps that is one reason why operations research analysts have had so little impact on strategy making (Mintzberg, 1979b).

Planners need not fall into the same trap. Those who wish to serve managers—people who, we noted earlier, often have to leap through "strategic windows" to seize opportunities, let alone deal with impending crisis—will necessarily do much of their strategic analysis in "real time," in other words, on the manager's schedule. But, as we noted in our article on the planning dilemma, that can still make use of the planner's natural comparative advantage:

> In part, the planner has done what the manager might do if he had the time. But he has done it more thoroughly and with far less time pressure. The manager has continued to manage as he must, giving attention to the mail and callers, while the planner gives attention to the problem. The key to this system is leverage. The manager may spend one hour defining the issue to the planner and one hour listening to the planner's recommendations one week later. During that one week, the planner and his staff of eight may be able to put in two man-months working on the problem. (Hekimian and Mintzberg, 1968:16)

The manager in a crisis situation or faced with a fleeting opportunity generally has only the choice between no analysis and "quick and dirty" analysis; thorough analysis is often impossible. Given a team of planners already in intimate contact with the manager and so thoroughly familiar with his or her concerns, it should be able to move quickly to analyze available hard data and assess certain consequences of proposed actions. Provided, of course, the team is prepared to forgo elegant techniques that have long start-up times and require data that are not readily available. "Quick and dirty" analysis can sometimes lead to cleaner, more thoughtful decisions.

Decision making can be considered in three stages—diagnosis, design, and decision (what Simon [1960:2] referred to initially as "intelligence, design, choice"). Our argument in the last chapter was that overall design—the creation of strategies themselves—is beyond planning (although proposals for subdesigns of particular components may sometimes be part of strategic analysis). But strategic analysis may have key roles to play in diagnosis before design and in the decision that follows it.

With respect to diagnosis, ad hoc strategic analysis could serve managers in two ways. One is to raise issues that they should be aware of but might have missed. Planners can expose managers to data in raw form (for example, that sales have been dropping in a key market segment), or analyze them to suggest their implications (for example, how marketing efforts might be reallocated in response to the sales drop). The other, more ambitious way is to attempt to shift the managers' perspectives on important issues, alter their "mental models," "mind-sets," "worldviews," by enabling them to become "more explicit about their key assumptions" (Marsh et al., 1988:28; see Lindberg and Zackrisson, [1991:272–274] with regard to the use of forecasting in this connection). The Shell scenario analysis discussed earlier informed management of a major shift that was likely to take place in the petroleum business. But more ambitiously, as the Wack account made clear, it sought to redefine the very way in which the Shell managers perceived their business:

> Every manager has a mental model of the world in which he or she acts based on experience and knowledge. When a manager must make a decision, he or she thinks of behavior alternatives within this mental model. . . .
>
> There is also a corporate view of the world . . . A company's perception of its business environment is as important as its investment infrastructure because its strategy comes from this perception. . . . [To change managerial behavior] the internal compass must be recalibrated.
>
> From the moment of this realization, we no longer saw our task as producing a documented view of the future business environment five or ten years ahead. Our real target was the [mental models] of our decision makers; unless we influenced the mental image, the picture of reality held by critical decision makers, our scenarios would be like water on a stone. (1985a:84; see also Makridakis, 1990:55)

Thus, in an interview on his view of future studies as "storytelling" (in Allio, 1986), Donald Michael claimed that since "we cannot know the future," indeed, since "there's no such animal" as "a most probable future" (6), forecasting should portray a variety of alternate futures for purposes of opening up the vistas of organizations and increasing their self-awareness (11). "The planner is best seen as an educator, especially in the organization that is trying to learn." One of his or her "main roles is to tell stories about long-range matters in such a way that they become today's strategic issues" (10).

In a paper entitled "Playful Plans," Rutenberg took this theme even further. He suggested how plans can be treated as "toys," which, when played with, can allow managers to better understand the situations they face.

> Following this metaphor a good corporate plan is one that executives will involve themselves with intently, envisioning different scenarios, forcing themselves to think differently, while struggling for a language by which they can talk with fellow executives about the uncertainty of a discontinuity. (1990:104)[16]

In general, we can distinguish three types of strategic analysis— environmental (external) studies, organizational (internal) studies, and strategy scrutinizing studies (the latter concerned with decisional choice after intended strategies have been conceived).

External Strategic Analysis

The world leaves behind all kinds of traces of its activity, many quite tangible and some indicative of things to come—at least to the insightful observer. In the Shell scenario planning experience, Wack provided us with one rich illustration of this.

There is a substantial literature on strategic analysis of the environment (some of it mentioned in the Chapter 2 discussion of the "external audit stage"). The popular (but perhaps unfortunate) term has been "environmental scanning," although the influence of Porter's work (1980, 1985) has caused many people to see this, in a more restricted way, as industry and competitive analysis. Indeed, the whole positioning school—for which Porter is the leading spokesman—depends to such an extent on this external strategic analysis, which serves to delineate the contexts in which its generic strategies can be applied, that it virtually replaces overall planning as the main activity.

In a recent paper entitled "Organizing Competitor Analysis Systems," Ghoshal and Westney (1991) presented the results of a

---

[16] De Geus, who headed the Shell planning department in which Wack worked, referred to one of the scenario analyses as "a licence to play" (1988:72).

"detailed study" of such systems in three large companies. They found three activity clusters: "information handling, or 'data management,' " concerned with "acquiring, classifying, storing, retrieving, editing, verifying, aggregating, and distributing information"; "analysis," to interpret the "higher-order" meaning of the information "to understand or predict competitor behavior"; and "implication," which "addressed the question of how the company could or should respond" (21). Problems involved especially the implications of activities, namely concerns about "the lack of relevance" of the whole process as well as "the lack of credibility of the analysts . . . and [the] analysis," also "a tendency to uncouple [hard and soft data], and in so doing to take the 'hard' data (the numbers) out of context, thereby creating serious problems in interpretation" (22).

Ghoshal and Westney went on to identify six different functions served by competitor analysis in organizations, all of which together make a nice list of the uses of strategic analysis in general:

- *Sensitization*, in order to "shake up the troops" by challenging "the organization's existing assumptions about particular competitors," including "in some cases changing the definition of the most significant competitor or of the most crucial dimensions of competition" (24, 25)
- *Benchmarking*, which "provides a set of specific measures comparing the firm with its competitors . . ."
- *Legitimization*, which means "to justify certain proposals and to persuade members of the organization of the feasibility and desirability of a chosen course of action."
- *Inspiration*, which gives "people new ideas about how to solve problems," in this process "by identifying what other firms had done in similar circumstances . . ." (25)
- *Planning*, namely "the use of competitor analysis to assist the formal planning process," interestingly enough "much more dependent on information from the formal [competitor analysis] function than any of the other uses."
- *Decision-making*, meaning "contribution . . . to operational and tactical decision-making by line managers," which provided the second largest number of examples cited (after planning) (26).

Besides those related to industry and competitor analysis, a host of other techniques for environmental analysis have been proposed, especially (as noted earlier) in the area of forecasting. Given the problem of coupling forecasting with the regular planning process, we suspect that forecasting in fact more often amounts to ad hoc analysis than to a systematic first step in a formal planning process. While we have not been optimistic about the harder techniques of forecasting, we do believe that some of the softer ones, such as scenario building, may be of use, especially when conducted by astute analysts in a descriptive way, by which we mean not to predict, but simply to interpret and clarify for managers what seems to be going on out there. Much as planners can study and interpret patterns in the organization's own behavior to identify its emergent strategies, so too can they study and interpret patterns in the external environment to identify possible strategic opportunities and threats (including, as already noted, the patterns in competitors' actions in order to identify their strategies).

Internal Strategic Analysis and the Role of Simulation

An organization can exhibit its own trends too, which are not always evident to its own managers. Thus, there is a role for strategic analysis in looking inside the organization. Such analysis can sometimes help to uncover the emerging pattern of behaviors and competences of the organization.

A good deal of formal analytical technology has been proposed for use here, in particular formal computer models as simulations of the firm. Models, in whatever form, are key to everything that planners do, for they describe how phenomena work, and all planning, forecasting, and analysis depend on such descriptions. Computer simulations are simply the most formal of these models (see Mockler, 1991, for a recent review of software), since all relationships have to be specified precisely in fully operational variables. But as we shall see, theories are models too, as are budgets, and managers also have models in their heads, some of them subconscious, on which everything they do likewise depends.

As we discussed Forrester's (1975) notion of the "counterintuitive behavior of social systems" in the last chapter, we suggested that managers may have difficulty dealing with certain types of intricate feedback loops. In other words, under certain circumstances their informal models may not be all that good. This might, in fact, suggest an important extension of the planning dilemma—beyond time, technique, and information, to the specific information processing capabilities of managers and planners. Thus, while organizations may have to fall back on the intuitive mind for synthesis, certain kinds of analysis may be better done, or at least aided, by the systematic efforts of nonmanagers. As Yavitz and Newman put it in discussing the dangers of "complete reliance on a 'great leader' to formulate strategy":

> Rarely can a single person comprehend upsets in social, political, technological, as well as economic areas. Moreover, a shift in strategy usually requires adjustments by several departments of a company, and predicting the likely impacts of these adjustments calls for specialized technical judgments. (1982:91)

As we concluded in our discussion of Forrester's paper, where there is little subtlety about the data in question (i.e., it tends to have been "hardened") and where the tacit knowledge of the manager is not critical for understanding, then formal computer models may constitute a preferable alternative. It should come as no surprise, therefore, that many of Forrester's earliest models, in *Industrial Dynamics* (1961), sought to simulate the flow of funds and the like through business organizations. Clearly a model that simulates the budgeting system of an organization may help a manager trace the financial consequences of proposed changes.

It should be noted, however, that systems dynamics models have been around for a long time, yet have hardly caught on. Perhaps they are difficult to construct, or perhaps faulty assumptions undermine many of the attempted applications. But a few interesting applications have been reported in the literature. The most famous was the Club of Rome's controversial study, *Limits to Growth* (Meadows et al., 1972), which projected various resource uses and the like to the next century, leading to predictions of catastrophic resource depletions. Closer to our concerns here is a fascinating study by Roger Hall (1976) that showed how such a simulation might have been used by the managers of the old *Saturday Evening Post* to change their mind-set concerning the magazine industry and so help save that publication from bankruptcy. In another paper, Hall teamed up with Menzies (1983) to simulate the activities of a small sports club in Winnipeg and so reportedly enabled it to adopt more effective membership strategies.

To return to the example of the budget (a form of plan), it should be noted that the budgeting system is a model of certain aspects of the organization, a simulation in its own right. That is what Cyert and March meant when they wrote of "plans as theories":

> plans, like other standard operating procedures, reduce a complex world to a somewhat simpler one. Within rather large limits, the organization substitutes the plan for the world . . . partly by making the world conform to the plan, partly by pretending that it does. (1963:112)

Plans, especially in the operational form of budgets, can be used to consider the impact of possible changes on the organization's current operations, including the testing of new strategies (e.g., Channon, 1979:125). In other words, plans can feed back into the strategy making process and so find a third role for themselves in the organization, namely as simulations (although this would seem to be less common than the roles of communication and control).

It should be emphasized, however, that models need not be so formal to be useful. Some of the best models that planners can offer managers are simply alternate conceptual interpretations of their world, for example, a new way to view the organization's marketing system or the behavior of its competitors. In other words, descriptive theories are simulations too, and planners can play the role of surveying the latest theoretical developments in various areas of interest and feeding the relevant perspectives to managers for their consideration. Thus Rutenberg suggested that planners can "help . . . managers to understand their mental 'maps'" (1990:4), while de Geus described "the real purpose of effective planning" as "not to make plans but to change the . . . mental models that . . . decision makers carry in their heads" (1988:71). We shall return to this point shortly.

As Forrester suggested and we have discussed elsewhere (Mintzberg, 1973), every manager models in his or her head all kinds of phenomena with which he or she must deal (for example, the response of the factory to customer pressures, or the flow of decisions through the organization's structure). We find (unlike Forrester) that some of these can be articulated clearly and easily while others remain locked deep in the mind's subconscious. Planners who wish to propose alternate, more formal models or conceptual theories to managers must be aware of these informal models, and consider their strengths (such as their ability to draw on privileged tacit knowledge) alongside their weaknesses (such as possibly being based on a narrow range of experience). To repeat what we believe to be an important point, systems can certainly be "counter-intuitive," but so too can they be "counter-analytic."

Scrutinization of Strategies

A third aspect of strategic analysis concerns the investigation and evaluation of proposed (intended) strategies. Unlike the first two aspects, this takes place *after* the strategy making process, for example, to confirm the results of managerial intuition or at least to cut its downside risks. In fact, from the perspective of the public sector, Cho argued that this is a more sensible activity for planners than the more obvious forms of analysis that feed into strategy making at the front end:

> Policy analysis is believed to have more value in policy evaluation ... than in policy formulation ... because it is better suited to systematic analysis of data and experiences than to prescribing a policy or program. Policy analysts—whether they come from political science, economics, sociology or other related fields—are primarily trained to discover a pattern, explain it, and develop a generalization, rather than to invent a new solution. (1989:212)

Gimpl and Dakin saw this as a process of rationalization, carried out "to legitimize decisions which have already been made on an intuitive basis" (1984:129). True though this often may be, scrutinization can also be used to sort out seemingly good and bad strategies. After all, conventional rationality is not always a bad thing! But Majone was not so quick to dismiss even such attempts at rationalization, finding them functional. He offered the interesting argument that such analysis is "needed *after* the decision is made to provide a conceptual basis for it, to show that it fits into the framework of existing policy, to discover new implications, and to anticipate or answer criticism." Majone considered "post decision arguments" to be "indispensable in policymaking . . . a means of increasing the persuasive force of a decision and exercising rational control over conclusions that may be suggested by extralegal considerations" (1989:31, 30).

The common term in the planning literature for this form of strategic analysis is "evaluation," and it is generally considered a step in the strategy formation process, after strategies have been codified and before they are implemented (i.e., programmed). We do not so consider it and prefer to label the activity *scrutinization*, to capture the idea that it extends beyond consideration of the numbers to assess the viability of strategies. As Quinn found:

> Only after an opportunity was thoroughly investigated and approved on a conceptual level—using a few broad numbers—was it thoroughly analyzed in financial terms and put through a separate, more detailed process for actual approval. (1980a:202)

There are several good reasons to view scrutinization as a process of ad hoc analysis rather than a step in the planning cycle (the way it is, in fact, treated, however implicitly, in the literature of the positioning school, which gives far more attention to the evaluation of individual strategies than to their integration in an overall process of planning). As we have described the strategy making process, strategies can appear at all kinds of odd times, in all kinds of odd ways, from all kinds of odd places. Strategy scrutinization must respond to this on a correspondingly ad hoc basis. Some strategies may be developed by managers on a speculative basis, others borrowed from competitors, still others uncovered as emerging patterns in the tracking of the organization's own action streams. Each strategy has to be considered on its own merits and in its own time, as well as compared with others. Planners must, therefore, look for possible strategies everywhere, and respond to them interactively, in order to pit one against the other to stimulate the fullest possible debate about their viability.

But even acceptable strategies do not generally move on to some kind of automatic programming step. Instead, through scrutinizations of various kinds they become part of the give-and-take that is strategy formation, with formulation and evaluation proceeding interactively. (This is implied even in Majone's comment about rationalization, when, for example, he mentioned the possibility to "discover new implications" in such analyses.) As a result, strategy scrutinization takes place *alongside* strategy making, in parallel with it, in a sense cycling around the process (as we have shown in our little figure below the subheading).

In fact, strategy scrutinization can extend (like other forms of strategic analysis) to the point of questioning planning itself.[17] In other words, planners should sometimes question conventionally formulated strategies no less than promote unconventionally formed ones. A clear intended strategy emanating from the executive suite on schedule should no more be automatically accepted as good than should a vague emergent one growing peripherally in the depths of the organization be automatically dismissed as bad.

Third Role of Planners: Catalysts

The planning literature, as we have already seen, has long promoted the role of planner as catalyst. "The role of a corporate planner . . . is more of a 'catalyst' and less of a 'strategist,' " wrote Chakravarthy (1982:22), citing Lorange (1980a), who, in another

---

[17] Schmidt (1988) considered what he called "strategic review," which he described as "*ad hoc* examination of a company's strategies and related capital investments," as a "replacement for formal corporate planning systems" (14).

publication, also referred to the planner as "a system 'catalyst' not a plans analyst" (1979:233).

Here, however, we take a view of the catalyst role that differs from conventional planning, which sees the planner as a "purveyor of planning methods among the decision makers of the firm," to quote a Gulf Oil planner (in Schendel and Hofer, 1979:501), that person who "manages the long-run planning system, insures that the plans are comprehensive, and promotes the ideas and techniques of planning" (Ackerman, 1972:140). In our view, it is not "planning" or "plans" that planners should be urging on organizations so much as the propensity "to plan." In other words, they should be promoting, not necessarily formalized procedure to produce articulated result so much as future thinking in its broadest sense.

Opening Up Strategic Thinking

To encourage strategic planning, as we have seen, is really to encourage strategic programming and thereby possibly to discourage strategic thinking. Of course, that may sometimes be appropriate. For example, entrepreneurial firms that have grown large sometimes suffer from their leaders' unwillingness to articulate and program the viable strategies they already have. Planners may thus appropriately promote strategic programming so that these strategies can be pursued more systematically and extensively. But such strategic programming is not always desirable, especially when critical strategic learning remains incomplete, when an external environment remains unsettled, or when an organization has the need to maintain its strategy as a rich and flexible personalized vision. In these circumstances—in effect, where it is paramount to avoid premature closure on strategy—planners who extort managers to engage in formal strategic planning may be doing their organizations a major disservice.

Let us, therefore, back up a few steps. What all of us want is more effective organizations. We all likewise believe that better strategies will help produce these (perhaps a tautology, because how are we to know that a strategy is better except that it makes an organization more effective?). And we all probably share the belief that better strategic thinking (in conjunction with better strategic acting) produces better strategies. But not all of us share the belief that better (or more) strategic planning produces better strategic thinking. Thus, in our opinion at least, the catalyst role is more appropriately focused on strategic thinking, in conjunction with strategic acting, than on strategic planning. Sometimes, of course, such thinking must be deliberate, whether visionary or somewhat more orderly. But at other times it has to be emergent, and then the planner, as catalyst, has to act in ways quite inconsistent with conventional planning. Arie de Geus, when the well-known head of planning at Royal Dutch/Shell, captured this well in his article on "Planning as Learning": ". . . we think of planning as learning and of corporate planning as institutional learning" (1988:70).

Thus we must conclude that planners are best off encouraging informal strategic behavior, as it comes naturally, in a way akin to Rutenberg's notion of play. In the catalyst role performed in this way, the planner does not enter the black box of strategy making so much as ensure that the box is occupied with active line managers. He or she, in other words, encourages others to think about the future in a creative way. As one company CEO put it: "the planner's role isn't to make policy. It's almost like a psychiatrist. . . . He's supposed to be a mirror, saying, 'What do you want to be when you grow up, David? Where do you want to move the company?' " (quoted in Blass, 1983:6–17).

In fact, this catalyst role sits at the edge of the other roles we have already discussed. Shift any one of them from a focus on the *content* of the planner's output to support for the *process* of the manager's work, and you begin to enter the catalyst role. (In other words, the content of the *planner's* work becomes an influence on the *manager's* process.) For example, what Rutenberg called the planner's role of "play therapist" seemed to sit at the interface of analyst and catalyst:

> The planning group's task in play is not to confront executives directly, but to create a triangular relationship between the planners, the executives, and the future. Sometimes the planner will interact with the future, in such a way that the executive sees that future differently. Sometimes the planner will interact with the executives, to help them disentangle inhibiting power relation-

ships. But the planners' long-term mandate is to improve the interaction between the executives and the future. (1990:23)

Similarly, Langley found in her research "the formal analysis and social interactive processes in organizations must be viewed as closely intertwined," that "formal analysis acts as a kind of glue within the social interactive processes of generating organizational commitment and ensuring action" (1989:626). Likewise, when strategic programming shifts from the planner doing it to helping line managers get it done, the planners have again entered the catalyst role. As Langley concluded, the "contribution [of formal planning] to strategy development is less direct than usually assumed" (1988:40).

Once planning as that "one best way" is replaced by a broader conception of the strategy making process, the planner's catalyst role can take on a new significance. In our experience, in some of the more interesting planning departments the planners have naturally become the organizations' conceptual thinkers about strategy formation. It is they who bring in the latest thinking about how the strategy process does and should work. As strategists, line managers are usually too busy making strategy to think about it in conceptual terms, let alone read its latest literature or attend its conferences. In other words, the chief executive has to worry more about the business he or she is in than the business of strategic management. But planners have the time and the inclination to develop such expertise and then to spread it through their organizations, as teachers of a sort. Thus Allaire and Firsirotu claimed that the "first task" of planners at the corporate level has to be "evaluating [and] challenging the adequacy of present definition of strategic systems" (1988:34), presumably also included the planning system itself. And "the most successful planners" that Quinn knows

were often among the company's most prolific conference goers and executive course attendees. Rather than build their own permanent staffs, they preferred to bring in a stream of outside experts on subjects of interest and to have special studies done by knowledgeable consultants or staff people elsewhere in the company. . . . Many had individual experts or teams come in and lead small

seminars on provocative topics well beyond the ordinary time horizons of their companies. (1980a:197)

Role for Formalization

So far we have described the catalyst role in a divergent sense—to
open up strategic thinking, in Rutenberg's terms, to become more
"playful." But there is a yang to the yin of this role as well, and that
is to bring some order to the loose ends of strategy formation. As
Langley wrote aptly, while it is people and not systems that create
strategy, systems can sometimes serve "as a discipline within
which to do this" (1988:48). And so here, at the risk of being
accused of contradiction, we wish to reintroduce the notion of
formalization.

In the messy world of management, things can fall between the
cracks. Agenda items can be forgotten, deadlines can be missed,
hard data can be overlooked. Consider again March and Simon's
" 'Gresham's Law' of planning: Daily routine drives out planning"
(1958:185), or, more accurately, again in their words, programmed
tasks "tend to take precedence" over unprogrammed tasks. Part of
the catalyst role, therefore, can be to introduce some degree of
formalization to avoid these problems, but only enough to avoid
impeding the natural flow of the process itself.

Formalization can pertain to time, to location, to participation,
to agenda, and to information, as well as, but with only the greatest
of care, to process itself. It can help to focus attention, stimulate
debate, keep track of issues, promote interaction, and facilitate
consensus. To quote one of the managers Langley interviewed:

> Ideas don't come out of planning . . . ideas are in the air. But the
> plan will force us to make an effort to group things together and to
> define these orientations more clearly. I don't think the plan will be
> a surprise. For most people it's just a chance to articulate their
> ideas. I've done research work and I think there's an analogy here.
> At some point, you have done a lot of work and collected a lot of
> data. Then the time comes when you have to present it some-
> where . . . you don't do anything new, but it forces you to put the
> data together, to synthesize it . . . to discuss things based on the

synthesis. And often, just getting the data together generates new ideas . . . (1988:48)

Consider, for example, the strategy "retreat," which brings various strategic actors together for one or several days in an isolated setting, to reflect on broader issues or perhaps address a few specific ones. We have made clear that strategy is not something made on demand at a meeting that happens to be labeled "strategy." There is no special time or place to make strategy. But organizations ripe for change sometimes find such retreats critical for the crystallization of the necessary consensus. These retreats formalize the *time* for discussion as well as the *participants* in the process. In 1986, Jack Welch of General Electric created "a Corporate Executive Council which brings together, every quarter, the fourteen business leaders and the heads of the corporate staff departments plus the CEO. Business plans are scrutinized, ideas exchanged, suggestions offered, practical ways of getting at synergies are sought, and implemented" (Allaire and Firsirotu, 1990:112).[18]

Less elaborate than even the retreat is the simple effort by planners to keep track of the issues on the strategic agenda, in order to remind managers of their progress. As one manager said, "planners are the guardians of the orthodoxy of the cycle. Something has to be started at this time and finished at this other time . . ." Moreover, while "we identify the broad outlines, they write it all down" (in Langley, 1988:49).

A system, moreover, can "structure discussions" and act as "a tool to facilitate organizational learning" (Allaire and Firsirotu, 1988:38). Thus, when it worked best, the OST system at Texas Instruments helped to focus the attention of managers on the need for innovation. Likewise, in the case of capital budgeting, Marsh et al. noted:

The formal systems, through annual budget rounds, and via the pre-set dates of the various committee and Board meetings . . . also

---

[18] Such an idea, it should be noted, is of course not new, Here is how Henri Fayol described a very similar activity almost a century earlier: "At these meetings each department head explains, in turn, the results obtained in his department, and the difficulties encountered. There is then discussion, and decisions are made by the Chief. At the end of the meeting each one knows he has the most up-to-date information, and co-ordination is ensured" (1949:xi–xii).

helped to set deadlines, and thereby force the project pace. They facilitated the movement of information up, down, and sideways within the organization, generating awareness of, and commitment to, the project. At the same time, they provided a scheduled set of occasions for face-to-face communication across multiple levels of the hierarchy. (1988:28)

Systems can also help in the generation of consensus. Indeed, "The politicians in ancient Greece used the oracle of Delphi as their main vehicle to achieve consensus" (Makridakis, 1990:56). And they can help in the communication of vision and the engendering of participation in it, a role that Langley labeled "group therapy" (1988:42): as "therapist," the planner structures experience; as analyst or "philosopher," he or she structures knowledge.

The Formalization Edge

Formalization may be necessary to strengthen some loose edges, but it has its own delicate edge beyond which planners should not go. Put another way, formalization is a double-edged sword, easily reaching the point where help becomes hindrance.

As we argued in the last chapter, there is something strange about formalization, something that can cause the very essence of an activity to be lost simply in its explication. Not all aspects of formalization need cause this—as we just noted, formalizing the time and participation of some event of a strategy process can be beneficial. But planners as catalysts need to be very sensitive to just where that edge may appear—for example, where the work of planners gets "out of phase with management needs." A case in point: "while senior managers . . . were ready to put forward their visions, planners were still collecting information" (Langley, 1988:49).

At the strategy retreat, even decomposing the process so that, for example, goals are discussed in the morning and strengths and weaknesses in the afternoon, may sometimes stifle creative discussion. The object of the exercise, to repeat, is not analysis but synthesis, not evaluation so much as design. Formal data inputs may help, as may a conceptual framework to consider the key issues. But efforts to force a loose process into sequential steps can kill it. Oftentimes formalization should not extend much beyond the specification of time, place, and participation.

Perhaps the two sides of this delicate edge can be identified as the difference between "systems that facilitate thinking" and "systems that (try to) do it" ("constituting it or replacing it" [Zan, 1987:191] or even "defining it" [see also Carrance, 1986:281]). The difference may be subtle but is often easy to identify. One serves the process already in place, responding to it in its own terms, while the other seeks to impose its own imperatives, becoming an exercise in exercising control. To quote one Texas Instruments executive on that company's systems, "We made 'em bureaucratic. We used the system as a control tool, rather than a facilitating tool. That's the difference" (in Jelinek and Schoonhoven, 1990:411). The formal planning process should be "a catalyst, not a cause" (Hurst, 1986:23). Thus, when Steiner and others of the planning school claimed that "it's the process that counts," they were correct, but not *their* process!

Figure 6–6 attempts to describe this edge graphically, showing types of formalization building up to an edge that drops off into the abyss once support becomes control.

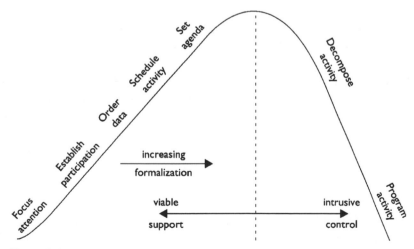

Figure 6–6
The Formalization Edge

Simons's Interactive Control

Langley found the formal approach of the planners to be "as much a social process as a rational analytic process" (1988:49). This was the theme pursued by Robert Simons in a series of papers that captured well the approach on the safe side of our formalization edge.

Simons contrasted what he called "interactive control" with the traditional "diagnostic control" (1987, 1988, 1990, 1991). His thesis was that top managers select one or a few systems as their own, usually "relatively simple and technically unsophisticated" ones, to which they give "a great deal of day-to-day . . . attention," interpreting the data they generate "in *face-to-face* meetings" of the concerned line actors (1988:8, 6). In effect, these systems are woven into their own natural ways of managing, providing that shade of formalization necessary to keep a large, complex organization running. They "provide guidance to organizational members" and "stimulate learning throughout the organization."

> The choice by top managers to make certain control systems interactive (and program others) provides signals to organizational participants about what should be monitored and where new ideas should be proposed and tested. This signal activates organizational learning and, through the debate and dialogue that surrounds the interactive management control process, new strategies and tactics emerge over time. (1990:137)

Simons (in personal correspondence in response to an earlier draft of this book) argued that "these systems do not take place 'alongside' strategy making; interactive systems drive strategy making—they are the box within which strategy is developed." (Bear in mind that these are the systems of the managers, not the planners.)

An example of a system favored for interactive control is that of budgets, "used, not as purely financial documents, but rather as agendas to discuss tactics, new marketing ideas, and product development plans throughout the organization" (1990:134). In this way other companies have used program management systems, broad revenue budgeting systems, intelligence systems (especially in pharmaceutical companies), and human development systems (1991). One company, Johnson & Johnson, where "there are no planning staff units,"

> uses two techniques to make long-range planning interactive instead of ritualistic. First, the planning horizon is fixed so that, over time, managers are held accountable for earlier estimates and plans. Second, long-range plans are subject to intense debate and challenge. . . . At Johnson & Johnson . . . the need for all managers to continually evaluate, revise, and present new commitments to action as part of the long-range and financial planning process makes these systems highly interactive. (1987:346, 348)

Playing the Catalyst Role

Serving as "corporate guru," as Litschert and Nicholson (1974:66) described the catalyst role in its broadest sense, requires skills quite different from those of the planners' more conventional roles. As Wack noted, changing the perceptions or mental models of the managers "was a different and much more demanding task than producing a relevant scenario" in the first place (1985a:84).

Such planners see their role as getting others to question conventional wisdom, and especially helping people out of conceptual ruts (which managers with long experience in stable strategies are apt to dig themselves into). Unconventional planners sometimes try to use provocation to do this—shock tactics if you like—raising difficult questions and challenging conventional assumptions. In this spirit, Huff developed a number of "metaphoric frames for planning." One is planning as counseling:

> Planners might be most useful if they would just concentrate on providing occasions for people to "see what they say." Uniting this idea with a counselling metaphor suggests that the planner might devote him/herself to the creation of low-threat, non-judgmental planning situations in which organization members can express themselves freely. (1980:37)

Another is planning as "vision testing," a kind of corporate "optometrist":

If we all filter information through a set of limiting beliefs and assumptions, then an optometrist-planner might provide a useful periodic check of the "lens" through which members of an organization make sense of activities. The planner could organize the search for flaws or inadequacies in present beliefs and assumptions, and could also help generate alternative assumptions that precipitate a different set of activities. (35)[19]

James Brian Quinn was particularly articulate on this creative catalyst role for planners, exhorting them to play it most actively. Under the heading, "teaching managers about the future," he wrote:

For good reasons, most line managers are preoccupied with urgent current problems. Successful planners learned when each key executive was most relaxed and likely to be open to more philosophical conversations or practical speculations about the future. After-hours talks, cocktails, lunch, golf links, carpools, and business trips all provided occasions for informally leading executives into the future. (1980a:198)

Next Quinn discussed "building awareness about new options" ("whispering in the ears of the gods" [198]), and then "broadening support and comfort levels for action," followed by "crystallizing consensus or commitment" (199, 200). This last aspect may reflect the step of codifying strategy in the programming role, but Quinn quoted a comment by the head of strategic planning at a large information products company that suggests the catalyst role as well:

I move when I know a top executive is about to make a speech or internal presentation where a reference about the future would be useful. I brief him or his speechwriters on potentially exciting developments or ideas I think may be ready for public exposure. Sometimes this is just a device to increase the executive's awareness of needs the company must respond to. Once an executive has spoken publicly about an issue, he is much more likely to feel he understands it and is committed to doing something about it. (200)

---

[19] See Mason and Mitroff (1981), also Mason (1969) and Mitroff et al. (1977) for a more formalized rendition of this, which they called "Strategic Assumptions Surfacing and Testing Planning Process," bearing in mind, however, that even this degree of formalization may have its problems.

The Planner as Strategist

Being organizational custodian of conceptual knowledge about the strategy making process may predispose planners to think about strategy. But being predisposed to think about strategy does not turn anyone into a strategic thinker. Information, involvement, and imagination do that—having the brain and the basis to synthesize. And nothing we have seen in the planners' other predispositions suggests that they have any comparative advantages over managers in these regards. Perhaps quite the opposite: their jobs limit planners' access to the right information, preclude the necessary involvement, and encourage analysis at the expense of synthesis.

Nevertheless, holding the title of "planner" does not preclude imagination either. Indeed, some planners—not caught up with planning technology—have been among the most creative people we have come across in organizations. Nor does it automatically preclude information (although it does make access to soft information more difficult). Some planners are successful at catching the ear of informed managers, while others have recently held line management positions and so have brought the requisite knowledge with them (for a time). And then there are the lucky planners who work for organizations where the hard data is paramount for strategy making (as perhaps in the treasury department of government, whose numbers are its products). Any of these planners may be strategists too—champions of specific strategies if not also creators of strategic visions—although none of this has anything to do per se with planning, plans, or even being planners. These may not be the traditional planners, but they are ones who have overcome the planners' comparative disadvantages at strategy making. That is why we mention "the planner as strategist" here but do not list it as a fourth role for planners.

We are now prepared to draw together our discussion of the roles for planning, plans, and planners, first by showing the roles in a comprehensive framework, then by introducing more formally our conventional and unconventional planners, finally by specifying the contexts in which the various roles and the two kinds of planners seem to be most appropriately used.

A Plan for Planners

We have discussed a variety of roles for planning, plans, and planners. These are summarized around the black box of strategy formation in Figure 6–7, which elaborates Figure 6–2 by combining all the little figures we have shown alongside the titles of each role. This diagram is meant to bring together our discussion of this chapter and represent a comprehensive framework for the planning function—if you like, a plan for planners.

Strategic programming—our one role for planning—is shown feeding out of the black box, starting from the strategies formulated, or found, and operationalizing them in the three steps of codification, elaboration, and conversion. The final results are detailed plans, which themselves serve the roles of communication and control, in three directions—out to the external environment,

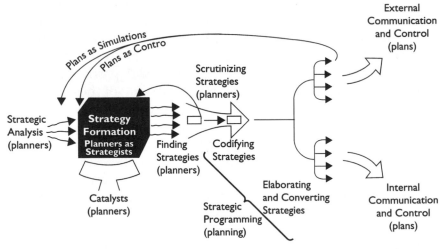

Figure 6–7
A Framework for Planning, Plans, Planners

down into the organization, and back to the input end of the strategy formation process in a feedback loop. Another role for the plans, as simulations, is also indicated as a loop back to strategic analysis.

Likely the most common role for planners—strategic analysis—is shown as a series of inputs to the black box of strategy formation at its front end. Also shown, at its output end and feeding back into it, is the scrutinizing of strategies—another aspect of this role. Just before this is shown the planner's role in finding strategies, indicated by tentative probes into the black box at its output end. Finally, the catalyst role is shown supporting the black box to encourage strategic thinking, while the planner as strategist is placed tentatively within that box for those planners who manage to get inside.

Thus our answer to the question of why organizations engage in planning with respect to strategy is (1) to program strategies, that is, to operationalize them in their behaviors. And they program strategies in this way (2) for purposes of communication and (3) for purposes of control (as well as coordination), which are the roles of plans. As to why organizations engage planners with respect to strategy, aside from their role in carrying out the above, the reasons are (4) to help find strategies (as logics in action), (5) to feed data and analyses into the strategy formation process, (6) to scrutinize the strategies that came out of it, and (7) to stimulate others to think strategically and be more knowledgeable about the strategy formation process in general.

A Planner for Each Side of the Brain

Our discussion suggests that planners can perform very different types of roles, which can call for two rather different orientations. On one hand, the planner must be a rather analytic, convergent type of thinker, dedicated to bringing order to the organization. Above all, this planner programs intended strategies and sees to it that they are communicated clearly and used for purposes of control. He or she also carries out studies to ensure that the managers concerned with strategy formation take into account the necessary hard data that they may be inclined to miss. And then this planner ensures that the strategies managers formulate are carefully and systematically evaluated before they are implemented. This kind of planner sees his or her role as "formalizing intuition," indeed often replacing it with analysis (Langley, 1982:26). This is the "conventional" planner we referred to in much of this book, who favors the analytic processes of the left hemisphere of the human brain. We might say that he or she engages in *right-handed planning*.

On the other hand, there is another type of planner, hardly conventional, at least as compared with most of the planning literature, but present nonetheless in a good many organizations. These planners are rather creative thinkers, more divergent, who seek to open up the strategy making process. As "soft analysts," they are prepared to conduct more "quick and dirty" studies. They like to find strategies in strange places and to scrutinize rather than just formally evaluate them. They encourage others to think strategically in Rutenberg's sense of play rather than other writers' sense of procedure. And they sometimes get themselves involved in the messy business of strategy formation. Unlike the other type of planner, this one is likely to be part of a group of "wild birds," as Quinn characterized them, established "to range throughout the organization stimulating offbeat approaches to issues" (1980a:106). This planner is somewhat more inclined toward the intuitive processes identified with the brain's right hemisphere. We might call him or her a *left-handed planner*.

Clearly, these two groups have to be differentiated, one for each of the manager's hands, so to speak. Those adept at carrying out procedures to program strategy and to conduct technical analyses of hard data will not likely promote creativity and playfulness. Planners who "are continuously asking the most searching, radical, and ridiculous questions," who have "unreasonable minds," to quote Churchman (in Mitroff et al., 1977:44), are unlikely to be the ones to work through the nitty-gritty of budgets and industry analyses. On the other hand, planners who are all play and creative divergence will hardly be the ones to see to it that strategies are properly operationalized when necessary or that the hard data are systematically considered in the strategy making process.

In fact, it may be a distortion for the two to share the label of "planner," since all they have in common is a concern with things that happen around the black box of strategy formation. Their purposes are different, as are their approaches, and even the positions they take around that box (one largely before and under the process, the other largely after it). Perhaps we should use adjectives to distinguish them, such as "analytical planner" or "strategic programmer" on one hand, "synthesis planner" or "strategic guru" on the other. (This comment should probably apply to the planning school in general, which could avoid a good deal of confusion by insisting that the word planning be used only with an adjective—other than "strategic"!)

That both types can be found in planning departments, even though the former predominates, is confirmed in Litschert and Nicholson's survey of 115 planning groups. Most conformed to the "norm," which they took to be "assisting the management [to] develop long-range plans and strategy" (1974:63). But 24 did vary "considerably . . . from the norm" (62), ten of them focusing on capital budgeting and other forms of capital control and eleven on project development, including the performance of project feasibility studies, closer to our planner role of analyst but not necessarily of the left-handed sort. But the remaining three planning groups sounded left-handed, being described as "think tank operations"—"musing about the long-range prospects of the company" and encouraging "line management to think and perceive in a more unorthodox manner and to ask less obvious questions" (65).

Who should fill planning positions? Some observers have argued against the notion of professional planners, believing that line managers should cycle into and out of planning jobs to give them limited periods of time to reflect. That way planning is carried out by people intimately linked to the operations of the organization (and who appreciate the demands of the management process). Dimma, as the CEO of a large firm commented:

> Never hire or employ professional planners, people whose sole career has been in planning. The ivory tower syndrome is bad at best and worse at worst. Use people in planning who have had good, i.e., successful line experience and who, after two or three years of broadening themselves, will want to go back into line. Never ever put tired executives into planning as a half-way house towards retirement. (1985:24)

We are sympathetic to this view—especially for the people who must head up planning groups and so link them with the line activities of the organization. Besides, as a well-known American general once remarked, "Nothing chastens a planner more than the knowledge that he will have to carry out the plan" (James Gavin, in King, 1983:263). We would add a qualification, however, at least for some of the specialized planning staff: the job also requires an orientation different from typical line management. As Ramanujam and Venkatraman pointed out, "It's a gross simplification to define planning as a line function" (1985:25). They argued for the benefits of a "detached perspective . . . to counter myopia and inertia" (16):

> Some aspects of corporate planning require specialists and people with an intimate knowledge of a business or function. However, other aspects require a detached, reflective perspective, and a willingness and ability to challenge the existing premises and assumptions of the business. In this case, a staff planner is needed rather than a line manager, whose specialized viewpoint can often be a liability. (25)

Interestingly, and evident in the above comments, these specialized planners can be left-handed as well as right-handed types. There is the need for people who can challenge and reflect in ways that managers require but may not do for themselves. Such planners can hardly be called "professional," but neither are they the typical organizational types. And then there is the need for specialized people who can carry out the more formalized roles of the planning function, analysts adept at "massaging the numbers," dealing with budgets, doing industry analyses, and so on. Again, line managers tend not to be so systematically analytic. While we are not sure what it even means for a planner to be "professional"—we know of no standardized set of entrance requirements for such jobs, no effective staff schools for such training[20]—these right-handed planners seem closer to some sense of formalized professionalism.

---

[20] However, it could reasonably be argued that MBA programs better prepare their students for right-handed staff planning jobs than for balanced line management positions (see "Training Managers Not MBAs," in Mintzberg, 1989:Chapter 5).

Planners in Context

Which type of planner should be favored in different organizations? Do all need both? Do any need only one, or neither? Lorange suggested the creation of "two different [planning] executives or offices," one to manage the planning processes, the other to counsel "the CEO in substantive strategizing matters" (1980a:269). Quinn saw two groups in a hierarchical relationship: "most successful planners learned to delegate the mechanics of the annual planning process to juniors and actively participated at the heart of strategic processes" (1980a:203). We believe, however, that organizations differ in their needs—for which planning, plan, and planner roles are most appropriately played in them—and so require different combinations of the two types of planners. It is to this last issue—the context of planning—that we turn here to complete our discussion.

Forms of Organization

Throughout this book, we have repeatedly criticized the "one best way" thinking that has been so prevalent in the management literature in general and the planning literature in particular. Organizations differ, just as do animals; it makes no more sense to prescribe one kind of planning for all organizations than it does to describe one kind of housing for all mammals (bears as well as beavers?). Part of the problem has been the absence of a widely accepted framework within which to discuss different forms of organization. In simple terms, the field of management has no less need for categories of species than does the field of biology.

In earlier work (Mintzberg, 1979a, see also, 1983 and 1989), we proposed a framework of five basic forms of organization, described below (using the labels from Mintzberg, 1989). We shall use this here to consider various postures that planning, plans, and planners might take under different circumstances.

The Machine Organization. Classic bureaucracy, highly formalized, specialized, and centralized, and dependent largely on the standardization of work processes for coordination; common in stable and mature industries with mostly rationalized, repetitive operating work (as in airlines, automobile companies, retail banks).

The Entrepreneurial Organization. Nonelaborated, flexible structure, closely and personally controlled by the chief executive, who coordinates by direct supervision; common in start-up and turnaround situations as well as in small business.

The Professional Organization. Organized to carry out expert work in relatively stable settings, hence emphasizing the standardization of skills and the pigeonholing of services to be carried out by rather autonomous and influential specialists, with the administrators serving for support more than exercising control; common in hospitals, universities, and other skilled and craft services.

The Adhocracy Organization. Organized to carry out expert work in highly dynamic settings, where the experts must work cooperatively in project teams, coordinating the activities by mutual adjustment, in flexible, usually matrix forms of structure; found in "high technology" industries such as aerospace and in project work such as filmmaking, as well as in organizations that have to truncate their more machine-like mature operations in order to concentrate on product development.

The Diversified Organization. Any organization split into semiautonomous divisions to serve a diversity of markets, with the "headquarters" relying on financial control systems to standardize the outputs of the divisions, which tend to take on the machine form (for reasons discussed in Mintzberg, 1979a:384–386).

Strategic Programming in the Machine Organization

Much of our discussion has focused on "conventional" planning and conventional "planners." Here we wish to argue that conventional planning (which we have identified as strategic programming) and conventional planners fit best with the machine form, which, in fact, is itself conventional organization. It would probably not be an exaggeration to claim that the vast majority of everything that has been written about management and organization over the course of this century—from Fayol and Taylor to Ansoff and Porter—has had as its model, usually implicitly, the machine form of organization. With its dominant vertical hierarchy, sharp divisions of labor, concentration on standardization, obsession with control, and, of course, appreciation of staff functions in general and planning in particular, the machine type has always constituted the "one best way " of the management literature, although its presence has usually been no more evident to its proponents than water is to fish.

As we described it in our 1979 book (Chapter 18), the machine form is a highly structured organization, generally with tightly coupled operations that break down its operating work into very fine tasks that can be easily understood and simply executed, without much expertise (as in the typical mass production assembly line). Its environment is generally stable and its industry mature, so that there is little uncertainty. Machine organizations are often large and capital-intensive as well. When we consider the organizations that have been most predisposed to planning, as discussed earlier in Chapter 3, the Air Canadas and many divisions of the General Electrics, the conventional military (especially in peacetime), the French government and its agencies, etc., we find that they tend to conform to all of these conditions, which were also the ones we described for strategic programming earlier in this chapter. In other words, the machine form is the configuration alluded to earlier, the context in which the characteristics associated with planning cluster most naturally.

Even in their functioning, these organizations fit the classic planning model. They tend to have well-developed "technostructures"—staff groups, including an important complement of planners—that are charged with developing the systems of formal planning and control that structure and coordinate everyone else's work. Moreover, machine organizations favor centralized control, with formal power resting at the apex of the hierarchy, where executives are expected to formulate the strategies that everyone else implements. These strategies usually have to be programmed precisely, their vagaries removed by the careful decomposition and specification of precise steps for each employee to execute.

Thus these organizations favor clear, consistent objectives and explicit strategies, and they rely on hard data for decision making, which, in any event, tend to be plentiful in sizable organizations with structured operations that function in stable, mature industries.

Above all, the machine organization, as we described it in our 1979 book, is obsessed with control, first of the workers but everyone else after that, through rules and regulations. No wonder that an attitude of "the system does it" prevails. All this is done to ensure the stability of the operations and the smooth functioning of the bureaucratic machine. Indeed, in their book on *The Neurotic Organization*, Kets de Vries and Miller called this the "compulsive" organization, with planning a prime manifestation of that compulsion:

> The strategy making style of the compulsive firm shows [a] preoccupation with detail and established procedures. First, every move is very carefully planned. There are generally a large number of action plans, budgets, and capital expenditure plans. Each project is very carefully designed, with many checkpoints, exhaustive performance evaluation procedures and extremely detailed schedules. There is often a substantial planning department which has representatives from many areas of functional expertise. (1984:29–30)

Now consider this depiction of the planning process by George Steiner:

> the formal planning system is organized and developed on the basis of a set of procedures. It is explicit in the sense that people know what is going on. Frequently, manuals of instruction are prepared to explain who is going to do what and when and what will happen with the information . . . Support for the decision making in the process is frequently documented and the result of the entire endeavor is a written set of plans. (1979:9)

What other form of organization is implied but the traditional machine?

Configuration implies system in a most integrated sense. There are no dependent and independent variables in a system; everything influences and is influenced by everything else. For example, the machine organization requires stability to function, but it also acts to ensure that stability. Indeed, planning serves it in both respects, since actively it works to impose stability on the operations (and sometimes on the environment as well), while passively it discourages the radical change that upsets the established stability. Thus planning is not an arbitrary component of this configuration but an integral element. The machine form not only *requires* planning (as planning requires the machine form), but planning also *enhances* its very nature, by formalizing its decision processes, encouraging the decomposition of its activities, and reinforcing its centralization of power.

Right- and Left-Handed Planners in the Machine Organization

Given the role of planning (and, therefore, of plans) as devices of communication and control in the machine organization, what about the roles of planners? Clearly, there is an important place for right-handed planners in this context, not only to do much of the strategic programming, but also to carry out strategic analyses of various kinds, especially in consideration of marginal adjustments to the organization's strategic positions (since machine organizations are more inclined to remain within a given strategic perspective than to promote strategic revolution). As Langley pointed out about the machine organization she studied, "the CEO here was well-known for defining in very clear terms exactly what was required in analysis" (1989:619). Further encouragement comes from the availability of hard data in this context and the propensity of the organization to respond to this type of analysis. Periodic industry reviews and the doing of competitive analyses seem well suited to the machine organization.

But is there any place for left-handed planners here, the ones who do more creative and radical analysis, as well as search for emergent strategies and serve as catalysts for novel strategic thinking? On one hand, these roles can be upsetting. Conventional planning is to the machine organization what blinders are to a horse—it keeps it pointed in the desired direction. Peripheral vision can be distracting. Creative planners can play havoc with organizations that know what they must do and need worry only about ensuring that they do it as efficiently as possible.

On the other hand, someone had better worry about change, about forces that can upset the given direction—new technologies, shifting customer tastes, the advent of unforeseen competition, etc.—and about the need for creative strategic response to them. The senior managers may not be so inclined. They, after all, have had to be the guardians of the (hitherto) successful strategic direction, not to mention possibly having been the creators of it. And so such worrying must often fall to left-handed planners, in their catalyst role.

But that is not an easy role to play here, for it necessarily challenges the status quo. It requires a good deal of delicacy: the left-handed planners must work behind the scenes, encouraging a broadening of perspectives while feeding in their ideas and the results of their analyses gently and subtly (as suggested in the earlier citations from the Wack article). Of course, when threats become imminent, so that radical changes must take place quickly, but senior management remains blind to them, then the left-handed planners may have to become more aggressive, broadening their catalyst role, perhaps even to include political behavior (such as taking their case directly to influential outsiders).

Bear in mind, however, that left-handed planners are inclined to see such threats, not only before the managers do, but often before the threats themselves have to be responded to (or, for that matter, even exist!). Machine organizations can happily exploit given strategies and stable conditions for years (our own research suggests decades), long after left-handed planners get restless. Having a clutch of creative planners running loose in an organization that is contentedly pursuing a viable strategy serves no one. Organizational machines, after all, exist to produce products and services efficiently, not to undergo change for its own sake. Left-handed planners can play a key role to signal the need for major change when it becomes necessary; otherwise they might best be kept in a corner of the organization's mind, perhaps developing scenarios and contingency plans for its future.

Strategic Programming Under Other Conditions

We have seen how the set of conditions favoring planning clusters to produce a particular type of organizational configuration. Before we consider the other forms of organization, let us review the conditions opposite to those discussed earlier.

The opposite of a stable environment is a dynamic one—an environment that changes frequently, if not constantly, in an unpredictable (and therefore uncontrollable) fashion. We need not dwell on a point already made at length: formalized planning makes no sense in such an environment. Strategic analysis may make good sense here, at least when conducted flexibly and creatively (by left-handed planners), but not the more inflexible form of planning. To program strategies when reliable forecasts cannot be made is only to impede the organization from being able to react to events as they unfold.

This may help to explain why the OST system eventually ran into difficulty at Texas Instruments, why Jack Welch at General Electric turned so strongly against planning, and why an organization like NASA, despite the need for the intricate coupling of many activities during the Apollo project, tended to plan far less formally and tightly than might have been expected (according to the study by Chandler and Sayles [1971:30–31, 33] to be discussed later). Left-handed planners may be useful in these circumstances— "in turbulent, political, noisy organizational situations planning analysts need to pose and create problems as much as analyze them" (Forrester, 1980/81:597)—but not right-handed planning.

Similarly, an emerging or even a declining industry is far less stable—with the jockeying for position, periodic shake-outs, possibly wild and unpredictable shifts in market growth—than a mature one, and so, for all the reasons given above, a difficult one in which to rely on formal planning. Likewise, the absence of elaborated structure renders planning difficult, since it depends on an established system of decomposed tasks on which to overlay its outputs. And the absence of tightly coupled operations may likewise remove a prime reason to engage in formal planning.

When the operations of an organization are complex instead of simple, meaning that they require the use of skilled experts, planning also runs into difficulty. As we noted earlier, especially with regard to Ashby's law of requisite variety, planning just does not have the sophistication of procedure to be able to program such work. For one thing, much of the critical information can be understood only by the trained experts. Lacking a means to internalize such information, planning systems and often planners themselves risk trivializing the work, for example by counting the publications by faculty members in a university as a surrogate measure for their research output in lieu of being able to judge the quality of research, or by imposing input controls on a research and development facility—working hours, budget categories, operating procedures, and the like—that in fact diminish the quality of the poorly understood outputs.

As for small organizations, we have already discussed the relatively high costs of planning in them and the lack of need for it if the necessary coordination can be effected informally, by mutual adjustment among the workers or direct supervision by the chief. Of course, there may be cases where the other forces override that of size to encourage a relatively small organization to engage in formal planning. There are, indeed, some rather small machine organizations. But for the most part, small size discourages reliance on formal planning. Finally, external control and capital intensity are both facilitating conditions whose presence may encourage planning but whose absence does not discourage it. The incidence of planning will depend on other factors.

With these conclusions in mind, let us now consider planning, plans, and planners in the other forms of organizations.

Strategic Analysis in the Professional Organization

As noted above, the field of planning, in its literature and its manifestations in practice, has generally taken the machine form for granted, and promoted formal planning as the "one best way" for all organizations. Such thinking has therefore spilled over to professional organizations, often with most unfortunate consequences. Thus we have books and articles on the need for formal strategic planning in universities (e.g., Dubé and Brown, 1983; Doyle and Lynch, 1979; Hosmer, 1978); in schools (Kaufman and Herman, 1991); and in hospitals (Peters, 1979; American Hospital Association, 1981). Almost all rely on the conventional assumptions of planning, namely that strategies should emanate from the top of the organization full-blown, that goals can be clearly stated, that the central formulation of strategies must be followed by their pervasive implementation, that the workers (in this case professors, teachers, and doctors, etc.) will (or must) respond to these centrally imposed strategies, and so on. It is almost as if the whole structure were supposed to be shifted to accommodate the needs of planning (as, indeed, governments sometimes seeks to do with public professional institutions).

In fact, these assumptions are wrong, stemming from a misunderstanding of (or an unwillingness to understand) how nonmachine forms of organization must function. The result has been a great deal of waste, trying to fit the square pegs of planning into the round holes of organization. At best, the pegs were damaged—the planners failed, they merely wasted their time. This seems to have been the common result in the universities, which have generally resisted extensive action planning (except, of course, in certain of their machine-like support services, where some of this may be appropriate). But at worst, the holes were damaged—the planners succeeded, and the *organization* wasted its time, possibly becoming dysfunctional in the process. To quote one university dean who probably spoke for many of his colleagues in educational systems, not to mention hospitals, etc.: "I see planning as an expanding bureaucracy, of very little assistance to me but capable of creating several structures of bullshit that I have to cope with" (in Hardy, 1987:72).

The reason for these problems are not difficult to understand, so long as one remains open to forms of organization other than the traditional machine. Universities, hospitals, engineering firms, and the like fit better a configuration called professional, driven by operating work that is highly complex if rather stable in execution. As a result of this one major difference, many of the basic cornerstones of the machine organization, and of right-handed planning, collapse, notably those of top-down control and centralized strategy making. Moreover, professional organizations are notoriously loosely coupled in their operating cores—professors teach and do research in almost complete isolation from one another, especially across different departments, and the same holds true for a good deal of medical practice in hospitals.

The result is a strategy making process almost diametrically opposed to that of the machine organization—and the conventional wisdom. We can summarize here the propositions of a model that we developed in an earlier article on "Strategy Formation in the University Setting" (Hardy et al., 1984). Many actors get involved in the process, including operating professionals, who create many of the key product-market strategies individually by deciding how they will serve their own clients. The direct influence of administrators is often restricted to strategies of support; and together with the operating professionals, they tend to enter into complex, interactive processes of collective choice that take on collegial as well as political colorings. The result is a rather fragmented process of strategy formation, with the organization's strategies typically being the aggregation of all kinds of individual and collective ones. March and his colleagues (e.g., March and Olsen, 1970) were inclined to see these processes as "organized anarchies," taking place in a kind of chaotic "garbage can." But we believe there is more order to them than that. Ironically, the overall strategic orientation of professional organizations seems to remain remarkably stable while individual strategies seem to be in a state of almost continual change.

The stability of the overall strategy may suggest a role for action planning, but the complexity of the professional work and its decentralization to the professional operating employees largely precludes this, or at least restricts it to the nonprofessional work of the support staff or to very broad or peripheral areas of organizational activity (such as the construction of new facilities, or the scheduling of space utilization).

But as Langley made clear in her own research (1986, 1988, 1989), as well as in her contribution to the Hardy et al. paper, strategic analysis has a major role to play in the professional organization, but not in the usual way. That is because much of the analysis is conducted, not by staff planners, but by the professionals themselves, and it is used, not so much for central control and coordination, as in the debate and interplay that make up the collective process of decision making. In other words, the "analysts" tend to be left- as well as right-handed.

> A [university] tenure planning model developed by a planning group reporting to central administration was vigorously "counter-analyzed" by a threatened faculty . . . and then counter-counter-analyzed by the planners. Several iterations took place in full view of the Council of Deans and of top administrators before the issue was resolved by a compromise, which at least in this case was largely in favour of the planners, although it incorporated some of

the faculty's concerns. The point is, however, that even when analysis is initiated by central administrations, it often becomes inextricably linked with the interactive processes of decision making. (Hardy et al., 1984:191)

Such use of analysis is, in fact, consistent with Mitroff's (1972) proposals for "partisan" analysis, in which analysts take sides and challenge each other, thereby drawing out the key arguments. Rondinelli referred to this as "advocacy planning," which "makes no pretense of objectivity," but instead represents "a policy position or the perceptions of a particular 'interested public' " (1976:80). Such analysis can help to expose biases and inconsistencies, and to "smoke out" ideologies (Schlesinger, 1968:298). Thus, Hardy et al. concluded that:

> ... analysis figures prominently in both collegial and political processes ... stimulated by the existence of ambiguous goals and multiple actors. Under ambiguity, there is more to be discovered by analysis, and there are more ways in which issues can be logically structured. And with multiple actors, there is more reason for each to attempt to structure issues in his or her own way in order to direct the thinking of others through the use of rational argument ... (1984:189)

As March and Simon put it, more simple, "bargaining (when it occurs) will frequently be concealed within an analytic framework" (1958:131).

> To summarize, analysis in universities serves more as a means of exerting influence in interactions rather than of resolving issues of its own. It may be used to aid personal understanding for individuals or groups, but it also serves as a means of communication and attention focusing, as a means of legitimizing decisions, as a means of consensus-building, and perhaps most importantly as a means of persuasion. In this way, analysis helps to ensure that what does get decided in fact has some justification in principle. (Hardy et al., 192)

In her doctoral dissertation, Langley (1986) looked carefully at the roles of planning as well as analysis in three organizations—

one professional (a hospital), one machine, and one adhocracy. In the professional organization she described what she called planning as a highly participatory activity carried out in good part by the professionals themselves. It served three purposes. The first was "public relations" (in sharp contrast with the machine organization, which kept its plans highly confidential). The second was informational, for purpose of "self-knowledge and input for strategic visions" (298), in other words, as a form of strategic analysis. And the third was "group therapy: consensus building, communication, and legitimization of strategic vision" (300), apparently with elements of both the catalyst role of planners and the communication role of plans.

Langley noted that hospital strategic plans in her experience amounted to "the concatenation of shopping lists from various medical departments that did not eliminate any possibilities, make any difficult choices, or establish any consistent patterns." This "did not provide a very clear guide for future action" (301). In the hospital studied in depth, she observed that while this phenomenon was present, the effort at persuasion and negotiation by the senior management did give the plan more legitimacy. The plan did "create some kind of focus," especially about which broad areas would be favored for funding (in other words, it served as a form of performance control). "Initiatives still had to come from professionals, but the plans served as a kind of filter to determine which initiatives should be favored and which discouraged" (1988:48). But despite that limited success, planning proved to be "a very blunt instrument for control here as compared with the machine bureaucracy" (303; see also Denis, Langley, and Lozeau, 1991).

Planning and Analysis in the Adhocracy Organization

Adhocracy is project structure, drawing together the complex skills of different experts to deal with a different environment—complex and dynamic. Planning would thus seem to lose out on all counts. Yet some adhocracies do require the intricate coupling of a myriad of tasks, as in NASA's race to put a man on the moon before 1970. The consequence seems to be a very loose form of strategic programming, which outlines broad targets and a set of milestones while leaving considerable flexibility to adapt to the dead ends and creative discoveries along what must remain a largely uncharted route. In a sense, these plans look more like general performance controls than specific action programs, or perhaps more fairly, something in between. To quote Chandler and Sayles, planning in NASA's Apollo project turned out to be

> a rather different function in these large developmental systems where uncertainties predominate. Traditionally, managers are taught to identify their ultimate ends and purposes, set objectives that will help attain these ends, and then develop operational plans. Unfortunately, this comforting and logical sequence gets upset in the real world of large systems. Clear objectives often disguise conflicting purposes reflecting the divergencies among the temporarily allied groups in the federation. . . . Planning turns out to be a dynamic, iterative process. This inevitably disperses authority, since a small group of expert, high-level "planners" cannot define strategy. (1971:7)

Thus, when Loasby wrote that to maintain flexibility, "perhaps the best way for firms to approach formal long-range planning is as something they should try to avoid," he may have been talking above all about adhocracy. "This does not mean as something they should try to dodge: it means so arranging the way they do things that as little as possible needs to be decided in advance" (1967:307).

Left-handed planners, on the other hand, may have more concerted roles to play here. Strategy formation is a most complex and nontraditional process in adhocracy, taking on especially shades of the grass roots model discussed earlier. There is thus great need to have the participants understand it, which highlights the importance of the catalyst role discussed earlier. And because the strategies of adhocracies tend to be rather emergent, the role of finding strategies likewise becomes crucial, again providing opportunities for left-handed planners. Moreover, conditions in adhocracy can be so complex and can change so rapidly that there tends to be an insatiable appetite for strategic analysis, according to Langley (1986), who summarized her findings on the three forms of organization as follows:

The study seems to indicate that different types of organizations may use formal analysis differently, in ways consistent with the nature of the structural configurations. Machine bureaucracies, with their top-down decision-making style, may use analysis most for information and direction and control purposes, to determine the substance of decisions, and to ensure that decisions made at top levels are detailed and implemented. Professional bureaucracies, in which strategic initiatives often come from the bottom up, may require analysis most for communication (direct persuasion) and information (reactive verification) as proposals move toward approval. Finally, in an adhocracy, the wide participation of individuals in decisions and the ambiguity surrounding formal authority may generate even greater uses of formal analysis for communication purposes (especially positioning and direct persuasion). (1989:622)

Creative planners will find no shortage of work in adhocracies. Indeed, we suspect that the truly creative left-handed planners are more likely to find hospitable homes here than in any other form of organization.

Minimal Roles in the Entrepreneurial Organization

Planning, plans, and planners are likely to meet considerable resistance in the entrepreneurial form of organization, which relies on very different means for coordination and control. Here, in the idealized version at least, everything revolves around the chief executive; that person controls activities personally, through direct supervision. Serious planning may get in the leader's way, impeding free movement, as we discussed in the study of the Steinberg supermarket chain and as was evident in the planning school's treatment of managerial intuition. Planners more interested in strategic analysis than formal planning may, however, be able to develop a niche for themselves here, if they can catch the ear of the chief executive. Indeed, the right-handed planner may have the advantage here, since the leader typically needs his or her intuition tempered by more systematic consideration of issues. But doing that analysis may not be easy, given the concentration of so much critical information in the leader's head, in addition to his or her inclination to move opportunistically.

As for the planner's other roles, the leaders of most entrepreneurial organizations do not relish someone telling them how to make strategy; the process tends to be locked into their own (subconscious) minds in any event. And they have little need for anyone to help them find strategies, since these are unlikely to develop outside of their own personal control. In any event, good intuitive leaders generally do this far better than staff people, particularly in these typically small, simple, and flexible organizations. Of course, as the entrepreneurial organization grows, settles down, and begins to take on the machine form, the visionary strategy of the leader may have to be pinned down through strategic programming, and so the influence of the planners may have to increase accordingly.

Performance Control in the Diversified Organization

Finally, we come to the diversified organization. As described in our earlier writings, this tends to be an elaborated version of the machine form. As the latter grows large, saturates its traditional markets, and looks elsewhere for expansion, typically it diversifies its product-market strategies and then divisionalizes its structures—splits itself into individual units, each dedicated to one of those strategies. Thus, while the coupling may be tight within divisions (as in machines), it tends to be loose across them.

Key to the diversified organization is the relationship between headquarters and the divisions. The former must exercise some kind of control, usually with regard to financing and performance, but loose enough to allow the divisions to manage their own businesses. The obvious solution is the imposition of objectives and budgets—in other words, use of systems of performance control. Thus the headquarters here tends to rely on planning not so much to program strategy per se as to effect financial control, although techniques such as the Boston Consulting Group's growth share matrix and capital budgeting do introduce a measure of the former as well. Of course, as discussed earlier, such external controls can have the effect of encouraging strategic programming within the divisions. So it is presumably not coincidental that a great deal of the popularity of "strategic planning" in American business developed in these very same diversified corporations.

But a little knowledge can be a dangerous thing, as the saying goes, and the more a headquarters distant from the running of a particular business tries to program its strategy, or encourage it to do the same thing for the wrong reasons, even to try to use directly the other roles of planners itself (especially strategic analysis), the more it may undermine the division's very effectiveness (as seems to have been the experience with the growth share matrix, now apparently largely a tool of the past). There may be a bit of a role for headquarters' planners as catalysts, to convey knowledge about the strategy process, but otherwise the roles seem logically left to planners within the divisions themselves.

Planning Under Politics and Culture

In a book on power (Mintzberg, 1983) that followed the one on the structural types, we added two more configurations to the initial five, discussed above. One we later came to call the *political* organization, the other the *ideological* organization (Mintzberg, 1989). The former is essentially captured by politics, while the latter is dominated by a powerful culture, which we prefer to call an ideology. It may be worth considering briefly here the propensity of each to engage in planning and to engage planners.

Within a context of intense politics, formal planning would seem logically to diminish. Here the assumptions of conventional planning—for example, that strategy emanates from legitimate authority at the top of a hierarchy, that goals can be agreed upon, and that courses of action can cascade down a well-ordered hierarchy—fail, and different means must be found to make decisions and evoke actions. For example, under what van Gunsteren called orthodox planning, "no politics at the level of implementation! Implementation of the plan should be neutral, apolitical, obedient" (1976:26). Otherwise it cannot happen. Accordingly, there is an important literature of public policy making which characterizes it as highly fragmented and politicized and so has been very critical of planning, promoting instead adaptive modes of policy making based on the informal mutual adjustments among a variety of independent actors (e.g., Lindblom, 1965, 1968; and Braybrooke and Lindblom, 1963; as well as van Gunsteren, not to mention the occasional earlier reference to Wildavsky!).

Of course, planners may be present in the political context too. They are, after all, common throughout government, while in business the established planners do not disappear just because political infighting has taken over. Some planners simply leap into the fray, using strategic analyses to protect and promote their own interests (as we discussed in Chapter 4). Those who try to stay neutral may be gobbled up by one side (or all), or else may be shunted off to a side: it is difficult to remain neutral under conditions of intense politics. (That planners can rise above the fray and do some kind of objective "stakeholder analysis" is, in our opinion and as we discussed in Chapter 3, sheer nonsense.) But overtly partisan analysis can hardly be considered regular work for planners either (except when they formally represent one particular side). As we concluded in Chapter 4, there are times, especially during severe change, when disruptive politics can be more functional for organizations than orderly planning.

Organizations with strong cultures, rooted in distinctive histories, tend to elicit strong commitment from their people, and so—to reintroduce the point about calculation versus commitment raised in Chapter 4—to diminish their propensity to accept the calculative nature of planning. Formal planning may seem excessively impersonal and technocratic in such ideological organizations, which prefer to rely for coordination on the standardization of norms through socialization and indoctrination (Mintzberg, 1983:Chapters 11 and 21). Even left-handed planners may have a difficult time here, since these organizations tend to discourage the divisions of labor that put staff planners on one side and line operators (let alone managers) on the other. This should be especially true of planners whose conclusions diverge from the accepted norms of the ideology!

To many people, the Japanese enterprise epitomizes the ideological organization, at least in the context of business. Consider, then, some evidence on its planning. Hayashi found that most of the Japanese firms he studied "had only strategic objectives and no explicit action programs"; "there was a lack of planning and forecasting technology"; and they "distrust[ed] corporate planning in general" (1978:221, 222). "One planning officer said that corporate planning at his company consisted of identifying major problems and of creating an atmosphere conducive to the development of creative ideas and hard work within the company" (217).

Writing initially in Japanese for a Japanese audience, Ohmae concluded that "most large U.S. corporations are run like the Soviet economy," with their emphasis on central plans and the details with which these spell out expectations for managers' actions. In his view, this is "a remarkably effective way of killing creativity and entrepreneurship at the extremities of the organization" (1982:224). In contrast, he described the Japanese firm as "less planned, less rigid, but more vision- and mission-driven than the Western organizations" (225), all indications of its ideological orientation.

Planning in Different Cultures

As a final point, let us consider the effect of national culture on the propensity to engage in planning, since there is evidence that some nations are more inclined to favor it than others, perhaps because of a predisposition to certain related forms of organization.

We have just discussed the example of the Japanese enterprises which, by favoring strong internal culture, seem to discourage action planning somewhat. It is interesting that Ohmae, in the passage quoted above, while associating Japanese firms with less action planning, also associated both the Soviet government and American business with more of it. We might have expected this of the defunct Communist regimes, whose political system was predicated on such planning. We might even have expected this of the French, who have long had their love affair with the Cartesian form of thought, or of the Germans and Swiss, given their preference for orderly structure. But why would this be so in the case of the pragmatic Americans, with a political ideology that is ostensibly so opposed to central planning?

That the relationship exists is hardly open to question: our discussion has made that quite clear. America is where the planning school first took root and grew: it is where the General Electrics and the Texas Instruments led the way with action planning, where ITT led the way with performance control, where the federal government led the way with PPBS. It is America that has generated the vast majority of the vast planning literature, America that has given birth to the huge planning societies, America that has spawned most of the strategy consulting boutiques.

In an international study, Steiner and Schollhammer (1975) found planning to be most common and most formalized in the United States, followed closely by England, Canada, and Australia, with Japan and Italy at the other end of the scale (Italy, perhaps, discouraged by its pervasive politics as well as its high incidence of entrepreneurial firms). Thus the propensity seems to be not just American but Anglo-Saxon, although the Americans have certainly been in the lead.[21]

How to explain this? Perhaps it is a reflection of the American (and general Anglo-Saxon) love affair with "professional management," itself perhaps reflecting an obsession with control—to bring under our control as people, at first things physical, later things social, and finally each other. Or perhaps the attention to planning simply reflects the quest for ways to manage the giant organizations that America has spawned by other means (namely entrepreneurial initiative). In other words, planning may represent the effort to exploit size through the systematic programming of strategy (a conclusion consistent with Chandler's [1962 and 1977] analysis of the evolution of the large American enterprise). If so, we believe—and have argued throughout this book—that it has been a failed effort, and a terribly costly one (whose full effect, in our view, has yet to be felt).

———————

To conclude this book, our discussion has made clear that "strategic planning" did not work, that the form (the "rationality" of planning) did not conform to the function (the needs of strategy making). Planning never was any "one best way." But reconceived as strategic programming, it can sometimes be a good way. It does

———————

[21] Al-Bazzaz and Grinyer (1981:163) also found the Swiss to be up there with the Americans, ahead of the British. Rieger (1986) also discussed "fatalism" as a factor that discourages planning in some cultures, such as the Hindu and the Islamic.

have an important role to play in organizations, as do plans and planners, when matched with the appropriate contexts. Too much planning may lead us to chaos, but so too would too little, and more directly.

We have learned a great deal in this wide-ranging discussion. Several decades of experience with strategic planning has taught us about the need to loosen up the process of strategy formation rather than try to seal it off through arbitrary formalization. Through all the false starts and excessive rhetoric, we have certainly learned what planning is not and what it cannot do. But we have also learned what planning is and can do, and perhaps of greater use, what planners themselves can do beyond planning. We have also learned about our need to solidify our descriptive understanding of complex phenomena—and to face up to our ignorance of them—before we leap into prescription. Only when we recognize our fantasies can we begin to appreciate the wonders of reality. And, ironically, our experiences with strategic planning have helped us to develop some of that understanding, even if inadvertently. Which is to conclude that this long exercise has had its benefits, both planned and unplanned.

References

Abell, D. F. "Strategic Windows." *Journal of Marketing* (July 1978:21–26).

Abell, D. F., and Hammond, J. S. *Strategic Market Planning* (Englewood Cliffs, NJ: Prentice-Hall, 1979).

Abernathy, W. J., and Utterback, J. M. "Innovation Over Time: Patterns of Industrial Innovation." *Technology Review* (June/July 1978).

Ackerman, R. W. Role of the Corporate Planning Executive (working paper, Graduate School of Business Administration, Harvard University, 1972).

———. *The Social Challenge to Business* (Cambridge, MA: Harvard University Press, 1975).

Ackoff, R. L. *A Concept of Corporate Planning* (New York: Wiley, 1970).

———. "Science in the Systems Age: Beyond IE, OR, and MS." *Operations Research* (XXI, 1973:661–671).

———. "Beyond Prediction and Preparation." *Journal of Management Studies* (XX, 1[January], 1983:59–69).

Aguilar, F. J. *Scanning the Business Environment* (New York: Macmillan, 1967).

Al-Bazzaz, S. J., and Grinyer, P. H. "Corporate Planning in the U.K.: The State of the Art in the 70s." *Strategic Management Journal* (II, 1981:155–168).

———. "How Planning Works in Practice: A Survey of 48 U.K. Companies." In D. E. Hussey, ed., *The Truth About Corporate Planning* (Oxford: Pergamon Press, 1983:211–236).

Allaire, Y., and Firsirotu, M. "Theories of Organizational Culture." *Organizational Studies* (V, 3, 1984:193–226).

———. Shaping the Firm's Destiny: Strategic Thinking and Planning for the Modern Corporation (working paper, Université du Québec à Montréal, January 1988).

———. "Coping with Strategic Uncertainty." *Sloan Management Review* (XXX, 3, Spring 1989:7–16).

———. "Strategic Plans as Contracts." *Long Range Planning* (23, 1, 1990:102–115).

Allen, M. G. "Diagramming GE'S Planning for What's Watt." *Planning Review* (V, 5[September], 1977:3–9).

———. "Strategic Management Hits Its Stride." *Planning Review* (September 1985:6–9, 45).

Allio, R. J. "GE = Giant Entrepreneur?" (Interview with GE planner M. A. Carpenter) *Planning Review* (January 1985:18–21, 46).

———. "Forecasting: The Myth of Control." *Planning Review* (May 1986:6–11).

Allison, G. T. *Essence of Decision: Explaining the Cuban Missile Crisis* (Boston, MA: Little, Brown, 1971).

American Hospital Association, Department of Hospital Planning and Society for Hospital Planning. *Compendium of Resources for Strategic Planning in Hospitals* (Chicago, IL: 1981).

Andrews, F. "Management: How A Boss Works in Calculated Chaos." *The New York Times* (October 29, 1976).

Andrews, K. R. *The Concept of Corporate Strategy* (Homewood, IL.: Irwin, editions 1971, 1980, 1987).

Ansoff, H. I. "A Quasi-Analytical Approach of the Business Strategy Problem." *Management Technology* (IV, 1[June], 1964:67–77).

———. *Corporate Strategy* (New York: McGraw-Hill, 1965).

———. The Evolution of Corporate Planning (working paper, Reprint #342, Graduate School of Industrial Administration, Carnegie-Mellon University, 1967).

———. "Managing Strategic Surprise by Response to Weak Signals." *California Management Review* (XVIII, 2, Winter 1975a:21–33).

———. An Applied Managerial Theory of Strategy Behavior (working paper, European Institute for Advanced Studies in Management, Brussels, 1975b).

———. "The State of Practice in Planning Systems." *Sloan Management Review* (Winter 1977:1–24).

———. *Strategic Management* (London: Macmillan, 1979a).

———. The Changing Shape of the Strategic Problem (working paper, European Institute for Advanced Studies in Management, Brussels, 1979b).

———. *Implanting Strategic Management* (Englewood Cliffs, NJ: Prentice-Hall, 1984).

———. "The Emerging Paradigm of Strategic Behavior." *Strategic Management Journal* (VIII, 1987:501–515).

———. *The New Corporate Strategy* (New York: Wiley, 1988).

Ansoff, H. I., and Brandenburg, R. C. "A Program of Research in Business Planning." *Management Science* (XIII, 6, 1967:B219–B239).

Ansoff, H. I., and Hayes, R. L. From Strategic Planning to Strategic Management, Management Under Discontinuity. (Proceedings from a conference at INSEAD, Fontainebleau, 1975.)

Ansoff, H. I., Avner, J., Brandenburg, R. C., Portner, F. E., and Radosevich, R. "Does Planning Pay? The Effect of Planning on Success of Acquisitions in American Firms." *Long Range Planning* (III, 2[December], 1970:2–7).

Ansoff, H. I., Eppink, J., and Gomer, H. Management of Strategic Surprise and Discontinuity: Problem of Managerial Decisiveness (working paper, European Institute for Advanced Studies in Management, Brussels, 1975).

Anthony, R. N. *Planning and Control Systems: A Framework for Analysis* (Division of Research, Graduate School of Business Administration, Harvard University, 1965).

Armstrong, J. S. "The Value of Formal Planning for Strategic Decisions: Review of Empirical Research." *Strategic Management Journal* (III, 1982:197–211).

Barnard, C. I. *Organization and Management: Selected Papers* (Cambridge, MA: Harvard University Press, 1948).

Barreyre, P. Y. "The Management of Innovation in Small and Medium-Sized Industries." *International Studies of Management and Organization* (Fall/Winter 1977/1978:76–98).

Bartlett, F. C. *Remembering* (Cambridge: The University Press, 1932).

Bass, B. M. "When Planning for Others." *Journal of Applied Behavioral Science* (VI, 2[April/May/June], 1970:151–171).

Baughman, J. P. Problems and Performance of the Role of Chief Executive in the General Electric Company, 1882–1974 (working paper, Graduate School of Business Administration Harvard University, 1974).

Baum, H. S. *Planners and Public Expectations* (Cambridge, MA: Schenkman, 1983).

Bello, F. "The Magic that Made Polaroid." *Fortune* (April 1959:124–164).

Bennett, R. C., and Cooper, R. G. "The Misuse of Marketing: An American Tragedy." *Business Horizons* (November–December 1981:51–61).

Benningson, L. A., and Schwartz, H. M. *Implementing Strategy: The CEO's Change Agenda* (The MAC Group, Boston, 1985).

Benveniste, A. *The Politics of Expertise* (Berkeley, CA: Glendessary Press, 1972:105–118).

Berg, N. "Strategic Planning in Conglomerate Companies." *Harvard Business Review* (May/June 1965:79–92).

Berle, A. A., Jr., and Means, G. C. *The Modern Corporation and Private Property*, rev. ed. (New York: Harcourt, Brace, 1968).

Blass, W. P. "Optimizing the Corporate Planning Function." In *The Strategic Management Handbook*, K. J. Albert, ed. (New York: McGraw-Hill, 1983:Chapter 6).

Bolan, R. S. "Mapping the Planning Theory Terrain." In O. R. Godschalk, ed., *Planning in America: Learning from Turbulence* (American Institute of Planners, 1974:13–34).

Boston Consulting Group Inc. (The) *The Experience Curve Reviewed: IV, The Growth Share Matrix or the Product Portfolio* (pamphlet, 1973).

Bourgeois, L. J., III. "Strategy and Environment: A Conceptual Integration." *Academy of Management Review* (V, 1, 1980a:25–39).

————. "Performance and Consensus." *Strategic Management Journal* (I, 1980b:227–248).

Bourgeois, L. J., III, and Brodwin, D. R. "Strategic Implementation: Five Approaches to an Elusive Phenomenon." *Strategic Management Journal* (5, 1984:241–264).

Bower, J. L. *Managing the Resource Allocation Process: A Study of Planning and Investment* (Boston: Graduate School of Business Administration, Harvard University, 1970a).

————. "Planning Within the Firm." *The American Economic Review, Papers and Proceedings* (1970b:186–194).

Boyd, B. K. "Strategic Planning and Financial Performance: A Meta-Analytical Review." *Journal of Management Studies* (XXVIII, 4[July], 1991:353–374).

Bracker, J. S., and Pearson, J. N. "Planning and Financial Performance of

Small, Mature Firms." *Strategic Management Journal* (VII, 1986:503–522).

Bracker, J. S., Barbara, K. W., and Pearson, J. N. "Planning and Financial Performance Among Small Firms in a Growth Industry." *Strategic Management Journal* (IX, 1988:591–603).

Braybrooke, D., and Lindblom, C. E. *A Strategy of Decision* (New York: Free Press, 1963).

Bresser, R. K., and Bishop, R. C. "Dysfunctional Effects of Formal Planning: Two Theoretical Explanations." *Academy of Management Review* (VIII, 4, 1983:588–599).

Broms, H., and Gahmberg, H. *Semiotics of Management* (Helsinki School of Economics, 1987).

Brunsson, N. *Propensity To Change: An Empirical Study of Decisions on Reorientations* (Goteborg, BAS, 1976).

———. "The Irrationality of Action and the Action Rationality: Decisions, Ideologies, and Organizational Actions." *Journal of Management Studies* (1, 1982:29–44).

Bryson, J. M. *Strategic Planning for Public and Nonprofit Organizations* (San Francisco: Jossey-Bass, 1988).

Bryson, J. M., and Einsweiler, R. C. Introduction. *Journal of the American Planning Association* (LIII, 1[Winter], 1987:6–8).

Bryson, J. M., and Roering, W. D. "Applying Private-Sector Strategic Planning in the Public Sector." *Journal of the American Planning Association* (LIII, 1[Winter], 1987:9–22).

Bunge, M. *Intuition and Science* (Westport, CT: Greenwood Press, 1975, © 1972).

Burgelman, R. A. "A Process Model of Internal Corporate Venturing in the Diversified Major Firm." *Administrative Science Quarterly* (XXVIII, 1983a:223–244).

———. "A Model of the Interaction of Strategic Behavior, Corporate Context, and the Concept of Strategy." *Academy of Management Review* (VIII, 1, 1983b:61–70).

———. "Corporate Entrepreneurship and Strategic Management: Insights from a Process Study" *Management Science* (XXIX, 12, 1983c:1349–1364).

———. Action and Cognition in Strategy-Making: Findings on the Interplay of Process and Content in Internal Corporate Ventures (working paper, #703, Graduate School of Business, Stanford University, 1984a).

———. Managing the Internal Corporate Venturing Process: Some Recommendations for Practice (working paper, Graduate School of Business, Stanford University, 1984b).

———. "Strategy Making as a Social Learning Process: The Case of Internal Corporate Venturing." *Interfaces* (18:3, May-June 1988:74–85).

Business Week. Texas Instruments Cleans up its Act (September 19, 1983:56–64).

———. The New Breed of Strategic Planner (September 17, 1984a:62–66, 68).

———. TI: Shot Full of Holes and Trying to Recover (November 5, 1984b:82–83).

Camillus, J. C. "Corporate Strategy and Executive Action: Transition Stages and Linkage Dimensions." *Academy of Management Review"* (VI, 2, 1981:253–259).

Cannon, J. T. *Business Strategy and Policy* (New York: Harcourt, Brace, 1968).

Capon, N., and Spogli, J. R. "Strategic Marketing Planning: A Comparison and Critical Examination of Two Contemporary Approaches." In A. J. Rowe, R. O. Mason, K. E. Dickel (eds.), *Strategic Management and Business Policy: A Methodological Approach* (Reading, MA: Addison-Wesley, 1982:165–171).

Caropreso, F., ed. Getting Value from Strategic Planning; Highlights of a Conference (New York, The Conference Board, 1988).

Carrance, F. "Les Outils de Planification Stratégique au Concrèt (Paris, Thèse de Doctorat, Centre de Recherche en Gestion, Ecole Polytechnique, 1986).

Chakraborty, S., and David, G. S. "Why Managers Avoid Planning." *Planning Review* (May 1979:17–35).

Chakravarthy, B. S. "Adaptation: A Promising Metaphor for Strategic Management." *Academy of Management Review* (VII, 1, 1982:35–44).

———. "On Tailoring a Strategic Planning System to its Context: Some Empirical Evidence." *Strategic Management Journal* (8, 1987:517–534).

Chamberlain, N. W. *Enterprise and Environment* (New York: McGraw-Hill, 1968).

Chandler, A. D., Jr. *Strategy and Structure: Chapter in the History of the Industrial Enterprise* (Cambridge, MA: MIT Press, 1962).

———. *The Visible Hand* (Cambridge, MA: The Belknap Press of Harvard University Press, 1977).

Chandler, A. D., Jr., and Sayles, L. R. *Managing Large Systems* (New York: Harper & Row, 1971).

Channon, D. F. *Business Strategy and Policy* (New York: Harcourt, Brace and World, 1968).

———. "Prediction and Practice in Multinational Strategic Planning." *Long Range Planning* (IX, 2[April], 1976:50–57).

———. "Commentary." In D. E. Schendel and C. W. Hofer, eds., *Strategic Management* (Boston: Little, Brown, 1979:122-133).

Chapman, R. B., Gabrielli, R. J. "Army Planning, Programming and Budgeting." In R. L. Cook, ed., *Army Command and Management: Theory and Practice, Volume II* (Carlisle Barracks, PA: US Army War College, 1976–1977: Chapter 12).

Cho, Y. H. Response to Peter May. *Public Administration Review* (March–April 1989:212).

Christensen, C. R., Andrews, K. R., Bower, J. L., Hamermesh, G., and Porter, M. E. *Business Policy: Text and Cases* Fifth edition (Homewood, IL.: Irwin, 1982).

Churchman, C. W. *The Systems Approach* (New York: Delacorte Press, 1968).

Clark, D. L. "In Consideration of Goal-Free Planning: The Failure of Traditional Planning Systems in Education." In D. L. Clark, Sue McKibbin, M. Malkas, eds. *New Perspectives on Planning in Educational Organizations* (Far West Laboratory, 1980).

Clausewitz, C. von. *On War*, Revised Edition, Volume I, II, III, Translated by
    J. J. Graham (London: Routledge and Kegan Paul, 1966).
Coffey, W. *303 of the World's Worst Predictions* (NY: Tribeca, 1983).
Cohen, M. D., and March, J. G. "Decisions, Presidents, and Status." In J. G.
    March and J. P. Olsen, eds., *Ambiguity and Choice in Organizations*
    (Bergen, Norway: Universitetsforlaget, 1976).
Cohen, S. M. "For G.E., Planning Crowned with Success" (interview with GE
    planner, W. E. Rothschild). *Planning Review* (March 1982:8–11).
Cohen, S. S. *Modern Capitalist Planning: The French Model* (Berkeley, CA: Uni-
    versity of California Press, 1977).
Collier, D. "How to Implement Strategic Plans." *Journal of Business Strategy*
    (Winter 1984:92–96).
Collier, J. R. *Effective Long Range Business Planning* (Englewood Cliffs, NJ:
    Prentice-Hall, 1968).
Cooper, C. L. "Policy Planning—National and Foreign." In *Commission on the
    Organization of the Government for the Conduct of Foreign Policy, Volume
    2, Appendix F* (United States Government Printing Office, June
    1975:228–233).
Corpio, D., Cohen, B., Elred, J., Gangavane, V., Greiner, J., Hall, J., Jayaraman,
    L. L., Joylekar, P., Levine, R., Noad, A., Prasow, S., Sagasti, F., and
    Smith, F. "A Student Appraisal of the Proposed Guidelines for Op-
    erations Research." *Management Science* (18, 1972:B618–B625).
Curtis, C. P., and Greenslet, F. *The Practical Cogitator* (Boston, MA: Houghton
    Mifflin, 1945).
Cyert, R. M., and March, J. G. *A Behavioral Theory of the Firm* (Englewood
    Cliffs, NJ: Prentice-Hall, 1963).
Davidson, D. "Dirty Hands and the Ivory Tower." *Interfaces* (7, 1977:31–33).
Davis, K. "Management Comments and the Grapevine." *Harvard Business
    Review* (September/October 1953:43–49).
de Geus, A. P. "Planning as Learning." *Harvard Business Review* (March/
    April 1988:70–74).
De Monthoux, P. G. "Modernism and the Dominating Firm" (paper prepared
    for Young and Rubicam seminar, Convergences et divergences cul-
    turelles en Europe, Paris, 1989).
de Montigny, J. Review of Speech by Harold Lardner, "Organizations and
    Misdirections." *Bulletin of the Canadian Operational Research Society*
    (1972:5).
Denis, J-L., Langley, A., and Lozeau D., "Formal Strategy in Hospitals," *Long
    Range Planning* (XXIV, 1, 1991:71–82).
Denning, B. W. "Strategic Environmental Appraisal." *Long Range Planning* (6,
    1, March, 1973:22–27).
Denning, B. W., and Lehr, M. E. "The Extent and Nature of Corporate Long-
    Range Planning in the United Kingdom II." *The Journal of Manage-
    ment Studies* (IX, 1, 1972:1–18).
deVillafranca, J. Patterns in Strategic Change: The Evolutionary Model Ver-
    sus the Revolutionary Model (Ph.D. Management Policy course pa-
    per, McGill University, 1983a).

————. Review and Comparison: Corporate Planning: An Executive Viewpoint by P. Lorange and Challenging Strategic Planning Assumptions by R. O. Mason and J. J. Mitroff (Ph.D. Management Policy course paper, McGill University, 1983b).

Devons, E. *Papers on Planning and Economics Management,* Sir Alec Cairncross, ed. (Manchester: Manchester University Press, 1970).

————. *Planning in Practice, Essays in Aircraft Planning in War-Time* (Cambridge: The University Press, 1950).

Dill, W. R. "Commentary." In D. E. Schendel and C. W. Hofer, eds., *Strategic Management: A New View of Business Policy and Planning* (Boston, MA: Little, Brown, 1979).

Dimma, W. A. "Competitive Strategic Planning." *Business Quarterly* (50, 1 [Spring], 1985:22–26).

Dionne, J. "Creativity, Planning, and Running a Business." In F. Caropreso, *Getting Value from Strategic Planning: Highlights of a Conference* (New York: The Conference Board, 1988).

Dirsmith, M. W., Jablonsky, S. F., and Luzi, A. D. "Planning and Control in the U.S. Federal Government: A Critical Analysis of PPB, MBO, and ZBB." *Strategic Management Journal* (I, 1980:303–329).

Doktor, R. H. "Problem Solving Styles of Executives and Management Scientists." *TIMS Studies in the Management Sciences* (VIII, 1978:123–134).

Doktor, R. H., and Bloom, D. M. "Selective Lateralization of Cognitive Style Related to Occupation as Determined by EEG Alpha Asymmetry." *Psychophysiology* (1977:385–387).

Doktor, R. H., and Hamilton, W. F. "Cognitive Style and the Acceptance of Management Science Recommendations." *Management Science* (XIX, 8[April], 1973:884–894).

Donnelly, J. H., Gibson, J. L., and Ivancevich, J. M. *Fundamentals of Management, Functions-Behavior-Models* 4th edition (Plano, TX: BPI, 1981).

Doyle, P., and Lynch, J. E. "A Strategic Model for University Planning." *Journal of Operational Research* (XXX, 1979:603–609).

Dror, Y. *Ventures in Policy Sciences* (New York: American Elsevier, 1971).

Drucker, P. F. "Long-Range Planning." *Management Science* (April 1959:238–249).

————. *Management: Tasks, Responsibilities, and Practices* (New York: Harper & Row, 1973).

Dubé, C. The Department of National Defence and the Defence Strategies from 1945 to 1970 (MBA Thesis, McGill University, 1973).

Dube, C. S., and Brown, A. W. "Strategic Assessment: A Rational Response to University Cutbacks. *Long-Range Planning* (XVI, 1983:105–113).

Duffy, M. F. "ZBB, MBO, PPB and Their Effectivenss Within the Planning/Marketing Process." *Strategic Management Journal* (X, 1989:163–173).

Durand, T. Strategic Planning In French Industry (working paper, Ecole centrale de Paris, 1984).

Dyson, K. H. F. "Improving Policy-making in Bonn: Why the Central Planners Failed." *The Journal of Management Studies* (May 1975:157–174).

Edelman, F. "Four Ways to Oblivion — A Short Course in Survival." *Interfaces* (II, 4[August] 1972:14–17).

Eigerman, M. R. "Who Should Be Responsible for Business Strategy?" *The Journal of Business Strategy* (November/December 1988:40–44).

Ekman, B. "The Impact of the Environment of Planning Technology." In E. Shlefer, ed. *Proceedings of the XX International Meeting* (The Institute of Management Sciences, Tel Aviv, Israel: Jerusalem Academic Press, 1972).

Emery, F. E., and Trist, E. L. "The Causal Texture of Organizational Environments." *Human Relations* (XVIII, 1965:21–32).

Emshoff, J. R. "Planning the Process of Improving the Planning Process: A Case Study in Meta-Planning." *Management Science* (XXIV, 11[July], 1978:1095–1108).

Emshoff, J. R., and Freeman, R. E. "Who's Butting Into Your Business?" *Wharton Magazine* (IV, Fall 1979:44–59).

Engledow, J. L., and Lenz, R. T. The Evolution of Environmental Analysis Units in Ten Leading Edge Firms (working paper, Strategy Research Center, Graduate School of Business, Columbia University, New York, 1984).

———. "Whatever Happened to Environmental Analysis?" *Long Range Planning* (XVIII, 2, 1985:93–106).

Enthoven, A. C. Annex A in D. Novick's "Long-Range Planning Through Program Budgeting." In E. Jantsch, ed., *Perspectives of Planning* (Paris: OECD, 1969a:271–284).

———. "Analysis, Judgment and Computers: Their Use in Complex Problems." *Business Horizons* (XII, 4[August], 1969b:29–36).

Fahey, L. "On Strategic Management Decision Processes." *Strategic Management Journal* (2, 1981:43–60).

Fahey, L. "Review of *The New Corporate Strategy* by H. I. Ansoff." *Academy of Management Review* XIV, 3, 1989:459–460.

Fahey, L., King, W. R., and Narayanan, V. K. "Environment Scanning and Forecasting in Strategic Planning—The State of the Art." *Long Range Planning* (XIV, February, 1981:32–38).

Fayol, H. *General and Industrial Management* (London: Pitman, 1949:43–53; first published in 1916).

Feld, M. D. "Information and Authority: The Structure of Military Organization." *American Sociological Review* (XXIV, 1, 1959:15–22).

Fincher, J. *Human Intelligence* (New York: Putnam's, 1976).

Forbes magazine, Edwin Land, "People Should Want More out of Life . . ." (June 1, 1975: 50).

Forrester, J. W. *Industrial Dynamics* (Cambridge, MA: MIT Press, 1961).

———. "Reflections on the Bellagio Conference." In E. Jantsch, ed., *Perspectives of Planning* (Paris: OECD, 1969a:503–510).

———. "Planning Under the Dynamic Influences of Complex Social Systems." In E. Jantsch, ed., *Perspectives of Planning* (Paris: OECD, 1969b, 237–254).

———. *Urban Dynamics* (Cambridge, MA: MIT Press, 1969c).

————. *World Dynamics* (Wright-Allen Press, 1973).

————. "The Counter-Intuitive Behavior of Social Systems." In *Collective Papers of J. W. Forrester* (Cambridge, MA: Wright-Allen Press, 1975).

————. "What Do Planning Analysts Do? Planning and Policy Analysis as Organizing." *Policy Studies Journal* (Special Issue 2, 1980/81:595–604).

Foster, M. J. "The Value of Formal Planning for Strategic Decisions: A Comment." *Strategic Management Journal* (VII, 1986:179–182).

Franklin, S. G., Rue, L. W., Boulton, W. R., and Lindsay, W. M. "A Grass Roots Look at Corporate Long-Range Planning Practices." *Managerial Planning* (May/June 1981:13–18).

Fredrickson, J. W. "The Comprehensiveness of Strategic Decision Processes: Extension, Observations, Future Directions." *Academy of Management Journal* (September 1984: 445–466).

Fredrickson, J. W., and Mitchell, T. R. "Strategic Decision Processes: Comprehensiveness and Performance in an Industry within an Unstable Environment." *Academy of Management Journal* (XXVII, 1984:399–423).

Freeman, R. E. *Strategic Management: A Stakeholder Approach* (London: Pitman, 1984).

French, R. *How Ottawa Decides: Planning and Industrial Policy-Making 1968–1980* (Toronto: J. Lorimer, 1980).

Friedman, J. "A Conceptual Model for the Analysis of Planning Behavior." *Administration Science Quarterly* (XII, 1967–68:225–252).

Fulmer, R. M., and Rue, L. W. "The Practice and Profitability of Long-Range Planning." *Managerial Planning* (1974:1–7).

Galbraith, J. K. *The New Industrial State* (Boston, MA: Houghton Mifflin, 1967).

Galbraith, J. R., and Nathanson, D. A. *Strategy Implementation: The Role of Structure and Process* (St. Paul, MN: West, 1978).

George, C. *The History of Management Thought* (Englewood Cliffs, NJ: Prentice-Hall, 1972).

Gershefski, G. W. "Corporate Planning Models—The State of the Art." *Managerial Planning* (1969:31–35).

Ghoshal, S., and Westney, D. E. "Organizing Competitor Analysis Systems." *Strategic Management Journal* (12, 1991:17–31).

Gilmore, F. F. *Formulation and Advocacy of Business Policy* (Ithaca, NY: Cornell University, 1970, 1st edition 1968).

Gilmore, F. F., and Brandenburg, R. G. "Anatomy of Corporate Planning." *Harvard Business Review* (November/December 1962:61–69).

Gimpl, M. L., and Dakin, S. R. "Management and Magic." *California Management Review* (Fall 1984:125–136).

Ginter, P. M., Rucks, A. C., and Duncan, W. J. "Planners' Perceptions of the Strategic Management Process." *Journal of Management Studies* (XXII, 1985:581–596).

Gluck, F. W., Kaufman, S. P., and Walleck, A. S. "Strategic Management for Competitive Advantage." *Harvard Business Review* (July/August 1980:154–161).

Glueck, W. F. *Business Policy: Strategy Formation and Management Action* (New York: McGraw-Hill, 1976).

Gluntz, P. The Introduction of Corporate Planning as a Cultural Change (working paper, CFSM, August 1971).

Glynn, L. "An Embattled General Sues for Peace." *Maclean's* (March 4, 1985:48).

Godet, M. *Scenarios and Strategic Management* (London: Butterworths, 1987).

Gomer, H. Corporate Planning in Action (doctorate paper, Institut d'Administration des Enterprises, Université de Grenoble, 1973).

———. L'Utilization des systèmes formèls de planification d'entreprise face à la "Crise Petrolière" (Thèse doctorat troisième cycle, Institut d'Administration des Entreprises, Université de Grenoble, 1974).

———. The Functions of Formal Planning Systems in Response to Sudden Change in the Environment (Ph.D. paper, Graduate School of Business Administration, Harvard University, 1976).

Goold, M. Strategic Control Processes (working paper, Strategic Management Center, London, 1990).

Goold, M. and Quinn, J. J. "The Paradox of Strategic Controls." *Strategic Management Journal* (11, 1990:43–57).

Gray, D. H. "Uses and Misuses of Strategic Planning." *Harvard Business Review* (January/February 1986:89–97).

Grinyer, P. H., and Norburn, D. "Strategic Planning in 21 U.K. Companies." *Long Range Planning* (August 1974:80–88).

———. "Planning for Existing Markets." *International Studies of Management and Organization* (Fall/Winter 1977/78:99–122).

Grinyer, P. H., and Spender, J.-C. "Recipes, Crises, and Adaptation in Mature Business." *International Studies of Management and Organization* (IX, 3, 1979:113–133).

Grossman, S. D., and Lindhe, R. "The Relationship Between Long-Term Strategy and Capital Budgeting." *The Journal of Business Strategy* (1984:103–105).

Guiriek, J. C., and Thyreau, A. Planification et Communication: l'Expérience d'Air France *Revue Française de Gestion* (novembre–decembre, 1984:135–139).

Gupta, A. The Process of Strategy Formation: A Descriptive Analysis (doctoral dissertation (Boston, MA: Graduate School of Business Administration, Harvard University, 1980).

Hafsi, T., and Thomas, H. Planning Under Uncertain and Ambiguous Conditions: The Case of Air France (working paper, Graduate School of Business, University of Illinois, 1985).

Halberstam, D. *The Best and The Brightest* (New York: Random House, 1972).

Hall, R. I. "A System Pathology of an Organization: The Rise and Fall of the Old Saturday Evening Post." *Administration Science Quarterly* (XXI, June 1976:185–211).

Hall, R. I., and Menzies, W. "A Corporate System Model of a Sports Club: Using Simulation as an Aid to Policy Making in a Crisis." *Management Science* (XXIX, 1983:52–64).

Hall, W. K. "Strategic Planning Models: Are Top Managers Really Finding Them Useful?" *Journal of Business Policy* (III, 2[Winter] 1972/73:33–42).

Hamermesh, R. G. *Making Strategy Work* (New York: Wiley, 1986).

Hardy, C. *Organizational Closure: A Political Perspective* (Doctoral dissertation, School of Industrial and Business Studies, University of Warwick, 1982).

———. "Using Content, Context, and Process to Manage University Cutbacks." *Canadian Journal of Higher Education* (XVII, 1, 1987:65–82).

Hardy, C., Langley, A., Mintzberg, H., and Rose, J. "Strategy Formation in the University Setting." In J. Bess, ed., *College and University Organization: Insights for the Behavioral Sciences* (New York: New York University Press, 1984:169–210).

Hax, A. C., and Majluf, N. S. *Strategic Management: An Integrative Approach* (Englewood Cliffs, NJ: Prentice-Hall, 1984).

Hayashi, K. "Corporate Planning Practices in Japanese Multinationals." *Academy of Management Journal* (XXI, 2, 1978:211–226).

Hayek, F. A. *The Road to Serfdom* (Chicago, IL: The University of Chicago Press, 1944).

Hayes, R. H. "Strategic Planning—Forward in Reverse?" *Harvard Business Review* (November/December 1985:111–119).

Hayes, R. H., Wheelwright, S. C., and Clark, K. B. *Dynamic Manufacturing* (New York: Free Press, 1988).

Hedberg, B. L. T., and Jonsson, S. A. "Strategy Formation as a Discontinuous Process." *International Studies of Management and Organization* (VII, 2, Summer 1977:88–109).

Heirs, B., and Pehrson, G. *The Mind of the Organization* (New York: Harper & Row, 1982).

Hekhuis, D. J. Commentary. In D. E. Schendel and C. W. Hofer, eds., *Strategic Management: A New View of Business Policy and Planning* (Boston, MA: Little, Brown, 1979).

Hekimian, J. A., and Mintzberg, H. "The Planning Dilemma." *Management Review* (May 1968:4–17).

Henderson, B. D. *On Corporate Strategy* (Cambridge, MA: Abt Books, 1979).

Herold, D. M. "Long-Range Planning and Organizational Performance: A Cross Valuation Study." *Academy of Management Journal* (March 1972:91–102).

Hertz, D. B., and Thomas, H. "Risk Analysis: Important New Tool for Business Planning." In R. B. Lamb, ed., *Competitive Strategic Management* (Englewood Cliffs, NJ: Prentice-Hill, 1984:597–610).

Higgins, R. B. "Reunite Management and Planning." *Long Range Planning* (August 1976:40–45).

Higgins, R. B., and Diffenbach, J. "The Impact of Strategic Planning on Stock Prices." *Journal of Business Strategy* (6, 2, Fall 1985:64–72).

Hilsman, R. "Policy-Making Is Politics." In J. N. Rosenau, ed., *International Politics and Foreign Policy* (New York: Free Press, 1969:232–238).

Hines, T. "Left Brain/Right Brain Mythology and Implications for Management and Training." *Academy of Management Review* (12, 4, 1987:600–606).

Hitch, C. J. *Decision-making for Defence* (Berkeley, CA: University of California Press, 1965).

Hofer, C. W., and Schendel, D. *Strategy Formulation: Analytical Concepts* (St. Paul, MN: West, 1978).

Hofstede, G. H. *Culture's Consequences, International Differences in Work-Related Values* (Beverly Hills, CA: Sage Publications, 1980).

Hogarth, R. M., and Makridakis, S. "Forecasting and Planning: An Evaluation." *Management Science* (XXVII, 2[Feb], 1981:115–138).

Holsti, O. R. "The Belief System and National Images: A Case Study." *Journal of Conflict Resolution* (VI, 3, 1962:244–251).

Hopwood, B. *What Ever Happened to the British Motorcycle Industry?* (San Leandro, CA: Haynes Publishing Co., 1981).

Horowitz, J. "Allemagne, Grande-Bretagne, France: Trois Styles de Management." *Revue Française de Gestion* (November/December 1978:45–53).

Hosmer, L. T. *Academic Strategy* (Graduate School of Business Administration, Ann Arbor, MI: University of Michigan Press, 1978).

Hrebiniak, L. G., and Joyce, W. F. *Implementing Strategy* (New York: Macmillan, 1984).

Huff, A. S. "Strategic Intelligence Systems." *Information & Management* (II, 1979:187–196).

———. "Planning to Plan." In D.L. Clark, S. McKibbin, and M. Malkas, eds., *New Perspectives on Planning in Educational Organizations* (Far West Laboratory, 1980).

Huff, A.S., and Reger, R. K. "A Review of Strategic Process Research." *Journal of Management* (XIII, 2, 1987:211–236).

Hurst, D. K. "Why Strategic Management Is Bankrupt." *Organizational Dynamics* (XV, Autumn 1986:4–27).

Hussey, D., ed. *The Truth About Corporate Planning* (Oxford: Pergamon Press, 1983).

Ijiri, Y., Jaedicke, R. K., and Knight, K. E. "The Effect of Accounting Alternatives on Management Decisions." In A. Rappaport, ed., *Information for Decision-Making* (Englewood Cliffs, NJ: Prentice-Hall, 1970:421–435).

Ives, B., and Olson, M. H. "Manager or Technician? The Nature of the Information System's Manager's Job." *MIS Quarterly* (5, December 1981:49–63).

Jantsch, E., ed., *Perspectives of Planning* (Paris: OECD, 1969).

Javidan, M. "Where Planning Fails—An Executive Survey." *Long Range Planning* (XVIII, 5, 1985:89–96).

———. "Perceived Attributes of Planning Staff Effectiveness." *Journal of Management Studies* (XXIV, 3[May], 1987:295–312).

Jelinek, M. *Institutionalizing Innovation* (New York: Praeger, 1979).

Jelinek, M., and Amar, D. Implementing Corporate Strategy: Theory and

Reality (paper presented at the Third Annual Conference of the Strategic Management Society, Paris, 1983).

Jelinek, M., and Schonhaven, C. B. *The Innovation Marathon: Lessons for High-Technology Firms* (Oxford: Basil Blackwell, 1990).

Jones, R. H. "The Evolution of Management Strategy at General Electric." In M. Zimet and R. G. Greenwood, eds., *The Evolving Science of Management* (New York: AMACOM, 1979:313–326).

Kaplan, A. *The Conduct of Inquiry* (San Francisco: Chandler Publishing, 1964).

Kast, F. E., and Rosenzweig, J. E. *Organization and Management: A Systems Approach* (New York: McGraw-Hill, 1970).

Katz, D., and Kahn, R. L. *The Social Psychology of Organizations* 2nd edition (New York: Wiley, 1978).

Katz, R. L. *Cases and Concepts in Corporate Strategy* (Englewood Cliffs, NJ: Prentice-Hall, 1970).

Kaufman, J. L., and Jacobs, H. M. "A Public Planning Perspective on Strategic Planning." *Journal of the American Planning Association* (LIII, 1[Winter], 1987:23–33).

Kaufman, R., and Herman, J. *Strategic Planning in Education* (Lancaster, PA: Technomic, 1991).

Keane, J. G. "The Strategic Planning External Facilitator: Rationales and Roles." In R. B. Lamb and P. Shrivastrava, eds., *Advances in Strategic Management, Volume 3* (Greenwich, CT: JAI Press, 1985:151–162).

Kennedy, C. "Planning Global Strategies for 3M." *Long Range Planning* (XXI/I, 107[February], 1988:9–17).

Kepner, C. H., and Tregoe, B. B. *The New Rational Manager* (London: John Martin, 1980).

Kets de Vries, M. F. R., and Miller, D., *The Neurotic Organization* (San Francisco: Jossey-Bass, 1984).

Khandwalla, P. N. *The Design of Organizations* (Harcourt, Brace, 1977).

Kiechel, W., III. "Sniping at Strategic Planning." *Planning Review* (May 1984:8–11).

Kiesler, C. A. *The Psychology of Commitment: Experiments Linking Behavior to Belief* (New York: Academic Press, 1971).

King, W. R. "Evaluating Strategic Planning Systems." *Strategic Management Journal* (IV, 1983:263–277).

Kissinger, H. A. "Domestic Structure and Foreign Policy." In J. N. Rosenau, ed., *International Politics and Foreign Policy*, Revised Edition (New York: Free Press, 1969).

Klammer, T. P., and Walker, M. C. "The Continuing Increase in the Use of Sophisticated Capital Budgeting Techniques." *California Management Review* (XXVII, 1[Fall], 1984:137–148).

Koch, S. J. "Nondemocratic Nonplanning: The French Experience." *Policy Sciences* 7 (1976:371–385).

Koontz, H. "A Preliminary Statement of Principles of Planning and Control." *Journal of the Academy of Management* (I, 1958:45–61).

Kotov, A. *Think Like a Grandmaster* (Trafalgar, U.K.: Batsford, 1971).

Kotler, P., and Singh, R. "Marketing Warfare in the 1980s." *Journal of Business Strategy* (Winter, 1981:30–41).

Kress, G., Koehler, G., and Springer, J. F., "Policy Drift: An Evaluation of the California Business Program." *Police Sciences Journal* (III, Special Issue, 1980:1101–1108).

Kudla, R. J. "The Effects of Strategic Planning on Common Stock Returns." *Academy of Management Journal* (XXIII, 1, 1980:5–20).

Kukalis, S. "Strategic Planning in Large US Corporations—A Survey." *OMEGA* (XVI, 5, 1988:393–404).

———. "The Relationship Among Firm Characteristics and Design of Strategic Planning Systems in Large Organizations." *Journal of Management* (XV, 4, 1989:565–579).

———. "Determinants of Strategic Planning Systems in Large Organizations: A Contingency Approach." *Journal of Management Studies* (XXVIII, 2, 1991:143–160).

Kundera, M. *The Unbearable Lightness of Being* (New York: Harper & Row, 1984).

Langley, A. "The Role of Rational Analysis in Organizations" (Ph.D. Theory Paper, Ecole des Hautes Etudes Commerciales de Montréal, December, 1982).

———. *The Role of Formal Analysis in Organizations* (Doctoral Thesis, Ecole des Hautes Etudes Commerciales de Montreal, 1986).

———. "The Roles of Formal Strategic Planning." *Long Range Planning* (21, 3, 1988:40–50).

———. "In Search of Rationality: The Purposes behind the Use of Formal Analysis in Organizations." *Administrative Science Quarterly* (XXXIV, December 1989:598–631).

Lauenstein, M. "The Strategy Audit." *Journal of Business Strategy* (IV, 3, 1984:87–91).

Laski, H. J. "The Limitations of the Expert." *Harper's Magazine* (162 [December 1930]:102–106).

Learned, E. P., Christensen, C. R., Andrews, K. R., and Guth, W. D. *Business Policy: Text and Cases* (Homewood, IL: Irwin, 1965).

Learned, E. P., and Sproat, A. T. *Organization Theory and Policy: Notes for Analysis* (Homewood, IL: Irwin, 1966).

Leavitt, H. J. "Beyond the Analytic Manager." *California Management Review* (17, 3, 1975a:5–12).

———. "Beyond the Analytic Manager: Part II." (17, [Summer] 4, 1975b:11–21).

Leff, N. H., "Strategic Planning in an Uncertain World," *The Journal of Business Strategy* (IV[Spring], 1984:78–80).

Lenz, R. T. "Strategic Capability: A Concept and Framework for Analysis." *Academy of Management Review* (V, 2, 1980:225–234).

———. "Environment, Strategy, Organization Structure and Performance: Patterns in One Industry." *Strategic Management Journal* (I, 1980b: 209–226).

Lenz, R. T., and Engledow, J. L. "Environmental Analysis Units and Strategic

Decision Making: A Field Study of Selected 'Leading-Edge' Corporations." *Strategic Management Journal* (XIX, 1986:69–89).

Lenz, R. T., and Lyles, M. A. "Paralysis by Analysis: Is Your Planning System Becoming Too Rational?" *Long Range Planning* (XVIII, 4[August], 1985:64–72).

Leontiades, M. "A Diagnostic Framework for Planning." *Strategic Management Journal* (IV, 1983:11–26).

———. "Strategic Theory and Management Practice." *Journal of General Management* (Winter 1979–80:22–32).

Leontiades, M., and Tezel, A. "Planning Perceptions and Planning Results." *Strategic Management Journal* (I, 1980:65–75).

Levitt, T. "Marketing Myopia." *Harvard Business Review* (July/August 1960:45–56).

Lewis, W. A. *The Principles of Economic Planning* (London: Allen & Unwin, 1969).

Lewis, W. W. "The CEO and Corporate Strategy: Back to Basics." In A. C. Hax, ed., *Readings on Strategic Management* (Cambridge, MA: Ballinger, 1984:1–7).

Lindberg, E., and Zackrisson, U. "Deciding About the Uncertain: The Use of Forecasts as an Aid to Decision-Making." *Scandinavian Journal of Management* (7, 4, 1991:271–283).

Lindblom, C. E. *The Intelligence of Democracy* (New York: The Free Press, 1965).

———. *The Policy-Making Process* (Englewood Cliffs, NJ: Prentice-Hall, 1968).

———. "Policy Making and Planning." In *Politics and Markets: The World's Political-Economic Systems* (New York: Basic Books, 1977).

Linneman, R. E., and Kennell, J. D. "Shirt-Sleeve Approach to Long-Range Plans." *Harvard Business Review* (March/April, 1977:141–150).

Lipsky, M. "Standing the Study of Public Policy Implementation on Its Head." In W. D. Burnham and M. W. Weinberg, eds., *American Politics and Public Policy* (Cambridge, MA: MIT Press, 1978:391–402).

Litschert, R. J., and Nicholson, E. A., Jr. "Corporate Long-Range Planning Groups—Some Different Approaches." *Long Range Planning* (1974:62–66).

Loasby, B. J. "Long-Range Formal Planning in Perspective." *The Journal of Management Studies* (IV, 1967:300–308).

Lorange, P. "Formal Planning Systems: Their Role in Strategy Formulation and Implementation." In D. E. Schendel and C. W. Hofer, eds., *Strategic Management: A New View of Business Policy and Planning* (Boston, MA: Little, Brown, 1979).

———. *Corporate Planning: An Executive Viewpoint* (Englewood Cliffs, NJ: Prentice-Hall, 1980a).

———. Roles of the CEO in Strategic Planning and Control Processes. In seminar on The Role of General Management in Strategy Formulation and Evaluation, cosponsored by E.S.S.E.C., E.I.A.S.M., and I.A.E. (CERGY, France: April 28–30, 1980b).

Lorange, P., and Vancil, R. F. *Strategic Planning Systems* (Englewood Cliffs, NJ: Prentice-Hall, 1977).

Lorange, P., Gordon, I. S., and Smith R. "The Management of Adaption and Integration." *Journal of General Management* (Summer 1979:31–41).

Lorange, P., and Murphy, D. C. "Strategy and Human Resources: Concepts and Practice." *Human Resource Management* (XXII, 1/2, 1983:111–133).

Mainer, R. The Impact of Strategic Planning on Executive Behavior (Management Consulting Division, Boston Safe Deposit and Trust Co., 1965).

Majone, G. "The Uses of Policy Analysis." In *The Future and the Past: Essays on Progress* (Russell Sage Foundation, Annual Report, 1976–1977:201–220).

————. *Evidence, Argument and Persuasion in the Policy Process* (New Haven, CT: Yale University Press, 1989).

Majone, G., and Wildavsky, A. "Implementation as Evolution." *Policy Studies Review Annual* (II, 1978:103–117).

Makridakis, S. *Forecasting, Planning, and Strategy for the 21st Century* (New York: Free Press, 1990); also extracts from 1979 draft.

Makridakis, S., and Hibon, M. "Accuracy of Forecasting: An Empirical Investigation." *Journal of the Royal Statistical Society* (CXLII, Part 2 [Series A], 1979:97–145).

Makridakis, S., and Wheelwright, S. C. "Forecasting an Organization's Futures." *Handbook of Organizational Design* (1981:122–138).

————. *Forecasting Methods for Management* (New York: Wiley, 1989).

Makridakis, S., Wheelwright, S. C., and McGee, V. *Forecasting, Methods and Applications* (New York: Wiley, 1983).

Makridakis, S., Faucheux, C., and Heau, D. What is Strategy? (paper presented at INSEAD, Fontainebleau, France, 1982).

Malik, Z. A., and Karger, D. W. "Does Long-Range Planning Improve Company Performance?" *Management Review* (LXIV, September 1975:27–31).

Malmlow, E. G. "Corporate Strategic Planning in Practice." *Long Range Planning* (V, 3, 1972:2–9).

March, J. G. "The Technology of Foolishness." In J. G. March and J. P. Olsen, eds., *Ambiguity and Choice in Organizations* (Bergen, Norway: Universitetsforlaget, 1976).

March, J. G. "Footnotes to Organizational Change." *Administration Science Quarterly* (XXVI, 1981:563–577).

March, J. G., and Olsen, J. P., eds., *Ambiguity and Choice in Organizations* (Bergen, Norway: Universitetsforlaget, 1976).

March, J. G., and Simon, H. A. *Organizations* (New York: Wiley, 1958).

Marks, M. "Organizational Adjustment to Uncertainty" *The Journal of Management Studies* (February 1977:1–7).

Marquardt, I. A. "Strategists Confront Planning Challenges." *The Journal of Business Strategy* (May/June 1990:4–8).

Marsh, P., Barwise, P., Thomas, K., and Wensley, R. "Managing Strategic Investment Decisions in Large Diversified Companies" (Centre for Business Strategy Report Series, London Business School, 1988).

Martinet, A. "Les discours sur la stratégie d'entreprise." *Revue Française de Gestion* (janvier/fevrier 1988:49–60).

Mason, R. O. "A Dialectical Approach to Strategic Planning." *Management Science* (XV, 8, 1969:B403–B414).

Mason, R. O., and Mitroff, I. I. A Teleological Power-Oriented Theory of Strategy (Prepared for Non-Traditional Approaches to Policy Research, University of Southern California, Los Angeles, 1981).

McCann, J. E., and Selsky, J. "Hyperturbulence and the Emergence of Type 5 Environments." *Academy of Management Review* (IX, 3, 1984:460–470).

McConnell, J. D. "Strategic Planning: One Workable Approach." *Long Range Planning* (IV, 2, 1971:2–6).

McGinley, L. "Forecasters Overhaul 'Models' of Economy in Wake of 1982 Errors." *The Wall Street Journal* (February 17, 1983:1).

McKenney, J. L., and Keen, P. G. W. "How Managers' Minds Work." *Harvard Business Review* (X, 4[May/June], 1974:79–90).

McNichols, T. J. *Policy Making and Executive Action: Cases on Business Policy* (New York: McGraw-Hill, 1972).

Meadows, D. H., et al. *The Limits to Growth* (New York: Universe Books, 1972).

Meek, L. "Organizational Culture: Origins and Weaknesses." *Organizational Studies* (9, 4, 1988:453–473).

Merton, R. K. "Limited Perspective of Staff Specialists." In R. Dubin, ed., *Human Relations in Administration* (Englewood Cliffs, NJ: Prentice-Hall, 1968:119–121).

Meyerson, M., and Banfield, E. C. *Politics, Planning and the Public Interest; The Case of Public Housing in Chicago* (Glencoe, IL: Free Press, 1955).

Miles, R. H. *Coffin Nails and Corporate Strategies* (Englewood Cliffs, NJ: Prentice-Hall, 1982).

Miller, D., and Friesen, P. H. *Organizations: A Quantum View* (Englewood Cliffs, NJ: Prentice-Hall, 1984).

Miller, D., and Mintzberg, H. "The Case for Configuration." In D. Miller and P. H. Friesen, eds., *Organizations: A Quantum View* (Englewood Cliffs, N.J.: Prentice-Hall, 1984).

Miller, G. A. "The Magic Number Seven Plus or Minus Two: Some Limits on Our Capacity for Processing Information." *Psychology Review* (March, 1956:81–97).

Miller, G. A., Galanter, E., and Pribram, K. H. *Plans and the Structure of Behavior* (New York: Henry Holt, 1960).

Millett, S. M., and Leppänen, R. "The Business Information and Analysis Function: A New Approach to Strategic Thinking and Planning." *Planning Review* (May/June, 1991:10–15).

Mintzberg, H. *The Nature of Managerial Work* (New York: Harper & Row, 1973).

———. "Impediments to the Use of Management Information" (Society of Industrial Accountants, 1975a).

———. "The Manager's Job: Folklore and Fact." *Harvard Business Review* (July/August 1975b).

———. "Planning on the Left Side and Managing on the Right." *Harvard Business Review* (July/August 1976:49–58).

———. Review of the "New Science of Management Decision" by Herbert Simon. *Administrative Science Quarterly* (June 1977).

———. "Patterns in Strategy Formation." *Management Science* (XXIV, 9, 1978:934–948).

———. *The Structuring of Organizations: A Synthesis of the Research* (Englewood Cliffs, NJ: Prentice-Hall, 1979a).

———. "Beyond Implementation: An Analysis of the Resistance to Policy Analysis." In K. B. Haley, ed., *OR '78* (Amsterdam: North Holland Publishing Company, 1979b:106–162).

———. "What Is Planning Anyway?" *Strategic Management Journal* (II, 1981:319–324).

———. *Power In and Around Organizations* (Englewood Cliffs, NJ: Prentice-Hall, 1983).

———. "Crafting Strategy." *Harvard Business Review* (July/August 1987:66–75).

———. *Mintzberg on Management: Inside Our Strange World of Organizations* (New York: Free Press, 1989).

———. "The Design School: Reconsidering the Basic Premises of Strategic Management." *Strategic Management Journal* (XI, 1990a:171–195).

———. "Strategy Formation: Schools of Thought." In J. Frederickson, ed., *Perspectives on Strategic Management* (Boston: Ballinger, 1990b).

———. "Learning 1, Planning 0: Reply to Igor Ansoff." *Strategic Management Journal* (12, 1991:463–466).

Mintzberg, H., Raisinghani, D., and Théorêt, A. "The Structure of 'Unstructured' Decision Processes." *Administration Science Quarterly* (XXI, June, 1976:246–275).

Mintzberg, H., and Waters, J. A. "Tracking Strategy in an Entrepreneurial Firm." *Academy of Management Journal* (XXV, 3, 1982:465–499).

Mintzberg, H., and McHugh, A. "Strategy Formation in an Adhocracy." *Administrative Science Quarterly* (XXX, 1985:160–197).

Mintzberg, H., Brunet, J. P., and Waters, J. A. "Does Planning Impede Strategic Thinking? Tracking the strategies of Air Canada from 1937 to 1976." In *Advances in Strategic Management*, 4, 3–41 (JAI Press, 1986).

Mitroff, I. I. "The Myth of Objectivity, or Why Science Needs a New Psychology of Science." *Management Science* (1972:B613–B618).

Mitroff, I. I., Barabha, V. P., and Kilmann, R. H., "The Application of Behavioral and Philosophical Technologies to Strategic Planning—A Case Study of a Large Federal Agency." *Management Science* (XXIV, 1, 1977:44–58).

Mockler, R. J. "A Catalog of Commercially Available Software for Strategic Planning." *Planning Review* (May/June, 1991:28–35).

Morse, P. M. "The History and Development of Operations Research." In G. J. Kelleher, ed., *The Challenge to Systems Analysis: Public Policy and Social Change* (New York: Wiley, 1970: 21–28).

Murray, E. A., Jr., "Strategic Choice as a Negotiated Outcome." *Management Science* (XXIV, 9[May], 1978:960–972).

Neustadt, R. E. *Presidential Power: The Politics of Leadership* (New York: Wiley, 1960).

Newell, A., and Simon, H. A. *Human Problem Solving* (Englewood Cliffs, NJ: Prentice-Hall, 1972).

———. "Computer Science as Empirical Inquiry: Symbols and Search." *Communication of the ACM* (19, 3, March 1976:113–126).

Newman, W. H. *Administrative Action: The Techniques of Organization & Management* (Englewood Cliffs, NJ: Prentice-Hall, 1951, 2nd edition, 1963).

Newman, W. H., Summer, C. E., and Warren, E. K. *The Process of Management* (Englewood Cliffs, NJ: Prentice-Hall, 2nd edition, 1967, 3rd edition, 1972).

Newman, W. H., and Logan, J. P. *Strategy, Policy, and Central Management* (South-Western, 1971).

Newman, W. H., Warren, E. K., and Schnee, J. E. *The Process of Management: Strategy, Action, Results* (Englewood Cliffs, NJ: Prentice-Hall, 5th edition, 1982).

Nonaka, I. "Toward Middle-Up-Down Management." *Sloan Management Review* (29, 3, Spring, 1988:9–18).

Norburn, D., and Grinyer, P. "Directors Without Direction." *Journal of General Management* (I, 2, 1973/74:37–48).

Normann, R. *Management for Growth* (New York: Wiley, 1977).

Normann, R., and Rhenman, E. *Formulation of Goals and Measurement of Effectiveness in the Public Administration* (Stockholm: SIAR, 1975).

Novick, D. "Long-Range Planning Through Program Budgeting." In E. Jantsch, ed., *Perspectives of Planning* (Paris: OECD, 1968:257–284).

Nutt, P. C. "Implementation Approaches for Project Planning." *Academy of Management Review* (8, 4, 1983a:600–611).

———. "A Strategic Planning Network for Non-profit Organizations." *Strategic Management Journal* (5, 1, January–March, 1984a:57–75).

———. "Planning Process Archetypes and Their Effectiveness." *Decision Sciences* (15, 1984b:221–238).

Nutt, P. C., and Backoff, A Contingency Framework for Strategic Planning (draft, Graduate Program in Hospital and Health Services Administration, Ohio State University, 1983b).

Nystrom, H. *Creativity and Innovation* (New York: Wiley, 1979).

Ohmae, K. *The Mind of the Strategist* (New York: McGraw-Hill, 1982).

Oliver, S. L. "Management by Concept." *Forbes* (November 26, 1990:37–38).

Orlans, H. "Neutrality and Advocacy in Policy Research." *Policy Science* (6, 1975:107–119).

Ornstein, R. F. *The Psychology of Consciousness* (New York: Viking, 1972).

Ozbekhan, H. "Toward a General Theory of Planning." In E. Jantsch, ed., *Perspectives of Planning* (Paris: OECD, 1969:47–155).

Paine, F. T., and Naumes, W. *Strategy and Policy Formation: An Integrative Approach* (Philadelphia: Saunders, 1974).

Pant, P. N., and Starbuck, W. H. "Review of Forecasting and Research Methods." *Journal of Management* (16, 2, June, 1990:443–460).

Pascale, R. T. "Our Curious Addiction to Corporate Grand Strategy." *Fortune* (105, 2: Jan. 25, 1982:115–116).

———. "Perspectives on Strategy: The Real Story Behind Honda's Success." *California Management Review* (Spring 1984:47–72).

Pearce, J. A., II, Freeman, E. B., and Robinson, R. B., Jr. "The Tenuous Link Between Formal Strategic Planning and Financial Performance." *Academy of Management Review* (XII, 4, 1987:658–675).

Pennington, M. W. "Why Has Planning Failed?" *Long Range Planning* (V, 1, 1972:2–9).

Perutz, P. Five Obstacles to Overcome in Order to Regain Initiative in the 1980s (presented at the 6th Ticimese Marketing Congress, Geneva, 1980).

Peters, J. P. A Guide to Strategic Planning for Hospitals (Chicago, IL: American Hospital Association, 1979).

Peters, J. T., Hammond, K. R., and Summers, D. A. "A note on intuitive vs. analytic thinking." *Organizational Behavior and Human Performance* (12, 1974:125–131).

Peters, T. H., and Waterman, R. H., Jr. *In Search of Excellence* (New York: Harper & Row, 1982).

Pfeffner, J. M. "Administrative Rationality" *Public Administration Review* (1960:125–132).

Piercy, N., and Thomas, M. "Corporate Planning: Budgeting and Integration." *Journal of General Management* (XX, 2, 1984:51–66).

Pines, M. "We Are Left-Brained or Right-Brained." *The New York Times Magazine* (September 9, 1973).

Polanyi, M. *The Tacit Dimension* (Garden City, NY: Doubleday, 1966).

Porter, M. E. *Competitive Strategy: Techniques for Analyzing Industries and Competitors* (New York: Free Press, 1980).

———. *Competitive Advantage: Creating and Sustaining Superior Performance* (New York: Free Press, 1985).

———. "Corporate Strategy: The State of Strategic Thinking." *The Economist* (303, 7499 [May 23, 1987]:17–22).

Potts, M. "New Planning System Aims to Boost Speed, Flexibility." *The Washington Post* (September 30, 1984).

Powell, T. C. "Strategic Planning as Competitive Advantage." *Strategic Management Journal* (XIII, 1992:551–558).

Prahalad, C. K., and Hamel, G. "The Core Competence of the Corporation." *Harvard Business Review* (May/June 1990:79–91).

Quinn, J. B. *Strategies for Change: Logical Incrementalism* (Homewood, IL: Irwin, 1980a).

———. "Managing Strategic Change." *Sloan Management Review* (Summer 1980b:3–20).

Quinn, J. B., Mintzberg, H., and James, R. M. *The Strategy Process* (Englewood Cliffs, NJ: Prentice-Hall, 1988).

Radosevich, R. A Critique of "Comprehensive Managerial Planning." In J. W.

McLuin, ed., *Contemporary Management* (Englewood Cliffs, NJ: Prentice-Hall, 1974:356–361).

Ramanujam, V., and Venkatraman, N. "Planning System Characteristics and Planning Effectiveness." *Strategic Management Journal* (XIII, 1987:453–468).

———. The Assessment of Strategic Planning Effectiveness: A Canonical Correlation Approach (paper presented at the TIMS/ORSA Joint National Meeting, Boston, 1985).

Rappaport, A. *Creating Shareholder Value: The New Standard for Business Performance* (New York: Free Press, 1986).

Rea, R. H. "The Design of Integrated Technological Forecasting and Planning Systems for the Allocation of Resources." In E. Jantsch, ed., *Perspectives of Planning* (Paris: OECD, 1969:203–233).

Reid, D. M. "Operationalizing Strategic Planning." *Strategic Management Journal* (X, 1989:553–567).

Reimann, B. C. "Getting Value from Strategic Planning." *Planning Review* (May/June 1988:42–48).

Rein, M., and Rabinovitz, F. F. "Implementation: A Theoretical Perspective." In W. D. Burnham and M. W. Weinberg, eds., *American Politics and Public Policy* (Cambridge, MA: MIT Press, 1979:307–333).

Restak, R. "The hemispheres of the brain have minds of their own." *The New York Times* (January 25, 1976).

Rhenman, E. *Organization Theory for Long-Range Planning* (New York: Wiley, 1973).

Rhyne, L. C. "The Relationship of Strategic Planning to Financial Performance." *Strategic Management Journal* (VII, 1986:423–436).

———. "Contrasting Planning Systems in High, Medium, and Low Performance Companies." *Journal of Management Studies* (XXIV, 1987:363–385).

Rice, G. H., Jr. "Strategic Decision-Making in Small Business." *Journal of General Management* (IX, 1[Autumn], 1983:58–65).

Rieger, F. Cultural Influences on Organization and Management in International Airlines (Doctoral dissertation, McGill University, Montreal, 1986).

Ringbakk, K. A. "Organized Corporate Planning Systems: An Empirical Study of Planning Practices and Experiences in American Big Business." (Dissertation abstracts) *Academy of Management Journal* (1968:354–355).

———. "Why Planning Fails." *European Business* (XXIX, Spring, 1971:15–27).

———. "The Corporate Planning Life Cycle—An International Point of View." *Long Range Planning* (September 1972:10–20).

Roach, J. D. C., and Allen, M. G. "Strengthening the Strategic Planning Process." In K. J. Albert, ed., *The Strategic Management Handbook* (New York: McGraw-Hill, 1983:Chapter 7).

Robinson, R. B., Jr., and Pearce, J. A., II. "The Impact of Formalyzed Strategic Planning on Financial Performance in Small Organizations." *Strategic Management Journal* (IV, 1983:197–207).

―――. "Planned Patterns of Strategic Behavior and their Relationship to Business-Unit Performance." *Strategic Management Journal* (IX, 1988:43–60).

Rogers, D. C. D. *Essentials of Business Policy* (New York: Harper & Row, 1975).

Rondinelli, D. A. "Public Planning and Political Strategy." *Long Range Planning* (IX, 2[April], 1976:75–82).

Rossotti, C. O. *Two Concepts of Long-Range Planning* (The Boston Consulting Group, Boston, MA, circa 1965).

Rothschild, W. E. *"Putting It All Together: A Guide to Strategic Thinking."* (New York: AMACOM, 1976).

―――. *Strategic Alternatives: Selection, Development and Implementation* (New York: AMACOM, 1979).

―――. "How to Ensure the Continued Growth of Strategic Planning." *Journal of Business Strategy* (I, Summer, 1980:11–18).

Rue, L. W., and Fulmer, R. M. Is Long-Range Planning Profitable? (Division of Policy and Planning, Proceedings of the National Meeting of the Academy of Management, Boston, 1973:66–73).

Rule, E. G. "What's Happening to Strategic Planning in Canadian Business?" *Business Quarterly* (LI, 4, 1987:43–47).

Rumelt, R. P. "Evaluation of Strategy: Theory and Models." In D. E. Schendel and C. W. Hofer, eds., *Strategic Management* (Boston, MA: Little, Brown, 1979a:196–212).

―――. Strategic Fit and the Organization-Environment Debate (paper presented at the Annual Meeting of the Western Region, Academy of Management, Portland, Oregon, 1979b).

Rutenberg, D. P. What Strategic Planning Expects from Management Science (working paper, Carnegie-Mellon University, Pittsburgh, 1976).

―――. Playful Plans (working paper 90–15, Queen's University, Kingston, Ontario, July 1990).

Saint-Exupéry, A. *Le Petit Prince* (New York: Harcourt, Brace, Jovanovich, 1943).

Sandy, W. "Link Your Business Plan to a Performance Plan." *The Journal of Business Strategy* (November/December 1990:4–8).

Sapp, R. W. "Banks Look Ahead: A Survey of Bank Planning." *The Magazine of Bank Administration* (July 1980:33–40).

Sarrazin, J. Le Role des Processus de Planification dans les Grandes Entreprises Françaises: Un Essai d'Interpretation (Thèse 3ieme cycle, Université de Droit, d'Economie et des Sciences d'Aix-Marseille, 1975).

―――. "Decentralized Planning in a Large French Company: An Interpretive Study." *International Studies of Management and Organization* (Fall/Winter 1977/1978:37–59).

―――. "Top Management's Role in Strategy Formulation: A Tentative Analytical Framework." *International Studies of Management and Organization* (XI, 2, 1981:9–23).

Saunders, C. B., and Tuggle, F. D. "Why Planners Don't." *Long Range Planning* (X, 3[June], 1977:19–24).

Sawyer, G. C. *Corporate Planning as a Creative Process* (Oxford, OH: Planning Executives Institute, 1983).

Sayles, L. *Managerial Behavior: Administration in Complex Organizations* (New York: McGraw-Hill, 1964).

————. "Whatever Happened to Management—Or Why the Dull Stepchild." *Business Horizons* (XIII, 2, April, 1970:25–34).

Schaffir, W. B. Introduction. In F. Caropreso, ed., *Getting Value from Strategic Planning* (New York: The Conference Board, 1988).

Schelling, T. C. *The Strategy of Conflict* 2d edition (Cambridge, MA: Harvard University Press, 1980).

Schendel, D. E., and Hofer, C. H., eds., *Strategic Management: A New View of Business Policy and Planning* (Boston, MA: Little, Brown, 1979).

Schlesinger, A. M. *The Bitter Heritage: Vietnam and the American Democracy, 1941–1968* (Greenwich, CT: Fawcett Publications, 1968).

Schlesinger, J. R. "Systems Analysis and the Political Process." *The Journal of Law and Economics* (1968).

Schmidt, J. A. "Case Study: The Strategic Review." *Planning Review* (July–August, 1988:14–19).

Schon, D. A., and Nutt, T. E. *Endemic Turbulence: The Future for Planning Education* (Chicago: American Institute of Planners, 1974:181–205).

Schumacher, E. F. *Small is Beautiful* (London: Abacus, 1974).

Schwartz, H., and Davis, S. M. "Matching Corporate Culture and Business Strategy." *Organizational Dynamics* (Summer 1981:30–48).

Schwendiman, J. S. *Strategic and Long-Range Planning for the Multi-National Corporation* (New York: Praeger, 1973).

Selznick, P. *Leadership in Administration; A Sociological Interpretation* (Evanston, IL: Row, Peterson, 1957).

Shank, J. K., Niblock, E. G., and Sandall, W. T. "Balance 'Creativity' and 'Practicality' in Formal Planning." *Harvard Business Review* (Vol. 51, 1[January–February], 1973:87–95).

Shapiro, H. J., and Kallman, E. A. "Long-Range Planning Is Not for Everyone." *Planning Review* (VI, 1978:27–34).

Sharp, J. A. "Systems Dynamics Applications to Industrial and Other Systems." *Operational Research Quarterly* (XXVIII, 1977:489–504).

Sheehan, G. A. Long-Range Strategic Planning and Its Relationship to Firm Size, Firm Growth, and Firm Growth Variabiity (Ph.D. Thesis, University of Western Ontario, 1975).

Shelling, T. *The Strategy of Conflict* 2d edition (Cambridge, MA: Harvard University Press, 1980).

Shim, J. K., and McGlade, R. "The Use of Corporate Policy Models: Past, Present and Future." *Journal of the Operational Society* (XXXV, 10, 1984:885–893).

Shrader, C. B., Taylor, L., and Dalton, D. R. "Strategic Planning and Organizational Performance: A Critical Appraisal." *Journal of Management* (10:2, 1984:149–171).

Siegel, D. "Goverment Budgeting and Models of the Policy-Making Process." *Optimum* (VIII, 1, 1977:44–56).

Simon, H.A. *The Shape of Automation: for Men and Management* (New York: Harper & Row, 1965).

———. Strategic Planning (Abstract from unpublished notes, Groningen, Holland, Sept. 11, 1973).

———. *The New Science of Management Decision* (Englewood Cliffs, NJ: Prentice-Hall, 1960, also Revised Edition, 1977).

———. "The Information Processing Explanation of Gestalt Phenomena." *Computers in Human Behavior* (II, 1986, 4:241–255).

———. "Making Management Decisions: The Role of Intuition and Emotion." *Academy of Management Executive* (I, February, 1987:57–64).

Simon, H. A., Dantzig, G. B., Hogarth, R., Plott, C. R., Raiffa, H., Schelling, T. C., Shepske, K. A., Thaler, R. A., Tversky, A., and Winter, S., "Decision Making and Problem Solving." *Interfaces* (XVII, 5, 1987:11–31).

Simons, R. "Planning, Control, and Uncertainty: A Process View." In W. J. Bruns, Jr., and R. S. Kaplan, eds., *Accounting and Management: Field Study Perspectives* (Cambridge, MA: Harvard Business School Press, 1987:Chapter 13.).

———. "The Role of Management Control Systems in Creating Competitive Advantage: New Perspectives." *Accounting, Organizations and Society* (XV, 1990:127–143).

———. "Strategic Orientation and Top Management Attention to Control Systems." *Strategic Management Journal* (XII, 1991:49–62).

———. Rethinking the Role of Systems in Controlling Strategy (presented at the 1988 Annual Meeting of the Strategic Management Society, Amsterdam, October 1988; published in 1991 by Publishing Division, Harvard Business School, #9-191-091).

Sinha, D. K. "The Contribution of Formal Planning to Decisions." *Strategic Management Journal* (XI, 1990:479–492).

Smalter, D. J., and Ruggles, R. L., Jr. "Six Business Lessons from the Pentagon." *Harvard Business Review* (March/April 1966:64–75).

Snyder, N., and Glueck, W. F. "How Managers Plan—The Analysis of Managerial Activities." *Long Range Planning* (XIII, February 1980:70–76).

Soelberg, P. O. "Unprogrammed Decision Making." *Industrial Management Review* (VIII, 2, Spring 1967:19–29).

Spender, J.-C. *Industry Recipes* (Oxford: Basil Blackwell, 1989).

Sperry, R. "Messages from the Laboratory." *Engineering and Science* (1974: 29–32).

Starbuck, W. H. "Acting First and Thinking Later: Theory versus Reality in Strategic Change." In J. M. Pennings and Associates, *Organizational Strategy and Change* (San Francisco: Jossey-Bass, 1985:336–372).

Starbuck, W. H., Greve, A., and Hedberg, B. L. T. "Responding to Crises." *Journal of Business Administration* (1978:111–137).

Starr, M. K. *Management: A Modern Approach* (New York: Harcourt, Brace, Jovanovich, 1971).

Steinbruner, J. D. *The Cybernetic Theory of Decision: New Dimensions of Political Analysis* (Princeton University Press, 1974).

Steiner, G. A. *Top Management Planning* (New York: Macmillan, 1969).
———. *Strategic Planning: What Every Manager Must Know* (New York: Free Press, 1979).
Steiner, G. A., and Kunin, H. E. "Formal Strategic Planning in the United States Today." *Long Range Planning* (XVI, 3, 1983:12–17).
Steiner, G. A., and Schollhammer, H. "Pitfalls in Multi-National Long-Range Planning." *Long Range Planning* (April 1975:2–12).
Stevenson, H. H. "Defining Corporate Strengths and Weaknesses." *Sloan Management Review* (Spring, 1976:51–68).
Stewart, R. *Managers and Their Jobs* (London: Macmillan, 1967).
Stewart, R. F. *A Framework for Business Planning* (Stanford, CA: Stanford Research Institute, 1963).
Stieglitz, H. *The Chief Executive—And His Job* (New York: The Conference Board, Personnel Policy Study No. 214, 1969).
Stokesbury, J. L. *A Short History of World War I* (New York: Morrow, 1981).
Strategic Planning Associates, "Strategy and Shareholder Value: The Value Curve." In R. B. Lamb, ed., *Competitive Strategic Management* (Englewood Cliffs, NJ: Prentice-Hall, 1984:571–596).
Summers, H. G., Jr., *On Strategy: The Vietnam War in Context* (Strategic Studies Institute, U.S. Army College, 1981).
Sun Tzu, *The Art of War* (New York: Oxford University Press, 1971).
Taylor, B. "Strategies for Planning." *Long Range Planning* (8, 4, 1975:27–40).
Taylor, F. W. "*Shop Management.*" In *Scientific Management* (New York: Harper and Brothers, 1947, reprint of 1911 book).
———. *The Principles of Scientific Management* (New York: Harper & Row, 1913).
Taylor, R. N. "Psychological Aspects of Planning." *Long Range Planning* (IX, 2, 1976:66–74).
Taylor, W. D. Strategic Adaptation in Low-Growth Environments (Ph.D. Thesis, Ecole des Hautes Etudes Commerciales, Montreal, 1982).
Terreberry, S. "The Evolution of Organizational Environments." *Administration Science Quarterly* (XII, 1968:590–613).
Thompson, V. A. "How Scientific Management Thwarts Innovation." *Transaction* (June 1968:51–55).
Thompson, A. A., Jr., and Strickland, A. J., III. *Strategy Formulation and Implementation: Tasks of the General Manager* (Dallas, TX: Business Publications Inc., 1980).
Thorelli, H. B., ed. *Strategy + Structure = Performance, The Strategic Planning Imperative* (Bloomington, IN: Indiana University Press, 1977).
Thune, S. S., and House, R. J. "Where Long-Range Planning Pays Off." *Business Horizons* (April 1970:81–87).
Tilles, S. "How to Evaluate Corporate Strategy." *Harvard Business Review* (July/August 1963:111–121).
———. "Corporate Strategic Planning—The American Experience." In B. Taylor and K. Hawkins, eds., *A Handbook of Strategic Planning* (London: Longman, 1972:65–74).
Time magazine, "The Most Basic Form of Creativity" (June 26, 1972:84).

Tita, M. A., and Allio, R. J. "3M's Strategy System—Planning in an Innovative Corporation." *Planning Review* (XII, 5, September, 1984:10–15).

Toffler, A. *Future Shock* (New York: Random House, 1970).

———. (1986) The Planning Forum Conference, Montreal, May 5, 1986: page 1 of handout.

Tregoe, B. B., and Zimmerman, J. W. *Top Management Survey* (New York: Simon & Schuster, 1980).

Turban, E. "A Sample Survey of Operation Branch Activities at the Corporate Level." *Operational Research* (1972:708–721).

Tversky, A., and Kahneman, D. "Judgment Under Uncertainty: Heuristics and Biases." *Science* (1974:1124–1131).

Unterman, I. "American Finance: Three Views of Strategy." *Journal of General Management* (I, 3, 1974:39–47).

Uyterhoeven, H. E. R., Ackerman, R. W., and Rosenblum, J. W. *Strategy and Organization: Text and Cases in General Management* (Homewood, IL: Irwin, 1977).

Vancil, R. F. "The Accuracy of Long Range Planning." In D. E. Hussey, ed., *The Truth About Corporate Planning* (Oxford: Pergamon Press, 1983).

Van Gunsteren, H. R. *The Quest of Control: A Critique of the Rational Control Rule Approach in Public Affairs* (New York: Wiley, 1976).

Venkatraman, N., and Ramanujam, V. "Planning System Success: A Conceptualization and an Operational Model." *Management Science* (XXXIII, 6[June], 1987:687–705).

Wack, P. "Scenarios: Uncharted Waters Ahead." *Harvard Business Review* (September/October 1985a:73–89).

———. "Scenarios: Shooting the Rapids." *Harvard Business Review* (November/December 1985b:139–150).

Wade, P. F. *The Manager/Management Scientist Interface* (Doctoral Theory Paper 1, McGill University, 1975).

Weick, K. E. *The Social Psychology of Organizing* (Reading, MA: Addison-Wesley, first edition 1969, second edition 1979).

———. "Managerial Thought in the Context of Action." In S. Srivastra and Associates, ed., *The Executive Mind* (San Francisco: Jossey-Bass, 1983:221–242).

———. "Cartographic Myths in Organizations." In A. S. Huff, ed., *Mapping Strategic Thought* (New York: Wiley, 1990:1–10).

Weizenbaum, J. *Computer Power and Human Reason* (San Francisco, CA: W. H. Freeman, 1976).

Welch, J. B. "Strategic Planning Could Improve Your Share Price." *Long Range Planning* (XVII, 2[April], 1984:144–147).

Westley, F. R. Harnessing a Vision: The Role of Images in Strategy-Making (working paper, McGill University, Montreal, 1983).

Wheelwright, S. C. "Strategy, Management, and Strategic Planning Approaches." *Interfaces* (XIV, 1[January/February] 1984:19–33).

Whitehead, T. C. Uses and Limitations of Systems Analysis (doctoral thesis, Sloan School of Management, MIT, 1967).

Wildavsky, A. "The Political Essay of Efficiency: Environmental Benefit Analysis, Systems Analysis, and Program Budgeting." *Public Administration Review* (1966:292–310).

———. "Does Planning Work?" *The Public Interest* (Summer, 1971:95–104).

———. "If Planning Is Everything Maybe It's Nothing." *Policy Sciences 4* (1973:127–153).

———. *The Politics of the Budgetary Process* 2d edition (Boston, MA: Little, Brown, 1974).

———. *Speaking Truth to Power: The Art and Craft of Policy Analysis* (Toronto: Little, Brown & Co., 1979).

Wilensky, H. L. *Organizational Intelligence: Knowledge and Policy in Government and Industry* (New York: Basic Books, 1967).

Williams, J. R. "Competitive Strategy Valuation." *The Journal of Business Strategy* (1984:36–46).

Wilson, J. H. "Reforming the Strategic Planning Process: Integration of Social Responsibility and Business Needs." *Long Range Planning* (XVII, 5, 1974:2–6).

Wise, T. A. "IBM's $5 Billion Gamble." *Fortune* (September 1966:118–123).

———. "The Rocky Road to the Marketplace." *Fortune* (October 1966:138–143).

Wood, D. R., Jr., and LaForge, R. L. "The Impact of Comprehensive Planning on Financial Performance." *Academy of Management Journal* (XXII, 3, 1979:516–526).

Woodward, J. *Industrial Organization: Theory and Practice* (Oxford: Oxford University Press, 1965).

Wootton, B. *Freedom Under Planning* (Chapel Hill, NC: The University of North Carolina Press, 1945).

Worthy, J. C. *Big Business and Free Men* (New York: Harper & Row, 1959).

Wrapp, H. E., "Business Planners: Organization Dilemma." In D. M. Bowman and F. M. Fillerup, *Management: Organization and Planning* (New York: McGraw-Hill, 1963).

———. "Good Managers Don't Make Policy Decisions." *Harvard Business Review* (September/October 1967:91–99).

Wright, R. V. L. "The State of the Art and Shortcomings in Planning Technology." In E. Schlefer, ed. *Proceedings of the IX International Meeting* (The Institute of Management Sciences, Tel Aviv, Israel: Jerusalem Academic Press, 1973:615–619).

Yavitz, B., and Newman, W. H. *Strategy in Action: The Execution, Politics, and Payoff of Business Planning* (New York: Free Press, 1982).

Zan, L. "What's Left for Formal Planning?" *Economia Aziendale* (VI, 2[March], 1987:187–204).

Index

Abell, D. F., 153, 155, 157, 241, 242n7, 244
Abernathy, W. J., 343
Acheson, Dean, 291
Ackerman, R. W., 195, 381
Ackoff, R. L., 8, 11, 54, 98, 138, 183, 192n7, 241, 246, 253, 298
Action planning, 78–79, 350, 414
Action program hierarchy, 62
Actions
  incentive for, 293–294
  paralysis of, 293
  performance control influences, 78
  tracking patterns of, 363–365
Ad hoc management, 148–149
Adhocracy organization, 398, 408–410
Agreements (on goals), 197–198
Aguilar, F. J., 261, 263
Air Canada, 112–114, 171, 176, 184–185, 334, 343–344
Air France, 112n9, 352–354
Al-Bazzaz, S. J., 345, 350, 367–368n15, 415n21
Albert, 222
Allaire, Y., 85–86, 126, 138n16, 170, 198, 222, 228, 274, 369, 383, 385
Allen, M. G., 102, 137, 180, 204, 224, 345n6
Allen, Woody, 1
Allio, R. J., 39, 102, 320, 335–336, 347n7, 372
Allison, G. T., 250–251, 263
Amar, David, 56, 294, 296n32
Analysis
  accuracy with, 327–328

associated with brain's left hemisphere, 324–325
compared with intuition, 325–329
coupled with intuition, 329–330
is not synthesis, 321
role of formal, 134
soft, 331–333
See also Decomposition
Analysis, ad hoc, 369
  forecasting as, 375
  scrutinization as, 378–380
  strategic, 371–372
Analysis, strategic
  defined, 367–368
  external and internal, 373–378
  in professional organization, 406–407
  types of, 373
Andrews, F., 244, 319
Andrews, K. R., 36, 38, 39, 152n19, 275, 335
Ansoff, H. I., 9n1, 12, 39–41, 53, 67, 89, 95, 99, 101–102, 136–137, 145–151, 152n19, 157–158, 161, 170–171, 178n3, 179, 192n7, 204–205, 229, 231–232, 236, 246, 251, 275, 290–291, 297, 334–335, 369
Ansoff model, 40–46, 56–58
Anthony, R. N., 86, 135, 179, 192n7, 241, 336
Armstrong, J. S., 93, 136n15, 343
Articulation
  effect of clear, 175
  forces, 216
  in formal planning, 13–15, 194
  of strategies, 338

About the Author

Henry Mintzberg is a visiting professor at INSEAD in France and a two-time winner of the prestigious McKinsey Award for the best *Harvard Business Review* article. A fellow of the Royal Society of Canada—the first fellow elected from a management faculty—he is the author of several seminal books including *Mintzberg on Management* (Free Press, 1989).